Eric Hirsch

D0574054

PRODUCTION OF CULTURE/ CULTURES OF PRODUCTION

Culture, Media and Identities

The Open University Course Team

Claire Alexander, Critical reader

Maggie Andrews, Tutor panel member, Study Guide author

Melanie Bayley, Editor

Veronica Beechey, Critical reader

Robert Bocock, Author

David Boswell, Critical reader

Peter Braham, Author

David Calderwood, Project controller

Elizabeth Chaplin, Tutor panel member, Study Guide author

Lene Connolly, Print buying controller

Jeremy Cooper, BBC producer

Margaret Dickens, Print buying co-ordinator

Jessica Evans, Critical reader

Martin Ferns, Editor

Paul du Gay, Book 1 Chair, Book 4 Chair, Author

Ruth Finnegan, Author

Stuart Hall, Course Chair, Book 2 Chair, Author

Peter Hamilton, Author

Jonathan Hunt, Copublishing advisor

Linda Janes, Course manager

Siân Lewis, Graphic designer

Hugh Mackay, Book 5 Chair, author

David Morley, Goldsmiths College, University of London, External assessor

Lesley Passey, Cover designer

Clive Pearson, Tutor panel member, Study Guide author

Peter Redman, Tutor panel member, Study Guide author

Graeme Salaman, Author

Paul Smith, Media librarian

Kenneth Thompson, Book 6 Chair, Author

Alison Tucker, BBC series producer

Pauline Turner, Course secretary

Kathryn Woodward, Book 3 Chair, Author

Chris Wooldridge, Editor

Consultant authors

Susan Benson, University of Cambridge

Paul Gilroy, Goldsmiths College, University of London

Christine Gledhill, Staffordshire University

Henrietta Lidchi, Museum of Mankind, London

Daniel Miller, University College, London

Shaun Moores, Queen Margaret College, Edinburgh

Keith Negus, University of Leicester

Sean Nixon, University of Essex

Bhikhu Parekh, University of Hull

Kevin Robins, University of Newcastle upon Tyne

Lynne Segal, Middlesex University

Chris Shilling, University of Portsmouth

Nigel Thrift, University of Bristol

John Tomlinson, Nottingham Trent University

This book is part of the *Culture, Media and Identities* series published by Sage in association with The Open University.

Doing Cultural Studies: The Story of the Sony Walkman by Paul du Gay, Stuart Hall, Linda Janes, Hugh Mackay and Keith Negus

Representation: Cultural Representations and Signifying Practices edited by Stuart Hall

Identity and Difference edited by Kathryn Woodward

Production of Culture/Cultures of Production edited by Paul du Gay

Consumption and Everyday Life edited by Hugh Mackay

Media and Cultural Regulation edited by Kenneth Thompson

The final form of the text is the joint responsibility of chapter authors, book editors and course team commentators.

The books are part of the Open University course D318 *Culture, Media and Identities*. Details of this and other Open University courses can be obtained from the Course Enquiries Data Service, PO Box 625, Dane Road, Milton Keynes MK1 1TY. For availability of other course components, including video- and audio-cassette materials, contact Open University Educational Enterprises Ltd, 12 Cofferidge Close, Stony Stratford, Milton Keynes MK11 1BY.

SAGE Publications
London • Thousand Oaks • New Delhi

in association with

The Open
University

PRODUCTION OF CULTURE/ CULTURES OF PRODUCTION

Edited by PAUL du GAY

The Open University, Walton Hall, Milton Keynes MK7 6AA

© The Open University 1997

First published in 1997

The opinions expressed are not necessarily those of the Course Team or of The Open University.

All rights reserved. No part of this publication may be reproduced, stored in a retrieval system, transmitted or utilized in any form or by any means, electronic, mechanical, photocopying, recording or otherwise, without permission in writing from the Publishers.

SAGE Publications Ltd
6 Bonhill Street
London EC2A 4PU

SAGE Publications Inc.
2455 Teller Road
Thousand Oaks
California 91320

SAGE Publications India Pvt Ltd
32, M-Block Market
Greater Kailash - I
New Delhi 110 048

British Library Cataloguing in Publication data

A catalogue record for this book is available from The British Library.

ISBN 0 7619 5435 X (cased)

ISBN 0 7619 5436 8 (pbk)

Library of Congress catalog card number is available.

Edited, designed and typeset by The Open University.

Printed in Great Britain by Bath Press Colourbooks, Glasgow

PRODUCTION OF CULTURE/ CULTURES OF PRODUCTION

edited by Paul du Gay

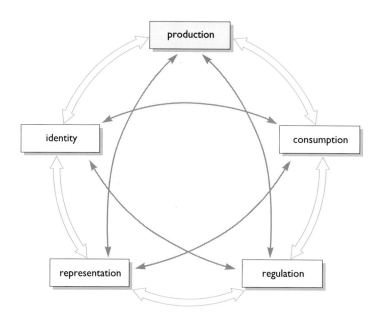

The circuit of culture

Introduction

The chapters in this book all deal, in their different ways, with the question of cultural production. This is one of the central processes and practices through which meaning is made and a key moment in what has been termed 'the circuit of culture' (see **du Gay, Hall et al.**, 1997)*. But what does production, industry, and the economic more generally, have to do with culture? What is the connection between them, and how are we to understand and conceive of this relation?

Economy and culture

If you were asked to list some of the key themes that had come to dominate discussion about wealth creation and successful business organization in the last decade or so, what would spring to mind? Terms like 'efficiency' and 'economy', almost certainly, 'flexibility' and 'de-regulation', quite probably, but what about 'culture'?

If this suggestion leaves you somewhat confused, try taking a quick flick through some of those popular management texts that seem to appear with such alarming regularity. Chances are a brief examination of their contents would soon reveal the primacy accorded to 'culture' in the battle to make enterprises more successful. In this literature, 'culture' is allotted such importance because it is seen to structure the way people think, feel and act in organizations. 'Culture' has thus come to be seen as a crucial means of ensuring organizational success because it is held that if you can effectively manage 'meaning' at work, so that people come to conceive of and conduct themselves in such a way as to maximize their involvement in, and hence their contribution to, the organization for which they work, you are more likely to have a profitable, effective and successful firm.

Perhaps one reason why we are somewhat surprised to hear that 'culture' has emerged as a crucial concept in the world of business organization is because we have come to think of these two terms – 'business' and 'culture' – as somehow mutually incompatible. Certainly there is a powerful tradition of thought which holds that 'culture' – and this normally means 'high' culture – is an autonomous realm of existence dedicated to the pursuit of particular values – 'art', 'beauty', 'authenticity' and 'truth' – which are the very antithesis of those assumed to hold sway in the banal world of the economy – the rational pursuit of profit, unbounded 'instrumentalism' and so on. Seen from this position any blurring of the boundaries between these two spheres is held to be potentially dangerous. The presumed 'higher' values of 'culture' are bound to be tainted if they come into contact with the brutal rationalities of the economic.

* A reference in bold indicates another book, or another chapter in another book, in the series.

You are probably aware of the basic tropes of this argument. They are invariably deployed when, for example, the government announces reductions in state funding for the arts and demands that arts organizations become more enterprising in their search for alternative sources of finance. In a somewhat different context, similar frames of reference are utilized when fans accuse 'indie' pop and rock bands of 'selling out' when they sign to major record labels. What these two examples share is a belief that 'economy' and 'culture' are absolutely autonomous entities and any merging of them is bound to demean and debase the latter.

A rather different approach to the relationship between 'culture' and 'economy', but one which nonetheless establishes an absolute hierarchy of values in which one term is privileged over the other, can be found within certain materialist and economistic traditions of thought within the social and human sciences. In these approaches, the language of the 'economy' is held to provide us with the possibility of 'hard', 'objective' knowledge of the world because it deals with seemingly 'transparent', 'factual' material processes. In contrast, the language of 'culture' is seen to deal with the 'soft', seemingly less tangible elements of life – meanings, representations and values, for example – and these are assumed to be incapable of generating clear, unambiguous and hence 'true' knowledge. For a long time, these approaches tended to view the 'cultural' dimensions of life as largely 'superstructural' phenomena – that is, as 'second order' processes and practices dependent upon and reflective of the material base. In this sense, the economy was assumed to completely dominate and determine the cultural domain.

These two approaches have come in for considerable criticism over time and it is fair to say that few people espouse the sort of simple 'ideal typical' versions outlined above. Nonetheless, it is also fair to say that traces of both continue to haunt contemporary academic debates about the relationship between 'economy' and 'culture' as well as everyday discussions concerning the relative merits of different cultural preferences and products.

This book is centrally concerned with exploring and analysing the relationship between economy and culture in the present. However, it attempts to sidestep positions which assume either an essential opposition between these two spheres of existence or an essentially deterministic relationship between them, where one side completely dominates the other. Instead, the contributors to this volume all acknowledge the mutually constitutive relationship between 'culture' and 'economy'.

In their different ways and in relationship to different objects of analysis they argue that in late modern societies such as our own the 'economic' and the 'cultural' are irrevocably 'hybrid' categories; that what we think of as purely 'economic' processes and practices are, in an important sense, 'cultural' phenomena – managers of business enterprises, as we saw earlier, are busy attempting to create appropriate organizational 'cultures' because they have come to see the very stuff of culture – meanings, norms and values – as crucial elements of economic success.

Similarly, contemporary material culture is predominantly 'manufactured'. After all, what films would we watch, what televisions would we view them on, what music would we listen to and so forth, if we were determined to enforce an absolute division between culture and economy? Our everyday cultural lives are bound up with mass-produced material cultural artefacts to such an extent that a principled opposition between the economic and industrial, on the one hand, and the cultural, on the other, is simply untenable.

If such principled oppositions have little practical or theoretical utility then the question arises as to how we can more productively conceptualize the relationship between the economic and the cultural in the present day. In this book, an attempt at reconstruction is conducted through the notion of 'cultural economy'[1].

'Cultural economy'

cultural economy

This phrase – **cultural economy** – may strike you as a little strange. So what does it mean; what is it meant to signify? One of the main reasons for using this term is to suggest both continuity and rupture with deterministic approaches to the study of 'economic life'. On the one hand, there are echoes in this phrase of the approach to analysing economic life commonly termed 'political economy', particularly in relation to the latter's opposition to the ahistoric and asocial tenets of neo-classical economics and its emphasis on a multi-paradigm analysis of the economy.

On the other hand, 'cultural economy' is also meant to signify a break with 'political economy' in one key respect – concerning the importance allocated to meaning in the conduct of economic life. For whereas 'political economy' has tended to emphasize features such as the distribution of income, patterns of corporate ownership and control, the dynamic nature of market economies, capital accumulation and the generation and uses of economic surplus, it has had rather less to say about the meanings these processes come to have for those involved in them. Because political economy approaches tend to represent economic processes and practices as 'things in themselves' – with certain 'objective' meanings – people are seen mainly as the 'bearers' of these. As a result of this process of 'objectification', the 'cultural' dimensions of economic activities – the meanings and values these activities hold for people – are evacuated.

As Stuart Hall has argued, however, 'culture is involved in all those practices ... which carry meaning and value for us, which need to be meaningfully interpreted by others, or which depend on meaning for their effective operation. Culture, in this sense, permeates all of society' (**Hall**, 1997, p. 3). The economic is a crucial domain of existence in modern societies, and it too is thoroughly saturated with culture. Indeed, this is precisely what the term 'cultural economy' is meant to signify. 'Economic' processes and practices – in all their plurality, whether we refer to management techniques for re-organizing the conduct of business, contemporary strategies for advertising goods and services, or everyday interactions between service employees and their customers – depend on meaning for their effects and have particular cultural 'conditions of existence'. Meaning is produced at 'economic' sites (at work, in shops) and circulated through economic processes and practices (through economists' models of how 'economies' or 'organizations' work, through adverts, marketing materials and the very design of products) no less than in other domains of existence in modern societies.

A crucial feature of this book, then, is the way it treats economic processes and practices as cultural phenomena, as depending on meaning for their effective operation. Just think, for a moment, about the entity we refer to as 'the economy'. How do we go about managing this entity? Well, one of the first things we need to do is to build a clear picture of what an economy looks like. We need to ask ourselves what its main components are, and how they work. In other words, before one can even seek to manage something called an 'economy', it is first necessary to conceptualize or **represent** a set of processes and relations as an 'economy' which is amenable to management. We need, in other words, a **discourse** of the economy, and this discourse, like any other, will depend on a particular mode of representation: the elaboration of a language for conceiving of and hence constructing an object in a certain way so that that object can then be deliberated about and acted upon. In this way, economics can be seen to be a cultural phenomenon because it works through language and representation. Discourses of the economy, like those of sexuality, 'race' or nationality, *carry meaning*.

representation

discourse

In the same vein, processes of production and systems of organization can be seen to be more than simply 'objective' structures that people inhabit and reproduce. Through a cultural lens they become assemblages of meaningful practices that construct certain ways for people to conceive of and conduct themselves at work. As indicated above, businesses have spent enormous time and money in recent years trying consciously and deliberately to change their organizational 'cultures'. Through the introduction of seemingly banal mechanisms and practices such as cost centres, performance appraisal and team-working, employers have sought to create new meanings for the work people do and thus to construct new forms of work-based identity amongst employees. In so doing they have indicated precisely how working practices are 'cultural' phenomena – how they are 'meaningful'. Organizational practices carry particular meanings and construct certain forms of conduct amongst people subjected to them.

The most important point to note about our term 'cultural economy' is therefore the crucial importance it allots to language, representation and meaning – to 'culture' – for understanding the conduct of economic life and the construction of economic identities.

However, the explanatory reach of the term does not end there, for 'cultural economy' carries another register of meaning. It doesn't simply suggest that economic phenomena are inherently 'cultural', that economic processes and practices are always meaningful practices; it also indicates something about the contemporary nature of economic life, namely that we live in an era in which the economic has become thoroughly 'culturalized'. So what does in mean to talk about a 'cultural economy' in this latter sense?

In this second manifestation, 'cultural economy' refers to the increasing importance of 'culture' to doing business in the contemporary world. This is evidenced at a number of different levels. First, and perhaps most obviously, by the way in which global entertainment corporations, such as Sony, Time-Warner, Bertelsmann, Disney and News Corporation, whose business is the production and distribution of 'cultural' hardware and software – such as music, film, television, print media and computer games – have become amongst the most powerful economic actors in the world. Today, 'culture' is a truly global business.

aestheticization

Secondly, more and more of the goods and services produced for consumers across a range of sectors can be conceived of as 'cultural' goods, in that they are deliberately inscribed with particular meanings and associations as they are produced and circulated in a conscious attempt to generate desire for them amongst end users. The growing **aestheticization** or 'fashioning' of seemingly banal products – from instant coffee to bank accounts – whereby these are sold to consumers in terms of particular clusters of meaning indicates the increased importance of 'culture' to the production and circulation of a multitude of goods and services.

cultural intermediary

This process has been accompanied by the increased influence of what are often termed the **cultural intermediary** occupations of advertising, design and marketing (see section 3 of **du Gay, Hall et al.**, 1997). These practitioners play a pivotal role in articulating production with consumption by attempting to associate goods and services with particular cultural meanings and to address these values to prospective buyers. In other words, they are concerned to create an identification between producers and consumers through their expertise in certain signifying practices.

The increased influence of these signifying practices to processes of production is closely linked to significant changes in manufacturing techniques. In contrast to mass production techniques, where particular products were manufactured in large batches on assembly lines that required great investment in inflexible plant, novel forms of flexible, electronics-based automation technologies, often referred to as 'flexible specialization technologies', make small batch production possible. So whereas in the past a company like Sony would produce one model of the Walkman, nowadays Sony uses computer-based technologies and a functionally flexible labour force to produce many different versions of the Walkman, each designed and marketed – or *lifestyled* – with a particular niche consumer grouping in mind (see **du Gay, Hall et al.**, 1997, section 3). In other words, *flexible specialization* and the increased culturalization of products go hand in hand. They are, in effect, mutually constitutive.

Finally, the growing importance accorded to signification in doing business is not only evident in the production, design and marketing of goods and services, for as we have already seen, the internal life of organizations is also the subject of cultural reconstruction. The turn to 'culture' within the world of business and organization is premised in part upon the belief that, in order to compete effectively in the turbulent, increasingly global markets of the present, a foremost necessity for organizations is to change they way they conduct their business and the ways people conduct themselves within organizations. 'Culture' is deemed to be crucial here because it is seen to structure the way people think, feel and act in organizations. The aim of managing organizational culture is to produce new sets of meanings through which people will come to identify with their employing organization in a way which enables them to make the right and necessary contribution to its success.

This focus on 'culture' as a means of changing the way people conceive of and relate to the work they perform and to their own sense of self indicates that its deployment as a managerial technique is intimately bound up with questions of *identity*.

In this second sense of the term, then, 'cultural economy' refers to the increasing 'culturalization' of economic life. From 'macro' level processes of 'economic globalization' to 'micro' level processes of individual work-based identity formation, cultural practices have come to play a crucial role in the conduct of many different forms of economic life in the modern world.

The structure of the book

As we have indicated, this book is structured by the notion of 'cultural economy'. Given the antipathy that has been held to exist between the terms 'culture' and 'economics', the notion of 'cultural economy' is designed to strike you as a little strange. However, we hope by now that you have begun to see why we are attaching such importance to it.

It is worth quickly re-capping the main themes and issues which we are gathering together under the rubric of 'cultural economy' before moving on to look at the content of each individual chapter.

The first thing to note is that the term draws attention to the ways in which forms of economic life are cultural phenomena; they depend on 'meaning' for their effects and have particular discursive conditions of existence.

Secondly, the term suggests that the production of 'cultural' artefacts in their contemporary manifestations cannot be divorced from economic processes and forms of organization. At the same time as making this point, however, we have also been keen to indicate that the **production of culture** cannot be reduced to a question of 'economics' alone. Processes of production are themselves cultural phenomena in that they are assemblages of meaningful practices that construct certain ways for people to conceive of and conduct themselves in an organizational context. These are the **cultures of production** referred to in the title of this book.

production of culture

cultures of production

Thirdly, it indicates the growing importance of 'culture' to doing business in the contemporary world. As we have seen, increasing numbers of goods and services across a range of sectors are 'cultural' goods in that they are inscribed with particular meanings and associations in the process of their production and circulation, in a deliberate attempt to generate desire for them amongst consumers. The growing importance of culture doesn't end here, though, as we have seen, for the internal life of organizations and their members is increasingly the subject of cultural reconstruction as well.

While each of the individual chapters in the volume focuses on different elements of 'cultural economy' they combine to present a distinctive analysis of the relationship between 'the economic' and 'the cultural' in the present day. The chapters are also ordered in a particular way to assist in this endeavour. Beginning with a macro-level focus on questions of cultural globalization and the emergence of global cultural industries, they move steadily towards a more micro-level focus at the end of the book where the cultural reconstruction of organizational life and the experience and identity of work are the main topics of analysis.

In Chapter 1, 'What in the world's going on?', Kevin Robins explores the relationship between culture and economy in the context of increasing globalization. He begins by considering the economic expressions of global change, focusing on the emergence of a 'global economy', on the nature of global corporations and on the significance of global markets. In analysing the forces and relations shaping the emerging global economic order, Robins is particularly concerned with the growing significance of media, communications, information, and cultural products and markets. Throughout the chapter he indicates how economic and cultural aspects of globalization interact with one another. Economic developments, he argues, provide the basis for many of the key developments in global culture, opening up certain cultural possibilities, and closing off others. At the same time, he also sees cultural forces as setting the conditions and limits of possibility for global economic and business developments. Robins shows how this interplay between economic and cultural logics gives rise to a globalizing process that is complex, uneven and uncertain.

In Chapter 2, 'The production of culture', Keith Negus picks up on Robins' analysis of the complex interplay between economic and cultural logics of globalization to explore the ways in which culture is produced in global times. In studying the production of culture, he argues, it is necessary to understand not only the technical processes and economic patterns of manufacturing, organization and distribution but also to understand the culture – the ways of life – through and within which music, films and other forms of cultural software and hardware are made and given meaning. In developing this argument, Negus draws attention to an important shift in approaches to how culture is produced: from earlier attempts to understand the impact of specific forms of industrial production on cultural artefacts (by applying notions of 'industry' to 'culture'), towards a perspective which approaches 'culture' not simply as a thing which is produced but as a meaningful 'form of life' (by applying theories of 'culture' to 'industry'). In particular, Negus indicates how the activities of staff working in the cultural industries are informed by a particular set of values, meanings and working practices – a 'culture of production' – which has a significant impact on the 'production of culture'.

This idea that there are 'cultural' limits to conceiving of production as a 'purely' economic phenomenon is developed by Peter Braham in Chapter 3, 'Fashion: unpacking a cultural production'. Through a 'case study' of one particular cultural industry – fashion – Braham indicates how practices of cultural production are not only shaped by an industry's 'internal' culture of production but also in relationship to the seemingly 'external' activities of cultural consumption. He argues that a comprehensive understanding of fashion in clothing can only be approached through an exploration of the mutually constitutive rhythms of production and consumption. In seeking to map the multiple worlds where the meaning of fashion is produced, Braham exposes the links that exist between production, distribution and retailing, on the one hand, and image, advertising, lifestyle and consumption, on the other. Focusing on the global fashion corporation, Benetton, the chapter shows how this particular producer and retailer of fashion clothing is involved in a constant attempt simultaneously to track *and* shape the cultural tastes and predispositions of consumers.

The question of how consumers are drawn into and implicated in the practices of cultural production also forms the central focus of Sean Nixon's Chapter 4, 'Circulating culture'. In this chapter, Nixon is concerned with exploring the increasing influence of the 'cultural intermediaries' of design, marketing and advertising, and with analysing their role in adding cultural value to an increasingly greater range of goods and services. He argues that 'cultural intermediaries' play a pivotal role in articulating production with consumption through their 'symbolic expertise' in making goods and services 'meaningful'. He notes that this 'culturalizing role' has increased considerably in recent years and links this to wider economic shifts associated with the transition from an era dominated by mass production and mass consumption to an emergent era of flexible specialization and market differentiation. Nixon notes that the intensified role of cultural intermediaries in contemporary economic life is not simply reflective of more fundamental shifts in manufacturing systems. Rather, he argues that shifts in production methods have been, in important ways, marketing-led. He suggests that both the dynamics of contemporary consumer culture and the emerging organizational forms of flexible specialization ensure an increased prominence for the expertise of the cultural intermediaries of design, marketing and advertising. Through their strategic location at the point of circulation – between production and consumption – these forms of symbolic expertise are able to affect the constitution both of processes of cultural production and of practices of cultural consumption.

In Chapter 5, 'Culturing production', Graeme Salaman argues that it is not simply goods and services that have been increasingly culturalized, for the processes and practices of organization and production have also become the subject of cultural change and reconstruction. Salaman analyses the ways in which senior managers of organizations increasingly sponsor attempts to define, for their employees, the meaning of employment, and the relationship they should have with their employing organization. They attempt to do this, he argues, because they are convinced that changing the 'culture' of organizations is an effective way of improving organizational performance – in terms of managers' objectives. These efforts (which Salaman refers to under the heading of 'Corporate Culture') arise from, and are encouraged by, managerial discourses developed by a particular sort of cultural intermediary – the management consultant. These discourses offer a way of thinking about how organizations work, what affects their performance, and how performance can be improved. However, as the chapter demonstrates, while 'Corporate Culture' discourse insists upon the essential reality of organizational consensus and harmony, this representation of organizational life is often contested and challenged by the very people at whom it is aimed – employees.

In the final Chapter 6, 'Organizing identity: making up people at work', Paul du Gay explores the ways in which attempts to change the culture of organizations impact upon and reconstruct economic identities, not only those of employees – whether workers or managers – but also those of consumers. Du Gay examines how contemporary changes in ways of representing and intervening in – what he terms 'governing' – organizational life create new ways for people to conduct themselves at work. In particular, he focuses upon the ways in which contemporary discourses of organizational change blur some established differences between the spheres of production and consumption, work and leisure, creating certain similarities in the forms of conduct and modes of self-presentation required of people across a range of different domains. Through an examination of contemporary organizational change in the service sector of the economy, where economic success is perhaps most visibly premised upon the production of meaning, du Gay delineates the emergence of novel 'hybrid' work identities. By the term 'hybrid work identities' he refers to the ways in which employees in contemporary service work are encouraged to take on both the role of worker and that of customer in the workplace. Throughout the chapter, he indicates the pitfalls of attempting to allocate an essential meaning to work and instead suggests that the experience and identity of work are historically and culturally constructed. What it means to be a 'worker', 'manager', or any other form of economic actor, varies across time and context in relationship to prevailing ways of governing economic life.

Where is meaning produced? Our 'circuit of culture' suggests that, in fact, meanings are produced at several different sites and circulated through several different processes and practices (the cultural circuit). This volume is primarily concerned with exploring the ways in which cultural meanings are made in *production*. However, while production, as we have seen, has its own particular 'forms of life', it is not wholly separate from other sites on our circuit. In discussing the production of culture we have not been able to avoid talking about consumption, representation or identity, for example. This suggests that meaning-making processes operating in any one site are always partially dependent upon the meaning-making processes and practices operating in other sites for their effect. In other words, meaning is not simply sent from one autonomous sphere – production, say – and received in another autonomous sphere – consumption. Meaning-making functions less in terms of such a 'transmission' flow model, and more like the model of a dialogue. It is an ongoing process. It rarely ends at a pre-ordained place. No doubt the producers of cultural goods and services wish it did and that they could permanently establish its boundaries! Why and how such an ambition remains forever thwarted is explored by each of the contributors to this volume.

Notes

1   This term is borrowed from John Allen.

References

DU GAY, P., HALL, S., JANES, L., MACKAY, H. and NEGUS, K. (1997) *Doing Cultural Studies: the story of the Sony Walkman*, London, Sage/The Open University (Book 1 in this series).

HALL, S. (1997) 'Introduction' in Hall, S. (ed.) *Representation: cultural representations and signifying practices*, London, Sage/The Open University (Book 2 in this series).

WHAT IN THE WORLD'S GOING ON?

Kevin Robins

Contents

1   Introduction

We are presently living through a period of extraordinary transformation. There is the growing sense that an older order is dissolving and a new world order taking shape around us. Familiar structures and orientations are weakening, and we are increasingly exposed to new and disorientating horizons of possibility. These dramatic developments are commonly described in terms of the logic of **globalization**. Globalization is about the dissolution of the old structures and boundaries of national states and communities. It is about the increasing **transnationalization** of economic and cultural life, frequently imagined in terms of the creation of a global space and community in which we shall all be global citizens and neighbours. With these globalizing dynamics we come upon new experiences and encounters, with the promise of new possibilities, but also the prospect of new uncertainties and anxieties.

globalization

transnationalization

In this chapter, we shall be exploring some of the key aspects of the globalization process, particularly as they relate to questions of culture, media and identities. We shall begin this endeavour, in the following section, by considering some particular and concrete examples of global change. I want you to think about globalization at this point in terms of your own experiences and encounters, and in terms of what you may see on television or read about in newspapers and magazines. Globalization is ordinary: we are all now exposed to, and increasingly aware of, its consequences. We are all immersed in the globalization process.

Section 2 stresses the complexities of the globalization process. Globalization is complex, first, in the sense that new (international) cultural elements are brought together with old (national) elements: globalization must be considered in terms of both change and continuity. And, second, globalization is complex in the sense that it is developing in multifarious (and often contradictory) directions, and is experienced differentially by particular social and cultural groups (according to such variables as gender, ethnicity, class, age and location). It is important to emphasize that there are diverse responses (which may take the form of resistances to the globalization process). You are studying a contemporary process of change that is the focus of contest and struggle, and which is consequently open-ended in its course and pace of development.

Globalization is both an economic and a cultural phenomenon, and this chapter proceeds to examine both aspects. In section 3, we shall consider the economic expressions of global change. What is meant by 'the **global economy**'? What is the nature of global corporations? What is the significance of global markets? Here we shall be particularly concerned with the growing significance of communications, information, cultural products and markets in the emerging global economic order. A number of commentators have described this transformation from industrial to information economy emblematically in terms of the shift from Fordism to

global economy

Sonyism. What are at issue here are the ideals and objectives of global corporate interests, and the extent to which these are succeeding in shaping the new order. To what extent, we must ask, are other constituencies of interest also able to influence the nature of the new global order? In dealing with this question, we shall pay attention especially to the interests of particular places (cities and regions) in the new economic context, considering the significance of the new relationship that is emerging between the global and the local.

Section 4 of this chapter then goes on to explore some of the cultural dimensions of global change. In line with the objectives of this series and this book in particular, I want to look first at the globalization of the media industries. A consideration of the emerging new spaces of global media will allow us to consider the relationship between economic and cultural developments in globalization. Here we shall examine those forces that are working towards standardization and homogenization in cultural forms, and, in contrast, those that are working to sustain particularity and difference. We shall also be concerned with cultural innovation, taking account of the new forms of hybrid culture arising as a consequence of global encounter and interaction. And we shall also pay attention to cultural continuities, taking seriously the reassertion of older (national, religious) identities in the new global context. What I shall emphasize is the great diversity of possibilities in global cultural change.

You will need to keep in mind the interrelation between economic and cultural aspects of globalization. Economic developments provide the basis for many of the key developments in global culture, opening up certain possibilities, and closing off other cultural possibilities. At the same time, we may see cultural forces as setting the conditions and limits of possibility for global economic and business developments. You should recognize that this interplay between economic and cultural logics gives rise to a process that is complex, uneven and uncertain. There is no way to predict what globalization will bring about. We must try to understand its complexities, in the hope that greater awareness of what is happening will allow us to realize the potentialities of globalization.

2   Global change

So, what exactly is it that's going on in the world now? What are the new experiences and encounters of global transformation? Let us begin to address these questions by considering global change in very concrete terms, in terms of our own context and experience.

2.1   Encountering globalization

Globalization is about growing mobility across frontiers – mobility of goods and commodities, mobility of information and communications products and services, and mobility of people. Walk down your local high street and you will be aware of global chains such as McDonald's or Benetton. You may buy the global products of Sony, Procter and Gamble or the Coca Cola Corporation. In your local supermarkets you will buy more or less exotic fruits and vegetables from almost anywhere in the world, along with ingredients for curries, stir-fries, pizzas, and other 'world foods'. If you go out to eat you can choose from restaurants providing a whole range of 'ethnic' cuisines (Italian, Chinese, Indian, Korean, Thai, etc.). Go to the off-licence and you cannot but be aware of the increasing globalization of the market for wines

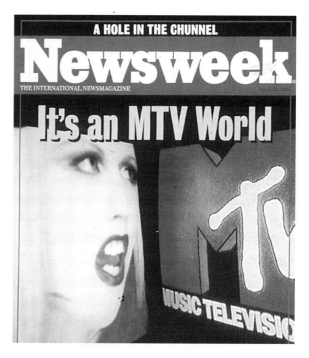

FIGURE 1.1
It's an MTV World
(*Newsweek* cover 24
April 1995; © 1995
Newsweek Inc.; all
rights reserved;
reprinted by
permission).

(not just French or Spanish, but now South African, Chilean, Australian, and even Crimean varieties) and beers (Italian, American, Indian, Brazilian, Japanese, and more). Your coat might be produced in Turkey, your hi-fi in Japan, and your car in Korea. And, of course, we could push this analysis back one stage further, for the various inputs into the production of these commodities (raw materials, labour, components, finance) are also likely to come from a range of geographical sources.

Through the development of satellite and cable services, and on the basis of more liberal media regulation, the television market is moving from national to transnational scale. CNN can bring you 'real-time' access to news stories across the world, as we clearly saw at the time of the Gulf War in 1991. The Disney Channel is targeted at a global audience. 'It's an MTV World' is the cover story of a recent issue of *Newsweek* magazine (24 April 1995) (Figure 1.1) – itself now a global media enterprise. The main headline: 'Rock around the clock and around the world with the ultimate New Age multinational'. Through the new telecommunications networks – from voice through to fax and e-mail – we can now enter into global communications 'at the touch of a button' (though paying for them is, of course, another matter). And if you have access to the Internet and the World Wide Web, you may gain access to global databases, and you can choose to become a member of a global user group. Instantaneous and ubiquitous communication is giving substance to the Canadian philosopher Marshall McLuhan's idea, first put forward in the 1960s, that the world is now becoming a 'global village'.

There are gathering flows of people, too, not just of physical and information products and goods. Members of the international business elite now undertake international travel on a routine and regular basis, constituting themselves as a global community of frequent-flier cosmopolitans. Far more numerous are those whose mobility and movement are precipitated by need or by despair, the migrants who take advantage of a cheap plane or train to seek work in the world's more affluent centres, establishing themselves there as minority communities in exile. Leisure pursuits, too, like the pursuit of employment, are associated with accelerating flows. If where you live is a tourist resort, you will be familiar with visitors from Europe or from the United States, increasingly from Japan and the Far East, and now, too, from Eastern Europe and Russia. And you will doubtlessly be aware of the relative ease with which you can undertake holiday travel, not just to the South of France, or the Costa Brava, but now to Florida Disneyland, or to Goa or the Caribbean. In their book on cultural tourism, Priscilla Boniface and Peter Fowler (1993, pp. 7, 5) refer to an advertisement for tourism in India which has the caption 'A world of difference only 9 hours away'. And they quote from an account of a holiday in The Gambia ('Advertised in its early days as "exotic". The Gambia is scarcely that now.') that has a truly global flavour: 'On Night One we were offered a Doncaster group dressed as cowboys who mimed country and western songs ... and a Russian pop band on a cultural exchange.' Mobility has become ordinary in the emerging global order. But it is also possible to see the world without having to move. For now 'the world' is able to come to where we are. As the writer Simon Winchester puts it in his introduction to Martin Parr's collection of photographs, *Small World*:

> A whole new industry has been born from the manufacturing of ... foreign-theme entertainment parks, the world brought to your doorstep by, first, the Americans (with both the outer world, and outer space, tucked into the more exotic corners of Disneyland) and then by the Japanese – who went on to develop the idea to a fine art, settling outside Tokyo an English village that is more brimming with thatch and swimming in bitter beer than anywhere in the Cotswolds. Soon the Europeans are to have such a *parc internationale*, with little great walls of China and petit Taj Mahals constructed in fields convenient for the fun-filled charabancs that converge on Cherbourg.
>
> (Parr, 1995, no pagination)

The photographs by Martin Parr (overleaf) provide a wonderful visual record of both these forms of tourist experience.

ACTIVITY 1

The examples of global culture that I have given above are simply ones that I have experienced or heard about. Examples could be multiplied almost endlessly. Before moving on, take some time to consider your own experience. Consider the things you own, and the food and drink you consume. Think about your own use of media and communications. And recall your own holidays and tourist excursions.

FIGURE 1.2   Happy Kingdom (German Theme Park), Japan

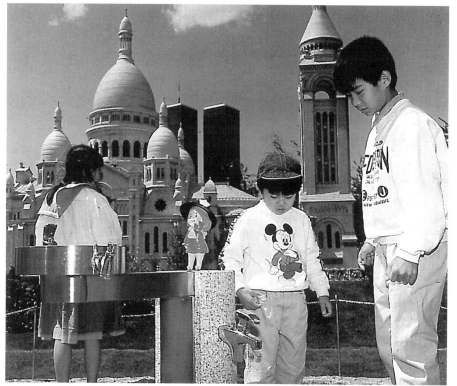

FIGURE 1.3   Tobu World Square, Japan

FIGURE 1.4   Grand Canyon, USA

FIGURE 1.5   Karnak Temple, Luxor, Egypt

With mobility, comes encounter. In many respects, this may be stimulating and productive. Global encounters and interactions are producing inventive new cultural forms and repertoires. Musical culture provides an excellent example: Salma and Sabine are Pakistani sisters who sing Abba songs in Hindi; Rasta-Cymru is a Welsh-speaking reggae band; El Vez is a Latino Elvis impersonator with attitude; Cartel is a Turkish–German group appropriating US West-coast rap music and style. The anthropologist Jan Nederveen Pieterse reflects on the significance of such musical and other cultural intermixtures:

> How do we come to terms with phenomena such as Thai boxing by Moroccan girls in Amsterdam, Asian rap in London, Irish bagels, Chinese tacos and Mardi Gras Indians in the United States, or Mexican schoolgirls dressed in Greek togas dancing in the style of Isidora Duncan? How do we interpret Peter Brook directing the Mahabharata, or Ariane Mânouchkine staging a Shakespeare play in Japanese Kubuki style for a Paris audience in the Théâtre Soleil?
>
> (Nederveen Pieterse, 1995, p. 53)

Nederveen Pieterse describes these phenomena in terms of the origination of 'third cultures', the 'creolization of global culture', the development of an 'intercontinental crossover culture'. Globalization, from this perspective, is conceived in terms of a process of creative and conjoining **hybridization**.   hybridization

Of course, this is only one aspect of the logic of globalization. The encounter between cultures can produce tension and friction. The globalization process can equally be associated with confrontation and the collision of cultures. At the present time, we can see some of the stresses of global change in the difficult relations between Western and Islamic worlds. It is there in the conflict between French people and Algerian migrants, or in the divisions between Germans and their Turkish 'guest workers'. The building of Europe's largest mosque in Rome, the historical centre of Christendom, has had some problematical repercussions. In Britain, the 'Rushdie affair' has testified to the difficulty of intercultural understanding. The Iranian government has sought to block American satellite broadcasting to prevent the 'Westoxification' of Iranian society (while many Iranians have been actively seeking to acquire satellite dishes in order to see Western programmes such as *Baywatch* and *Beavis and Butthead*). In August 1995, the socialist mayor of Courcouronnes, south of Paris, put a ban on satellite dishes to prevent the reception of programmes from North Africa. 'Integration', he maintained, 'does not mean transforming France into a nation of the Maghreb' (*The Observer*, 17 September 1995).

But there are also cultural confrontations within the Western world itself. It is apparent in the ambivalence and anxiety felt in Europe towards American cultural exports: in 1995, the Uruguay Round of GATT (General Agreement on Tarriffs and Trade) negotiations almost broke down on account of French intransigence about maintaining restrictive quotas on US film and television products. 'Are we all Americans now?' Andrew Billen wondered (*The Observer*, 17 September 1995), as the Disney Channel arrived in Britain. There is the clear sense in some quarters that 'Americanization' – from Hollywood to Coke and McDonald's – is a threat to the integrity of European cultural life (see **Tomlinson**, 1997). In these defensive and protective responses to cultural encounter, we are a long way from the celebration of cultural hybridization.

2.2   Complexities of globalization

Having argued that globalization and global encounter constitute a new logic of economic and cultural development, I want now to make two important qualifications to what would otherwise risk being too facile an argument. Media researcher Marjorie Ferguson exhorts us not to succumb to what she calls the 'mythology about globalization':

> To whatever extent globalization (however defined) actually is occurring (and to whom), its alleged positive benefits or negative costs are difficult to assess. The deeper questions are: 'cui bono?' and 'who is being globalized (or de-globalized), to what extent and by whom?'
>
> (Ferguson, 1992, p. 69)

Let us not imagine global economy and culture in terms of a simple and schematic ideal type. 'Globalization,' as Ferguson argues, 'defined either as a journey or a destination demands a critical approach' (p.87).

The first point of qualification that should be made is that globalization does not supersede and displace everything that preceded it. As well as recognizing social innovation, we must have regard to the evident continuities in social and cultural life. Globalization may be seen in terms of an accumulation of cultural phenomena, where new global elements coexist alongside existing and established local or national cultural forms. This is nicely illustrated in the anthropologist Ulf Hannerz's description of a small Nigerian town where he has undertaken anthropological field work over the past twenty years. Consider the local record shops:

> What struck me about them was that you could inspect the stock, and then predict to what ethnic group the store owner belonged. Nigerian popular music has tended to be ethnically marked, again mostly Yoruba, Ibo, or Hausa. But most likely you will find some imported records as well. West Indian reggae has been very popular in Nigeria, and there may be some recordings by American religious vocalists, of the televangelist type. Recorded tapes have also become popular in Kafanchan in recent times. You could pick them up from a hawker who sells pirated copies out of a tall stack mounted on the back of his bicycle.
>
> (Hannerz, 1992, p. 24)

Or take the example of television broadcasting:

> Switch on a television set in Kafanchan at night, and you may see
> newscasts in English and Hausa, an old episode of *Charlie's Angels*, a
> concert by Hausa drummers, commercials for detergents and bicycles, and
> a paid announcement of a funeral to take place in the nearest big city, where
> the TV station is located. The notion of funeral commercials struck me as
> innovative at first, but obviously it is an extension of the concept of the full-
> page advertisements wealthy Nigerians take out in their daily newspapers
> to announce the burials of their loved ones. Death and conspicuous
> consumption often go together in Nigeria.
>
> (ibid., pp. 24–25)

What is being emphasized is the juxtaposition and combination of both old
and new elements – cultural persistence as well as cultural innovation. It is
something we must recognize in relation to the continuing significance of
national culture. One of the rhetorical generalizations of globalization
mythology – probably the one that is most commonly and assertively
proclaimed – is that the national point of reference has been rendered
obsolete in the contemporary world. Here the qualifying observation of
Anthony Smith is highly apposite. 'In the modern world', he notes, '[the] felt
and perceived collective past is still pre-eminently ethnic and national ... .
This is only to be expected, given the centrality of memory in forging
identities and cultures, which is why the basic motifs, ideas and styles of
post-modern cosmopolitanism are folk or national in origin' (Smith, 1991,
p. 159). Whatever the progress of cosmopolitan orientations, the warm
appeal of national affiliations and attachments remains tenacious.

In the second of my qualifying observations on the logic of globalization, I
want to emphasize its complexity and diversity (which make it particularly
unamenable to ideal-type categorizations). The processes of global change are
multifarious, and they are also experienced differentially by all those who
confront them. Something of this multifariousness is brought out in another
text of Ulf Hannerz's, in which he seeks to clarify some of the different ways
of experiencing globalization.

READING A

Turn now to Reading A: Ulf Hannerz, 'Varieties of transnational
experience'. This is a section from an article entitled 'The withering
away of the nation?', which puts forward the argument that the nation is
in decline and that the transnationalization of culture is of growing
significance.

Note Hannerz's recognition of the complexity of global experience, as he
documents the different manifestations of post-national experience.

What is your response to the arguments of Reich and Ohmae (the like of
which we shall come across again in Ian Angell's arguments in Reading

B)? Do you agree with Jo-Jo's argument that 'there's no such thing as "England" any more'? What of the idea of 'hybridity' (which we shall come back to in section 4) as preferable to the 'purity' of traditional (national, religious) identities?

Hannerz's concern is with the 'various kinds of people for whom the national works less well'. Do you think there are those for whom it still works at least well enough? What are your own thoughts concerning the merits of cosmopolitan versus national identity?

For an argument that the nation remains an important and valuable point of reference, you might look up the work of Anthony D. Smith, to which Hannerz refers.

What Hannerz makes clear is that how a person experiences and responds to the forces of globalization will be a consequence of their economic, social and geographical position in the world. He describes two categories of person who are most likely to respond to the challenge of globalization. There is Reich's '**symbolic analyst**', who holds an occupation involving the non-standardized manipulation of symbolic information (data, words, oral and visual representations), and who continuously accumulates mobile, transferable and hence highly valued skills, skills that are autonomous of fixed organizational or national location. Or there is Ohmae's '**transnational organization man**', who unlike the 'symbolic analyst' is not autonomous in relation to every *organizational* context, but who rather is mobile between the multiple locations of the truly global (i.e. non-national) corporation, possessing skills which are at a premium in relation to that corporation, and hence whose sense of identity and solidarity is bound up with the life of that corporation. These categories of person are most likely to evaluate detachment from the national culture of origin in a positive light, while those in more place-based occupations – in 'routine production services' and 'person services' – are, we infer, more likely to react defensively and negatively to the disruptions of global change.

The statements of Jo-Jo and Salman Rushdie are again responsive, in their different ways, to the possibilities inherent in globalization, though each is a world away from the aspirations of Reich's and Ohmae's privileged business executives. But Hannerz would surely recognize – if he were to move beyond his objectives simply to note some of the varieties of cosmopolitanism – that there are those who will defiantly refuse cosmopolitan cultural experiences in favour of the perceived certainties of ethnic or national containment.

There are more and less benign encounters with the forces of globalization. The geographer Doreen Massey captures this inequality well in relation to the experience of human mobility and movement, which I have described as being one of the phenomena at the heart of the globalization process. At one end of the spectrum, she argues, there are those 'at the forefront' of what is going on: 'the jet-setters, the ones sending and receiving the faxes and the e-mail, holding the international conference calls, the ones distributing the

symbolic analyst

transnational organization man

films, controlling the news, organizing the investments and the international currency transactions.' At the other end are those who are out of control:

> The refugees from El Salvador or Guatemala and the undocumented migrant workers from Michoacán in Mexico crowding into Tijuana to make perhaps a fatal dash for it across the border into the USA to grab a chance of a new life. Here the experience of movement, and indeed of a confusing plurality of cultures, is very different. And there are those from India, Pakistan, Bangladesh and the Caribbean, who come halfway round the world only to get held up in an interrogation room at Heathrow.
>
> (Massey, 1993, pp. 61–2)

'Some initiate flows and movement', Massey observes, 'others don't; some are more on the receiving end of it than others; some are effectively imprisoned by it' (ibid., p. 61). Globalization is an uneven and an unequal process.

So far, I have tried to emphasize the complexity of the globalization process. And I have sought to emphasize the differing experience and perceptions of this process. For some (Reich's symbolic analyst, for example), globalization represents a positive development. For others, it can be a frightening and disorientating experience, and it may be resisted (and, of course, old identities are still there to hang on to).

Now I want to move on to a more theoretical level of discussion, considering first the economic and then the cultural dynamics of the globalization process.

3   Economic globalization

Globalization is a complex process, involving both economic and cultural dynamics. Already, from the above discussion, you should have some initial sense of the interaction between economic and cultural factors in the logic of globalization. It is these that I want to explore more fully in the next two sections. First, we should consider the economic restructuring that is driving global transformation, before going on, in section 4, to consider cultural dynamics in more detail. Section 3.1 will be concerned with one of the most powerful scenarios for the global future, associated with the idea of an emerging **global information economy**. This constitutes one of the bleakest projections for a new world system, envisaging and forecasting an economic order characterized by division, fragmentation and inequality. In section 3.2, we shall explore some further aspects of economic globalization, seeking to open up more promising and creative possibilities in the global logic. Here, we shall be concerned with what happens as global businesses have to negotiate the gravity and resistance of the real world. The processes of globalization do not evolve in the abstract and empty space of a *tabula rasa*.

global information economy

The global economy exists in the context of, and must come to terms with, the realities of actually existing societies, with their accumulated – that is to say historical – cultures and ways of life. In different locations, different contexts, different circumstances, the nature and configuration of the globalization process will vary. The focus here will be on the relationship between global and local, on what has been called the **global–local nexus**.

global–local nexus

Throughout sections 3 and 4, as we explore the interrelationships between economy and culture, you should take note of the diverse possibilities inherent in the processes of globalization. While a great many business and economic projections encourage us to think that the logic of globalization is fixed and determined, approaches which are attentive to the cultural dimensions of globalization suggest a variety of possible developments and outcomes. Globalization is an unfinished project, and it is also, as I have argued, a contradictory and contested one. There are different and competing narratives and projects for globalization. So, you should not think that the nature of the global future is pre-ordained.

3.1   The new world information economy

Globalization is about the organization of economic production and the exploitation of markets on a world scale. (See the discussion of 'globalization' in **du Gay, Hall et al.**, 1997.) Of course, this entrepreneurial aspiration does not come out of the blue. The development of the world economy has a long history, dating from at least the sixteenth century, and associated with the economic and imperial expansion of the great powers. From the late nineteenth century, multinational or transnational corporations emerged as the key shapers of the international economy, and it was the ever more extensive and intensive integration of their business activities that set in motion the dynamics of the globalization process. What we are witnessing in the late twentieth century, with the advent of global corporations, is the continuation and culmination of the constant aspiration to overcome national boundaries and achieve world-scale advantages. If multinational or transnational corporations operate across national frontiers and from the perspective of the national economy in which they originate, global corporations seek to operate as if there were no national frontiers and with what Kenichi Ohmae (1989) refers to as 'equidistance of perspective'.

What distinguishes global accumulation now from the earlier forms of international or world economic organization? What is new and unprecedented about the global economic order of the late twentieth century? 'What is new,' Carnoy, Castells et al. (1993, p. 6) suggest, 'is not so much that international trade is an important part of each nation's economy, but that national economies now work as units at the world scale in real time.' Or, as Manuel Castells expresses it elsewhere:

> By global economy we mean an economy that works as a unit in real time on a planetary scale. It is an economy where capital flows, labour markets, commodity markets, information, raw materials, management and organization are internationalized and fully interdependent throughout the planet ...
>
> (Castells, 1994, p. 21)

The global economy combines instantaneous electronic transactions with the accelerated distribution of physical goods through 'just-in-time' delivery systems. Driving this process forward are the new global corporations, which have the organizational and technological capacity to operate on this real-time basis across the world's key markets.

Carnoy, Castells et al. argue, further, that this global transformation is closely linked to the growing significance of knowledge and information in the changing world economy – their concern is with 'the new global economy in the information age'. 'Production in the advanced capitalist societies', they argue, 'shifts from material goods to information-processing activities, fundamentally changing the structure of these societies to favour economic activities that focus on symbol manipulation in the organization of production and in the enhancement of productivity' (Carnoy, Castells et al., 1993, p. 5). As Castells (1994, p. 21) puts it, 'information becomes the critical raw material of which all social processes and social organizations are made'; what is critical in all economic activities now is 'the capacity to retrieve, store, process and generate information and knowledge.' The global information economy is 'based less on the location of natural resources, cheap and abundant labour, or even capital stock, and more on the capacity to create new knowledge and to apply it rapidly, via information processing and telecommunications, to a wide range of human activities in ever-broadening space and time' (Carnoy, Castells et al., 1993, p. 6). Economic organizations thereby have a new basis for flexibility and mobility. And you should note that this economic development is precisely what brings to the fore Reich's 'symbolic analyst' and Ohmae's 'transnational organization man' (as described in Reading A). The global information economy creates a new international elite of knowledge producers and processors.

An absolutely crucial factor in the transnational organization of this post-industrial economy has been the development of information and communications technology, increasingly integrated now into a global technological infrastructure. The new telecommunications and computer networks make possible the instantaneous, real-time coordination of economic activities, permitting organizational decentralization to coexist with functional coordination and integration. The frictions of time and space are significantly transcended. Castells (1994, p. 29) writes of the emergence of 'the space of flows, superseding the space of places.' Other writers frequently refer to conquest of distance in terms of 'time-space compression'. Taking up Marshall McLuhan's phrase, Linda Harasim (1994, p. 8) sees them as implicated in the phenomenon of 'global villagization'. And the assumption made by all is that these information and communication networks have now become the main conduits of all economic activities and functions. There are predictions of a world characterized by network transactions, involving a whole array of 'tele'-activities (tele-work, tele-shopping, tele-education, tele-medicine, tele-viewing, etc.). With the development of such electronic networks, William Mitchell (1995, pp. 139–40) argues:

> the necessary connection between buyers and sellers is established not through physical proximity but through logical linkage. It is all done with software and databases. Merchants get to potential customers by accessing lists of electronic addresses; the key to successful marketing is not being in the right neighbourhood with the right sorts of customers for whom to lay out wares, but ... having the right lists for sending out advertising.

This growing centrality of electronic transactions underpins the construction of 'information superhighways' in the world's developed countries. 'So a new logic has emerged,' Mitchell concluded. 'The great power struggle of cyberspace will be over network topology, connectivity, and access – not the geographic borders and chunks of territory that have been fought over in the past' (ibid., p. 151).

ACTIVITY 2

There is something quite seductive about this idea that economic actors have become increasingly 'disembedded' from local contexts, and have assumed a growing autonomy *vis-à-vis* particular places. It is an idea that is frequently put forward these days. Are you persuaded by such techno-rhetoric? Do you believe that new technological capacities and organizational forms can actually transcend geographical constraints? Do you think that we are really seeing a decline in the significance of borders and territorial attachments? In many parts of the world, there seems to be evidence of the growing significance of such allegiances.

My own view is that it is preferable to say, not that the new technologies are overcoming spatial constraints, but, rather, that they are changing the basis on which global corporations relate to place and territory. To see what this means, let us consider the organization of production and of service provision in the new global environment (in section 3.2 we shall go on to consider the organization of markets). The key point is that the significance and influence of national territory and the nation-state have been considerably weakened. Global enterprise no longer functions in terms of the national economy, but across national frontiers, and national governments are increasingly powerless to regulate and control its activities. 'Does Government Matter?' is the front-page headline on a recent issue of *Newsweek* magazine (26 June 1995) (Figure 1.6). 'A brash new world economy is shoving the old statist structures aside,' the lead story observes. 'It is private, it is fast-paced and it is, by and large, averse to government meddling.' The management consultant Kenichi Ohmae (already referred to in Reading A) puts this argument even more strongly:

> The nation-state has become an unnatural, even dysfunctional, unit for organizing human activity and managing economic endeavour in a borderless world. It represents no genuine, shared community of economic interests; it defines no meaningful flows of economic activity.
>
> (Ohmae, 1993, p. 78)

This has now become a commonplace observation, and we must recognize that it does, indeed, contain a significant truth.

But this by no means translates into unconditional freedom and mobility and the transcendence of geographical constraints as such. Global corporations are, in fact, coming into closer relationship with sub-national territories – leading to what Ohmae (1993) calls 'the rise of the **region-state**'. Particularly significant is the rise of what the urban sociologist Saskia Sassen (1991) calls the **global city** – cities like London, New York or Tokyo, which are the command centres of corporate organizations and the strategic nodes in corporate networks. These cities are where the symbolic analysts congregate. 'The more national states fade in their role,' Castells (1994, p. 23) observes, 'the more cities emerge as a driving force ... Thus we are witnessing the renewal of the role of regions and cities as locuses of autonomy and political decision.' Global corporations have reason to draw on the skills and resources held by particular cities and regions. And cities and regions have, by the same token, the clear motivation to ensure that they are 'plugged into' the global economy and networks. In the words of business consultant Rosabeth Moss Kanter (1995, p. 154), they must learn 'how to harness global forces for local advantage', for success 'will come to those cities, states and regions that do the best job of linking the businesses that operate within them to the global economy.' Castells is somewhat optimistic in claiming that cities and regions are places of autonomy. For some cities, this may, indeed be the case, but for the great majority, power lies in the hands of corporate interests. Most cities and regions are forced to compete with each other to attract the attention of increasingly mobile investors, and are always vulnerable to the loss of what they have attracted. Those that fail in this inter-urban competition – this race between cities – are relegated to the margins of the global economy.

region-state

global city

READING B

Turn now to Reading B by Ian Angell, 'Winners and Losers in the Information Age'. Ian Angell is a Professor of Information Systems, and you might read this text as representing the perspective of the new class of symbolic analysts. The ideas of Reich and Ohmae, which you encountered in Reading A, are further developed here, though in a somewhat bleaker scenario, it might be argued.

What is your reaction to this projection for a global information order? Do you agree that the nation-state is mutating into the corporate state? What is likely to be the response of those who lose out – whether it be the 'poor areas', the 'expanding underclass' or the 'untrained migrants'? Consider particularly Angell's observation on the competition between cities and regions. Have you yourself observed anything of this new form of global competition? Angell's observations on the relationship between globalization and localization will be relevant to the discussion in section 3.2.

Ian Angell's argument acknowledges the bleak scenario I have outlined in this section as both necessary and inevitable. It accepts Reich's distinction between symbolic analysts, on the one hand, and those engaged in in-person or routine production services, on the other. Moving beyond Reich's more moderate position, Angell sanctions the privilege of the former group – 'the real generators of wealth' – accepting that they will expect just rewards and that they will show no loyalty to anything so anachronistic as the nation-state. His global information society is divided between those who belong to this footloose elite – always ready 'to move on to more lucrative and agreeable climes' – and those burdened by their immobility. Even further down the hierarchy comes the 'expanding underclass' and the 'untrained migrants'. As Castells (1994, p. 39) puts it from his more critical perspective, there is an 'increasing lack of communication between the directional functions of the economy and the informational elite that performs such functions, on the one hand, and the locally orientated population that experiences an ever deeper identity crisis, on the other.'

FIGURE 1.6
Does Government Matter? (*Newsweek*, cover 26 June 1995; © 1995 Newsweek Inc.; all rights reserved; reprinted by permission).

As well as an employment and social divide, Angell accepts the inevitability of growing divisions between cities and regions. 'Any area with independent aspirations will use economic weapons against its neighbours,' he argues – area against area, town against town, even suburb against suburb. The fundamental and brutal principle is that 'rich areas will dump poor areas'. This is what Castells, again critically, describes as the 'uneven integration' of cities and regions into the global system. 'Thus,' he argues, 'the global economy embraces the whole planet, but not all regions and all people on the planet' (Castells, 1994, pp. 21–2). In Angell's scenario, there are networked places, and there are those that no longer work as places – those that have become non-places in the global information economy.

3.2   The global–local nexus

Now I want to move on to consider another way of thinking about economic globalization, and one that might offer some more optimistic possibilities than the perspective (of Ohmae and Angell) that we have just encountered in the previous section. This second approach involves recognition that the global economy cannot simply override existing social and historical realities: global entrepreneurs must negotiate, and come to terms with, particular local contexts, conditions and constraints. This is something we have already come upon indirectly in section 3.1, in relation to global business's need for local expertise and resources (see Angell, 1995). In this section, we shall explore this relationship between the global and the local more fully.

Globalization is frequently seen in terms of the 'disembedding' of ways of life from the narrow confines of locality. But, increasingly, we are coming to recognize that it is – paradoxically, it seems – also associated with new dynamics of re-localization. Globalization is, in fact, about the creation of a new *global–local nexus*, establishing new and complex relations between global spaces and local spaces (see the discussion of Sony's strategy of global–localization in **du Gay, Hall et al.**, 1997). I should immediately emphasize that 'local' should be seen here as a relational, and a relative, term, which was once significant only in relation to the national territory, but now is being recast in relation to the global. The emerging global–local nexus is about the relation between globalizing and particularizing dynamics in the strategies of global corporations – thus in the context of global business strategies, the local might correspond to a region, to a national, or even to a multinational, sphere of activity (the European Union, for instance).

The global–local agenda has become particularly significant in the context of corporate marketing and promotional strategies. First, we shall consider the marketing and advertising of goods and services in the new global context. And then we shall proceed to look at the marketing of places, which has become increasingly significant as cities and regions seek to position themselves favourably in the new global hierarchies. In pursuing this line of inquiry, we shall begin to confront some of the cultural issues that will then be more fully examined in section 4.

Global corporations must now operate and compete in the world arena in terms of quality, efficiency, product variety, and the close understanding of markets. And they must operate in all markets simultaneously, rather than sequentially, as they once did. One significant aspect of this logic has been the development of the 'global product' – the Walkman, Coca-Cola, Levi jeans, McDonald's hamburgers, or Benetton clothes. Such consumer goods give substance to the idea that, as people gain access to global information and become more globally aware, so they acquire global tastes and become 'global consumers'. And let us note incidentally that these world brands are not just being developed by legitimate corporate entrepreneurs: it is apparent that global mafias are also competing in the development of their own global products – cocaine, heroin, crack. ('The Russian Mafia Goes Global' was the front-page headline of *Newsweek* magazine on 2 October, 1995.)

But the story is still more complex, and is about more than just the creation of global brands. In an interview in *Harvard Business Review*, the chief executive of the US white goods manufacturer, Whirlpool, makes clear his company's strategy 'to be one company worldwide'. What this involves, he argues, is global integration at the level of technology and organization, but when it comes to marketing, there is recognition of the need for decentralization: 'a company may need plants in Europe, the United States, Latin America, and Asia to make products that meet the special needs of local markets ... [V]arying consumer preferences require us to have regional manufacturing centres' (Whitwam, 1994, pp. 136–7). In the marketing context, the global corporation must relate to the local. Take also the example of the new global strategy of Ford. The corporation is aiming to 'transform itself from a multinational organized by geography with regional profit centres into a global car manufacturing business organized by product line' (*Financial Times*, 3 April 1995). Global product teams are being put in place to design cars to be sold around the world. But, as far as marketing strategies are concerned, it is still necessary to take account of regional differences and local customer preferences. As Ford chairman, Alexander Trotman acknowledges, 'the design and feel of our vehicles can be made very different to suit local tastes ... And we will still have regional vehicles like the Lincoln Town Car in North America and the Ford Transit van in Europe' (ibid.). Again, the global strategy entails a compromise with the local.

We can see the same tension in the outlook of advertising and promotional executives (for a more detailed clarification of the work of these symbolic occupations, by Sean Nixon, see Chapter 4 of this book). These are some of the key members of the class of symbolic analysts, actively involved in promoting the mythology of globalization. Advertising executive Theodore Levitt has been one of the most fervent among these activists. 'Widespread communication and travel pound the same constant drumbeat of modern possibilities into the human consciousness everywhere,' he argues in his influential book, *The Marketing Imagination*. 'Everywhere everything gets more like everything else, as the world's preference structure gets pressed into homogenized commonality' (Levitt, 1983, pp. 22, 24). The global corporation 'seeks constantly in every way to standardize everything into a common global mode', giving rise to an increasing number of 'world-standard products' (ibid., pp. 28, 27). Today's global corporation, in contrast to the antiquated multinational corporation of yesterday, operates 'as if the entire world (or major regions of it) were a single, largely identical entity; it ... sells the same things in the same single way everywhere' (ibid., p. 22).

But even the militant globalist Levitt has to recognize the persistence of local differences. Thus, he acknowledges the growth in ethnic markets, though he then manages to accommodate this within his global perspective: 'Everywhere there is Chinese food, pitta bread, country and western music, pizza, and jazz. The global pervasiveness of ethnic forms represents the cosmopolitanization of speciality segments. Again, globalization does not mean the end of segments. It means, instead, their expansion to worldwide proportions' (ibid., pp. 30–31). And where there is still a heavy presence of multinational (as opposed to global) corporations – in the real world of today, that is to say, as opposed to the imagined and desired global order of the future – Levitt has to acknowledge that 'vast differences in products and product features remain between different nations' (ibid., p. 31). This, as far as Levitt is concerned, merely reflects 'the respectful accommodation of multinational corporations to what they believe are fixed local preferences' – a problematical accommodation in so far as 'such differences as remain are vestiges of the hardened inherited past as to cultural preferences, national tastes and standards, and the institutions of business itself' (ibid., pp. 31, 30). But many other advertising executives are more willing to accept this actually existing world, with all its compromises between global and local elements, as what the reality of globalization is all about. They have recognized that global advertising must be diverse and flexible in its scope. As geographer Deborah Leslie (1995, p. 416) observes, global campaigning 'can fall anywhere on the continuum from a totally standardized strategy and execution to a standardized strategy with modified executions (different images, cast, script) to totally localized strategies and executions'. The reality of the global–local nexus is underpinning strategies for what has been called 'global advertising'.

What we see, then, in the pursuits of global business and marketing, is the formation of a new global–local nexus, representing a pragmatic compromise between the aspiration to expand market spaces and the realities of cultural gravity and resistance. The new consumer and advertising philosophies show us how global entrepreneurs relate to questions of space and place. But we can, and we should, look at things the other way round, in terms of how particular spaces and places now relate to the global economy. We have already touched on this issue indirectly in relation to Ohmae's observations on the rise of the region-state; to Angell's thoughts about areas 'with independent aspirations'; and to Moss Kanter's arguments about harnessing global forces for local advantage. It is a question of how, and how successfully, cities and city-regions can insert themselves into the new global system.

'Links are increasingly developed between region-states and the global economy,' notes James Mittleman (1995, p. 291). 'Formed by parts of states, as in "the third Italy" and Baden-Württemberg, or by economic patterns that overlap state boundaries, such as the cross-border zone radiating across the Straits of Malacca and joining parts of Laos, Vietnam and Thailand, region-states hook into and seek to derive advantage from market expansion in a global division of labour'. Entrepreneurial cities and regions compete to present themselves as preferential locations. It is a matter of exploiting local assets and resources to attract, not only industrial and business investment, but also other kinds of mobile venture (conferences and conventions, sporting events, science parks, theme parks, expositions, etc.). Place-specific differences become weapons in what have been called the 'place wars' of the 1990s. In the rivalry between cities and regions, image and profile can be of critical competitive advantage. And because image has become so decisive, as Haider (1992, p. 131) observes, 'image marketing [has become] perhaps the most frequently employed marketing approach to place development used by states, cities, and various places. Image marketing can be used to reinforce existing positive images, neutralize and change unfavourable ones, or create new images where [few] or no images exist.'

This question of image relates to the broader agenda of developing – and exploiting – the kind of urban culture that will help a major city to position itself favourably in the new global setting. As Jack Behrman and Dennis Rondinelli (1992, pp. 119, 116) put it, cities must 'adapt their culture to attract and accommodate the types of international economic activities they desire... "Great cities" in the future will be those that can adapt their cultures to become part of a new international urban network with global economic and cross-cultural ties.'

Image and culture are not just crucial in attracting investment in industry and services. They are also important in attracting the spending power of global tourists. This, declares a feature article in *Time* magazine (12 June 1995), is 'an age of voyaging on a truly global mass scale. As the 21st century unfurls, people of every class and from every country will be wandering to every part of the planet.' Places throughout the world find themselves competing to attract the tourist dollar. For many parts of the world – those that are marginalized in the global industrial and information economy – this may even seem the only way to survive in the global era:

> Tourism is often presented as the last chance. Thus, through international tourism, poor regions which have been removed from any focus of activity, closed in on themselves, and condemned to certain death by economists, find themselves rediscovered and thrust into the path of development, linked to the international market and propelled on to the world scene.
>
> (Lanfant, 1995, p. 3)

In all regions, poor and rich alike, competitive advantage will be gained through the exploitation of local sites (and sights), culture and heritage. And some places may choose to exploit the local particularities of other global regions. Thus, the town of Windsor has its royal tradition and heritage, but also something more, in its Safari Park. Priscilla Boniface and Peter Fowler (1993, p. 6) refer to an advertisement for it:

An African Adventure ...
... in Berkshire?
The new Windsor Safari Park is all this and more.
You'll find everything from a Moroccan Bazaar
to the Serengeti Plain and discover a host of
thrilling rides in the Port Livingstone Village.

Tourism brings the global economy into encounter with local culture.

ACTIVITY 3

Think of a city or region that you know, which has sought to position itself in the new global context. Perhaps it has endeavoured to attract international business and investment. Or it may have campaigned to attract tourists and cultural visitors, or to host a major sporting event. What strategy and slogans has it used to market itself? To what extent has it made use of its particular history and heritage? How much has the image of place played a role in its self-promotion? How successful do you think it has been? What are the disadvantages in such place-marketing?

In our discussion of economic globalization, we began with the corporate ambition to establish global markets, centred on global cities and linked through global information networks. As the discussion has developed, it has become apparent that these aspirations are too simplistic, failing to take into account the realities of both economic and cultural geographies. It has been necessary to acknowledge the relationship between global and local. What I have sought to emphasize – first in relation to global marketing, and then in relation to the role of cities and regions in the global economy – is the way in which the global and local are integrally related. As Roland Robertson (1995, p. 30) observes, 'globalization has involved the simultaneity and the interpenetration of what are conventionally called the global and the local or – in more abstract vein – the universal and the particular.' Localization is an 'aspect' of globalization'. This opens up possibilities beyond what seemed possible in the scenarios outlined in section 3.1. It also opens up questions of culture and identity, which will be the focus of attention in section 4.

4   Cultural globalization

Let us now move on to consider the cultural aspects of globalization. Increasingly we hear about the development of a global culture. But, as with the idea of a global economy, we must exercise caution. Rather than wielding slogans, we need to undertake careful analysis to understand the phenomenon in its complexity. What precisely, we must ask, is changing in the cultural sphere through the development of global forces?

In section 4.1 we shall consider the media industries – where, of course, we find some of the most dynamic global corporations, driven by basic economic imperatives. In the case of commercial media (film and television, popular music, etc.) there are certainly aspirations towards creating a unitary, worldwide market. Global media corporations, such as Time Warner, Sony and Rupert Murdoch's News Corporation, are thinking in terms of global products and global audiences. This is only possible with certain kinds of programming, however, and for the most part global media interests operate in terms of transnational media spaces (e.g. the 'Eurovision' region; the 'Asian' region served by Murdoch's Star TV). At the same time we shall see that there are contrary tendencies, towards the proliferation of national and also regional (e.g. Basque, Gaelic) media. This may be seen in terms of the (re)assertion of cultural difference and distinction in the face of globalizing tendencies. Again, then, it is the relation between the global and local that is significant: the globalization of the media should be understood in terms of the construction of a complex new map of transnational, national and sub-national cultural spaces.

In section 4.2, we shall move on to consider questions of culture and identity in the new global context. In one of its aspects, cultural globalization is bringing about convergence and **homogenization** in world culture. But, at the same time, there are also more cosmopolitan developments, with new cultural encounters across frontiers creating new and productive kinds of cultural fusion and hybridity. In yet another of its aspects, cultural globalization manifests itself as the revalidation of particular cultures and identities (often against the perceived threats of either homogenization or cosmopolitanization), reinforcing **diversity**. Across the world, there are those who are responding to global upheaval by returning to their 'roots', reclaiming what they see as their ethnic and national homelands, or recovering the certainties of religious tradition and fundamentals. Globalization pulls cultures in different, contradictory, and often conflictual, ways. It is about the 'de-territorialization' of culture, but it also involves cultural 're-territorialization'. It is about the increasing mobility of culture, but also about new cultural fixities.

homogenization

diversity

4.1   New spaces of global media

Since the 1980s, as a consequence of regulatory, economic and technological change, dramatic upheavals have taken place in the media industries, laying the basis for what must be seen as a new media order. No longer constrained by, or responsible to, a philosophy of public service, media corporations are pursuing commercial and marketing objectives.

Driven now by the logic of profit and competition, the overriding objective of the new media corporations is to get their product to the largest number of consumers. There is, then, an expansionist tendency at work, pushing all the time towards the construction of enlarged media spaces and markets. The imperative is to break down the old boundaries and frontiers of national communities, which now present themselves as arbitrary and irrational obstacles to this reorganization of business strategies. Media geographies are thus becoming detached from the symbolic spaces of national culture, and realigned on the basis of the more 'universal' principles of international consumer culture. The free and unimpeded circulation of programmes – television without frontiers – is the great ideal in the new order. It is an ideal whose logic is driving ultimately towards the creation of global programming and global markets – and already we are seeing the rise to power of global corporations intent on turning ideal into reality. The new media order is set to become a global order.

What does this actually mean? Let us first consider what I would call the mythology of global media. In his 'Worldview Address', delivered at the 1990 Edinburgh International Television Festival, the late Steven Ross, then head of the world's largest media business, Time Warner, argued that the global media corporations of the 1990s were finally realizing Marshall McLuhan's vision of the 'global village'. 'The competitive market place of ideas and experience can only bring the world together,' Ross argued. 'With new technologies we can bring services and ideas that will help draw even the most remote areas of the world into the international media community.' The free flow of media and information products would make national frontiers seem a relic of the past. We are, says Ross, 'on the path to a truly free and open competition that will be dictated by consumers' tastes and desires ... [T]he new reality of international media is driven more by market opportunity than by national identity.' And, of course, Ross (whose arguments should recall those of Theodore Levitt) believes that Time Warner's products will play an important role in the 'interconnection of cultures'.

FIGURE 1.7
Walt Disney's Mickey Mouse as media tycoon (Newsweek cover, 14 August 1995; © 1995 Newsweek Inc.; all rights reserved; reprinted by permission).

That is one particular vision of media globalization. It is the operating philosophy of Time Warner and of other media giants, such as Sony, Viacom, News Corporation, and the Walt Disney Company. Global corporations are manoeuvring for world supremacy. It is a process that has brought about major take-overs and mergers: Sony's acquisition of Columbia Pictures, Viacom's purchase of Paramount, Disney's take-over of Capital Cities/ABC, Time Warner's merger with Turner Broadcasting. A fundamental objective of these manoeuvres and machinations has been to bring into existence a global media space and market. In the 1980s, the global advertising company Saatchi and Saatchi was talking about 'world cultural convergence'. Taking up Levitt's arguments about the standardization of culture into a 'common global mode', it was argued that 'convergences in demography, behaviour and shared cultural elements are creating a more favourable climate for acceptance of a single

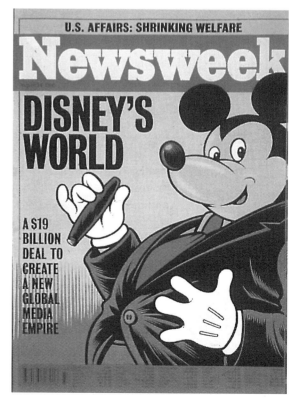

product and positioning across a wide range of geography'. Television programmes such as *Dallas*, or films such as *Star Wars* or *ET* were then seen as exemplary cases, 'hav[ing] crossed many national boundaries to achieve world awareness for their plots, characters, etc.' (Winram, 1984, p. 21). It is a logic that is still at work in the 1990s, with the global television music of MTV, the 'global village' news of CNN, and global box-office hits like *Jurassic Park* and *Pocahontas*. The pursuit of economies of scale through the creation of universal media products is a developing imperative.

But, even as they pursue this ideal of world standardization, these media corporations have to recognize that global reality is more complex (see also the discussions in **du Gay, Hall et al.**, 1997, and in Chapter 2 of this book). They must compromise the mythology of globalization. Let us consider how the globalizing logic proceeds as it comes to encounter and negotiate with the actual world, the world of already existing and established markets and cultures. Consider two examples. The first is that of CNN, which has been considered the very paradigm of a global operator. Launched in 1980 by the American entrepreneur, Ted Turner, its phenomenal success has been achieved through the worldwide distribution of a single English-language news service. The rationale was explained by a CNN representative at the end of the 1980s:

> There has been a cultural and social revolution as a consequence of the globalization of the economy. A blue-collar worker in America is affected as much as a party boss in Moscow or an executive in Tokyo. This means that what we do for America has validity outside America. Our news is global news.
>
> (*Guardian*, 12 November 1989)

In the 1990s, however, the channel is confronting the accusation that it is too American in its corporate identity. CNN's global presence is interpreted as an expression of American cultural domination, and this clearly raises problems about its credibility as a global news provider. Back at company headquarters, this translates into a fundamental dilemma over market strategy and position. CNN's present news service has been successful in reaching the world's business and political elites, but it has not significantly penetrated mass markets, where local affiliations and attachments are far stronger. To reach such viewers, one commentator observed 'CNN would have to dramatically change its vision of a single, English-speaking global network', and 'to effect that change Turner would need to seek partners and would need to localize' (Auletta, 1993, p. 30). What CNN is having to recognize is that the pursuit of further success will entail the production of different editions, in different languages, in different parts of the world. To this end, collaboration with local partners is essential. CNN is having to reconcile global ambitions with local complexities.

The second example is that of MTV, which is also recognized as one of the really successful global operators. Like CNN, MTV has also been forced to respond to the complexities of culture and taste in the global market by regionalizing its output (MTV Europe, MTV Asia, MTV Latino, as well as the American original).

READING C

Turn now to Reading C: Marc Levinson, 'It's an MTV World'. Marc Levinson here provides an excellent journalistic account of the corporate strategies of MTV, described as 'the ultimate New Age multinational'.

What can we learn from the example of MTV about the pragmatics of global marketing? Many commentators see MTV's global strategy as simply extending the domination of US culture – and of the English language – on a global scale. Do you agree with this assessment? Or is globalization about more than this cultural imperialism? What are the cultural factors that resist and set limits to MTV's global aspirations? What evidence is there of the continuing significance of national musical cultures?

What Marc Levinson brings out very well in his article is the difficult balance that has to be managed between economic imperatives (achieving economies of scale) and cultural imperatives (responding to diverse consumer preferences). What is apparent is the tension between globalizing and localizing logics. There are strong pressures to respond to much smaller markets than MTV's global regions. The German music station, Viva, mentioned by Levinson, competes with the global giant by catering for the distinctive taste of German youth (including pop songs in German regional dialects).

READING D

Reading D is a short article 'Gut, Gut, Alles Super Gut!', also by Marc Levinson, which describes Viva in more detail. This article suggests that globalization in fact opens up a whole array of possibilities for more localized marketing strategies.

The relation between global and local dynamics is not just an issue for corporate marketing strategies, however. It also concerns the relation between global cultural industries and those local interests that experience globalization in terms of standardization and the loss of identity. Globalization gives rise to active cultural campaigning to defend local and particularistic identities. In Europe, such campaigns have been directed against American media interests – the global corporations of Hollywood – which are seen as a force that is eroding European national cultures and traditions. This was a crucial issue in the Uruguay round of GATT negotiations (completed in 1995). Whilst the United States called, in the name of free trade, for the free circulation of ideas (Steven Ross's message too, if you recall), European interests were endeavouring to preserve quotas and restrictions, in order, as they saw it, to defend the specificity and integrity of European culture. It was a particularly big issue for France, which was extremely critical of Britain for having afforded Ted Turner's CNN access to European audiences. Here is how one critic articulated the European defensiveness (perhaps even paranoia): 'Turner is only the avant-garde of the big US companies who are sitting back to see how Europe reacts. If he gets in, Disney and Time Warner will follow' (Powell, 1993). The European stance has been articulated as a battle for freedom of expression: 'We want the Americans to let us survive. Ours is a struggle for the diversity of European culture so that our children will be able to hear French and German and Italian spoken in films' (ibid.). The emphasis is on particularity and difference, in the face of the logic of standardization that seems to threaten their erosion.

But, within Europe, defences are not only mobilized against the global corporations of Hollywood. There are also those who see the development of global media interests within Europe itself as a threat to their particular cultures and identities. Their argument on behalf of 'decentralization in the global era' is about culture in the regions and small nations of Europe: 'There are strong cultural reasons for communications policies recognizing and supporting the existence of television in the regions. In the modern communications system it is impossible to maintain small cultural identities (and their respective languages) without the corresponding local media of the regions in which they exist' (de Moragas Spà and Garitaonandía, 1995, p. 15). There is an appeal to the kind of situated meaning and belonging that seem to be dissolved by the forces of globalization. This new regionalism puts value on the diversity and difference of identities in Europe, and seeks to sustain and conserve the variety of cultural heritages, both regional and national.

Broadcasting has been seen as a major resource in the pursuit of this objective, and since the 1980s we have seen a growing interest in promoting media industries and activities within the regions and small nations of Europe. In most cases, principles of local cultural interest have been mobilized against the market interests of transnational economic forces. In lobbying for support from the European Community, the argument has been put that 'in the particular case of regional TV programming in the European vernacular languages, the criteria should be based on both audience ratings and percentages of the language-speaking population, not on strict, economic cost-effectiveness' (Garitaonandía, 1993, p. 291). Since the late 1980s, a certain level of support has been elicited from the European Union, particularly through its MEDIA programme, which provides loans and support for small producers across the continent. Within the Union there has been increasing sensitivity towards cultural difference and commitment to the preservation of cultural identities in Europe.

Here again, we have an example of the global–local nexus. 'Local' in this case, however, means something quite different from what it means in the corporate lexicon. In this context, it relates to the distinctive identities and interests of local and regional communities. In these global times, there are those who desire to 're-territorialize' the media, that is to re-establish a relationship between media and territory. They are determined that the media should contribute to sustaining both the distinctiveness and the integrity of local and regional cultures against the threatening forces of 'de-territorialization' and homogenization. 'Local' in this sense constitutes a challenge to the strategies of global corporate interests.

ACTIVITY 4

Before moving on to the next section, I would like you to reflect on your own viewing habits. Consider the pattern of your viewing across the spectrum of global, national, regional/local. What are the respective merits and limits of global and national television? Is local or regional television important to you? Your answer to this question may vary according to where you live in the UK. Why might this be? What do you consider to be the most appropriate scale of regional/local broadcasting in this country? Do you think that we have the right balance between global, national and regional/local broadcasting? Do you think there is a future for regional television in the new European context?

4.2   A world of difference

Finally, I want to go on to look at some broader aspects of globalization in relation to culture and identity. For it is surely clear that the global shift — associated with the creation of world markets, with international communication and media flows, and with international travel — has profound implications for the way we make sense of our lives and of the changing world we live in. For some, the proliferation of shared or common cultural references across the world evokes cosmopolitan ideals. There is the sense that cultural encounters across frontiers can create new and productive kinds of cultural fusion and hybridity. But, where some envisage and enjoy cosmopolitan complexities, others perceive, and often oppose, what they see as cultural homogenization and the erosion of cultural specificity. Globalization is also linked to the revalidation of particular cultures and identities. Globalization is, then, transforming our apprehension of the world in sharply contrasting ways. It is provoking new senses of disorientation and of orientation, giving rise to new experiences of both placeless and placed identity.

Old certainties and hierarchies of identity are called into question in a world of dissolving boundaries and disrupted continuities. Thus, in a country that is now a container of African and Asian cultures, can the meaning of what it is to be British ever again have the old confidence and surety it might once have had? And what does it mean now to be European in a continent coloured not only by the cultures of its former colonies, but also by American and Japanese cultures? Is not the very category of identity itself problematical? Is it at all possible, in global times, to sustain a coherent and unified sense of identity? Continuity and historicity of identity are challenged by the immediacy and intensity of global cultural confrontations. Of course, we should not believe that these developments are entirely unprecedented; as I made clear at the outset, globalization has a long history, and a great many cultures have historical experience of global intrusion (perhaps the shock of globalization is greater for the 'First' world than the 'Third'?). Nonetheless, we should have regard to what is without precedent at the end of the twentieth century: the scale, the extent, the comprehensive nature, of global integration. We should consider – in the terms I set out in section 2 – the particular complexities of global encounter at this century's end.

One very powerful dimension of global cultural change has been that which has sought to dissolve the frontiers and divisions between different cultures. It has been actively promoted by global corporate interests, and we have already come across it in the pronouncements of Ohmae, Ross and Levitt – it is an ideal that is particularly sympathetic to those members of the class of symbolic analysts working in the creative areas of media, advertising, and so on. We could consider it in terms of the global culture and philosophy associated with 'McDonaldization' or 'Coca-colonization'. But a particularly good example – because it is so explicit and self-aware about its objectives – is that of Benetton advertising. Through its 'United Colours of Benetton' slogan, the company has actively promoted the idea of the 'global village', associated with global consumer citizenship. What is advocated is the ideal of a new, 'universal' identity that transcends old, particularistic attachments. But transcendence is through incorporation, rather than through dissolution. Michael Shapiro describes it as 'a globalizing, ecumenical impulse':

> Ever since [Oliviero] Toscanini [the artistic creator of the campaigns] produced the slogan, *The United Colours of Benetton*, the Benetton company has made explicit its desire to dominate the mediascape with a symbolism that comprehends nationalities, ethnicities, religions, and even tribal affiliations. The world of geopolitical boundaries – boundaries transversed by Benetton's enterprises – is no impediment to the production of media-carried global symbolism.
>
> (Shapiro, 1994, p. 442)

This global corporate philosophy is further refined in Benetton's most recent campaign, concerned with global threats and disasters:

> In this case, the interpretative work locates the observer in a global community, trying to make sense of the violent clashes of ethno-nationalists. This global self-identification is precisely the difference-effacing stance that Benetton is trying to achieve. The interpretative contemplation of global threats and catastrophes cuts across ethnicities, nationalities, and tribalisms, allowing Benetton to position its products in a universalizing thematic that transcends cultural inhibitions.
>
> (ibid., p. 448)

What the example of Benetton makes clear is the resourcefulness of global advertising, both incorporating and effacing cultural difference in its endeavours to put in place the new global acumen.

A second dimension of cultural globalization that we should consider is that which promotes cultural encounter and interaction. Here, in stark contrast with the first dimension that we have just looked at, we are concerned with the active interpenetration, combination and mixture of cultural elements. These processes are, as Akbar Ahmed makes clear, a consequence of both communication flows and human flows:

> The mixing of images, interlocking of cultures, juxtaposition of different peoples, availability of information are partly explained because populations are mobile as never before. The mobility continues in spite of increasingly rigid immigration controls. Filipino maids in Dubai, Pakistani workers in Bradford, the Japanese buying Hollywood studios, Hong Kong Chinese entrepreneurs acquiring prime property in Vancouver testify to this. The swirling and eddying of humanity mingles ideas, cultures and values as never before in history.
>
> (Ahmed, 1992, p. 26)

Cultures are transformed by the incorporations they make from other cultures in the world. Salman Rushdie (1991, p. 394) has famously written of 'the transformation that comes of new and unexpected combinations of human beings, cultures, ideas, politics, movies, songs'; '*Mélange*, hotchpotch,' he declares, 'a bit of this and a bit of that is *how newness enters the world*' (see also Hannerz in Reading A for this chapter). This process of hybridization is particularly apparent now in developments within popular culture. The sociologist Les Back (1994, p. 14) describes the bhangramuffin music of the singer/songwriter Apache Indian as 'a meeting place where the languages and rhythms of the Caribbean, North America and India mingle producing a new and vibrant culture'. 'Artists like Apache Indian are expressing and defining cultural modes that are simultaneously local and global,' Back observes. 'The music manifests itself in a connective supplementarity – raga plus bhangra plus England plus India plus Kingston plus Birmingham' (ibid., p. 15). Places too can be characterized in terms of hybridity: places of encounter, meeting places, crucibles in which cultural elements are turned into new cultural compounds. Doreen Massey (1993, p. 66) argues for the recognition of 'a sense of place which is extraverted, which includes a consciousness of its links with the wider world, which integrates in a positive way the global and the local'. A 'global sense of place' involves openness to global dynamics and also an acceptance of cultural diversity and the possibilities of cultural encounter within.

The third dimension of cultural globalization that I want to put before you concerns developments that apparently involve a rejection or turning away from the turbulent changes associated with global integration. These developments express themselves in a turn, or return, to what are seen as traditional and more fundamental loyalties. In the recent period, we have become increasingly aware of the resurgence of national, regional, ethnic and territorial attachments. In Eastern Europe, particularly in the former Yugoslavia, we have witnessed the growth of neo-nationalism in its most militant form, but it has also been a feature of Western Europe, with the assertion of Basque, Breton or Scottish identities. It has now become a journalistic commonplace to describe such regionalist or nationalist reassertion in terms of a reversion or regression to tribal loyalties. These loyalties and attachments seem to go against the grain of globalization; they appear to articulate the desire and need for stability and order, as a refuge from the turbulence and upheaval of global transformation. And, of course, there is a great deal of truth in this theory of resistance through roots. But we might, at the same time, also see this as itself an expression of the globalization process – Anthony Smith (1991, p. 143) writes of the 'globalization of nationalism'. Resurgent nations are also seeking to position themselves in the new global space.

We may see the same contradictory relation to the globalization process in the case of resurgent religious cultures and identities. While there has been a return to fundamentals within Hinduism, Judaism and Christianity, it is the case of Islamic fundamentalism that has been made to stand out for its opposition to global times. The attempts by some Islamic countries to ban satellite television have seemed to symbolize resistance to global information and communication flows (those for which Steven Ross was such a powerful advocate). A *Guardian* headline (5 August, 1994) expressed it perfectly: 'As satellite television shrinks the world, traditionalists from Tehran to Bollywood [India] take on the dishes in a war of the heavens'. At one level, of course, this does indeed represent a defensive and protective response to the disruptions of global modernity. As Akbar Ahmed (himself a Muslim) makes clear in his book *Postmodernism and Islam*, we must see such actions in the context of the struggle by traditional cultures, and particularly Islam, to come to terms with Western globalization:

> The West, though the dominant global civilization, will continue to expand its boundaries to encompass the world; traditional civilizations will resist in some areas, accommodate to change in others. In the main, only one, Islam, will stand firm in its path. Islam, therefore, appears to be set on a collision course with the West.
>
> (Ahmed, 1992, p. 264)

But we must see this as far more than just closure and retreat from global culture. What we must also recognize is the aspiration to create a space within global culture. For many Muslims, Ahmed argues, the objective is 'to participate in the global civilization without their identity being obliterated' (ibid.). As Peter Beyer (1994, pp. 4, 3) argues:

[The] revitalization of religion is a way of asserting a particular (group) identity, which in turn is a prime method of competing for power and influence in the global system... [T]he central thrust is to make Islam and Muslims more determinative in the world system, not to reverse globalization. The intent is to shape global reality, not to negate it.

The point is to create a global civilization on a different basis to that which is being elaborated by the symbolic analysts of the West.

What I am trying to bring out in all of this is the factor of diversity and difference in the cultural experience of global modernity: new forms of universal culture, new kinds of particularism, new hybrid developments, all of them gaining their significance from their new global context. We should not think of globalization in terms of homogenization, then, in line with what is commonly believed and feared.

But nor should we see it just in terms of diversity and differentiation, which is the opposite temptation that many more critical spirits have succumbed to. What globalization in fact brings into existence is a new basis for thinking about the relation between cultural convergence and cultural difference. This new basis is brought out very well in Richard Wilk's discussion of beauty pageants in the Caribbean country of Belize.

READING E

Turn now to Reading E: 'The local and the global in the political economy of beauty'. In this reading, Richard Wilk, an anthropologist, makes some very interesting observations on the question of homogenization versus differentiation with respect to beauty competitions in the Caribbean country of Belize. Wilk provides a textured and historically-informed analysis that does justice to the real complexities and tensions involved in this cultural phenomenon.

In the opening section, he makes some preliminary observations about the American Double-Dutch League Jump Rope Championships. Before proceeding beyond this, try to clarify in your own mind the issues he is seeking to elaborate.

When you read Wilk's more sustained account of beauty contests, you should try to understand the *complexity* of the relationship between local and global dynamics.

Wilk summarizes his argument thus:

Beauty pageants are an exemplar of global cultural flow, and the tensions between local and supranational production and reception of media events ... The pageants are portrayed as sites where Belizean identity is recast in a universalized language of difference and distinction. The political econ- omy of beauty allows local production and interpretation only within a narrow semantic frame provided by the metropole.

(Wilk, 1995, p. 117)

What are emerging in the global system, Wilk argues, are new **structures of common difference**. Here is how he explains what this means:

> The new global cultural system promotes difference instead of suppressing it, but selects the dimensions of difference. The local systems of difference that developed in dialogue with western modernism are becoming globalized and systematized into structural equivalents of each other. This globalized system exercises hegemony not through content, but through form. In other words, *we are not all becoming the same, but we are portraying, dramatizing and communicating our differences to each other in ways that are more widely intelligible.* The globalizing hegemony is to be found in what I call *structures of common difference, which celebrate particular kinds of diversity while submerging, deflating or suppressing others.*
>
> (ibid., p. 124)

Jan Nederveen Pieterse develops a similar line of argument. He reconsiders some examples of hybridization – the ones we have already come across in section 1:

> Ariane Mânouchkine's use of Kabuki style to stage a Shakespeare play leads to the question, which Shakespeare play? The play is *Henry IV,* which is set in the context of European high feudalism. In that light, the use of Japanese feudal Samurai style to portray European feudalism makes a point about transcultural historical affinities.
>
> 'Mexican schoolgirls dressed in Greek togas dancing in the style of Isidora Duncan', mentioned before, reflects transnational bourgeois class affinities, mirroring themselves in classical European culture. Chinese tacos and Irish bagels reflect ethnic crossover in employment patterns in the American fast food sector. Asian rap refers to cross-cultural convergence in popular youth culture.
>
> (Nederveen Pieterse, 1995, p. 50)

What appears from one perspective as hybridization can, from another, be interpreted in terms of transnational affinities in sensibility or attitude. 'In other words', says Nederveen Pieterse, 'the other side of cultural hybridity is transcultural convergence' (ibid.).

5   Conclusion

In drawing the present chapter to a close I want to sustain this argument about complexity, finally with respect to the relation between economic and cultural aspects of the globalization process. Kenichi Ohmae (with whose perspective you should now be familiar) puts forward the epigrammatic argument that globalization is about the choice between Sony and soil. And how global folk will choose is, for Ohmae, obvious: 'People don't want nationalism or soil; they want satellites and Sony' (Ohmae, 1991, p. 72). He proceeds to illustrate what he means by this:

> It was this consumerist urge that underlay German reunification. Information never respected the Berlin Wall. Antennas on what were recently East German roofs brought images of the West German good life into the homes of millions of people. The impulse to tear down the Wall did not originate from any sense of nationalism but from a desire for blue jeans and more consumer choices.
>
> (ibid.)

From this corporate symbolist perspective, achieving global awareness means realizing that you were 'born not to belong but to buy' (ibid.) .

I have three major objections to such formulations, the presentation of which will, I hope, summarize the arguments I have sought to put forward as a counter to the global business perspective. First, it is surely problematical to present the contemporary situation in terms of such a stark and simplistic choice. (How, for example, would we account for the equal impulse among West Germans to tear down the Berlin Wall?) Globalization, as I have argued, is about a great deal more than just achieving consumer consciousness on a new scale. I can see no inconsistency between wanting Sony *and* soil. And I would not regard not wanting Sony as disqualifying anyone from being a global citizen. My second objection is to Ohmae's assumption that we can all participate equally in the global consumer culture that he is promoting. Globalization, in fact, occurs as a contradictory and uneven process, involving new kinds of polarization – economic, social, cultural, political, geographical. Some will clearly win out, but others will lose or be marginalized, and may well react against the disruption and destabilization of global change. The confrontation of social and cultural groups is an inevitable consequence. Third, Ohmae's account assumes that the future is already mapped out (Sony is the future, and soil an anachronism). His vision expresses what he, from the perspective of the corporate symbolic analysts, wants the future to be (and, of course, from his position he may have a disproportionate influence on what unfolds). But there are a great many other interests now working to have their say too. Far from being determined, the global era is still in the process of being invented.

What I have sought to emphasize in this chapter is the complexity in the development of global culture. There are corporate projections for the creation of new global cultural industries and markets. But global businesses, and cultural businesses especially, have to take account of the inflexibilities and resistances of existing cultural realities. And then there are other constituencies of interest that have quite different conceptions of what the new cultural order might look like. Some of these invoke possibilities that are beyond the corporate imagination, while others are drawn into defensive postures against the forces of globalization. The globalization process must be seen in terms of the complex interplay of economic and cultural dynamics, involving confrontation, contestation and negotiation. The global future is therefore sure to have surprises in store for us.

References

AHMED, A. (1992) *Postmodernism and Islam*, London, Routledge.

ANGELL, I. (1995) 'Winners and losers in the information age', *LSE Magazine,* Vol. 7, No. 1, pp. 10-12.

AULETTA, K. (1993) 'Raiding the global village', *The New Yorker*, 2 August, pp. 25-30.

BACK, L. (1994) 'The sounds of the city', *Anthropology in Action,* Vol. 1, No. 1, pp. 11-16.

BEHRMAN, J. and RONDINELLI, D. (1992) 'The cultural imperatives of globalization: urban economic growth in the 21st century', *Economic Development Quarterly*, Vol. 6, No. 2, pp. 115-26.

BEYER, P. (1994) *Religion and Globalization*, London, Sage.

BONIFACE, P. and FOWLER, P. (1993) *Heritage and Tourism in 'the Global Village'*, London, Routledge.

CARNOY, M., CASTELLS, M., COHEN, S. and CARDOSO, F. H. (1993) *The New Global Economy in the Information Age*, University Park, PA,Pennsylvania State University Press.

CASTELLS, M. (1994) 'European cities, the informational society, and the global economy', *New Left Review*, 204, pp. 18-32.

DE MORAGAS SPÁ, M. and GARITAONANDÍA, C. (1995), 'Television in the regions and the European audio-visual space' in de Moragas Spà, M. and Garitaonandía, C. (eds), *Decentralization in the Global Era: television in the regions, nationalities and small countries of the European Union,* London, John Libbey.

DU GAY, P., HALL, S., JANES, L., MACKAY, H. and NEGUS, K. (1997) *Doing Cultural Studies: the story of the Sony Walkman*, London, Sage/The Open University (Book 1 in this series)

FERGUSON, M. (1992) 'The mythology about globalization', *European Journal of Communication*, Vol. 7, No. 1, pp. 69-93.

GARITAONANDÍA, C. (1993) 'Regional television in Europe', *European Journal of Communication*, Vol. 9, No. 3, pp. 277-94.

HAIDER, D. (1992) 'Place wars: new realties of the 1990s', *Economic Development Quarterly*, Vol. 6, No. 2, pp. 127-34.

HANNERZ, U. (1992) *Cultural Complexity*, New York, Columbia University Press

HANNERZ, U. (1993) 'The withering away of the nation?' *Ethnos*, Vol. 58, Nos. 3–4, pp. 377-91.

HARASIM, L. (1994) 'Global networks: an introduction', in Harasim, L. (ed.), *Global Networks: computers and international communication*, Cambridge, MA, MIT Press.

LANFANT, M. F. (1995) 'Introduction' in Lanfant, M. F., Allcock, J. and Bruner, M. (eds) *International Tourism: identity and change*, London, Sage.

LESLIE, D. (1995) 'Global scan: the globalization of advertising agencies, concepts and campaigns', *Economic Geography*, Vol. 71, No. 4, pp.402-26.

LEVINSON, M. (1995) 'It's an MTV world', *Newsweek*, 24 April, pp. 44-9.

LEVITT, T. (1983) *The Marketing Imagination*, London, Collier Macmillan.

MASSEY, D. (1993) 'Power-geometry and a progressive sense of place' in Bird, J. et al. (eds) *Mapping the Future: local cultures, global change*, London, Routledge.

MITCHELL, W. (1995) *City of Bits: space, place and the Infobahn*, Cambridge, MA, MIT Press.

MITTELMAN, J. (1995) 'Rethinking the international division of labour in the context of globalization', *Third World Quarterly*, Vol. 16, No. 2, pp. 273-95.

MOSS KANTER, R. (1995) 'Thriving locally in the global economy', *Harvard Business Review*, September–October, pp. 151-60.

NEDERVEEN PIETERSE, J. (1995) 'Globalization as hybridization' in Featherstone, M., Lash, S. and Robertson, R (eds) *Global Modernities*, London, Sage.

OHMAE, K. (1989) 'Managing in a borderless world', *Harvard Business Review*, Vol. 67, No. 3, pp. 152-61.

OHMAE, K. (1991) 'Global consumers want Sony not soil', *New Perspectives Quarterly*, Fall, pp. 72-3.

OHMAE, K. (1993) 'The rise of the region-state', *Foreign Affairs*, Vol. 72, No. 2, pp. 78-87.

PARR, M. (1995) *Small World*, Stockport, Dewi Lewis.

POWELL, N. (1993) 'French redskins take on the cowboys', *Observer*, 19 September.

ROBERTSON, R. (1995) 'Globalization: time-space and homogeneity-heterogeneity' in Featherstone, M., Lash, S., and Robertson R. (eds) *Global Modernities*, London, Sage.

RUSHDIE, S. (1991) *Imaginary Homelands*, London, Granta/Penguin.

SASSEN, S. (1991) *The Global City*, Princeton, NJ, Princeton University Press.

SHAPIRO, M. (1994) 'Images of planetary danger: Luciano Benetton's ecumenical fantasy', *Alternatives*, Vol. 19, No. 4, pp. 433-54.

SMITH, A.D. (1991) *National Identity*, Harmondsworth, Penguin.

STRANGE, S. (1995) 'The limits of politics', *Government and Opposition*, Vol. 30, No. 3, pp. 291-311.

THOMPSON, K. (ed.) (1997) *Media and Cultural Regulation*, London, Sage/The Open University (Book 6 in this series).

TOMLINSON, J. (1997) 'Internationalization, globalization and media imperialism', Chapter 3 in Thompson, K. (ed.).

WHITWAM, D. (1994) 'The right way to go global' (interview), *Harvard Business Review*, March-April, pp. 134-45.

WILK, R. (1995) 'The local and the global in the political economy of beauty: from Miss Belize to Miss World', *Review of International Political Economy*, Vol. 2, No. 1, pp. 117-34.

WINRAM, S. (1984) 'The opportunity for world brands', *International Journal of Advertising*, Vol. 3, No. 1, pp. 17-26.

READING A:
Ulf Hannerz, 'Varieties of transnational experience'

Let us consider some recurrent varieties of personal experience today; experiences which touch on issues of time, space, loyalty and identity and which relate somehow uneasily to national boundaries.

Increasingly in the current era, Robert Reich has argued in *The Work of Nations* (1991), work in advanced societies falls into three main categories: those he calls routine production services, in-person services, and symbolic-analytic services. The first of these entail the endlessly repetitive tasks of a great many blue-collar as well as white-collar workers. The major difference between these and the in-person services is that the latter must be provided, if not face to face with customers, at least in their immediate environment; in-person services include the jobs of retail sales people, waiters and waitresses, janitors, secretaries, hairdressers, taxi drivers, and security guards. The third category is that with which Reich is most directly concerned: the symbolic-analytic services, including for example research scientists, various kinds of engineers, investment bankers, lawyers, any number of kinds of consultants, corporate headhunters, publishers and writers, musicians, television and film producers ... 'even university professors'.

What the symbolic analysts have in common, Reich suggests, is the non-standardized manipulation of symbols – data, words, oral and visual representations. They are problem-identifiers, problem-solvers, strategic brokers; highly skilled people whose continuously cumulative, varied experience is an asset which makes them relatively autonomous *vis-à-vis* particular places and organizations.

The symbolic analysts, in the contemporary picture which Reich draws, are linked to global webs of enterprise. They are no longer particularly dependent on the economic performance of other categories of people in their national context, such as people in routine production services. And in the American case, which is Reich's major concern, he finds that the 'symbolic analysts have been seceding from the rest of the nation' (1991, p. 252).

It has been a secession taking place gradually and without fanfare. The symbolic analysts may pledge allegiance to the flag with as much sincerity as ever, yet 'the new global sources of their economic well-being have subtly altered now they understand their economic roles and responsibilities in society'.

Among the tribes of symbolic analysts we seem to get the close up view of the nation retreating, as suggested by Hobsbawm. They build their own monuments – the convention centres, the research parks, the international airports – and withdraw into their own private habitats, enclaves with security guards if need be. If they are less concerned with local routine production services, which are liable to be replaced more cheaply somewhere else in the world, they may on the other hand be more interested in the quality of the in-person services.

The tendency toward a withdrawal of the symbolic analysts is not only American, although Reich sees some variations of degree in different places (1991, p. 202). It is not a tendency which pleases him. Symbolic analysts, he believes, are not likely to exchange an old commitment to the nation for a new global citizenship, with an even more extended sense of social responsibility. There are no strong attachments or loyalties here but more likely a sense of resignation. 'Even if the symbolic analyst is sensitive to the problems that plague the world, these dilemmas may seem so intractable and overpowering in their global dimension that any attempt to remedy them appears futile' (1991, p. 310). What Reich argues for, then, is a revitalized commitment to the nation, more especially a shared investment in the productivity and competitiveness of all its citizens, within the framework of the globalized economy.

When Reich's book was published he was a Harvard political economist. Since then, he has become Secretary of Labor in the Clinton Administration, and thus he is perhaps now in a position to do something about all this. Yet it is hardly obvious how such a renewed political will, including the symbolic analysts in the alliance, is to come about. In any case, if we consider Reich's ethnography of recent trends rather than his enlightened nationalist call to action, we see that the symbolic analysts, in all their internal diversity, would appear to have distanced themselves from much of what Smith, as quoted above, sees as characteristic of the nation. The latter hardly 'provides the most inclusive community, the generally accepted boundary within which social intercourse normally takes place', it is questionably 'the basic unit of moral economy'. The possibility of fraternity does not seem to be embraced. Yet there is no doubt room for some symbolic ambiguity even among symbolic analysts – national allegiance may be proclaimed even when not really practised, and to the problem of personal oblivion, for example, a better answer may still be waiting to be found.

Again, the ideal-type symbolic analyst according to Reich is fairly autonomous in relation to organizations as well as places. This would seem to be not quite the kind of person, then, that another commentator on the contemporary restructuring of the world, Kenichi Ohmae, has in mind. Ohmae, author of *The Borderless World* (1990) and several other books, and a frequent contributor to *Wall Street Journal* as well as *Harvard Business Review*, is an international management consultant – 'guru' is a term that comes to mind – concerned in particular with the workings of corporations in the global market. What he has to say about the internal life of a corporation reaching the higher stage of globalism also reflects interestingly, I think, on our assumptions about the national. The global corporation, in Ohmae's view, must loosen its ties to any particular country, 'get rid of the headquarters mentality', 'create a system of values shared by company managers around the globe to replace the glue a nation-based orientation once provided' (1990, p. 91). It needs an 'amoebalike network organization'. This organization depends on a shared unofficial culture which cannot be learned by reading the same manual or going to the same brief training programme. It can only grow over time, Ohmae argues, as people develop a broad range of common references and experiences. They must meet face to face over the years, they must stay at each others homes, their families must know each other; and at the same time formal structures – training programmes, career planning, job rotation, evaluation systems – must also be the same wherever the corporation first finds you, and wherever it then places you. Only thus is the highest stage of corporate globalism reached:

The customers you care about are the people who love your products everywhere in the world. Your mission is to provide them with exceptional value. When you think of your colleagues, you think of people who share that mission. Country of origin does not matter. Location of headquarters does not matter. The products for which you are responsible and the company you serve has been denationalized. [...]

You really have to believe, deep down, that people may work 'in' different national environments but are not 'of' them. What they are 'of' is the global corporation.

(Ohmae, 1990, pp. 94, 96)

Ohmae admits that few if any corporations have quite reached this far, although 'the signs of movements in this direction are numerous and unmistakable' (1990, p. 91). It is interesting, in any case, that here the vision seems to go beyond that of Robert Reich, who sees among the symbolic analysts mostly an attenuation of nationalities. Here the corporation apparently becomes an alternative, a transnational source of solidarity and collective identity, a basic unit of moral economy in Smith's terms again, while the nation at the same time becomes defined as little more than an environment, a local market (and moreover, not the only one). In the shared life and personal ties of a corporation, it is implied, cultural resonance can again be found. The corporation may even have a history, a mythology of the past, and celebrate it. More certainly, it will offer some vision for the future.

Ohmae's transnational organization man and Reich's symbolic analyst are two recognizable social types of the present, fairly closely related. But listen now to another voice, the reggae fan Jo-Jo, as recorded by Simon Jones (and quoted by Dick Hebdige, 1987, pp. 158–9) in Birmingham's multi-ethnic Balsall Heath neighbourhood:

... there's no such thing as 'England' any more ... welcome to India brothers! This is the Caribbean! ... Nigeria! ... There is no England, man. This is what is coming. Balsall Heath is the centre of the melting pot, 'cos all I ever see when I go out is half Arab, half Pakistani, half Jamaican, half Scottish, half Irish. I know 'cos I am (half Scottish/half Irish) ... Who am I? Tell me who do I belong to? They criticize me, the good old England ... Alright, where do I belong? You know I was brought up with blacks, Pakistanis, Africans, Asians, everything, you name it ... who do I belong to? I'm just a broad person.

Jo-Jo, I take it, is a young man of the streets not a self-conscious and well-read intellectual. Nonetheless, his point of view reminds me strikingly of some formulations in Salman Rushdie's collection of essays, *Imaginary Homelands* (1991). [...] Commenting on his best known novel and the controversy to which it gave rise, Rushdie notes that the characters at the centre of the book are people struggling with problems of ghettoization and hybridization, of reconciling the old and the new:

> *The Satanic Verses* celebrates hybridity, impurity, intermingling, the transformation that comes out of new and unexpected combinations of human beings, cultures, ideas, politics, movies, songs. It rejoices in mongrelization and fears the absolutism of the Pure. Mélange, hotchpotch, a bit of this and a bit of that is *how newness enters the world*. It is the great possibility that mass migration gives the world, and I have tried to embrace it.
>
> (Rushdie, 1991, p. 394)

It seems to me that Jo-Jo and Rushdie are on to the same thing. But Rushdie, of course, gets both more reflective and more elaborate and so we may record a little more of his comments. Here and elsewhere, in commenting on his own writing, Rushdie sees it as drawing on the migrant condition. Before writing the earlier novel, *Midnight's Children*, he had spent months trying to recall as much as he could of his childhood Bombay. He was thrilled to see how much had in fact been stored somewhere in his memory, and yet it was precisely the partial nature of his recollections that made them so evocative to him:

> The shards of memory acquired greater status, greater resonance, because they were remains; fragmentation made trivial things seem like symbols, and the mundane acquired numinous qualities ... it may be argued that the past is a country from which we have all emigrated, that its loss is part of our common humanity. Which seems to me self evidently true; but it suggests

that the writer who is out of country and even out of language may experience this loss in an intensified form. It is made more concrete to him by the physical fact of discontinuity, of his present being in a different place from his past, of his being 'elsewhere'. This may enable him to speak properly and concretely on a subject of universal significance and appeal.

> (1991, p. 12)

The migrant looks here to a past which is spatially as well as temporally distant; it may be reflected in his present in different ways. For the Mauritian in Paris or the Belizian in Los Angeles, we have seen, it may intensify the sense of nationhood and national identity, rooted back home. Rushdie, it appears, is also concerned with a more general human experience of migration and uprootedness. Yet he sees the possibility of a continuous reconstruction of the past of his adopted country as well. Others have become British before him – the Hugenots, the Irish, the Jews; Swift, Conrad, Marx. 'America, a nation of immigrants, has created great literature out of the phenomenon of cultural transplantation', Rushdie (1991, p. 20) concludes, and suggests that the example can be followed elsewhere.

Indeed it seems that much of the most gripping in recent fiction and autobiography thematizes what Rushdie calls 'hybridity, impurity, intermingling'. If the great literature also becomes national literature may be another matter. It is one thing for the United States, more accustomed to defining itself as a nation of newcomers, to find its identity in a master narrative of migration and melting pot (yet even here we see the current problems of multiculturalism and the canon). In Britain, the dominance of other ideas of historical roots would seem much more difficult to challenge successfully. As Jo-Jo of Balsall Heath has it, 'they criticize me, the good old England'.

In any case, my general point is this. From Reich to Rushdie, by way of Ohmae and Jo-Jo, we seem to see that there are now various kinds of people for whom the nation works less well, or at least less unambiguously, as a source of cultural resonance. In the instance of the symbolic analyst and perhaps for some variety of others, it may even turn out to be less a richly imagined community than what Maurice Janowitz (1967, pp. 210 ff.), in an entirely different context, referred to as a 'community of limited liability' – one has a largely transactional relationship to it, and one withdraws if it fails to serve one's needs. So the big question would be, what can your nation do for you that a good credit card cannot do?

If the nation as an idea is culturally impoverished here, we cannot be quite certain whether it is replaced by anything else. Reich has little to say on this point. Ohmae, on the other hand, suggests that the global corporation should turn itself into something like a nation. Perhaps we disapprove of this, seeing it only as the business consultants' utopia, a manipulative product of corporate managerial ideology (but then some measure of manipulation has certainly gone into the building of other nations as well). With Jo-Jo and Rushdie, however, it seems undeniable that much of the most deeply felt, highly resonant, personal experience is at odds with ordinary notions of the national. It may be that this experience, and the shared understandings which grow out of it, are 'eclectic', as Smith (1990, 1991) has it in his portrayal of transnational culture, but it does not appear either 'fundamentally artificial', 'indifferent to place and time', or 'carefully calculated'. To say that it 'lacks any emotional commitment' is hardly correct. Admittedly, we are looking here at something other than the commercial, bureaucratic or technical transnationalism, of large-scale, impersonal organizational characteristics, which Smith has in mind. The argument, however, is that transnationalism and globalization nowadays have more varied characteristics, and that sometimes, for some people (a growing number), they include precisely the kinds of sites where cultural resonance is generated.

It used to be, more often, that people's more real communities, those made up of people known personally to one another, primarily through enduring face-to-face relationships, were contained within the boundaries of those entities which could be made into nations and imagined communities. There was no great obstacle to a symbolic transformation of the concrete experience of the former into the imagery of the latter; hence, for example, 'peasants into Frenchmen' (Weber, 1976). Now a great many real relationships to people and places may cross boundaries. Intimate circles and small networks can be involved here, the

transnational is not always immense in scale. These relationships are sensed not to fit perfectly with established ideas of the nation, and in this way the latter becomes probably less pervasive, and even compromised. The feeling of deep historical rootedness may be replaced by an equally intense experience of discontinuity and rupture, as in the case of the transcontinental migrant; the fraternity of the present as in Balsall Heath and innumerable places like it, is in opposition to the sedimented differences of history.

We should not take for granted, either, that such personal experiences come in only a few varieties. It seems, rather, that in the present phase of globalization, one characteristic is the proliferation of kinds of ties that can be transnational; ties to kin, friends, colleagues, business associates and others. In all that variety, such ties may entail a kind and a degree of tuning out, a weakened personal involvement with the nation and national culture, a shift from the disposition to take it for granted; possibly a critical distance to it. In such ways, the nation may have become more hollow than it was.

On the other hand, in all their diversity, these outside linkages tend not to coalesce into any single conspicuous alternative to the nation. The people involved are not all 'cosmopolitans' in the same sense; most of them are probably not cosmopolitans in any strict sense at all (cf. Hannerz, 1990). It is also in the nature of things that we are not always sure who is affected by these linkages. Some may be of a more dramatic and conspicuous kind, others apparently mundane and hardly noticeable to anyone not in the know, not intimately familiar with the other's network and biography. Globalization of this kind, diffused within social life, is opaque. The deep personal experiences of an individual, and their distribution within his transnational habitat of meaning, can be in large part a private matter.

What we may find in the present time, then, if I try to summarize the gist of this part of the paper, is a situation where to some people, no doubt a great many, the idea of the nation is still largely in place, where it has been perhaps for some centuries. In some ways, here and there, it may even be strengthened. It still encompasses virtually all their social traffic, and offers a framework for thinking about past and future. Yet interspersed among those most committed, encapsulated nationals, in patterns not always equally transparent, are a growing number of people of more varying experiences and connections. Some of them may wish to redefine the nation; place the emphasis, for example, more on the future and less on that past of which they happen not to have been a part. Of such desires, and their clash with established definitions, cultural debates may be made. Others again are in the nation but not of it. They may be the real cosmopolitans, or they are people whose nations are actually elsewhere, objects of exile or diaspora nostalgia (and perhaps of other debates), perhaps projects for the future. Or they may indeed owe a stronger allegiance to some other kind of imagined transnational community, an occupational community, a community of believers in a new faith, of adherents to a youth style. There may be divided commitments, ambiguities, and conflicting resonances as well. It may work at the personal level and at the situational. All this need not come to a withering away of the nation, but would seem to make it an entity rather different from the one that possibly used to be.

References

HANNERZ, U. (1990) 'Cosmopolitans and locals in world culture', in M. Featherstone (ed.) *Global Culture*, London, Sage.

HEBDIGE, D. (1987) *Cut 'n' Mix*, London, Comedia/ Methuen.

HOBSBAWM, E. (1990) *Nations and Nationalism Since 1780*, Cambridge, Cambridge University Press.

JANOWITZ, M. (1967) *The Community Press in an Urban Setting*, Chicago, University of Chicago Press. (First published 1952.)

OHMAE, K. (1990) *The Borderless World*, New York, Harper Business.

REICH, R.B. (1991) *The Work of Nations*, New York, Knopf.

RUSHDIE, S. (1991) *Imaginary Homelands*, London, Granta.

SMITH, A.D. (1990) 'Towards a global culture?' in M. Featherstone (ed.) *Global Culture*, London, Sage.

SMITH, A.D. (1991) *National Identity*, London, Penguin.

WEBER, E. (1976) *Peasants into Frenchmen*, Stanford, CA, Stanford University Press.

Source: Hannerz, 1993, pp. 380–7.

READING B:
Ian Angell, 'Winners and losers in the Information Age'

Just open any newspaper, or switch on the radio or television, and you'll find journalists worldwide bemoaning a crisis of confidence in social, political and economic institutions. There is a deep feeling that it is all coming to an End. For they know we are on the verge of an Information Revolution that is taking us out of the Machine Age, into ... who knows what.

Many commentators are deeply pessimistic; they see only chaos ahead. In Britain, both press and politicians keep asking themselves (and us interminably) 'where is the "feel good" factor?' Even when the 'numbers' look good, with the economy growing, low inflation, and unemployment falling ... the country is still miserable. A malaise has contaminated the national consciousness. The British people aren't stupid. They know that for the majority of our society, any society, it has gone forever – and there is nothing anyone can do about it. Everywhere the socio-economic certainties of the twentieth century are collapsing. The world as we know it is changing: it may even be moving in reverse.

'History is the natural selection of accidents' (Trotsky) and our world today is full of accidents just waiting to happen. The very nature of work, of institutions, of society, and even of capitalism itself, are mutating. These mutations are confronting each other in the political power vacuum left by the fall of communism, and the increasing impotence of liberal democracy, as the utopia promised by science and technology has turned into a nightmare for the 'common man'. Poverty, unemployment, pollution, overpopulation, mass migration, global plagues etc. have left us with a world full of frightened people. For the masses will not win in the natural selection for dominance of an increasingly elitist world. Naturally the politicians don't like it. For the past two centuries 'the values of the weak prevail[ed] because the strong have taken them over as devices of leadership' (Nietzsche). But no longer. The politicians may promise, but now the markets decide.

Globalization and localization

But why is it happening now? The answer is quite simple: a new order (which many will call disorder) is being forced upon an unsuspecting world by advances in telecommunications. The future is being born in the so-called *information superhighways*. Very soon these electronic telecommunication networks, covering the world via cable and satellite, will enable everyone in the world to 'talk' to everyone else. We are entering a new elite cosmopolitan age. Global commerce will force through the construction of multi-media highways, and anyone bypassed by these highways faces ruin. Information technology, together with speedy international travel, is changing the whole nature of political governance and its relationship to commerce, and commerce itself.

One major consequence emerging out of the new freedoms bestowed by global telecommunications is the *globalization* of organizations and not merely their *internationalization*. Individuals and companies are setting up large transnational networks that pay absolutely no heed to national boundaries and barriers. The commercial enterprise of the future will be truly global, it will relocate (physically or electronically) to where the profit is greatest and the regulation least. The umbilical cords have been cut: the global company no longer feels the need to support the national aspirations of the country of its birth. Recently this new business paradigm was expressed most forcibly by Akio Morita, causing uproar in Japan, when he announced that Sony was a global company and not Japanese!

But paradoxically, globalization is resulting in a trend towards *localization* or, as Morita calls it, 'global localization'. Global companies are setting themselves up within *virtual enterprises,* at the hub of loosely knit alliances of local companies, all linked together by global networks, both electronic and human. These companies assemble to take advantage of any temporary business opportunity; and then separate, searching for the next major deal. Apart from local products, local companies also deliver local expertise and access to home markets for other products created within the wider alliance. Companies and countries outside such networks have no future.

International trading now includes new forms of barter and exchange on these networks, particularly in superior scientific and technological expertise and knowledge. Money, which is merely a means of facilitating economic transactions, has itself become electronic information, and what constitutes money can no longer be monopolized by national governments. This inevitably lowers the transaction costs of money – a real competitive advantage for any virtual enterprise with a moveable centre of gravity; and for those individuals who are willing to trade their expertise in this electronic market.

Knowledge workers vs. service workers

With the rise of teleworking/telecommuting/televillages Peter Drucker has a very interesting forecast. He says that humanity is polarizing into two employment categories: the intellectual, cultural and business elite (the mobile and independent *knowledge workers)*, and the rest (the immobile and dependent *service workers*). In a similar vein, Robert Reich believes in the Information Age there will be three categories: *symbolic-analytic services* (the knowledge workers who are problem identifiers, solvers and brokers), *in-person services,* and *routine production services.* The latter two groups roughly correspond to Drucker's service workers.

Routine production services can either be replaced by robots or exported anywhere on the globe. Wages in this sector are already beginning to converge worldwide to Third World levels. British Polythene Industries is to close its factory at Telford with the loss of 150 jobs, and switch to China. BPI's payroll bill will be cut by 90%. Even the Home Office at one time was seriously considering subcontracting a large but straightforward data-entry job to the Philippines. Such 'social dumping' is dragging down the wages of in-person service workers, a sector which is itself being increasingly automated. It is estimated that 150,000 UK bank jobs will eventually be lost because of automation. Millions of jobs will be lost if teleshopping takes off. Inevitably the slow redistribution of wealth that has occurred over the last centuries is being reversed, rapidly. Societies are stratifying; new elites are appearing. The future is inequality; at the very bottom of the heap, western societies are already witnessing the emergence of a rapidly expanding underclass.

Now we can see that knowledge workers are the real generators of wealth. The income of these owners of intellectual and financial wealth will increase substantially, and they will be made welcome anywhere in the world. As from October 1994, foreign 'entrepreneurial investors' with £1 million at their disposal could bypass the usual entry rules into Britain. But Britain has been slow off the mark, with the added embarrassment that none of the migrant rich want to live here. In the United States, there is a fast-track immigration policy for businessmen and women who can offer $1 million and guarantee to employ 10 people. Six hundred millionaires emigrated to America in 1993. It is only a matter of time before intellectual capital, such as scientific and technological expertise, will be included on the balance sheet.

On the other side of the coin, there is a growing realization that each service worker is a net loss both to the state and to the company – they cost far more than they generate. Service workers will now be expected to add far more value to the company, unlike in the past where service work meant just turning up. Companies will be reducing the wages and staffing levels of service workers, and it is no accident that most Western companies are presently instigating major *downsizing* programmes.

This is all happening against a background of an exploding population in the Third World (95% of the world's population increase is in developing countries). To combat the inevitable mass migrations, state barriers will be thrown up everywhere to keep out alien service workers: each state has a surplus of its own to support. It is already happening. Canada is to impose a c$1000 tax on people seeking landed immigration status, thus sending out a message which is likely to reduce applications from poor service workers but increase applications from richer knowledge workers. In California, proposition 187 intends to bar the nearly two million illegal immigrants from schools, welfare services, and all but emergency health care. How long will it be before there are 'differential rights' for 'differentiated citizens', identified in a data base and policed by smart cards? How long before the notion of 'Human Rights' is as outdated as the 'Divine Right of Kings'?

[...]

A role for the nation-state?

Everywhere the nation-state is in retreat. All the while citizens are losing their faith in the nation-state, seeing it as a peculiarly twentieth century phenomenon. For the state is failing to deliver its side of the Faustian pact, where the individual submits to the legitimate violence of the state in return for protection and security. Globalization has shown the James Bond myth, that the state is good and global corporations (Spectre) are bad, to be blatant propaganda on behalf of the nation-state. James Bond, the patron saint of the nation-state, is now just another dirty old man.

The nation-state is based on the premise that the state owns the individual and that the leaders of the state can dispose of his property as they see fit. But knowledge workers call it social injustice: for there is no justice in equality. All taxation is theft. It is the state obtaining money with menaces. They say with derision that the 'Common Good' isn't good, it is merely common! The protection of the interests and independence of the knowledge workers is going to be big business in the Information Age.

The very nature of the nation-state itself is mutating; increasingly it will have to behave as merely another form of commercial enterprise. According to western sentiment some states are becoming criminal enterprises, but these too will be part of global trade. That the roles of governments and organizations are converging was unconsciously highlighted in *The Guardian* of 10 December 1993. They asked the question: 'what's the difference between Zambia and Goldman Sachs'. The answer: 'One is an African country that makes $2.2 billion a year and shares it among 25 million people. The other is an investment bank that makes $2.6 billion [...] and shares it between 161 people. FAIR ENOUGH!' Of course the 'bleeding heart' liberals of *The Guardian* haemorrhage at such gross unfairness and make snide comments about 'Goldmine Sachs'. Unfairness? They fail to see that the symbolic-analysts of Goldman Sachs earned that money. Yes, they earned it, and they earned it fairly.

To the knowledge workers, this call for fairness is the mere whinging of failures and parasites. They say it is time to rid ourselves of that backward looking idea, that work involves physical effort. Of course labour is needed – but there is a world full of labourers out there. It is that rare commodity, human intellect, which is the stuff of work in tomorrow's world. Politicians really must stop saying 'nanny knows best' and playing to the sentimentality of the herd. Governments, like all other organizations, will have to survive economically on the efforts of an elite few – and no nation-state has an automatic right to exist.

A future for democracy?

Because of the need to employ local workers, the major social problem for politicians in the coming decades is going to be how to attract global employers to partner local companies, and how to keep them attracted. Governments will have no choice other than to acquiesce to the will of global enterprises. A new paradigm is upon us, in which the nation-state has mutated into just another form of organization, which will delegate market regulations to continent-wide bodies such as North American Free Trade Agreement or the European Union, which in turn will use their economic muscle and conspire with local communities to undermine each member state. Not only will state be pitted against state, but also area will compete against area, town against town, even suburb against suburb. It will be inevitable that nation-states will fragment: rich areas will dump the poor areas. Such shakeout trends can be interpreted as *downsizing*, a strategy that is being considered by most shrewd major corporations these days. As Daniel Bell so eloquently put it, 'the nation-state is too small for the big things and too big for the small things'. Some futurologists, such as Heineken, expect that early in the next century the number of states in the United Nations will increase from the present number of 184 to over 1,000. Each state will permit entry to holders of 'UN style' company passports. Tax holidays and reduced regulation aimed at attracting employers will be 'the name of the game' everywhere. Already different states in Europe have embarked on 'regulatory arbitrage' to tempt financial sector companies away from their 'European partners'. Inevitably this trend will undermine national legislation and taxation policies. Any area with independent aspirations will use economic weapons against its neighbours and distance itself from their legislative oppression.

One inevitable consequence of global trade will be the rise of the New City State at the hub of global electronic and transport networks. The non-democratic model of Hong Kong is an exemplar, even though the city itself doesn't yet realise that it has defined the future. Singapore under the enlightened leadership of Lee Kuan Yew is another. What European city will be the first to break ranks with the nation-state mentality holding back progress? A number of European cities can make the leap. Liechtenstein has already started: what about Monaco? And let us not forget Venice, perhaps it will rediscover former glories. What about Lisbon? They have the singular example of attracting the Gulbenkian wealth earlier this century. The Corporation of the City of London too has enormous potential and could be revitalized. However, the dead hand of the 'Mother of Parliaments' will make this far more difficult.

To protect their wealth, rich areas will also undertake a *rightsizing* strategy, ensuring a high proportion of (wealth generating) knowledge workers to (wealth depleting) service workers. Rich areas have to maintain and expand a critical mass of scientific and technological expertise, and use it to underpin an effective education system to regenerate the resource. These rich areas will reject the liberal attitudes of the present century, as the expanding underclass they are spawning, and the untrained migrants they welcomed previously, are seen increasingly as economic liabilities. 'Many too many are born. The state was devised for the superfluous ones' (Nietzsche). Mass-production methods needed an over-supply of humanity; in a sense the Machine Age spawned the nation-state, but with its demise what is to be done with the glut as we enter the Information Age?

As far as global enterprises are concerned liberal democracy is an artefact of the Machine Age, an ideology from a time when the masses were needed – but it will soon mutate into an irrelevancy. It will be merely the means of governing the immobile and dependent service workers. That citizens elect their slave masters makes democracy slavery none the less.

Global companies have no interest in populism, unless it adversely affects their business, when they will simply leave: in the Information Age 'democracy is bad for business'. The Marxist myth that labour creates wealth has been buried once and for all. A large population, particularly an uneducated and ageing population, has now become the major problem facing all Western governments. The masses themselves will put employment and economic well-being before the dubious privilege of electing powerless representatives. Even Karl Marx anticipated politicians becoming ineffective, but for other reasons!

As the nation-state mutates into corporation-states in the new order, the role of each corporation-state is to produce the right people, with the right knowledge and expertise, as the raw material for the global companies that profit from the Information Age, to service these companies, and to provide them with an efficient infrastructure, a minimally regulated market and a secure, stable and comfortable environment. If a state cannot produce a quality 'people product', in sufficient quantities, then it must buy them from abroad. Each state will have to view education, not as the right of every citizen, distributed arbitrarily, but as an investment on which it must expect a return: they must invest in success and not failure.

If the state can convince the commercially attractive elite of knowledge workers and local entrepreneurial companies to stay, then a virtuous circle of success is ensured. For then, migrating global players and their wealth will also be attracted into that country. If, however, the state maintains a greedy collectivist and populist stance, under the defunct motto 'power to the people', then the entrepreneurial and knowledge elite will move on to more lucrative and agreeable climes, and, in the long-term, leave that country economically unviable, composed solely of the unproductive masses, sliding inevitably into a vicious circle of decline.

Source: Angell, 1995, pp. 10–12.

READING C:
Marc Levinson, 'It's an MTV world'

What words fit a band like Los Fabulosos Cadillacs? Back home in Buenos Aires, fans use the term *musica de onda* to describe the Cadillacs' hard-rocking combination of reggae, salsa and samba. In Bogota they call it *chévere*. In Mexico City, it's *suave*. But if you're a television company broadcasting the Cadillacs' music from California to Chile, you need a form of praise that will be universally understood. Something like: *coolisimo!*

Don't bother checking your Spanish-English dictionary. Coolisimo isn't there. It's an invention of MTV Latino. Americans know MTV as the deliberately obnoxious voice of the next generation, the channel that features heavy metal and the juvenile dialogue of those animated antiheroes, Beavis and Butt-head. Behind that calculated hipness, though, Viacom Inc.'s music network has become the ultimate New Age multinational. It has more viewers in Europe than in the United States, pumps out music videos in Brazil and Japan, and, starting this week, will rock around the clock in Mandarin Chinese.

Its strategy is unique. While McDonald's serves up the same burgers everywhere and Procter & Gamble sells soap under a variety of names, MTV combines a global presence and a single global brand with a product designed for separate regional markets. 'The container's the same,' says chair Tom Freston. 'The contents are different.' But they may not be different enough in a world where people who supposedly speak the same language cannot even agree on how to say 'cool'. MTV's worldwide strategy offers an intriguing and unusual map for information-based companies seeking riches abroad. It also reveals some unexpected bumps in the road.

For an entertainment company that wants to keep growing fast, there's no alternative to going international. In America where MTV reaches 60 million households, the network is running out of growing room: most of the 18- to 24-year-olds who might be induced to watch MTV already tune in. Overseas, where cable is still a novelty, the potential is almost unlimited. MTV and its two sister networks. VH-1 and Nickelodeon, harvested 28 percent of last year's $852 million in revenue from abroad. By the end of the century, Freston predicts, that figure will be around 50 per cent. Much of the growth will come from Asia, where the number of homes reached by cable or satellite TV will grow from 44 million to 206 million by 2004, according to Paul Kagan Associates. MTV's Mandarin-language service makes its debut this week in Taiwan. MTV Asia, produced in English in Singapore for viewers from the Philippines to India, will take to the air May 3.

The man behind MTV's global ambitions is Freston lieutenant William Roedy. A West Point grad and Vietnam vet who commanded NATO missile bases – 'If my classmates could see this now, they wouldn't believe it,' he says – Roedy took charge of a struggling MTV Europe in 1989, two years after its creation, and built it into a money-maker. Now, as president of London-based MTV International, he jets from production sites in Chile to dinners with Mongolian cable operators to meetings in Istanbul (where the Turkish government has partially retreated from a ban on MTV Europe). 'One of the things I've had to grapple with is this stereotype image of MTV,' he says. 'It makes such a difference when you sit down with a head of state and explain, 'You may not like it,' but also explain, 'It not only brings culture to your country; it also takes music and culture from your country and exposes it to others.'

Back in the USA: Roedy's biggest complaint is about provincialism back in the USA. The 23-year-old production assistants crowding the cubicles at Viacom headquarters in New York's Times Square don't much care about things foreign. Only a handful of non-American supergroups, such as Ireland's U2, get much air time on MTV USA; the 'demo', MTV's core 18- to 24-year-old audience, prefers its music homegrown. Drop by the morning meeting where a dozen young staffers plan MTV's 15 daily minutes of news and you'll hear about Soul Asylum's new drummer and hazing at US fraternities – but barely a word about anything happening abroad.

Management thinks very differently. MTV gains no advantage from its global scope unless it can find economies of scale in programming. The design of 'MTV News's' New York set was meant to save money by doubling as the set for 'Semana Rock', the two-month-old music-news show on MTV

Latino. As soon as Tabitha Soren records the day's news briefs in a New York studio, 'MTV News' comes down from behind the anchor desk and 'Noticias MTV' goes up. Budget-minded executives are pushing insular producers to craft shows to please Lübeck as well as Los Angeles. 'As we develop new programs, the idea is, let's see how we can make this work around the world,' says program-development chief Doug Herzog. The first fruits will be visible next fall on 'The Real World', MTV's real-life soap opera about seven young adults who live together. The show's three previous seasons were filmed in the United States. The next series, partly financed by MTV Europe, is now being shot in a West London flat with a mostly non-American cast. The housemates speak English – but will American viewers turn off when one of them chats with his mom on the phone in German? Stay tuned.

MTV Europe's London headquarters pulses with internationalism. Located hard by the rocker-boot and leather-jacket shops that pull hordes of youthful globe trotters to Camden Road. MTV Europe draws its staff from a generation of worldly youths for whom English is a second language and national borders are outdated relics. The mix of music videos, news briefs and zany promotional spots is instantly recognizable as MTV. But the content is largely produced in London for trend-conscious viewers like Graciela, who recently rang up 'MTV's Most Wanted', a live music show, from Bucharest, Romania. Her on-air question for host Ray Cokes: where could she find someone to install a nose ring? 'In my country there are not these possibilities,' Graciela lamented.

No one espouses the ideal of a united continent more fervently than MTV Europe. It is a single program shown in 37 countries. The network must find common denominators – or even build them by such means as a slick get-out-the-vote drive before last year's Euro-Parliament elections. The more young viewers think of themselves as Europeans, rather than Spaniards and Italians, the more likely they are to crave MTV's international chic and its big helpings of English-language rock. On-air video jockeys (VJs) such as 22-year-old heartthrob Enrico Silvestrin, who sports a blond goatee and dreadlocks, have deliberately emptied their on-camera personalities of national character. They could come from any place on the continent.

The Music Goes Round and Round

Since it was first exported eight years ago, MTV has accelerated its push into markets outside the U.S.

Company	Start-up-date	Households reached (millions)	Languages
MTV (U.S.)	Aug. 1, 1981	59.7	English
MTV Europe	Aug. 1, 1987	61.0	English
MTV Brazil	Oct. 20, 1990	9.7	Portuguese
MTV Japan	Dec. 24, 1992	1.1	Japanese, English
MTV Latino	Oct. 1, 1993	5.0	Spanish, English
MTV Mandarin	April 21, 1995	3.0	Mandarin Chinese
MTV Asia	May 3, 1995	n/a*	English, Hindi

* Deals with broadcasters still pending. (Source MTV.)

Exults Dutch-born VJ Simone Angel, a hyperkinetic bottle blonde with a Cockney accent: 'All those politicians are still sitting in stuffy old buildings talking about how to unite Europe. We're doing it.'

Animated blobs: MTV Europe creates unity mostly by speaking English. Almost all of its music videos are in English. So are the news, the intros and the animated blobs called The Brothers Grunt. Continental bands are welcome – but groups such as Sweden's Ace of Base, which MTV Europe helped propel to stardom, would get scant air time if they sang in their native tongues. There's just not much room for minority tastes.

This is not because Viacom worships English. The company offers VH-1, its music channel for the 35-and-older crowd, in German, and a Swedish VH-1 may come soon. MTV Europe already beams separate commercials to Germany, but Brent Hansen, a former New Zealand schoolteacher who is now MTV Europe's creative director, insists that MTV Europe's youthful, internationally minded audience wouldn't accept separate shows. 'The audience would say, "You've taken away the real thing and given us a watered-down product"', he explains. The choice of English leaves room for astute competitors to segment the market, siphoning off viewers with narrower tastes. A global company has a hard time playing that nationalist game. The German music-television company Viva is playing it masterfully [see Reading D below].

Language isn't the only obstacle to MTV's strategy of building regional music networks. Most of Latin America speaks Spanish – MTV Brasil, partially owned by Viacom, offers a Portuguese program for São Paulo – but musical traditions are so varied that few Spanish-language artists have managed regionwide breakthroughs. By default, American videos dominate MTV Latino's playlist. The frenzy of Metallica and the rancor of grunge don't resonate in Quito the way they do in Chicago: VJs such as Daisy Fuentes play mellower acts, like singer Phil Collins and blues trio G. Love & Special Sauce, along with such Latin stars as Juan Luis Guerra. Old regime rockers like the Rolling Stones are popular too. Where MTV USA is designed to repel parents, MTV Latino draws a family audience. Interviews with stars, most of them taken from the US network and presented in English with subtitles, knit the music videos together. While American viewers won't tolerate subtitles, MTV's research shows that Latins detest dubbing. They also want programs that, by US standards, seem slow-paced. 'We haven't developed the short attention span that US viewers have,' jokes Gabriel Baptiste, MTV Latino's Venezuelan-born music director. 'But give us time.'

Imported music, though, is only a stop-gap. To draw more viewers, the 18-month-old network is creating an entire new genre, a Latin rock that can jump from Mexico to Chile as easily as the Beatles jumped the Atlantic. Five years ago, Latin rock didn't exist. Today, heavy play on MTV Latino has made Los Fabulosos Cadillacs, from Argentina, one of Mexico's hottest acts, while Mexican groups like Caifanes are gaining popularity in South America. 'In Mexico, there's a whole new generation of bands. That's interesting in Argentina, because the same thing happened there four or five years ago', says Javier Andrade, the young Argentine music journalist who hosts 'Semana Rock'.

Adman's dream: MTV Latino's 5 million subscribers are an advertiser's dream, the wealthiest households in a region of sharp contrasts between rich and poor. But the network has yet to turn a profit. Its prospects are directly linked to an ongoing revolution in the way Latin America shops. Most Latin countries are still filled with locally owned companies targeting local consumers, and not a single one of them advertises on MTV Latino. The network draws just a handful of multinationals – Levi's, Coca-Cola, Kodak – that want to reach young people from Paraguay to Puerto Rico with a single sales pitch. Region-wide advertising is still in its infancy, and few ad agencies are equipped to mount campaigns in 23 countries at once. MTV's regionalism is ahead of its time.

But in Latin America, MTV has one strong advantage: there is no major competition. In Asia, the competition promises to be fierce. It is led by one of the most powerful men in the media business, Rupert Murdoch.

Murdoch has longstanding ties with Viacom. They are partners in Britain, where Murdoch has a half-interest in MTV's children's network, Nickelodeon. They used to be partners in Asia, where an MTV program briefly ran on Murdoch's satellite network, Star TV. But after the Star-MTV venture blew apart a year ago, Murdoch quickly launched his own Asian music service, Channel V. MTV India, which transmits two-and-a-half daily hours of Hindi rock on a government-owned station, competes head to head with V's Indian Middle Eastern service. MTV Asia, the new English service, will go up against V as well. And when MTV Mandarin takes to the air in Taiwan on April 21 – a date chosen after April 15, the original target, proved to have unlucky portents – it will find V firmly entrenched in 6 million homes on the island nation. The competition is spreading to mainland China, too, where some viewers already watch Channel V on illegal satellite dishes. MTV Mandarin, which is racing to lock up time on over-the-air stations serving tens of millions of households, is expected to be available in China later this year.

That is only the beginning. Last January, three of the four record companies that control MTV's German competitor, Viva, took a 50 per cent stake in Channel V. 'The majority of the music we sell in Southeast Asia is Chinese music', explains Robert Morgado of Warner Music Group. That means Warner wants Asian channels that given ample play to Asian music. 'If we were not there, there would be less pressure to customize locally', he says. MTV sees more sinister motives, fearing that the music companies will withhold their videos to favor Channel V. Sony Entertainment and MTV recently signed a ceasefire in the form of a worldwide licensing pact that protects MTV's access to videos and gives Sony higher fees. Relations with the other music companies, though, remain frosty.

Channel V, like Viva, is betting that MTV's bigness is its Achilles' heel. While MTV will run its Asian services from Singapore, V is opening studios in Bombay, Dubai and Taipei and talks of supplementing its two current networks with five more. While MTV's shows will have its international feel, V doesn't much care whether Arab-speaking viewers know that V is big in Taiwan. While MTV hopes its Mandarin program will appeal in Taiwan, Hong Kong and across the Chinese mainland, V is testing shows in the Cantonese dialect of south China.

Source: Levinson, Newsweek, 24 April 1995, pp. 45–9.

READING D:
Marc Levinson, 'Gut, Gut, Alles Super Gut!'

If MTV has an antithesis, Viva is it. Based in an industrial park on the outskirts of Cologne, hard by a construction-equipment yard, Viva has none of MTV's insistent hipness. Where visitors to the headquarters of MTV Europe are subjected to the blare of a multiscreen projection television, Viva offers them only a bank of mail-boxes. MTV Europe's studio is boisterous, chaotic and smoke-free; Viva's is quiet, efficient and dense with tobacco fumes. But hipness isn't everything. Since it went on the air 16 months ago, Viva has succeeded in challenging MTV's basic credo: that young people are young people pretty much wherever you go.

Viva is decidedly German. It vehemently rejects MTV's vision of a Europe with one musical taste and one common language. 'It's cool to throw in three or four words of English,' says program director Michael Kreissl. 'It's not cool to do it all in English. It's an illusion that everybody in Europe is speaking English.' American music does, however, occupy about a fifth of Viva's air time. In a nod toward internationalism, Viva conspicuously uses a black veejay, Nigerian Mola Adebisi. But he speaks German.

Viva's dominant fare is technopop, with an urgent disco beat and lowest-common-denominator lyrics. MTV Europe carries technopop in very limited quantities; most young Europeans detest the synthetic sounds and the mechanical, computer-generated videos. Young Germans, on the other hand, adore it. For those who want to watch E-Rotic's techno-hit 'Fred Come to Bed,' or the recent chart-topper 'Super Gut,' by the Italian group Mo-Do (lyric: *Gut, Gut, Alles Super Gut/Gut, Gut Alles Super Gut*), Viva is the place to turn. MTV does well with the affluent, trend-setting university crowd. But since its start in late 1993, Viva has grabbed the lead among high-school students and young adults who haven't gone to college – the groups least likely to be fluent in English. Says Dieter Gorny, a onetime rock bassist who runs the network, 'We've proved that this global pop-music internationalism hasn't really gone that far.'

Viva starts with some major disadvantages. MTV can economize by sending shows or promotional spots across the Atlantic; Viva cannot. MTV can strike worldwide deals with advertisers. But Viva isn't exactly defenseless. Most of its shares are owned by four of the biggest names in music: Sony, EMI, PolyGram and Warner. Last year Viacom – the U.S. company that started MTV – filed an anti-trust complaint with the European Commission, claiming that these record giants withheld videos from MTV Europe in order to aid Viva. Viva denies the charge, which is still under investigation. Gorny says people who think Viva's owners want the channel just to promote their records are missing the point. 'We're talking about an audiovisual product that is developing toward an interactive product,' he says. 'Viva is a logical step in this direction, just as the purchase of MTV by Viacom was.'

Dialects: MTV expects more Vivas to emerge across Europe as cable networks spread. Meanwhile, Viva itself is vulnerable to the same decentralizing forces that strengthened it against MTV. Germany's latest fashion is dialect rock, with south German artists singing in Schwäbisch and Bavarians singing in a Bayerisch that leaves Berliners clueless. The group Bap, performing in the Cologne region's Kölnisch dialect, has even had its turn on Viva's playlist – to less than universal praise. 'I don't understand a single word from Bap,' confesses programmer Kreissl. 'I could understand better if they sang in English.'

Source: Marc Levinson, Newsweek, 24 April 1995, p. 48.

READING E:
Richard Wilk, 'The local and the global in the political economy of beauty: from Miss Belize to Miss World'

Structures of common difference

If [...] there is a growing global system of common difference, busy incorporating and colonizing existing distinctions between people, where might we look for its advancing edges? I would like to bring up two examples, the first based on a single observation and the second resulting from several months of fieldwork and observation. One night in 1993 I happened to stay up late watching cable television, which I do not have at home, but remember from my last stay in Belize. Long after midnight I strayed onto ESPN, the sports channel, and to my surprise encountered the final events of the American Double-Dutch League Jump Rope Championships, for the 4th grade through high school.

I had thought jumping rope was a simple recreation, the unregulated fun of kids at play, but here it was presented with all the features of a professionalized contest – the moves were named and standardized, along with a precision scoring system based on skill and difficulty. The performances were divided into required compulsory patterns, and 'free style' expressive and artistic performances, graded separately. There were corporate sponsors, a panel of judges, computerized scores flashed on the screen following slow-motion replays, and truly dazzling, well practiced performances by teams of young people in matching costumes and designer sportswear.

Stepping back and looking at the contest as a cultural system, it is clear how it organizes both time and space – there is a hierarchy of regional competitions from local through state, regional and nationals, an annual season starting in the spring, and a sense of continuity as teams come back year after year, and players become coaches. The events classify performers by age grades – all team members have to be in a narrow range, and they can only compete within that category. At the same time, other kinds of distinctions were deliberately muted; boys and girls could be on the same team

together though most competitors were girls. There was no explicit mention of race or ethnicity, though all the teams but one were all-black or all-white, and there was a powerful subtext of rich white suburbs pitted against the black city. The teams were surrounded by adult coaches, clearly family members and friends, tied together by intensely local networks in which they invested tremendous energy and large amounts of money with little hope of reward.

We heard interviews with the winners and coaches after each competition; they spoke of the way the sport uplifted and disciplined performers, 'developing self-respect' and giving the kids a chance for travel and experience. But besides becoming cosmopolitans, they developed a sense of local pride: 'Seein ourselves last year on TV was real important, especially comin from a small town like we do.' As performance, play becomes cultural work, part of the rhythm of discipline and release that is such a familiar part of capitalist consumerism (see Nichter and Nichter, 1991).

I have to say I am not much of a sports fan, but I found this program riveting. Before a tiny late-night insomniac audience, I found the cutting edge of global capitalist culture, and a model for what I have been seeing and experiencing over the last twenty years of work in Belize. The National Double-Dutch League (based in Washington DC) is professionalizing jump rope as a public performance, taking a lived, contextualized tradition of play and turning it into a commodity. The contest formalizes a particular set of distinctions and places them in the foreground, while moving others into the background. It reifies and emphasizes particular kinds of hierarchy based on time and geopolitical space, and it groups people according to some kinds of physical biological characteristics, but not others. The competition is exactly what Bourdieu (1984) means as a practice that 'classifies and classifies the classifier'.

Since watching the rope jumpers, I've noted other similar events, from professional ballroom dancing to the national mixed doubles free style canoe championships (covered in *Paddler* magazine). The contest seems to be an especially potent social form in which difference is expressed, commodified, and contained, a crucial site where difference is rationalized and naturalized to create equivalency between different social groups. The jump rope contest calls attention to a process which I have been studying in Belize, where beauty pageants have become extremely popular public events.

These pageants began in Belize right after the Second World War. They were sponsored and organized by two contending political parties, who made the crowning of queens the centerpieces of their respective annual patriotic celebrations. The first pageant was started by a loyalist middle-class Creole political movement which arose during the 1930s and 1940s.[1] As nationalist and anti-British sentiment grew more prevalent during the Second World War, the urban middle class, who dominated the civil service, reacted by forming the 'Loyal and Patriotic Order of the Baymen' in 1945. This group organized neighborhoods into 'lodges' modelled on existing fraternal and Masonic organizations. The lodges functioned as social and political clubs, whose main public activities revolved around the annual celebration of the Battle of St George's Cay on 10 September. While the nationalists and trade unionists argued that the British were dominating and exploiting the country, the LPOB stressed their pride in being part of the British Empire. Celebrating the Battle of St George's Cay dramatized the identity of British Hondurans with the British, for this heavily mythologized eighteenth-century event was supposedly a time when Baymen (as the local white inhabitants were then known), slaves and British troops stood 'shoulder to shoulder' to drive back an armed Spanish attempt to enforce their (quite legal) claim to the area. The Baymen were eulogized by the LPOB for their 'Deeds that won an Empire'.

The Queen of the Bay pageant was added to the annual celebration in 1946 at the instigation of several older women in the LPOB. They conceived of the Queen competition to bring the lodges together, and add respectability to the parade. One of the organizers told me the goal was to 'bring up' (give status to) the celebration; she kept careful track of the girls' family background and personal character and made sure they had no babies: 'we were looking for a real queen'. A contemporary contestant looking back said: 'The black colonials acted like she was the real Queen Elizabeth, they wanted someone who would be like royalty as part of their celebrations.' The neighborhoods competed

not only to select a winning contestant, but also to raise money to clothe her in the latest imported fashions.

The LPOB strategy in staging the pageant was consistent with its general policy of trying to merge the political issue of independence and self-government, with the cultural arena of respectability, education and 'taste'. Beneath both the political and cultural agenda was the unspoken social agenda of continuing the privileged position of a small, educated middle class in a stagnant and marginal local economy. Faced with rapidly increasing populist and anti-British sentiment, the LPOB tried to broaden the appeal of the pageant to include contestants from outside Belize City. In 1950 they relabeled the selection of the Queen of the Bay as the 'National Beauty Pageant'.

The nationalist Peoples' Committee, prevented from direct economic or political action through harsh libel and labor laws, attacked the colonial order in its symbolic heart. In 1950 their supporters attended the tenth celebration, but wore the Committee's colors of blue and white instead of the Union Jack. They refused to participate in the celebration of the Battle of St George's Cay, and publicly questioned whether the battle had ever really occurred (this is still a heated controversy in the newspapers every September). The political party (the Peoples United Party) that emerged from this movement quickly created its own flag and song. The colonial governor responded to their demonstrations with a state of emergency, and in 1950 jailed most of its leaders for sedition. Amidst this turmoil, as the British rewrote the colonial constitution, with its leaders in jail, the Peoples United Party plotted not a revolution, but a beauty pageant – 'Miss British Honduras'. The PUP committees in each district selected contestants, who were presented in local meetings that were notable more for their lack of British trappings than for the presence of anything local (American styles and popular songs were prominent). Significantly, the winner's prize was a trip to Guatemala, a strong statement of the PUP's policy of seeking closer ties with its Hispanic neighbors instead of the British Caribbean.

The spread of beauty pageants went along with the extension of political parties into the countryside. The very first local beauty pageants in many towns and villages in 1950 sparked heated controversies, for the selection of a single local Queen in public made it clear what faction was locally dominant. The newspapers were full of letters complaining that Queens were selected 'undemocratically', in a secretive way, favoring candidates for their political connections rather than beauty or elegance.

[...]

Today the organizers and sponsors of the major national pageants see them as events that unite the nation in diversity – following the official pluralist line of the state that each ethnic group contributes something to a unique mix. As Miss Teen Belmopan 1990 put it: 'Even though we all a different race, Belize da one place.' The pageants attempt to organize and domesticate differences between Belizeans, by an appeal to objective standards of beauty and talent. They also provide a common code for the expression of differences between Belizeans.

Contestants often dress in fancied regional or ethnic costumes, perform 'ethnic' dances or sing 'ethnic' songs, and may themselves be considered official representatives of particular groups (though this is by no means universal). Sometimes a person of one ethnic group will dress in the costume of another. Where no recognizable 'traditional' folk-dress exists, they are created. But as each pageant progresses towards the semi-finals, the ethnic themes are dropped and national unification takes over. Speeches, songs and discussion focus on Belizean culture and nationalism. In the semi-final interviews, contestants are often asked questions about the country which call for patriotic answers. In 1990 the aspiring Miss Belize candidates were asked 'What would you as a Belizean, selling your country to tourists, tell them about Belize?' The responses mentioned the democratic government, the harmony among diverse people, and the natural environment's touristic attractions. 'Belize is rich in natural beauty and we should be proud of it.' 'Belize is peaceful and democratic.' 'Belize is truly a paradise.' 'Belize is a curious colorful mixture of cultures such as the Maya, the Mestizo, Garifuna, Creole, Lebanese and East Indians. I am proud to be part of this mixture.' Such questions explicitly situate Belize in the foreigner's gaze; they project Belize outwards as a unique place, in the common

descriptive terms of all the unique places that make up a global pageant.

The pageant is one means by which the government has sought to make ethnicity, a potentially dangerous and divisive issue, into something ornamental and safe (see Wilk and Chapin, 1989). As long as it remains focused on artistic performance, the government sponsors ethnic expression. Safe ethnic culture is attractive to tourists, part of an international genre of 'our nation's wonderful diversity'; it is safely disengaged from the inequities in land, labor and rights which are so visible to a social scientist in the countryside, but which are rarely spoken of in public life. When ethnicity takes on a political, economic or territorial nature, the government has reacted with repression, bribery or cooptation that takes the form of support for 'safe' projects (Moberg, 1992). When the Maya in the southern districts formed an organization to press for land rights in 1984, the government response was to offer them money and equipment for videotaping their ritual dances (Wilk and Chapin, 1989).

Pageants also make ethnicity safe by subordinating cultural identity to gender and sexuality. The contestants first appear clothed in ethnic garb, as representatives of their 'people'. But in the next step the contestants appear in bathing suits, as bodies stripped of their external cultural costume. Since skin color and features are so heterogeneous among Belizeans, in bathing suits ethnicity is gone; the woman remains. Gender transcends the ethnic, but what transcends gender? The final transformation of the image of woman in the pageant occurs when symbolically naked essentialized sexual objects are reclothed, but this time as creatures of modernity and fashion. The evening-gown competition brings the contestants back on stage transformed into cosmopolitans, wearing the latest expensive imported dresses, showing their sophistication and knowledge of the world outside Belize.

The flow of imagery in the pageant makes representational order by linking together different feminine images. We start with woman submerged in the localized, ethnic and 'primordial' community, strip away that identity to reveal woman-as-body as something supposedly more basic and essential, and end with woman transformed by modernity into a transcending figure ready to move outwards to the global stage. (There is a clear structural parallel to the classic stages of a rite of passage).

Beauty pageants also organize and objectify other kinds of differences. Like the jump rope contests they channel space and time, space into a hierarchy and time into annual cycles of competition, linked by the careers of the participants. They provide regular institutions that link small communities of competitors and supporters together into larger and larger structures reaching upwards to a global level. Like jump rope, pageants make an appeal to objectivity in their competitive distinctions, through 'objective' judges, a scoring system, and displays of both innate talent and acquired skill. Like other competitions, they classify the participants by essentialized characteristics – originally the pageants were open only to 16 to 24-year-olds, but now there is a full array of Miss Teen, Miss Preteen, Ms Elegant, Ms Middle Age and Ms Maturity pageants. One organizer told me she planned a 'Miss Big and Beautiful' pageant for 'larger' women. And also like the rope jumpers, they publicly justify pageantry as educational and uplifting for the contestants, a chance for them to become cosmopolitan, gain poise and begin careers.

The cultural forms of pageants do not speak with a single voice, nor is their message always effective or convincing. Their ostensible purpose is to bring people together as equals, to promote a common identity and build support for a particular party, goals that are themselves contradictory in a highly stratified, factionalized and ethnically divided nation. The pageants inevitably dramatize particular kinds of difference in ways that the organizers do not intend. Doubt and division enter the pageant partly because the event derives some of its power from the tension between foreground and background, onstage and backstage. The audience knows that the public performance is only a part of the story, and that there is a world 'behind the scenes' where the competition is anything but objective and fair (Cohen, 1991). On the one hand there is a public contest of open democracy, with a public display of bodies and talents, and experts who vote on contestants according to ostensibly objective standards. On the other hand there is a hidden, covert process of the

exercise of power and privilege, where factions scheme and manoeuvre for advantage and influence, in ways the public can only imagine or gossip about. Public conversation about the pageant is dominated by speculation about influence and conspiracy. Both systems of power, the objective stage and the scheming backstage, share legitimacy, and in many ways they are dependent on each other.

One consequence of these mixed messages is that selecting a beauty queen always brings forward existing divisions within the community. The crowd at a pageant identifies candidates with factions – ethnic, class, political and familial – and acts as if the pageant is a struggle for power. When the winner is unpopular, the crowd is angry, and complains that the contest was rigged, that the process was not really open or democratic. So the pageant foregrounds both the divisions between factions in the community and the differences between the politics of public democracy and those of private power and influence. In a similar way, the jump rope competition builds on the tensions between the 'natural' physical abilities of some contestants, and others' privileged access to trainers, facilities, practice time and expensive equipment and clothing.

While there is controversy and difference among organizers, participants and audiences at pageants and beauty competitions, these disputes are inherently local. They draw their power from an array of local powers and participants, and they cannot be decoded without local knowledge. This is the context in which the global, foreign institution of the beauty pageant has been appropriated and localized, made Belizean. If analysis stopped at this point, we would have a story about how foreign models of gender and identity are absorbed into the local scene and given a new cultural content (Arnould and Wilk, 1984). But a second level of complexity emerges more clearly when we look at the highest level of competition in Belize to choose the candidates that will go onwards to the global stages. Here we find that pageants simultaneously look inwards to the kinds of distinctions Belizeans make among themselves, and outward through the ways they portray themselves to the global 'Other's' gaze.

Local and global difference

An inescapable reality of Belize's global position is that it simply has no chance of winning a major contest. These days winning requires professional coaches and fabulously expensive wardrobes. In twenty years only one Belizean contestant even made it to the final group of twelve in the Miss Universe pageant (in 1979 – most Belizeans still remember her name). So why participate? The local organizer of the Miss Universe pageant said it concisely: 'To show we can compete with the rest of the world.' Even for the losers, the contest asserts a kind of categorical equality, and being the underdog can have more of a nationalizing effect than winning. How else can one explain the role of that famous Olympic performance by the Jamaican bobsled team?

This categorical equality has a key focus on the concept of beauty, and the encounter between the local and the global hinges on the way beauty organizes and objectifies relations of similarity and difference. In interviews with organizers and contestants, I was told that Belizeans cannot win international competitions because they have different standards of beauty from foreigners. As one organizer said,

> The international judges like tall, thin and beautiful girls. In Belize they like girls who are shorter – here 5 feet 6 inches is tall, and stockier. To qualify for Belizean men, you must have some shape, you must have bust and hips. It's something completely different. If you choose a girl for the international competition the Belizean men will say 'E too maaga.' [She's too thin.] Bones alone, not enough flesh. But them [foreign] judges will look at the Belizean girl and say 'E too fat.'

Part of the drama of the contest, then, is the collision between local standards of beauty, deeply embedded in cultural constructs of gender and sexuality, and international standards which are widely believed to be those of the dominant white nations of the North. But these separate realms are also unified through the common notion of beauty; the differences between local and global become different 'standards' within a single framework.

Standards of beauty in Belize are inherently difficult and dangerous social and political territory because, as elsewhere in the Americas, color has always been indexical with social status (e.g. Graham, 1990). Blackness, and features labeled 'black', are unequally distributed, are actively discriminated against and/or considered 'ugly' by many Belizeans. Thus, the national pageants can highlight class and ethnic discrimination based on color, rather than resolving or eliminating it.

The organizers of Belizean national pageants are frustrated by differences in 'standards'. They say they could find Belizean women who could be 'Miss World', but the local pageants must first please a Belizean audience with a different agenda. This discourse about beauty emphasizes the highly local, contextualized nature of Belizean pageants. Local organizers told me that 'the real reason' why Belizean pageants don't produce international competitors, is because the judges and crowds favor contestants because of political, ethnic, class and kinship connections. In a country as small as Belize, nobody is anonymous – all the contestants' connections are known. The most common public discussion of the reasons why one woman won are comments on the contestants' wealth, ethnicity, political patronage or family connections.

[...]

The key point here is not that the pageants and competitions eliminate differences. They are not hegemonic tools that create homogeneity. All they do is provide a common channel and a point of focus for the debate and expression of differences. They take the full universe of possible contrasts between nations, groups, locales, factions, families, political parties and economic classes, and they systematically narrow our gaze to particular kinds of difference. They organize and focus debate, and in the process of foregrounding particular kinds of difference, they submerge and obscure others by pushing them into the background. They standardize a vocabulary for describing difference, and provide a syntax for its expression, to produce a common frame of organized distinction. They essentialize some kinds of differences as ethnic, physical and immutable, and portray them in objective categories of Beauty and Talent, washing them with legitimacy. By focusing on the female body, they attribute culture to nature – but not one particular culture. In doing this they might be seen as the gender reversal of international sporting competitions, which map cultural geography onto the physical capabilities of male bodies.

I would argue that in accomplishing these tasks, competitions serve political and polemic purposes for many different and contending interests. They are not hegemonic in the sense that they allow one group to simply extend and exercise its power over others. They are hegemonic only in the way they involve disparate groups in a common contest, and thereby limit their ranges of possible action and domesticate conflict. In Belize we see this reflected in the 'anti-pageants' of minority groups and movements over the last twenty years. The American-inspired black power movement of the early 1970s selected 'Miss Afro-Honduras'. The Garinagu, an excluded minority in the country, started their separate 'Miss Garifuna' pageant in the 1950s, but now their winners compete for Miss Belize. The expatriate Belizean community in the United States, excluded from national politics, selected a 'Queen of the Belize Honduran Association of New York' in 1954, and the expatriate Queens now attend the national pageants every year. The pageants have become a common frame for the expression of deep cultural and political divisions. In the meantime, a whole series of fundamental economic issues that underlie Belize's ability to chart an autonomous future, that divide its people more dramatically than any pageant, are out of the public eye. The country is vastly dependent, dominated and impoverished, but this economic reality remains dimly and poorly perceived.

Note

1   The term 'Creole' refers in Belize to a broad group of people of mixed African and European descent, though the merchant and professional elite of mostly European descent also use the term. The historical change in the use of the term is tracked by Judd (1989).

References

ARNOULD, E. J. and WILK, R. (1984) 'Why do the Indians wear Adidas?', *Advances in Consumer Research*, Vol. 11, pp. 748–52.

BOURDIEU, P. (1984) *Distinction: a social critique of the judgement of taste*, Cambridge, MA, Harvard University Press.

COHEN, C. (1991) 'Queen contestants in a contested domain: staging national identity in the post-colonial Caribbean', paper presented at the Annual Meeting of the American Anthropological Association, Chicago.

GRAHAM, R. (1990) *The Idea of Race in Latin America, 1870–1940*, Austin, TX, University of Texas Press.

JUDD, K. (1989) 'Who will define us? Creole history and identity in Belize', paper presented at the Annual Meeting of the American Anthropological Association, Chicago.

MOBERG, M. (1992) *Citrus, Strategy and Class*, Iowa City, IA, Iowa University Press.

NICHTER, M. and NICHTER, M. (1991) 'Hype and weight', *Medical Anthropology*, Vol. 13, pp. 249–84.

WILK, R. and CHAPIN, M. (1989) 'Ethnic minorities in Belize: Mopan, Kekchi and Garifuna', Monograph No. 1, Society for the Promotion of Education and Research, Belize City.

Source: Wilk, 1995, pp. 124–33.

THE PRODUCTION OF CULTURE

Keith Negus

Contents

l   Introduction

During 1988 and 1989 Sony, the company that had for many years produced and marketed a range of audio-visual products which included the world's first transistor radio and the Walkman, purchased Columbia Studios and CBS Records. The acquisition of these two US-based companies was accompanied by a flurry of corporate announcements in which Sony declared that it was pursuing a new strategy, referred to as **synergy**. No longer would Sony simply be known as a manufacturer of technology, it would now be a 'total entertainment' company that provided both the hardware (compact disc players, video-recorders, televisions) and the software (films and music) that featured on them. Like many other media and communication corporations, Sony had recognized that the links between the manufacture of technologies and the production of sounds, words and images had always been close (no-one would buy a Walkman or compact disc player without the recorded music or words to play on it) and they now intended to bring these connections even closer by putting them together within one corporation. At the same time as creating these hardware–software connections (or 'synergies') Sony would – proclaimed company founder Akio Morita – forge new links between cultural texts, by bringing together moving image, music, written word and computer programming in new products.

synergy

Just over five years later, things were not looking as positive as when this strategy was first announced. The Columbia/Tri Star Studios division (re-named Sony Pictures Entertainment) had incurred large losses and the company had written off a deficit of Y265 billion ($2,979 million) and acknowledged other losses of Y50 billion ($562 million) due to abandoned projects and the settlement of legal claims (Sony, 1995). At the same time, Sony Music Entertainment (formerly CBS Records) was engaged in a very public court case with one of their major artists, George Michael. As part of his case, Michael had issued a public statement declaring that since the Sony acquisition he had seen CBS Records 'become a small part of the production line for a giant electronics corporation, who quite frankly, have no understanding of the creative process' (*Music Week*, 21 November 1992, p. 3).

The promised synergy – the mutually enhancing bringing together of texts and technologies – was not occurring in the way that Sony's management had anticipated. In an editorial commentary on the situation, *The Financial Times* suggested that its readers should be sceptical about the long-term prospects for such synergistic connections, particularly in this case which had involved 'culture clashes between technology and programming companies, and between Japanese hierarchies and Hollywood egos' (18 November 1994). As Sony discovered, bringing together hardware and software in one company involves much more than formally matching products (movies with video machines, songs with CD players). It also entails trying to link up complex organizational activities and management practices. It does not merely involve bringing together media technologies and possibly incompatible techniques of production; it also entails bringing into contact different working practices and 'cultures of production'.

I have begun by referring to Sony's predicament (which will be covered in a little more detail later) because it highlights the key theme and argument that I will be pursuing throughout this chapter: in studying the production of culture it is necessary to understand not only the technical processes and economic patterns of manufacturing, organization and distribution. It is also important to understand the culture – the ways of life – through and within which music, films and hardware technologies are made and given meaning. In following this theme I will be drawing your attention to an important shift in approaches to how culture is produced: from earlier attempts to understand the impact of specific forms of industrial production on cultural artefacts (a method which initially involved applying notions of 'industry' to 'culture'), towards a perspective which approaches 'culture', not simply as a thing which is produced but as a 'way of life' and, as such, refers to the constitutive meanings and practices through which the creation and circulation of texts and technologies occurs (a method that involves applying theories of 'culture' to 'industry').

The chapter will be divided into two broad sections.

In section 2 I shall direct you to one of the most influential theoretical approaches to the production of culture: that developed and schematically elaborated by Theodor Adorno and Max Horkheimer during the 1940s. I shall explain two of their key concepts (*standardization* and *pseudo individuality*) and provide examples which point to the enduring relevance of their arguments. I shall also be highlighting a number of problems with this type of approach.

In section 3 I shall give a more detailed and descriptive sense of some of the working practices within the contemporary culture industry. The story of the Sony Walkman (see **du Gay, Hall et al.,** 1997) could be seen as the story of a company's great success, but this section will give a contrasting perspective as I point to some of the problems encountered by Sony when they attempted to create connections between hardware and software divisions of the company. Finally, I will indicate how the activities of staff working in the cultural industries are informed by particular sets of values, beliefs and working practices – a 'culture of production' which has a significant impact on the 'production of culture'.

Overall, this chapter will trace a broad theoretical shift from approaching the production of culture through a *macro* perspective which stresses social and organizational *structures* and *economic* relationships, towards a more *micro* approach which focuses on everyday human *agency* and the making of *cultural* meanings. The first approach foregrounds the issue of control over production and constraint on creative practices; the second emphasizes human autonomy and the active ability to engage in creative activities despite such constraints. The challenge for empirical research and theoretical understanding is to regard both as equally important and *related* through the ways in which products are circulated and given particular meanings via the range of production–consumption relationships (i.e. the 'cultural circuit' of representation, identity, production, consumption and regulation – see the Introduction to this volume).

2   The culture industry

The idea of a **cultural industry** was first widely used as a concept by Theodor Adorno and Max Horkheimer in a work written in 1944 and first published in 1947. Writing against those who believed that the arts were independent of industry and commerce, Adorno and Horkheimer adopted the term 'culture industry' to argue that the way in which cultural items were produced was analogous to how other industries manufactured vast quantities of consumer goods. All products were produced with the aim of profit-making uppermost and according to the same rationalized organizational procedures. Adorno and Horkheimer argued that the culture industry exhibited an 'assembly-line character' which could be observed in 'the synthetic, planned method of turning out its products (factory-like not only in the studio but, more or less, in the compilation of cheap biographies, pseudo documentary novels, and hit songs)' (Adorno and Horkheimer, 1979[1947], p. 163).

culture industry

This metaphor of the 'culture industry' has endured and comparable phrases such as 'production line' and 'sausage machine' have often been used (both inside and outside the academy) to refer to the music industry, book publishing business and to characterize Hollywood film production.

Adorno and Horkheimer, though, were doing more than just highlighting how culture had been industrialized, they also sought to explain the impact that this process was having on how cultural items were created and consumed. In doing this they linked the idea of the 'culture industry' to a model of 'mass culture' in which cultural production had become a routine, standardized repetitive operation that produced undemanding cultural commodities which in turn resulted in a type of consumption that was also standardized, distracted and passive.

Adorno and Horkheimer's view of cultural production has, with some justification, often been portrayed as the pessimistic lament of cultural elitists who were dismayed at what they perceived to be the homogeneity and vulgarity of 'mass' taste, and who were concerned that the potential for artistic creativity in music, literature and painting had been co-opted and corrupted by the production methods and administrative regimes of industrial capitalism. However, it would be wrong to dismiss the work of these writers so hastily and entirely because of their apparent elitism. For one thing, the ideas that they introduced have continued to have a resonance within contemporary discussions about how culture is produced. In addition, Adorno and Horkheimer produced their theory during a particularly significant historical period in the twentieth century. In this sense, their theory and argument was both a product of its times and an attempt to understand those times. Before I direct you to a reading in which you will get a feel for their 'despair', let me briefly preface the details of their argument with some background information which should give you an insight into the trajectory of their analysis and why they reached some of the conclusions that they did.

Adorno and Horkheimer were members of a group of predominantly German-Jewish intellectuals who have become widely known as the Frankfurt School and who produced a substantial body of analysis between the 1920s and the 1960s. The term Frankfurt School comes from the School of Social Research, an independently financed institute affiliated to the University of Frankfurt that was first established during the early 1920s. The use of this label tends to suggest a unity to a group of writers who in fact had a diverse range of interests and who pursued many different empirical and theoretical studies. However, members of the Frankfurt School did share a similar orientation and a common desire to develop a philosophically informed analysis which was explicitly opposed to the behaviourist and positivist thinking of some of their sociological contemporaries who were basing their approaches on the methods of the natural sciences.

The critique of the 'culture industry' appeared in *Dialectic of Enlightenment*, a book which identified and then outlined the emergence of a particular form of 'instrumental rationality' which the authors believed had become dominant within European thought since the Enlightenment. Like the sociologist Max Weber, they were concerned about a type of reasoning through which groups and individuals were encouraged to pursue particular aims in a 'logical' and calculated way untouched by sentiment. Adorno and Horkheimer argued that this had resulted in a type of science which sought to dominate and subordinate the natural world. This instrumental approach to means/ends had also led to exploitative relationships between human beings; this was particularly noticeable in the relationship between employers and workers, where the workers' value was judged, unsentimentally, solely in terms of its use and function for the process of production and generation of profits. Hence, Adorno and Horkheimer were opposed to a particular type of 'scientific' rationality which sought to control and impose a predictable order on both the natural and social world.

Adorno and Horkheimer did not arrive at such a theoretical orientation just from philosophical reflection. The impact of this type of instrumentalist scientific rationality was quite tangibly apparent as they were writing. Both had lived through the bloodshed of the 1914–18 War, and the failure of the working-class revolutions that had spread across Europe after the Russian Revolution of 1917. As they questioned the potential of working-class movements to bring about progressive social change (as anticipated by Marx), Adorno and Horkheimer were also aware of the growth of fascist parties across western Europe. When the Nazi Party seized power in 1933, both writers had to flee Germany and eventually relocated in the United States. In exile, Adorno and Horkheimer observed what was occurring across Europe and asked how the development of modern European thought, instead of enabling the development of a more enlightened and liberated society, was leading to what they called 'a new kind of barbarism', the epitome of an instrumentalistic approach to the world which they observed in the logic of totalitarianism and fascism.

In addition, Adorno and Horkheimer were living at a time when technological changes had led to the improvement and increasing popularity of recorded music on the phonograph disc, and when radio broadcasting and the introduction of sound in the cinema had provided increased opportunities for commercial marketing and political propaganda. While the Nazi party were making maximum use of these media technologies in Germany, Adorno and Horkheimer arrived in the United States to find the same media being used to produce and distribute forms of commercial culture such as movies, jazz and inexpensive high circulation magazines. Their resulting theory of the 'culture industry' was thus also written at a formative moment in the development of the modern culture and communications media.

Adorno and Horkheimer made a connection between what they had observed in Europe and then in the United States and developed an argument in which the domination and manipulation of the people (who are thought of as undifferentiated 'masses') was explicitly connected to the production and dissemination of a particular form of homogeneous culture (characterized as 'mass culture'). Informing this argument was the belief that specific forms of culture might have contributed to the appearance of authoritarian patterns of domination.

READING A

With the above contextual information in mind, you should now turn to the Readings at the end of the chapter and read the extract from *Dialectic of Enlightenment* by Adorno and Horkheimer, entitled 'The culture industry: enlightenment as mass deception'.

As you read, jot down what you take to be the key themes and issues that the authors are raising. What are they suggesting about the relationship between public, talented performer and industry, for example?

You should also bear in mind that this extract is a small part of a complex and highly philosophical work which was written in an often elliptical and dense prose style. You are strongly recommended to read the original, if you have the opportunity.

In their essay, Adorno and Horkheimer make a number of specific empirical points which are related to three main threads of a central argument:

1   From a political-economy analysis which draws on Marx, they argue that the concentration of culture production in a capitalist industry results in a standardized commercial commodity.

2   This they connect to an argument which draws on a tradition of romantic aesthetic thought which had counterposed free and autonomous art against the repetitive and unchallenging culture produced as a commodity.

3   They then connect this to a theory of the experience of this type of 'mass culture'. Drawing on the psychological theories of Freud, Adorno and Horkheimer argue that cultural consumption has become a de-concentrated activity leading to passive and 'obedient' types of social behaviour.

Despite its complexity this essay formed a starting-point for many subsequent discussions about cultural activity and social behaviour. In my brief introduction to this work, I want to focus on the way in which Adorno and Horkheimer conceived of cultural production (saying less about consumption and little about aesthetics).

Let me highlight some of the key points that drive Adorno and Horkheimer's argument in this article. The capitalist corporation seems to enjoy an almost omnipotent form of domination and both the consumers and the creative artists are not separate from but are directly connected to this system of production. Adorno and Horkheimer wrote of how artists and audiences 'belong' to the culture industry: the 'talented performer' and the 'attitude of the public' are not independent from but are 'inherent in the technical and personnel apparatus which, down to its last cog, itself forms part of the economic mechanism of selection' (1979, p. 122). Hence, the argument here is that the activities of consumers are as pre-made and determined a 'part' of the culture industry, as is the activity of producers.

Adorno and Horkheimer stressed the structures of economic ownership and control of the means through which cultural products are produced and argued that this directly shapes the activities of creative artists and consumers. From this perspective, the activities of artists (musicians, actors, novelists) and various audiences (in the cinema, reading novels, watching television, listening to recorded music) are directly explicable in terms of the way in which culture has become administered in production. Consumption and creative activity are not in any way independent from production, and the implication of Adorno and Horkheimer's approach is that it would simply be misleading to think of them as such; the 'audience' and creative work only exist as they are defined and made by the culture industry.

This is an approach characterized by **du Gay, Hall et al.** (1997) as 'the production of consumption perspective'. However, the idea that there is such a neat fit (or fusion) between production and consumption, and that we can explain the activities of consumers or the meaning of films or songs simply from the way in which they are produced, is open to challenge. **Mackay** (ed.,

1997) deals with the complex of human actions that are condensed into the simple term 'consumption' and the range of representations that can become attached to commercial objects. In this chapter, however, I am not going to challenge Adorno and Horkheimer's assumptions about consumption in any detail. Rather, I shall confine my discussion to the sphere of production.

One of the ways I will be challenging this 'production of consumption' argument is by highlighting how the process of production is by no means as standardized, rational and predictable as suggested by this approach. Before I move on to this, however, I want to provide you with a little more detail about some of the arguments that were advanced by Adorno and Horkheimer (and Adorno alone) to support their case. In criticizing this particular emphasis on production, I will not be rejecting it in its entirety.

2.1   Co-opting culture: standardization and pseudo individuality

You will recall from the discussion in the previous section that Adorno and Horkheimer argued that the 'culture industry' operated in the same way as other manufacturing industries. All work had become formalized and products were made according to rationalized organizational procedures that were established for the sole purpose of making money. The metaphor of the 'assembly-line' was used to stress the repetitive and routine character of cultural production. This theme was then pursued in more detail in relation to two additional concepts – standardization and pseudo individuality. These concepts, outlined by Adorno and Horkheimer in 1947, were also employed by Adorno in his own writings on music. I shall discuss each in turn.

Adorno and Horkheimer argued that all products produced by the culture industry exhibited **standardized** features. They wrote: standardization

> As soon as the film begins, it is quite clear how it will end, and who will be rewarded, punished, or forgotten. In light music, once the trained ear has heard the first notes of the hit song, it can guess what is coming and feel flattered when it does come. The average length of the short story has to be rigidly adhered to. Even gags, effects, and jokes are calculated like the setting in which they are placed. They are the responsibility of special experts and their narrow range makes it easy for them to be apportioned in the office.
>
> (Adorno and Horkheimer, 1979, p. 125)

The argument here is that there is nothing spontaneous about the process of cultural production: it has become a routine operation that can be carried out in an office by the application of specific formulae. This is a theme that Adorno pursued in more detail in his writings on popular music, particularly when he evoked the terminology used in contemporary books that offered guidance to budding hit songwriters. Adorno (1976) observed that ambitious songwriters were advised that their melodies and lyrics should fit strict formulae. He also noted that songs which became successful over time were often referred to as 'standards', a category that clearly drew attention to their formulaic character. From the 'plan' to the details, songs were based around repetitive sequences and frequently recurring refrains (Adorno, 1976, p. 25). This was done for quite calculated commercial reasons, so that the song would imprint itself on the mind of the listener and then provoke a purchase. For Adorno, the production of hit songs had become a mechanical and manipulative operation motivated purely by commercial gain. An instrumental approach to the production of culture had resulted in songs, films and novels being rationalized into component parts that could then be substituted for each other, just like the cogs in a machine.

ACTIVITY 1

Think about the popular songs that you might hear throughout an average day (on the radio, when out shopping, on television or when in a club or bar). Do you agree with Adorno's argument about standardized songs? Are some songs more predictable than others? Or is such an analysis simply irrelevant today?

pseudo individuality

Adorno and Horkheimer were also critical of what they referred to as **pseudo individuality**. By this they meant the way that the culture industry assembled products that made claims to 'originality' but which when examined more critically exhibited little more than superficial differences. The following quotation will remind you of their reasoning:

> The constant pressure to produce new effects (which must conform to the old pattern) serves merely as another rule to increase the power of the conventions ... Pseudo individuality is rife: from the standardized jazz improvization to the exceptional film star whose hair curls over her eye to demonstrate her originality ... The defiant reserve or elegant appearance of the individual on show is mass-produced like Yale-locks, whose only difference can be measured in fractions of millimeters.
>
> (Adorno and Horkheimer, 1979, pp. 128, 154)

Here Adorno and Horkheimer evoked the image of the lock and key – an item that is mass produced in millions, whose uniqueness lies in only very minor modifications (the analogy is with the way in which generic love songs, detective novels and formulaic movies such as westerns have been produced). Adorno again pursued this theme in his critiques of music, and in particular in his writing about jazz. Adorno contended that when jazz performers were engaging in what was referred to as 'free improvization', this was merely a conceit. He argued that 'what appears as spontaneity is in fact carefully planned out in advance with machine-like precision' (1967, p. 123). As a musical form, jazz had come to be administered by the 'experts' of the culture industry whose instrumental approach had resulted in a generic music in which 'the formal elements of jazz have been abstractly pre-formed by the capitalist requirement that they be exchangeable as commodities' (Adorno, 1989, p. 52).

In making this argument he was not implying that such deceptions were inevitable, nor was he suggesting that this process was peculiar to jazz alone. Adorno also argued that a similar fate had befallen many forms of music: the performance of 'sacrosanct traditional music' had 'come to resemble commercial mass production' (1973, p. 10) and the consumption of opera had become an act of recognition. Instead of understanding an opera in its totality, Adorno (1976) contended that listeners were encouraged to respond as they would to the refrains and hooks of a hit song. Radio broadcasting was threatening to do the same thing to a Beethoven symphony. Important motifs that were introduced within the context of a complete and unique symphonic composition had been abstracted and transformed into little more than easily recognized 'trade marks' (Adorno, 1945).

ACTIVITY 2

Think again about the music you listen to in terms of Adorno's argument about pseudo individuality. To what extent do you think that you recognize singers, songs, composers and symphonies by their 'trade marks'?

There is, however, yet a further step in the argument: Adorno and Horkheimer were not only arguing about how culture had become standardized and robbed of any unique qualities, they also suggested that this resulted in a particular type of consumption in which few demands were made of the listener, viewer or reader. The 'mass culture' that was being produced by the culture industry encouraged consumers to reject everything that was not familiar. Again Adorno put forward evidence for this in his writings about music, pouncing on the category of 'easy listening' (1976, p. 30) and arguing that this was clear evidence that music was being deliberately created to encourage distracted audience activity: easy listening music was made up of the most familiar harmonies, rhythms and melodies and this provided a music which had a 'soporific' effect on the minds of those consuming it. Like other cultural products, this provided mere diversion and distraction and prevented people from reflecting on their position in the world. This resulted in what Adorno (1991) called 'regressive listening' whereby audiences were pacified by a type of music that merely provided a temporary escape from the boredom of the factory or daily drudgery of the office. Such 'mass culture' made people accept the status quo and engendered obedience towards authoritarianism. It was, ultimately, the products of the culture industry, with their pacifying effects and unchallenging qualities, that were allowing people to become 'masses' and be easily manipulated by capitalist corporations and authoritarian governments.

Adorno and Horkheimer thus present us with a powerful argument about what happens to culture when it is subject to the structural control and organization of industrial capitalist production: it becomes merely a standardized, formulaic and repetitive element of 'mass culture'. It has no aesthetic value whatsoever and leads to a very specific type of consumption that is passive, obedient and easily manipulated for the purpose of propaganda or advertising.

ACTIVITY 3

Before moving on to the next section, think about the argument that I have just summarized. Does this type of reasoning sound familiar? Have you ever defended your own cultural preferences (books, films, music, television programmes, opera, theatre) as complex and demanding, while criticizing other peoples' as standardized and repetitive? Have you heard people explain the worldwide popularity of performers such as Madonna, films like *Batman* or the novels of Jackie Collins by arguing that the audiences are being manipulated by the marketing and promotional mechanisms of the culture-producing corporations?

2.2   Cultural industries and current anxieties

If you think that Adorno and Horkheimer's ideas still have a certain relevance for contemporary discussions of cultural production, then you are not alone. Whilst subsequent concerns about cultural production have not been quite so apocalyptic nor as totally pessimistic as those advanced by Adorno and Horkheimer, a concern with the consequences of concentrated corporate cultural production has continued and can be found in critiques of the film industry, book publishing and the music business.

Such concerns were clearly expressed by UNESCO (United Nations Educational, Scientific and Cultural Organization) in 1982 with the publication of *The Culture Industries: a challenge for the future of culture*. The UNESCO volume took Adorno and Horkheimer's essay as its starting-point and adopted the concept of the culture industries (pluralized) as a way of explaining how cultural activities throughout the world are being increasingly subject to the influence of the major media and communication companies. In this book, UNESCO expresses concern that the growth and international spread of the culture industries over the previous forty years had resulted in the gradual 'marginalization of cultural messages that do not take the form of goods, primarily of value as marketable commodities' (UNESCO, 1982, p. 10). Echoing Adorno and Horkheimer's thesis, the 'basic problem' was identified as:

... that of the ownership and control of the means of production and of distribution circuits, the trends towards the concentration and internalization of the most representative firms, and the subordination of creative artists to market forces or to more or less overtly dictated consumer demand.

(UNESCO, 1982, p. 21)

However, unlike Adorno and Horkheimer's ultimately pessimistic conclusions, the various contributors to the debate which UNESCO was attempting to re-kindle, adopted a range of positions. Whilst highlighting the constraints and manipulative power of the industries who controlled the production of culture, there was also a recognition that opportunities had been provided for the distribution of cultural products of an educative and informative character. UNESCO noted that many people had acquired literary skills and knowledge through their access to books, radio and television broadcasts. Such potentials, however, were also continually haunted by anxieties about the way that the culture industries were increasingly having a detrimental influence on the attitudes and values of young people. UNESCO also expressed concern about the distribution of entertainment products which were contributing to the inequalities between men and women and between people in different parts of world.

Although recognizing the possibilities that the widespread distribution of cultural products such as movies, books and music might bring, UNESCO's conclusions were not very far away from the arguments that had been made by Adorno and Horkheimer some forty years earlier. This was particularly apparent in the assessment that 'standardization and production on a massive scale ... and ... the tendency towards uniformity and mass culture is undermining one of the foundations of the cultural heritage of mankind [sic], namely, the very diversity of the conceptions, values and customs of which it is composed' (UNESCO, 1982, pp. 202, 235).

Whilst Adorno and Horkheimer were largely writing about what they had observed to be happening in the United States and western Europe, UNESCO extended this concern about the power of the culture industries into a more international perspective. UNESCO's final call was for member-states to develop and initiate 'response strategies' that might counter the international influence of the culture industries. The argument was for explicitly national policies that might unite the shared interests of the citizens of nations and hence formally regulate the way in which the culture industries were being allowed to produce and distribute standardized cultural products that were threatening the amount of cultural diversity in the world.

Herbert Schiller (1989) has noted that UNESCO's call for a concerted response from an 'international public sector' occurred at the very moment when the Reagan administration in the United States was forcefully promoting ideas about 'privatization and deregulation'. Schiller has argued that because the US government was hostile towards the United Nations system in general and explicitly opposed to UNESCO's aims in particular, their unilateral withdrawal from UNESCO in 1984 was a quite deliberate attempt to promote privatization and deregulation both at home and in an international context. Sharing the anxieties of Adorno and Horkheimer about the power of the culture industries, which he characterized as the 'corporate take-over of public expression', Schiller argued that because of the importance of revenues generated by US corporations from the worldwide distribution of cultural products, by withdrawing from UNESCO the United States government had made a deliberate attempt to weaken 'the capability of an international organization to defend the informational interests of its members against transnational corporate activity' (1989, p. 115).

As Kevin Robins (1995) has pointed out, the attempt to actively promote what has been called 'deregulation' in both Britain and the United States during this period should more accurately be seen as involving a process of 're-regulation': there has in fact been a shift from regulatory principles based on notions of the public interest and citizenship towards those based on the idea of people as customers and the public as consumer markets. Throughout the 1980s, as the growing media corporations of North America and Europe began to search for new sources of income beyond their own national borders, so the culture industry became more oriented towards a 'global media space and market' (Robins, 1995, p. 246).

At the very moment when UNESCO was giving a voice to the concerns of those who felt subject to the increasingly international influence of the culture industries, business analysts were advocating the adoption of 'globalization' strategies which would contribute to this process. As Theodore Levitt wrote in a book entitled *The Marketing Imagination*, the 'global corporation' should not approach the nations of the world in terms of their differences but in terms of their similarities: 'the global corporation ... seeks to standardize everything into a common global mode' (Levitt, 1983, p. 28).

This significant shift towards 'global' business strategies which gained momentum during the 1980s (see Chapter 1 of this volume) was identified by those who were concerned about the possible consequences (such as Schiller and UNESCO) and also by those who were advocates of such changes (such as Levitt). Whilst Levitt wrote of the possibilities for 'global' business that were being opened up by the standardization of products (such as global branding) and wrote of the marketing opportunities provided by a convergence and homogenization of 'the world's needs and desires' (1983, p. 93), Schiller was concerned about the increasing commodification of 'public expression' and cultural forms by the major corporations and UNESCO were concerned about the threat that this was posing to cultural diversity across the world.

By the middle of the 1990s similar anxieties were being voiced about media and culture industries being able to monopolize processes of production and distribution and seemingly being able to operate without any constraints on their activities. When in August 1995, the Walt Disney corporation merged with Capital Cities/ABC to create what (at that moment, anyway) was the world's largest media conglomerate, the comments of a *Financial Times* journalist provided yet more contemporary echoes of Adorno and Horkheimer's anxieties:

> The union of America's most famous film studio and most powerful TV network is seen in Wall Street terms as a win–win situation. What is good for investors, however, need not be good for the wider world. A win–win situation is like a free lunch; someone has to pay in the end. In this case, it could turn out to be the consumer. ... [I]t is worth recalling why it is taking place now rather than earlier. As in so much of the US economy at present the answer is simple: deregulation.
>
> For more than two decades, TV networks in the US were subject to a battery of restrictions to prevent them from exploiting their hold on the public. Over the past two years, the system has been dismantled ... From Disney's standpoint two of these restrictions were crucial. First, networks could fill only a fraction of their primetime entertainment with programmes they had made themselves. Second, they were not allowed to exploit those programmes fully through syndication ... Disney would not have been able to push its shows over a network which it owned. It can now do so without limit. ...
>
> One is left with the question of how media giants such as the new Disney are to be policed. The simple answer is that no one knows yet, because no one knows where the industry is going. Hence the bewildering number of strategies being pursued by the big players in the communication industry ... [I]n a shifting world of technologies, alliances and regulations, it is not impossible that the media world will throw up monsters. If so, it is in everyone's interest that they should be controlled. Disney's magic kingdom might be fun to visit, but few people would want to spend their lives there.
>
> (Jackson, 1995, p. 15)

This extract from a daily newspaper indicates how current anxieties about the production of culture continue to draw on themes that can be found in the arguments of Adorno and Horkheimer. This journalist stresses the concentration of resources, economic power and the means of cultural production and distribution in one corporation. It is then argued that such structures give the company the ability to dominate cultural production and distribution on a global scale in ways that will ultimately have detrimental consequences for consumers – evoked here through the image of corporate monsters and the viewing and listening public being confined to Disney's magic kingdom.

Such anxieties were heightened by the way that Disney had grown into one of the major culture-producing corporations and, at the time of writing, was strategically establishing systems of manufacture and distribution to take full advantage of the possibilities of the 'global' distribution of motion pictures,

FIGURE 2.1
Part of the wide range of products marketed along with Disney's film version of *The Hunchback of Notre Dame.*

videos, television programmes, computer software, musical recordings, magazines, theme parks and a plethora of consumer products. This range of interests was being consolidated into a 'global' strategy and, as the company informed shareholders in its 1994 Annual Report, 'despite differences in national taste, most American hits become hits everywhere ... Disney books, merchandise are hits in every corner of the world' (Disney, 1994, pp. 23–7). It is proclamations such as these that have so concerned contemporary critics who worry about the power of global culture-producing corporations.

So far in this chapter I have travelled from an argument about the production of culture that was written as a result of very specific circumstances during the 1940s and arrived at more contemporary anxieties about the power of the culture industries in the 1990s. The overriding theme of this part of the chapter has been that of the concentration of cultural production within an industry that is dominated by a few corporate producers who manufacture, own the rights to and distribute a vast number of the mass-mediated cultural products that are found in the world. The consequences of such concentration are viewed as leading to a process of standardization of form and homogeneity of content. The impact is perceived as, at best giving the consumer little real choice, at worst promoting cultural forms that are dulling our ability to think critically about the world in which we live and reducing the diversity of values, beliefs and customs across the world.

2.3 Standardized culture and the porous perimeter of production

In the remainder of this chapter I will be portraying cultural production and its possible impact as more complex, unstable and less predictable than implied so far. In **Mackay** (ed., 1997) you will find arguments that connect with this discussion in terms of activities of consumption (a challenge to the idea that consumption is 'produced') and you will find extensive discussion of processes of regulation (which should give you some ideas about the degree to which the spread of Disney's 'magic world' might need policing and how it might be done) in **Thompson** (ed., 1997).

To conclude this section I want to begin questioning some of the ideas that I have presented so far by directing you to an essay which attempts to assess Adorno's relevance for the contemporary discussion of music, and which focuses in particular on the issue of standardization.

READING B

You should now read the article by Bernard Gendron, 'Theodor Adorno meets the Cadillacs' which you will find provided as Reading B at the end of the chapter.

In this article Gendron takes issue with a specific essay by Adorno on popular music. However, the main themes should be familiar to you from the discussion above. As you read, note the distinction that Gendron makes between 'music texts' and 'functional artefacts' and how he compares the standardization of parts for an automobile with the components of hit songs. Note what he has to say about the contrasts between the functional utility and cultural meanings of standardization and how standardization might be thought of as a source of pleasure.

In this article Gendron plays on the terminology of the Cadillac (referring to both the automobile and a group of doo-wop musicians) and makes a distinction between the standardization of 'functional artefacts' such as a car and 'music texts' such as songs. While he does not dispute that both convey a range of cultural meanings and that both are functional (i.e. he does not simply present a naïve dichotomy between function and meaning), his point is that the standardization of components in the car is qualitatively different to that in a song. An automobile has standard parts for the benefit of continual production, maintenance and for the need of replacement parts. This is quite different to songs which are not 'standardized' in the same way. Furthermore, he highlights an important issue that Adorno and Horkheimer neglected – the fact that standardization is actually a source of pleasure for both musicians and audiences.

Gendron raises a very interesting question about standardization here, by suggesting that we need to understand the 'part interchangeability' of music elements and the repetition that is so integral to many musical forms (folk, blues and country traditions over a long time – and rock, rap and techno more recently) as more than simply the consequence of the administration by a culture industry. The ultimate point he makes is that we cannot simply understand what the 'repetition' of elements or the 'standardization' of song forms might mean by simply referring to the 'assembly-lines' of production. Before we can make any judgement about what a standardized product might result in, or even what a constant diet of Disney-produced programmes might mean for its viewer, we need to know much more about how they are circulated and connected with audiences. In short, we need to ask questions about how production is connected to or made to fit with consumption in quite specific ways. Here, Gendron points to the limits of a 'productionist' perspective and highlights how production is directly related to such issues as representation, circulation, consumption and regulation. Having reminded you that production is just one part of the 'cultural circuit', let me now shift levels slightly and examine some of the activities taking place within the culture industries in a less abstract way.

3   Inside the culture industries

In the section above I have referred to how 'the culture industry' is mainly made up of a few large corporations which account for the vast majority of commercial cultural products that are manufactured and distributed in the world. It has also been noted that these companies have been pursuing a variety of strategies since the end of the 1980s as they attempt to take full advantage of new technological developments, changing regulatory systems and greater opportunities for 'global' marketing to different parts of the world simultaneously. In this section I am going to focus on one company that has been pursuing such strategies, the Sony Corporation (see **du Gay, Hall et al.**, 1997, for a cultural study of the Sony Walkman). Here I shall outline some of the problems which the Sony Corporation encountered when pursuing a strategy of synergy. In doing this I shall be starting to take the theoretical shift which I signalled earlier. I will be moving from the macro to the micro, from the structures of control to the actions of producers, and from questions of economic ownership to issues of cultural meaning.

While reading this section you should bear in mind that major entertainment companies rarely expose their internal problems to public scrutiny. Fearing that share prices will fall, or that investors will get cold feet, the press releases and annual reports that are regularly issued by companies such as News Corporation, Polygram, Time-Warner or Fujisankei usually contain tales of corporate success. Only occasionally do we catch glimpses of things going wrong or not working quite as smoothly as the company's management and directors would like. When we do, the picture we are presented with is of a culture industry that is not quite as unified or powerful as Adorno and Horkheimer envisaged. The ability to direct the production of culture is not simply imposed but has to be negotiated and struggled for. In this brief overview of some of the consequences of Sony's attempt to bring together hardware and software I will suggest that the concentration of economic resources and technological capability (stressed by Adorno and Horkheimer and their followers) of itself by no means leads to a greater ability to direct or 'control' the processes of cultural production.

Hence, the main point I want to make in the following section is that it is unwise to assume too much from formal structures of ownership. A company may own a film studio, publishing company and record label along with disc manufacturing and audio assembly plants, but this is only a start – these then have to be made to work together. This involves bringing together staff who are engaged in different working practices and it also entails working with 'creative artists' who do not act and think like 'raw materials' that can be dispatched along an assembly-line. In short, we need to understand how *structures* are produced through particular human *actions* and how *economic* relationships simultaneously involve the production of *cultural* meanings.

3.1   The dream of synergy: more than integration

Adorno and Horkheimer identified a trend which they described as 'the fusion of all arts into one work', noting how the culture industry was attempting to integrate all elements of production 'from the novel (shaped with an eye to the film) to the last sound effect' (1979, p. 124). Such observations have become even more pertinent over recent years, causing Ben Bagdikian, writing in 1989, to evoke a 'dream sequence' which he believed was tantalizing 'the lords of the global village':

> Giant Corporation Inc. owns subsidiaries in every medium. One of its magazines buys (or commissions) an article that can be expanded into a book, whose author is widely interviewed in the company magazines and on its broadcast stations. The book is turned into a screenplay for the company movie studios, and the film is automatically booked into the company's chain of theatres. The movie has a sound track that is released on the company's record label. The vocalist is turned into an instant celebrity by cover features in the company magazines and interviews on its television stations. The recording is played on the company's chain of Top 40 radio stations. The movie is eventually issued by the firms video-cassette division and shown on company television stations around the world. And it all started with an article in the company magazine, whose editor selected it because it was recognized as having other uses within the company. The editor of the magazine is given a generous stock option. Every other editor and producer in the empire takes notice.
>
> (Bagdikian, 1989, p. 812)

Bagdikian was caricaturing the possibilities of what was becoming known as 'synergy', a strategy of synchronizing and actively forging connections between directly related areas of entertainment. In theory, synergy provided the corporation with opportunities for extending the presentation of and gaining the maximum exposure and revenue from specific cultural products and people. By the early 1990s there were four discrete but interrelated potential synergies that were attracting major culture producers (and also leading to the 'bewildering' array of strategies that the *Financial Times* journalist referred to earlier when writing about the Disney Corporation):

1   *Textual connections or synergies of software.* The talent which is signed up by the culture industry now, whether a musical performer, actor or author, is acquired with the knowledge that his/her sounds, words and images can be presented and promoted simultaneously across a range of media, entertainment products and leisure goods: through audio recordings, still images and words in books and magazines and on T-shirts, sounds and moving images in advertisements, films, in television broadcasts and in video and on computer games.

2   *Connections between hardware and software, or between the text and the technology.* The importance of such connections became apparent following the struggles between Sony and Matsushita to introduce domestic video equipment. Although Sony's Betamax system was technically superior to Matsushita's VHS format, the latter managed to reach agreements for its technology to be used for film and music distribution far quicker than Sony. Both companies realized that it was no use producing a technology if they did not have direct and quick access to the sounds to be listened to and images to be viewed. This was one of the key factors which motivated both Sony and Matsushita to acquire film studios and music production companies so that, as new technologies are introduced, the company would have direct access to the audio and visual material to be used on these technologies.

3   *Convergence of previously distinct hardware components.* This has been facilitated by the development of small microprocessors and digital technology which has enabled various cultural texts to be converted into digital information and then stored in binary code, as a series of pulses in a computerized memory. This has resulted in music, films, photographs, paintings and books being digitized and stored and recalled in a similar way. Since the early 1990s many companies have been developing home entertainment–information systems that combine audio and visual media in various combinations of 'multi-media'.

4   *Connections between technologies of distribution.* The development of fibre optic cable, digital broadcasting and satellite transmission, and the introduction of the so-called information highways has meant that digitized music, films, words and video images can now be rapidly distributed over space via cable, satellite and telecommunications equipment. This is drawing music and film companies into negotiations with the telecommunication corporations who already have such

networks in place and who can transmit sounds and images without the need of conventional networks of distribution (warehouses, trucks and storekeepers) and retail outlets.

In many respects, these types of connections are merely the latest examples of processes of integration, of which the twin dynamics of **'vertical' and 'horizontal' integration** have characterized the culture industry for many years. Horizontal integration refers to a process whereby one company acquires and integrates into its operations numerous firms that are producing the same product – whether it is one firm buying up high-street shoe-shops or a company acquiring as many film studios, record labels or publishing houses as possible. An example of horizontal integration would be the way that (in 1995) EMI owned 65 record companies in 37 countries around the world, including the highly successful Virgin, Chrysalis and Capitol record labels. This enables the company to monopolize the market for particular products, in this case musical recordings.

vertical integration
horizontal integration

In contrast, vertical integration involves the consolidation of processes occurring at different levels of an industry. This entails acquiring the means by which a particular product (and it could be films as much as cars or breakfast cereals) is manufactured, distributed and sold. An example here would be the way that the Disney Company owns film production studios, film distribution networks and cinemas along with video production companies, distribution outlets and television channels. This enables the company to monopolize different stages of the production–distribution process.

However, there is a difference between the strategy of synergy and that of vertical and horizontal integration. Processes of integration do not necessarily imply, nor are they aimed at, bringing the different elements together. Record labels are acquired and horizontally integrated in an attempt to enlarge market share and to increase profits from monopolizing the market outlets, not necessarily to make the staff from different music labels or movie studios work together. Similarly, vertical integration is pursued as a way of reducing the costs paid to distributors or retailers, and to gain an advantage over competitors, but not necessarily to give retailers, or distributors, a say in the content of a company's products. Hence, under a strategy of vertical integration a record retailer usually neither has a say in what is recorded, nor is under any obligation to take a recording just because it is from a label in the same parent group.

Synergy has been proposed as an attempt to make such connections and to get the different divisions to work more closely with each other. So, for example, during the early 1990s it was reported that some companies were bringing software designers together with record company staff to discuss integrating the recordings of new artists into computer games. Similarly, teams of games' designers were beginning to regularly visit the sets during the production of feature films to advise on what colours would be most suitable for transferring to the computer game.

Sony's acquisition of Columbia/Tri Star and CBS Records was touted as an attempt to pursue such synergies to the full. Rather than simply distributing the sounds and images of movies and musicians on hardware equipment after they have been recorded, films and music were now seen as vehicles for promoting hardware. The general aim was to bring different parts of the company together and to create new ways of marketing and making products that took full advantage of the 'synergistic' connections that were being created within the corporation through their merger and acquisition activities. This strategy is informed by an assumption similar to the beliefs that guided Adorno and Horkheimer's critique of cultural production: the idea that monopolizing the ownership of technical processes will lead to a decisive type of control over, and ability to shape, processes of cultural production. The following section focuses on some of the problems and pitfalls that arise when a company attempts to pursue such a strategy.

3.2   Last action heroes: Sony's synergy nightmare

One of the ways in which Sony started to pursue the possibilities that might be provided by synergy was by holding regular 'opportunities meetings' at which staff from different parts of the company were brought together with the aim of developing new product ideas and marketing strategies that could make use of the company's combinations of hardware and software. A notable instance of the company attempting to cultivate the synergistic potentials of their new film studios was reported when they were planning the production of *Last Action Hero*. The article on pages 88–9 is an extract from an account of one of the planning meetings for this movie, observed and written up by a journalist writing for the *Wall Street Journal*.

As this article makes clear, drawing staff from different occupations and different corporate locations does not necessarily lead to harmonious collaborative relations or the most imaginative of ideas. These 'synergies' were bringing together people who had quite different experiences of working life, contrasting ideas and outlooks on what they were doing and little or no experience of working together on projects – and often, it seemed, no particular desire to do so. An engineer involved in developing televisions or tape recorders inhabits a different working culture to the producer of rock music or the film director: they talk a different language, dress differently, work according to different temporal logics and have contrasting outlooks. But there was more to Sony's problems with synergy than styles of dress, vocabularies and beliefs.

Sony's movies were made within the context of a management philosophy and approach to appointing staff which, although proving successful in Tokyo, took on a different form and dynamic when translated into the cultural world of Hollywood. Sony developed an organizational culture which depended upon recruiting 'bright eccentrics', regardless of theirtraining or background; Sony recruited people who were judged to be

MISSING LINKS

Entertainment Giants, Like Sony, See Little Of Synergy's Benefits

Next Schwarzenegger Co-Stars May Be Games, MiniDiscs; Corporate Tensions Arise

Rattled by Hollywood Culture

When about 40 executives of Sony USA gathered here for a meeting last November, the culture clash couldn't have been more stark.

From 'hardware' came the marketing experts, buttoned-down types from the company's East Coast consumer-electronics business. Also present – in Italian-cut suits or laid-back casual gear – were the executives from 'software', Sony's West Coast movie studios and music labels.

Over a sumptuous buffet in a meeting room on the sprawling Sony Pictures studio lot, each group made presentations on projects, many of them still months or even years away from reality. They talked of new movies and recordings, of consumer-electronics hardware and video games.

The aim of the meeting: to capture the elusive 'synergy' between operating units, to use software to sell hardware to sell software to sell …

It was synergy, after all, that drove companies like Sony Corp., Time Warner Inc. and News Corp. to take on billions of dollars of debt in the 1980s to acquire other entertainment and media companies. It was synergy that spurred Sony to pay more than 56 billion for record and movie operations – and hundreds of millions more to finance their expansion.

Thunder and Wind

But Sony and the other behemoths of global entertainment are often finding that synergy works better on paper than in practice. Conflicting cultures aren't just about what people wear to meetings: more important, they have made it difficult for different divisions to work together to help the corporate whole.

'Synergy: big wind, loud thunder, no rain,' says securities analyst Jeffrey Logsdon of Sadler Amdec in Los Angeles. 'It's great to talk about conceptually … but at the end of the day it's minimal.' Managers responsible for profit centers, he says, are focused on 'their own interests and not necessarily the corporate interest.'

Some also question whether the benefits of synergy could have been achieved at much lower cost by simply entering partnerships or joint ventures with other

companies. They also worry that the quest for synergy may force a company to use one product to promote another that might not be right for the market. Sony, for example, has put its movies on miniature video-cassettes to support its eight-millimeter video-cassette record, but that product hasn't been much of a hit.

Gauging a 'Hero'

But the companies insist that synergy will work, and they are pushing more meetings like the November gathering at Sony to make sure that it does.

Much of that meeting focused on the synergy possibilities from 'The Last Action Hero,' a big-budget movie due out this summer from Sony's Columbia Pictures. The movie, a spoof on action heroes, stars Arnold Schwarzenegger. 'It was clear to us that to make this picture meant recommending [to the Sony bosses] that you have a franchise that goes well beyond the movie,' says Mark Canton, chairman of Columbia Pictures. 'This isn't the type of movie you want to do in isolation.' Prior to the November meeting, Mr Canton says, he 'asked people to go back to their divisions and calculate what they could bring to the party, and the prospective profit margins that made sense for all of this.'

As the Sony meeting begins, 'software' takes the floor first. 'We came to the meeting to let us, Sony, know about it,' says Sid Ganis, Columbia's top marketer. The movie, he adds, holds 'heavy-duty [business] opportunities' for all of the assembled Sony family.

Music Weighs In

Sony's music marketers quickly seize the opportunity to produce the movie's sound-track album, which will feature a rock star from a Sony Music label. 'We think this will be a major soundtrack,' one music marketer says. Another asks whether the yet-to-be-named rock star could be in the movie, and whether Mr Schwarzenegger would appear in a music video. The answer to both is, 'quite possible'.

Marketers from Sony Electronic Publishing, which produces video games, see an opportunity for a video game based on 'The Last Action Hero.' As for the hardware marketers, perhaps the movie could promote their latest potential hit in consumer electronics – the MiniDisc player. The MiniDisc plays a new music format, a 2.5 inch optical disk that records music and delivers pre-recorded music with near compact-disc sound quality. 'The Last Action Hero' could use the MiniDisc as a snazzy prop, the hardware people suggest.

The meeting goes well. But there's an undercurrent of tension, and privately some executives express reservations about 'the other side.' One hardware marketer frets that the software types are making too much of the synergistic possibilities of this one movie. After all, it's just one movie, he says. It may give a little push to the MiniDisc, but the MiniDisc has the potential to be a long-term blockbuster anyway. 'My concern about all of this,' he says, 'is that we not end up focusing on synergy through one movie. MiniDisc will provide the most big-business opportunities for the big long-term payoff.'

Even Mr Ganis, the movie marketer, who is one of Sony's most ardent advocates of synergy, notes the difficulties. 'Software is brand new stuff for Sony,' he says. 'The hardware company takes a look at the movie guys and says: "Boy, these guys don't look like us, don't do business like us, and live in Hollywood, unlike us."

[...]

Don't Say 'Synergy'

Some entertainment-industry executives cringe at the use of the word 'synergy,' which they say suggests an unnatural force-fit of businesses and people. 'It connotes something artificial; things have to work because they feel right,' says Michael P. Schulhof, chairman of Sony USA, Sony's U.S. subsidiary. 'I'd love to find another synonym.' Time Warner, which denies that it ever embraced the notion of synergy, prefers the fuzzily defined term 'intersection.'

At News Corp., 'we prefer to call it integration,' says Ms Wall, adding that integration 'suggests merging components that create truly new products as opposed to just marrying two [existing] products and hoping the result is a new product.' When synergy first 'emerged as a concept and opportunity two or three years ago,' she notes, 'there initially were unrealistic expectations about the result.'

Sony, for one, is candid about the obstacles it has encountered in fostering synergy. Among the most critical, Mr Schulhof indicates, has been the electronic group's 'strong sense of deserved pride.' The electronics employees believe that 'they are Sony,' he says, and that profits from their efforts provided the financial muscle for the company's multibillion-dollar foray into entertainment software. Thus, 'there is a certain amount of resentment,' Mr Schulhof says.

The hardware employees have also been rattled by the Hollywood culture, particularly its heavy spending and rich salary structure. 'The electronics group reads the gossip about the parties and Schwarzenegger's and [Tom] Cruise's salaries,' Mr Schulhof says. He notes, however, that he has been careful to explain to the group that spending levels are appropriate for the industries and that benefit packages are consistent across Sony's businesses. 'By and large, the electronics group is taken care of,' Mr Schulhof says. 'That was important to me.'

What's in a Name?

Despite his efforts, however, some problems remain. For example, Sony continues to suffer confusion over its corporate name in the U.S. Currently, Sony Corp. of America is the name for the electronics group, while the music operation is called Sony Music and the film operations Sony Pictures. Mr Schulhof would like to rename the electronics operations 'Sony Electronics Group', but such a change might upset that side of the business.

Mr Schulhof is still trying to overcome resistance in the electronics group to having performers under contract with Sony Music endorse its products. 'They have never used artist endorsements and have felt that the only name that should be associated with their products is Sony,' he says. 'They are nervous. They have no experience in the last 30 years with artists.'

But some performers, wanting to extend their public association with Sony, have actually asked to do Sony ads. In Japan, Billy Joel and Michael Jackson, among Sony Music's biggest stars, have appeared in Sony ads. So far, however, the U.S. electronics group is still balking.

The electronic group has agreed to use Sony music to demonstrate its electronics products at trade shows. At one point, the group was using a tape of 'Murphy Brown', which is produced by rival Time Warner, to demonstrate professional video equipment. Through the opportunities meetings, the company has now arranged for the group to use clips from 'Married with Children' and 'Designing Women', both of which are produced by the television unit of Sony's Columbia Pictures.

Says Mr Schulhof: 'I think we are making headway. In the beginning, there was very little contact between the groups. I try to make sure those meetings take place now. All of the negatives we've overcome, more or less. We put our own electronics products in films. The electronics group now uses Sony software in demonstrations of equipment. On the music side, we use Sony [professional recording] products with artists all the time.'

(Source: Johnnie L. Roberts, *The Wall Street Journal*, 30 March 1993)

open-minded and who could be moved around the company, acquiring and drawing on different experiences and knowledge (see discussion of the Walkman in **du Gay, Hall et al.**, 1997). Through this, the company had developed a strategy of blending 'mavericks' with trained specialists. This policy had seemed successful in Japan where it was introduced within the context of a series of culturally specific codes, practices and beliefs which involved a commitment to the workplace and a collective sense of responsibility, within a tightly organized company structure. However, this approach – which ignored experience, background and training, and the context within which this would be employed – did not achieve the same type of working practices when applied to Hollywood.

When Sony acquired Columbia Studios they did indeed recruit a 'bright eccentric' rather than a trained expert when appointing Michael Schulhof as Chairman. Schulhof was a trained physicist with twenty-five years' experience of working in technical jobs at Sony and described as a 'protegé' of company founder, Akio Morita. He was someone who fitted well into the culture of 'techno-wizardry' that characterized Sony in the 1970s (Landro et al., 1994) but who had no experience of the entertainment side of the business.

Virtually unknown in Hollywood, one of Schulhof's first decisions was to hire Jon Peters and Peter Gruber to run the newly acquired studio. Peters (who had entered film from a hairdressing business) and Gruber (a lawyer by training) had worked as movie producers and were known to have many contacts within the industry, but they had no previous experience of running a studio. Under Schulhof's chairmanship, Sony purchased the two men's production company for $200 million. Almost instantly a writ was issued by rival conglomerate Time-Warner because this purchase had infringed an existing contract. As a result, Sony were forced to pay Time-Warner $500 million as a settlement for breaking a legal contract. Hence, right at the outset, Sony's total cost of hiring these two producers worked out at $700 million, a figure estimated to be nearly three times the annual profits of a leading studio in a 'reasonable year' (Reeves, 1994, p. 7).

According to numerous newspaper articles, Peters and Gruber relished the freedom that they had acquired from their new employers and embarked upon a major spending spree. They paid $100 million to have MGM studios refurbished, invested millions in locating and restoring old movie posters, and spent considerable sums on renovating offices and increasing catering and corporate hospitality facilities. What they did not do, however, was come up with the 'blockbuster' hit – the major money-making movie that was required to justify the money invested in employing them.

Peters very quickly returned to independent production, whilst Gruber stayed on and initiated a series of highly publicized 'hiring and firings' which involved senior executives, all of whose dismissal had to be settled with the payment of millions of dollars in compensation (such is the character of Hollywood contracts). It was reported that staff within the company were very dissatisfied and felt that both Gruber and Schulhof were out of touch. Finally, with no significant major blockbuster success and Sony's share of the US box office falling from 14.7 per cent in 1990 to 9.8 in 1994, Gruber left the company, with Sony agreeing to finance his new company as part of his leaving settlement (Rawsthorn, 1994; Reeves, 1994).

It was a few months after Gruber's departure that Sony announced losses of $562 million on abandoned projects and settling lawsuits and wrote off $2,979 million 'in goodwill in its Pictures Group' (Sony, 1995, p. 3). By this time the value of the studio had fallen to half of the $6 billion that Sony had paid for it just a few years earlier.

One of the major flops that Sony had under this management culture was the film referred to in the *Wall Street Journal* article above, *Last Action Hero* (released June 1993). This film was a particularly notable failure within the industry, partly because it was presented as *the* movie that would show the potentials of hardware–software synergies (Grover and Landler, 1993). The film starred Arnold Schwarzenegger and was directed by John McTiernan (who had directed *Die Hard*). Its initial production costs were estimated to be anywhere between $60 and $120 million. Here are some of the key elements of this movie's 'synergies' that you should recall from the above *Wall Street Journal* article:

- The film would include a soundtrack which would feature artists signed to Sony Music Entertainment (formerly CBS Records). These included Cypress Hill, AC/DC and Alice in Chains.

- Sony Consumer Products would have items prominently featured in the movie. In particular, the MiniDisc player would be listened to by Schwarzenegger's sidekick (and be playing music by Sony artists) and the new Sony cellular phone would be used by the main character, Jack Slater (played by Schwarzenegger).

- Film footage from the movie would be used to create an interactive video game.

- Film footage would also be used to make an amusement ride.

- A virtual reality version of the film would be made for showing in the Loews Theatre chain (owned by Sony).

- Prints of the film would be produced with Sony's new digital sound system and these would then be used to market this system to cinemas and theatres.

The marketing of this film included a major deal with Burger King whereby the film was promoted with *Last Action Hero* cups and the placing of Schwarzenegger's image and the movie title on a NASA rocket. The company had invested a lot of importance in the movie and when the *Los Angeles Times* reported that a test screening had resulted in a very negative audience response, Columbia threatened to cut off contact with the newspaper and withdraw their advertising if the writer of the piece, Jeffrey Wells, was allowed to write anything else about Columbia movies (*Empire*, August 1993, p. 7).

Despite all of the synergistic potentials, having a major star, using expensive marketing and adopting aggressive public relations, the film was very poorly received by critics. It was described by *Variety* as a 'joyless, soulless machine of a movie ... a mish-mash of fantasy, industry in-jokes, self-reverential parody, and too-big action set pieces' (cited in Hibbert, 1993, p. 68). Three months after its initial release the film was reported to be in debt to the cost of $124 million. The movie was a critical and commercial failure and an example of how Sony's synergy was not working. Indeed, this film contributed to the perception amongst senior business analysts and corporate advisers in both the United States and Japan that Sony did not know what they were doing by buying into Hollywood. The company was, according to critics, pursuing the wrong style of management (a contrast with the days of the Walkman). The attempt at 'synergy' had merely forced a series of short-term 'culture clashes' rather than created any new ways of working with hardware or software. As the *Wall Street Journal* observed: 'Instead of mining US studios as sources of software for a new generation of electronic gadgets, the Japanese found themselves trying to manage an unruly and uneven set of companies whose operations never meshed well with those of their new parents' (Landro et al., 1994, p. A12).

3.3   Classification struggles and culture clashes within the corporation

Let me now step back from this narrative for a moment and relate this example more directly to the argument I am making in this chapter as a whole. The first point to make here is that Sony's strategy was based on acquiring particular production organizations and then bringing these together within one corporation. It was a rational approach to expansion whereby the company sought to build by exerting direct control over the different technical production processes when combining them through 'synergies' to create new products.

However, as anthropologist Kathleen Gregory (1983) has argued, one of the problems of viewing organizational activities in such rational and overtly structural terms is that the activities of people within the organization and the meanings that they give to their work are often not equally as harmonious – they do not necessarily fit together homogeneously simply because everyone is working for the same company. Gregory has argued that companies should be viewed as 'multi-cultural' in the sense of having distinct 'occupational communities' that cut across the organization and which provide employees with a range of distinct and differentiated senses of identity. This is particularly so in large multi-divisional companies, such as Sony and other entertainment conglomerates, which are internally differentiated and often forced to continually change working practices as they respond to new technological developments, markets for new products and new aesthetic practices in movie-making, film production and industrial design.

Gregory argues that, as a result of working in this way, such companies often only command a 'part-time commitment' from staff members who are in turn inclined to a type of 'ethnocentrism' on an occupational level. By this she means that different occupational groupings tend to take for granted their own cultural views and assess the behaviour of others within the organization on these terms. Gregory's argument, which was drawn from a study of technical professionals within the computer industry, is particularly relevant to the way that the synergies that Sony had been trying to create had involved bringing together two distinct 'occupational communities' – engineers and movie producers – who had different perspectives not only due to working in different locations within the same company but as a result of the distinctive geographical variations in working practices between Tokyo and Hollywood.

The division here is part of a broader divide that can often be found within the culture industries between the software divisions and the hardware divisions. Notable here is the contrast between those working in films, music and book publishing who often enjoy a large degree of occupational independence, and the engineers and designers who tend to be subject to closer supervision, and who work far more collaboratively in teams and with other divisions within a company. Rosabeth Moss Kanter of the Harvard Business School, observing people within the book publishing and film industry in the United States, has remarked that: 'They resist like crazy the idea that they owe any allegiance and cooperation to anyone in any other part of the business, even if they are at the same company' (quoted in Sims, 1993).

Sociologist Pierre Bourdieu (1986) has argued that such occupational divisions are not simply the result of what goes on within organizations but are at the same time part of broader social divisions which are expressed in different lifestyles, values and beliefs. Bourdieu argues that when these contrasting ways of life and cultural beliefs are brought into close proximity, this can result in what he has called **classification struggles**. Bourdieu has suggested that this can involve 'a struggle for supremacy' between staff working in such occupations as production and publicity or between engineers and marketing people 'in which each category of managers seeks to advance its occupational interests by imposing a scale of values which sets at the top of the hierarchy the functions for which it feels itself best equipped' (Bourdieu, 1986, p. 309). Such struggles then become 'inseparable from conflicts of value which involve the participants' whole world views and arts of living' (ibid., p. 310).

classification
struggles

The way in which such occupational struggles involve broader sets of cultural values and beliefs can be glimpsed by considering the difference between the cultures of hardware and software production in terms of approaches to risk taking and contrasting concepts of 'research and development'. Hollywood's version of 'research and development' involves acquiring and funding hundreds of scripts, from which only a few will eventually be made into movies and a very small number of which will be economically successful and bring the necessary return on investment. It is easy to predict that people will go to the cinema, but it is very difficult to predict the success of particular movies, all of which, from the perspective of Hollywood marketing, are judged as individual items.

Research and development for televisions and tape machines, in contrast, can be more carefully planned and the potential market success can be assessed with more precision. Although new products are introduced and either succeed or fail in ways that have not been anticipated, most new products are variations on a theme; it is relatively easier to predict the market for televisions, tape machines and hi-fis. As Kazuhiko Nishi, President of the Ascii Corporation observed (in Turner and Ono, 1993, p. 6), following reports of Sony's problems, 'many Japanese companies think that Hollywood is part of Las Vegas' – all 'risk strategies', while 'research and development' is little more than speculative gambling.

Yet it is partly because of the risks involved that successes in Hollywood bring far higher financial rewards. The executives in Hollywood earn vastly higher sums of money than their 'colleagues' working within the hardware divisions of the same corporation. Such distinctions contribute to the resentment and lack of understanding which emerge when the two sides are brought together in an attempt to collaborate on a project (as indicated in the newspaper article above).

In Sony's case the contrasts between these different ways of working in hardware and software were compounded by the contrasts between working life in Hollywood and Tokyo. This is perhaps captured by the comments of an entertainment business analyst based in New York who, when Sony's financial losses were reported in November 1994, remarked, 'These LA guys seem like a flakey bunch of prima donnas here in Manhattan. Over in Tokyo they must seem completely crazy' (Rawsthorn, 1994, p. 25). A caricature, of course, yet such contrasts were apparently neglected by Sony who perhaps did not anticipate that the management methods which had been effective in Japan would not necessarily produce the same type of working behaviour in California.

The general point I am making here is about the lack of 'fit' between the rational, macro structures of ownership which are put in place by the corporation through formal acquisitions, and the more messy informal world of human actions, working relationships and cultural meanings through which the companies' goals have to be realized on a day-to-day basis. Proponents of the 'corporate control' argument such as Adorno and Horkheimer certainly have a point about the way in which large corporations own the technical means of producing and distributing products and reap the economic rewards of the products created by staff. But what they neglect is the way that cultural production is not simply a technical and economic activity but one that involves particular 'occupational communities' (Gregory, 1983) whose cultural beliefs and 'arts of living' (Bourdieu, 1986) are often a source of division and antagonism within the company. This can then result in a lack of shared goals and lead to the abandonment of projects. Company success and corporate control is not guaranteed simply through ownership of technical means and economic resources; it has to be worked for.

To pursue this issue in more detail I shall remain with the same company, Sony, and consider how the culture of the organization also became an issue that was partly responsible for George Michael, the British singer and songwriter, initiating court proceedings against Sony's newly acquired record label at the very time when the company was having problems in Hollywood.

3.4   George Michael on the production line

In the remainder of this chapter I am going to be focusing on the music industry and building on what I have been arguing so far by pointing to some of the ways in which culture-producing organizations cannot simply control creative activities in any straightforward manner. As such, this part of the chapter is a further challenge to Adorno and Horkheimer's argument that the all-powerful corporation can simply standardize and de-individualize the work of creative artists. Again I focus on micro day-to-day activities and start by referring to the case of George Michael.

When Sony purchased CBS Records at the end of the 1980s, the acquisition came at a time when one of the company's most successful performers, George Michael, was re-considering his long-term prospects and future direction as a recording artist. For many years Michael had attracted a young following and had played on his physical appearance and sex appeal. By the late 1980s he had decided that it was time for him to make the transition, difficult for many performers (from Frank Sinatra onwards), from 'teenage idol' to 'more serious adult artist'.

Michael's first album after Sony's acquisition was *Listen Without Prejudice* (1990) a deliberate attempt to challenge his audience to listen to songs that covered a range of social issues and wider blend of musical styles than on previous recordings. This album was accompanied by a serious *South Bank Show* documentary which focused on Michael's songwriting, creative influences and techniques of recording in the studio. The album sold 7 million copies (half the number of the previous LP *Faith* which had been released in 1987). Although Michael had expected the new album to sell fewer copies than the previous release, and though he had not allowed his face to appear on the cover (in an attempt to emphasize the music over the image), he began to accuse the company of deliberately not promoting *Listen Without Prejudice* and argued that Sony were trying to 'kill it' in an effort to convince him to return to his older musical styles and visual presentation.

Michael began to give interviews in which he publicly stated that the company was not allowing him to develop as a long-term artist but merely treating him as short-term 'software' for their hardware, arguing that Sony's acquisition had changed the company: 'Sony have developed hard-sell, high-profile sales techniques, and their stance is that if an artist does not wish to conform to Sony's current ideas, there are plenty of hungry young acts who will' (Michael, quoted in Garfield, 1995, p. 7).

In October 1992 Michael called a meeting with the aforementioned Michael Schulhof, head of US Sony, and Norio Ohga, Sony's International President. At this meeting Michael voiced his concern about the amount of creative control he had over his work, his concerns about his future musical direction, the misunderstandings he was having with personnel at the company and he asked to negotiate a release from his contract. Four days later he filed a High Court writ claiming restraint of trade and inequality of earnings and bargaining power.

Michael's publicly voiced concerns were about the way in which the company was working with him and were directly related to his attempt to make the transition to a mature artist. He was, in short, mainly concerned about the working culture within the company. Yet the writ that he served merely attempted to prove that his contract was unfair. According to all his public statements up to this time, the issues that he was concerned about were the more intangible aspects of his working relationship with people at the company, yet such issues are difficult to encapsulate in a legal challenge. Hence, the way he ultimately tried to resolve these was to attempt a more formal, legal extrication from his contract.

FIGURE 2.2
George Michael arriving at the London High Court, November 1993.

The court case began in October 1993 and finally finished in June 1994 when Michael lost and boldly left the court declaring that he would never record for Sony again. This outburst was initially taken with a pinch of salt and Sony's top executives subsequently met with Michael and promised him more money and his own record label. But Michael maintained that he would stick by his word and Sony were faced with having an artist under contract who was unlikely to deliver any recordings and who was publicly talking about how unhappy he was with the way the company was being managed.

One year later, after months of financial negotiations, George Michael signed a new deal whereby he would record for Virgin Records in the UK and Dreamworks (a company newly set up by film director Steven Spielberg, record label boss David Geffen and former Disney film producer Jeffrey Katzenberg) in the United States. The contract included a substantial pay-off to Sony and a complex series of clauses through which certain future royalties and song copyrights would also go to Sony. The reported details of this final settlement tended to dwell on the financial aspects (perhaps because such details are often not circulated so publicly), but underlying Michael's departure was a breakdown in the relationship between recording artist and record company.

Like Sony's problems in Hollywood, when dealing with George Michael prior to, during and after the court case, the issue of dispute was usually reported as involving 'culture clashes'. Many people within the recording industry – working at the point where the structures of ownership meet the individual actions of creative artists – were reported to be commenting on how the style of management which had been adopted by Sony was simply not capable of dealing with the type of working relationships required to motivate performers and make good recordings. *The Sunday Times* quoted an 'insider' who said that 'Sony thought it was all about money. But for George it was all about emotions and personalities' (Lynn and Olins, 1995, p. 8).

Likewise, *The Daily Telegraph* observed that: 'The company's failure to placate its sensitive star is a puzzle. Record contracts have never been set in stone. Companies know that most acts seek to re-negotiate after every successful album. Record industry logic should have brought them to an accommodation. But commercial logic ceased to apply.' Reporting on the court case, the same journalist observed that as the 'sensitive star' clashed with the 'hard-headed businessman', so the 'clash of cultures spawned misunderstandings and widely circulated rumours all of which served to make things worse' (Muir, 1994, p. 4). In a similar way *The Financial Times* also reported:

> Senior executives at rival companies believe Sony should never have allowed its relationship with one of its leading artists to deteriorate to the point where he decided to go to court ... If you cannot deal with touchy, sensitive individuals, they say, you should not be in the music business. Most artists go through periods of insecurity. Many feel they are not appreciated by their companies, the press or the public. The job of the music company manager is to make sure that these feelings do not grow to the point where the artist can no longer perform. If music companies cannot get on with their successful artists any longer, some executives

believe they should consider ending their relationship. To reach this point is widely seen as a failure. To go further and engage in a widely publicized acrimonious legal battle is regarded by many as worse.

(Skapinker, 1994, p. 22)

There are a number of theoretical issues here which are of direct relevance to the theme of 'culture, media and identities'. First, you should bear in mind that we cannot know of George Michael and of his dispute with Sony in any transparently accessible sense, but through a quite particular series of mediations and representations (see the discussion of Sony's culture in **du Gay, Hall et al.**, 1997). Here, journalists in the print media played a crucial role as 'cultural intermediaries' (a concept that will be explored in more detail in Chapter 4). Journalists mediate between the activities of music corporations and its artists; they provide us with interpretations and a pool of 'knowledge' from which we accumulate information and form our own judgements as fans and observers. What has particularly interested me about this case has been the way that George Michael's dispute with Sony was given a particular representation which focused not so much on arguments about money or accusations of a 'rip-off' (the staple of so many recording industry stories that hit the news pages), as on the 'culture' of the working environment within the company and the muddled series of misunderstandings that were occurring as different people and company divisions were simply not cooperating with each other in working towards the same goal.

A central issue concerned the identity of the artist (and his autonomy to determine his own self-representation and select his own preferred career path). At the same time, the identity of the company was also at stake. This court case and the resulting settlement highlighted that recording artists do not sign to record companies for money alone. The 'culture' of the company and the way it works with its artists have a significant impact on the decision. It is due to this that different record companies actively attempt to develop and cultivate particular working environments and styles of working. Michael eventually signed to Virgin and Dreamworks, not for more money than he could have gained at Sony but because they offered a working environment that appealed to him as an artist. Virgin has been acutely aware of its 'alternative' and 'creative' image over many years and this has attracted many artists to sign to them rather than to their competitors. The image and the culture of a company is thus of strategic importance to record companies when trying to attract and keep artists. Because all the major companies can usually match each other's financial offers, the final decision often rests on less tangible aspects, such as the other artists who are signed to a label and the quality and commercial success of the work they have produced, what the working environment is like, the level of enthusiasm and general characteristics of the staff in the company buildings. Even a rude receptionist has been known to put off artists from signing to a record company.

I have presented this discussion of Sony's film and music divisions in these last two sections as a deliberate contrast with the first part of this chapter. Rather than stress the way that Sony is able to concentrate and integrate technical production processes at a macro corporate level I have emphasized the messy, micro day-to-day working world. Rather than emphasize economic relationships I have stressed the importance of cultural meanings. In contrast to the argument about structural constraints I have highlighted human agency. In place of successes and the ability to control production, I have focused on the failures and inability of a company to manage its technical, human and artistic resources (it is worth bearing in mind that all movie companies, record labels and hardware manufacturers generally produce more commercial failures than successes). Throughout this part of the chapter I have started to introduce you to the idea that there is a 'culture of production' within which the production of culture takes place. In doing this I have raised questions about how the company attempts to manage this process. This issue will be pursued in more theoretical detail in later chapters which introduce you to concepts of organizational culture and the way in which companies attempt to influence the subjective outlook of their staff. My main concern in this chapter has been to raise this issue in a very broad way by highlighting how Sony's attempt at synergy involved more than just a technical process but also cultural activities. I now want to conclude this chapter by following George Michael's tracks and considering their implications for how we think about the music industry.

3.5 The culture of production and the production of popular music

From Adorno and Horkheimer's despair about the cultural 'assembly-line' to George Michael's experience on the 'production line', one of the most enduring images of what goes on inside the recording industry has involved variations on a mechanical transmission model of products being shifted sequentially from artists to audience. A formal sociological account of this was developed by Paul Hirsch (1972), who proposed a 'filter-flow' model of music production whereby artistic creators provide the 'raw material' that is then processed and passed through the system to the public.

Not long after Hirsch proposed this model, it was challenged by Richard Peterson (1976) who called for a 'production of culture perspective' which he advocated in opposition to the idea that cultural artefacts are simply the work of individual artists (from whom they are then filtered to the public). Peterson wished to stress the way that 'elements' of culture are 'fabricated' amongst occupational groups and within social milieus for whom 'symbol-system production is most self-consciously the centre of activity' (1976, p. 10).

Peterson illustrated his approach in a case-study of country music, jointly written with John Ryan. Employing a familiar mechanical metaphor, they considered the work of 'a number of skilled specialists [who] ... have a part in shaping the final work as it goes through a series of stages which, superficially at least, resemble an assembly line' (Ryan and Peterson, 1982, p. 11). Ryan and Peterson then followed the progress of country music songs along a 'decision chain' of discrete activities which involved writing, publishing, recording, marketing, manufacture, release and consumption. At each stage they observed that a number of choices were confronted and a number of modifications might be made to the songs. Hence, unlike the 'filter flow model', Peterson and Ryan allowed for music to change as it passed along the chain.

Ryan and Peterson argued that the making of country music was being coordinated around the idea of a 'product image'. This involved the different staff involved in the process (from studio producers to promotion people) using their judgement to shape 'a piece of work so that it is most likely to be accepted by decision makers at the next link in the chain' (Ryan and Peterson, 1982, p. 25). Hence, according to Ryan and Peterson, all the personnel involved in the chain were adopting a pragmatic, strategic and commercially oriented approach, organized around a 'product image', which then enabled them to collaborate in a very practical way.

Such an approach draws heavily on the 'professional' ideas of senior record company executives who often explain that their organizations work in these very terms – staff united in shared, commercially defined goals (the product image) which override any personal or departmental divisions. Useful as this approach might be for suggesting how popular music is produced through the adherence to a few routine working practices and shared goals, it seems in stark contrast to the numerous accounts of musical production which have appeared over the years in popular biographies and the trade press. These indicate that music is often produced from situations characterized by a total lack of consensus or shared goals.

Whilst music industry staff may have some notion of a 'product image' as a type of professional ideal, this idea may often be contested, challenged and transformed as a recording is produced, rather than acting simply as an organizing principle. Think of the account of the synergy meeting that was held to discuss *Last Action Hero*. Whilst staff clearly had some notion of a 'product image', there were a number of different ideas about the *meaning* of this 'product image' and how it should be pursued in practical terms. This point is particularly relevant to the music industry where, during my own research on the development of artists between 1988 and 1992, I often found staff referring to what they were doing in a more fragmentary and less unified way and using the analogue of 'a jigsaw' in which their own interests were focused on just one part of the picture. The pieces of the jigsaw often did not come together and the process was often not successful because the jigsaw was continually being changed as it was being put together. (This research is reported in more detail in Negus, 1992.)

My point, in drawing on the jigsaw metaphor, is to argue that the contribution of different personnel to cultural production does not merely involve 'filtering' or contributing to an identifiable 'product image'. Instead, it entails actively intervening, mediating and changing the sounds and images of popular music as they are being made and put together. The general point here, building on what I have already written in this chapter, is that producing culture does not simply involve making a 'product' (a functional artefact, in Gendron's terms) which has an 'image' (an agreed and shared meaning). As Joli Jensen has argued, 'culture' is not simply 'a product that is created, disseminated and consumed ... a "product" which is "processed" like soap by organizational, technical, and economic "factors"' (1984, pp. 104–10). Instead, she argues that culture should be understood more broadly as the means through which people create meaningful worlds in which to live. These 'cultural worlds' are constructed through interpretations, experiences and activities whereby material is 'created in connection with its consumption' (Jensen, 1984, p. 111).

In adopting this approach Jensen was drawing on Howard Becker's theories of the 'worlds' within which art is produced (1982). Becker had argued that the creation of works of art (painting, films, novels, music) involves 'collective' practices which are 'coordinated' by shared 'conventions' and 'consensual definitions' that were arrived at as various people formed, were attracted to and actively recruited to inhabit different 'art worlds' (1982). For Becker it was often the cultural life and social values of the art worlds (overlapping across production, distribution and consumption) that created the conditions for creative collaboration and hence the 'production of culture' to take place as it did, and not the formal organizational criteria and 'product images' as identified by Peterson.

Jensen's critique also drew on Raymond Williams' (1965) important writings about culture as involving a 'whole way of life' and this leads me towards the final point I want to emphasize in this chapter. In studying the 'production of culture' we need to do more than understand culture as a 'product' which is created through technical and routine processes and practices. We need to do more than simply read off or assume the characteristics of culture from patterns of ownership or the way commodity production is organized. We need to understand the meanings that are given to both the 'product' and the practices through which the product is made. Culture, thought of more broadly as a way of life and as the actions through which people create meaningful worlds in which to live, needs to be understood as the constitutive context within and out of which the sounds, words and images of popular music are made and given meaning.

4   Summary and conclusion

The aim of this chapter has been to contrast the 'production of culture' and the 'culture of production' in order to highlight a significant theoretical shift in approaches to cultural production and to trace this shift with reference to empirical examples of specific cultural activities. Adorno and Horkheimer's analysis of the impact of the corporate control of production provided the starting-point, with their characterization of the culture industry as an assembly-line producing standardized products which lack any originality. This emphasis on macro structures of ownership informed anxieties about the globalization of cultural production and distribution during the 1980s and 1990s. The recent concern – similar to that of the 1940s when Adorno and Horkheimer first wrote on this theme – is about the ability of large corporations to dominate the ownership of cultural production; this in turn is perceived to have a detrimental impact on creative activity, leading to a decline in aesthetic diversity and ultimately offering consumers very little choice.

The culture industry can, however, also be portrayed as a less stable and predictable entity by focusing on micro relations and the cultural worlds within which the production of culture takes place. This was illustrated through the detailed descriptive information and analysis of Sony's attempt to create 'synergies' by bringing together hardware and software through the combination of different production processes – and the less than happy consequences of this strategy in film production and in George Michael's dispute with Sony over his contract.

Throughout this discussion I have challenged the idea that the corporations of the culture industry are able to directly 'control' production and creative work simply through their formal ownership of the 'means' of production. In doing this, and whilst maintaining an 'analytical' boundary around the sphere of production, I have indicated at various points how the practices of production take place in relation to the activities of consumption. You should also have become aware of the ways in which the issue of identity is important for occupational groups, companies and artists, who all seek to define and represent themselves to others in very particular ways. It is important to consider the culture of production, not only within the organization in terms of particular occupational cultures but in terms of how these connect with broader social divisions and how these are given specific cultural meanings within the production process. Production does not take place within a completely separate sphere but in relation to the broader social contexts of consumption. The next chapter pursues this theme by exploring the relationship between production and consumption in a particular 'cultural industry' – that of fashion.

References

ADORNO, T. and HORKHEIMER, M. (1979) *Dialectic of Enlightenment*, London, Verso (first published 1947).

ADORNO, T. (1945) 'A social critique of radio music', *Kenyon Review.* Vol. 11., Spring, pp. 2, 208–217.

ADORNO, T. (1967) 'Jazz – perennial fashion' in *Prisms*, translated by S. and S. Weber, Saffron Walden, Neville Spearman.

ADORNO, T (1973) *The Philosophy of Modern Music*, New York, Seabury Press.

ADORNO, T. (1976) *Introduction to the Sociology of Music*, translated by E. B. Ashton, New York, Seabury Press.

ADORNO, T. (1989) 'On jazz', *Discourse*, Vol. 12, No. 1. pp. 44–69 (first published 1936).

ADORNO, T. (1991) *The Culture Industry: selected essays on mass culture*, edited by J. Bernstein, London, Routledge.

BAGDIKIAN, B. (1989) 'The lords of the global village', *The Nation*, 12 June, pp. 805–20.

BECKER, H. (1982) *Art Worlds*, Berkeley, University of California Press.

BOURDIEU, P. (1986) *Distinction: a social critique of the judgement of taste*, London, Routledge.

DISNEY CORPORATION (1994) *Annual Report.*

DU GAY, P., HALL, S., JANES, L., MACKAY, H. and NEGUS, K. (1997) *Doing Cultural Studies: the story of the Sony Walkman*, London, Sage/The Open University (Book 1 in this series).

GARFIELD, S. (1995) 'The battle for George Michael' *The Independent*, 15 July, p. 7.

GENDRON, B. (1986) 'Theodor Adorno meets the Cadillacs' in Modelski, T. (ed.) *Studies in Entertainment*, Bloomington and Indianapolis, IA, Indiana University Press.

GREGORY, K. (1983) 'Native-view paradigms: multiple cultures and culture conflicts in organizations', *Administrative Science Quarterly*, Vol. 28, No. 3, pp. 359–76.

GROVER, R. and LANDLER, M. (1993) 'Last Action Hero – or first $60 million commercial', *Business Week*, April 12.

HIBBERT, T. (1993) 'Not to be ...', *Empire*, August, pp. 64–71.

HIRSCH, P. (1972) 'Processing fads and fashions: an organizational set analysis of cultural industry systems', *American Journal of Sociology*, Vol. 77, No. 4, pp. 639–59.

JACKSON, T. (1995) 'Masters of the moving image', *Financial Times*, 2 August, p. 15.

JENSEN, J. (1984) 'An interpretative approach to cultural production' in Rowland, W. and Watkins, B. (eds) *Interpreting Television*, London, Sage.

LANDRO, L., HAMILTON, D., TRACHTENBERG, J. and WILLIAMS, M. (1994) 'Sony finally admits billion dollar mistake: its messed-up studio', *Wall Street Journal*, 18 November, pp. A1–12.

LEVITT, T. (1983) *The Marketing Imagination*, New York, The Free Press.

LEVITT, T. (1983) 'The globalization of markets', *Harvard Business Review*, May–June, pp. 92–102.

LYNN, M. and OLINS, R. (1995) 'Harmony restored as Michael sheds Sony', *Sunday Times Business*, 16 July, p. 8.

MACKAY, H. (ed.) (1997) *Consumption and Everyday Life*, London, Sage/The Open University (Book 5 in this series).

MUIR, H. (1994) 'Courtroom blues for the star who changed his tune', *Daily Telegraph*, 22 June, p. 4.

NEGUS, K. (1992) *Producing Pop*, London, Edward Arnold.

PETERSON, R. (1976) 'The production of culture: a prolegomenon' in Peterson, R. (ed.) *The Production of Culture*, London, Sage, pp. 7–22.

RAWSTHORN, A. (1994) 'Sony's Hollywood romance dies', *Financial Times*, 18 November, p. 25.

REEVES, P. (1994) 'Welcome to Tinseltown, Mr Morita', *Independent on Sunday*, 10 April, pp. 7–8.

ROBINS, K. (1995) 'The new spaces of global media' in Johnston, R., Taylor, P. and Watts, M. (eds) *Geographies of Global Change*, Oxford, Blackwell.

RYAN, J. and PETERSON, R. (1982) 'The product image: the fate of creativity in country music songwriting' in Ettema, J. and Whitney, D. (eds) *Individuals in Mass Media Organizations: creativity and constraint*, London, Sage, pp. 11–32.

SCHILLER, H. (1989) *Culture, Inc.: the corporate takeover of public expression*, London, Oxford University Press.

SIMS, C. (1993) 'Synergy: the unspoken word', *New York Times*, 5 October, pp. D1–20.

SKAPINKER, M. (1994) 'Designer stubble that got burnt', *Financial Times*, 22 June , p. 22.

SONY CORPORATION (1995) *Annual Report*.

THOMPSON, K. (ed.) (1997) *Media and Cultural Regulation*, London, Sage/The Open University (Book 6 in this series).

TURNER, R. and ONO, Y. (1993) 'Japan lays an egg', *Wall Street Journal*, 26 March, pp. R6–12.

UNESCO (1982) *Culture Industries: a challenge for the future of culture*, Paris, UNESCO.

WILLIAMS, R. (1965) *The Long Revolution*, Harmondsworth, Penguin.

READING A:
Theodor Adorno and Max Horkheimer, 'The culture industry: enlightenment as mass deception'

The sociological theory that the loss of the support of objectively established religion, the dissolution of the last remnants of precapitalism, together with technological and social differentiation or specialization, have led to cultural chaos is disproved every day; for culture now impresses the same stamp on everything. Films, radio and magazines make up a system which is uniform as a whole and in every part. Even the aesthetic activities of political opposites are one in their enthusiastic obedience to the rhythm of the iron system. The decorative industrial management buildings and exhibition centers in authoritarian countries are much the same as anywhere else. The huge gleaming towers that shoot up everywhere are outward signs of the ingenious planning of international concerns, toward which the unleashed entrepreneurial system (whose monuments are a mass of gloomy houses and business premises in grimy, spiritless cities) was already hastening. Even now the older houses just outside the concrete city centers look like slums, and the new bungalows on the outskirts are at one with the flimsy structures of world fairs in their praise of technical progress and their built-in demand to be discarded after a short while like empty food cans. Yet the city housing projects designed to perpetuate the individual as a supposedly independent unit in a small hygienic dwelling make him all the more subservient to his adversary – the absolute power of capitalism. Because the inhabitants, as producers and as consumers, are drawn into the center in search of work and pleasure, all the living units crystallize into well-organized complexes. The striking unity of microcosm and macrocosm presents men with a model of their culture: the false identity of the general and the particular. Under monopoly all mass culture is identical, and the lines of its artificial framework begin to show through. The people at the top are no longer so interested in concealing monopoly: as its violence becomes more open, so its power grows. Movies and radio need no longer pretend to be art. The truth that they are just business is made into an ideology in order to justify the rubbish they deliberately produce. They call themselves industries; and when their directors' incomes are published, any doubt about the social utility of the finished products is removed.

Interested parties explain the culture industry in technological terms. It is alleged that because millions participate in it, certain reproduction processes are necessary that inevitably require identical needs in innumerable places to be satisfied with identical goods. The technical contrast between the few production centers and the large number of widely dispersed consumption points is said to demand organization and planning by management. Furthermore, it is claimed that standards were based in the first place on consumers' needs, and for that reason were accepted with so little resistance. The result is the circle of manipulation and retroactive need in which the unity of the system grows ever stronger. No mention is made of the fact that the basis on which technology acquires power over society is the power of those whose economic hold over society is greatest. A technological rationale is the rationale of domination itself. It is the coercive nature of society alienated from itself. [...] It has made the technology of the culture industry no more than the achievement of standardization and mass production, sacrificing whatever involved a distinction between the logic of the work and that of the social system. This is the result not of a law of movement in technology as such but of its function in today's economy. The need which might resist central control has already been suppressed by the control of the individual consciousness. The step from the telephone to the radio has clearly distinguished the roles. The former still allowed the subscriber to play the role of subject, and was liberal. The latter is democratic: it turns all participants into listeners and authoritatively subjects them to broadcast programs which are all exactly the same. No machinery of rejoinder has been devised, and private broadcasters are denied any freedom. They are confined to the apocryphal field of the 'amateur', and also have to accept organization from above. But any trace of spontaneity from the public in official broadcasting is controlled and absorbed by talent scouts, studio competitions and official programs of every kind selected by professionals.

Talented performers belong to the industry long before it displays them; otherwise they would not be so eager to fit in. The attitude of the public, which ostensibly and actually favors the system of the culture industry, is a part of the system and not an excuse for it. If one branch of art follows the same formula as one with a very different medium and content; if the dramatic intrigue of broadcast soap operas becomes no more than useful material for showing how to master technical problems at both ends of the scale of musical experience – real jazz or a cheap imitation; or if a movement from a Beethoven symphony is crudely 'adapted' for a film sound-track in the same way as a Tolstoy novel is garbled in a film script: then the claim that this is done to satisfy the spontaneous wishes of the public is no more than hot air. We are closer to the facts if we explain these phenomena as inherent in the technical and personnel apparatus which, down to its last cog, itself forms part of the economic mechanism of selection. In addition there is the agreement – or at least the determination – of all executive authorities not to produce or sanction anything that in any way differs from their own rules, their own ideas about consumers, or above all themselves.

In our age the objective social tendency is incarnate in the hidden subjective purposes of company directors, the foremost among whom are in the most powerful sectors of industry – steel, petroleum, electricity, and chemicals. Culture monopolies are weak and dependent in comparison. They cannot afford to neglect their appeasement of the real holders of power if their sphere of activity in mass society (a sphere producing a specific type of commodity which anyhow is still too closely bound up with easygoing liberalism and Jewish intellectuals) is not to undergo a series of purges. The dependence of the most powerful broadcasting company on the electrical industry, or of the motion picture industry on the banks, is characteristic of the whole sphere, whose individual branches are themselves economically interwoven. All are in such close contact that the extreme concentration of mental forces allows demarcation lines between different firms and technical branches to be ignored. The ruthless unity in the culture industry is evidence of what will happen in politics. Marked differentiations such as those of A and B films, or

of stories in magazines in different price ranges, depend not so much on subject matter as on classifying, organizing, and labeling consumers. Something is provided for all so that none may escape; the distinctions are emphasized and extended. The public is catered for with a hierarchical range of mass-produced products of varying quality, thus advancing the rule of complete quantification. Everybody must behave (as if spontaneously) in accordance with his previously determined and indexed level, and choose the category of mass product turned out for his type. Consumers appear as statistics on research organization charts, and are divided by income groups into red, green, and blue areas; the technique is that used for any type of propaganda.

How formalized the procedure is can be seen when the mechanically differentiated products prove to be all alike in the end. That the difference between the Chrysler range and General Motors products is basically illusory strikes every child with a keen interest in varieties. What connoisseurs discuss as good or bad points serve only to perpetuate the semblance of competition and range of choice. The same applies to the Warner Brothers and Metro Goldwyn Mayer productions. But even the differences between the more expensive and cheaper models put out by the same firm steadily diminish: for automobiles, there are such differences as the number of cylinders, cubic capacity, details of patented gadgets; and for films there are the number of stars, the extravagant use of technology, labor, and equipment, and the introduction of the latest psychological formulas. The universal criterion of merit is the amount of 'conspicuous production,' of blatant cash investment. The varying budgets in the culture industry do not bear the slightest relation to factual values, to the meaning of the products themselves. Even the technical media are relentlessly forced into uniformity. Television aims at a synthesis of radio and film, and is held up only because the interested parties have not yet reached agreement, but its consequences will be quite enormous and promise to intensify the impoverishment of aesthetic matter so drastically, that by tomorrow the thinly veiled identity of all industrial culture products can come triumphantly out into the open, derisively fulfilling the Wagnerian dream of the *Gesamtkunstwerk* – the fusion of all the arts in one work. The alliance of word, image, and music is all the more perfect than in *Tristan* because the sensuous elements which all approvingly reflect the surface of social reality are in principle embodied in the same technical process, the unity of which becomes its distinctive content. This process integrates all the elements of the production, from the novel (shaped with an eye to the film) to the last sound effect. It is the triumph of invested capital, whose title as absolute master is etched deep into the hearts of the dispossessed in the employment line; it is the meaningful content of every film, whatever plot the production team may have selected.

[...]

The whole world is made to pass through the filter of the culture industry. The old experience of the movie-goer, who sees the world outside as an extension of the film he has just left (because the latter is intent upon reproducing the world of everyday perceptions), is now the producer's guideline. The more intensely and flawlessly his techniques duplicate empirical objects, the easier it is today for the illusion to prevail that the outside world is the straightforward continuation of that presented on the screen. This purpose has been furthered by mechanical reproduction since the lightning takeover by the sound film.

Real life is becoming indistinguishable from the movies. The sound film, far surpassing the theater of illusion, leaves no room for imagination or reflection on the part of the audience, who is unable to respond within the structure of the film, yet deviate from its precise detail without losing the thread of the story; hence the film forces its victims to equate it directly with reality. The stunting of the mass-media consumer's powers of imagination and spontaneity does not have to be traced back to any psychological mechanisms; he must ascribe the loss of those attributes to the objective nature of the products themselves, especially the most characteristic of them, the sound film. They are so designed that quickness, powers of observation, and experience are undeniably needed to apprehend them at all; yet sustained thought is out of the question if the spectator is not to miss the relentless rush of facts. Even though the effort required for his response is semi-automatic, no scope is left for the imagination.

Those who are so absorbed by the world of the movie – by its images, gestures, and words – that they are unable to supply what really makes it a world, do not have to dwell on particular points of its mechanics during a screening. All the other films and products of the entertainment industry which they have seen have taught them what to expect; they react automatically. The might of industrial society is lodged in men's minds. The entertainments manufacturers know that their products will be consumed with alertness even when the customer is distraught, for each of them is a model of the huge economic machinery which has always sustained the masses, whether at work or at leisure – which is akin to work. From every sound film and every broadcast program the social effect can be inferred which is exclusive to none but is shared by all alike. The culture industry as a whole has molded men as a type unfailingly reproduced in every product. All the agents of this process, from the producer to the women's clubs, take good care that the simple reproduction of this mental state is not nuanced or extended in any way.

[...]

Amusement and all the elements of the culture industry existed long before the latter came into existence. Now they are taken over from above and brought up to date. The culture industry can pride itself on having energetically executed the previously clumsy transposition of art into the sphere of consumption, on making this a principle, on divesting amusement of its obtrusive naïvetés and improving the type of commodities. The more absolute it became, the more ruthless it was in forcing every outsider either into bankruptcy or into a syndicate, and became more refined and elevated – until it ended up as a synthesis of Beethoven and the Casino de Paris. It enjoys a double victory: the truth it extinguishes without, it can reproduce at will as a lie within. 'Light' art as such, distraction, is not a decadent form. Anyone who complains that it is a betrayal of the ideal of pure expression is under an illusion about society. The purity of bourgeois art, which hypostasized itself as a world of freedom in contrast to what was happening in the material world, was from the beginning bought with the exclusion of the lower classes – with whose cause, the real universality, art keeps faith precisely by its freedom from the ends of the false universality. Serious art has been withheld from those for whom the hardship and oppression of life make a mockery of seriousness, and who must be glad if they can use time not spent at the production line just to keep going. Light art has been the shadow of autonomous art. It is the social bad conscience of serious art. The truth which the latter necessarily lacked because of its social premises gives the other the semblance of legitimacy. The division itself is the truth: it does at least express the negativity of the culture which the different spheres constitute. Least of all can the antithesis be reconciled by absorbing light into serious art, or vice versa. But that is what the culture industry attempts. The eccentricity of the circus, peepshow, and brothel is as embarrassing to it as that of Schönberg and Karl Kraus. And so the jazz musician Benny Goodman appears with the Budapest string quartet, more pedantic rhythmically than any philharmonic clarinettist, while the style of the Budapest players is as uniform and sugary as that of Guy Lombardo. But what is significant is not vulgarity, stupidity, and lack of polish. The culture industry did away with yesterday's rubbish by its own perfection, and by forbidding and domesticating the amateurish, although it constantly allows gross blunders without which the standard of the exalted style cannot be perceived. But what is new is that the irreconcilable elements of culture, art and distraction, are subordinated to one end and subsumed under one false formula: the totality of the culture industry. It consists of repetition. That its characteristic innovations are never anything more than improvements of mass reproduction is not external to the system. It is with good reason that the interest of innumerable consumers is directed to the technique, and not to the contents – which are stubbornly repeated, outworn, and by now half-discredited. The social power which the spectators worship shows itself more effectively in the omnipresence of the stereotype imposed by technical skill than in the stale ideologies for which the ephemeral contents stand in.

Nevertheless the culture industry remains the entertainment business. Its influence over the consumers is established by entertainment; that will ultimately be broken not by an outright decree, but by the hostility inherent in the principle of entertainment to what is greater than itself. Since all the trends of the culture industry are profoundly embedded in the public by the whole social process, they are encouraged by the survival of the market in this area. Demand has not yet been replaced by simple obedience. As is well known, the major reorganization of the film industry shortly before World War 1, the material prerequisite of its expansion, was precisely its deliberate acceptance of the public's needs as recorded at the box-office – a procedure which was hardly thought necessary in the pioneering days of the screen. The same opinion is held today by the captains of the film industry, who take as their criterion the more or less phenomenal song hits but wisely never have recourse to the judgement of truth, the opposite criterion. Business is their ideology. It is quite correct that the power of the culture industry resides in its identification with a manufactured need, and not in simple contrast to it, even if this contrast were one of complete power and complete powerlessness. Amusement under late capitalism is the prolongation of work. It is sought after as an escape from the mechanized work process, and to recruit strength in order to be able to cope with it again. But at the same time mechanization has such power over a man's leisure and happiness, and so profoundly determines the manufacture of amusement goods, that his experiences are inevitably after-images of the work process itself. The ostensible content is merely a faded foreground; what sinks in is the automatic succession of standardized operations. What happens at work, in the factory, or in the office can only be escaped from by approximation to it in one's leisure time. All amusement suffers from this incurable malady. Pleasure hardens into boredom because, if it is to remain pleasure, it must not demand any effort and therefore moves rigorously in the worn grooves of association. No independent thinking must be expected from the audience: the product prescribes every reaction: not by its natural structure (which collapses under reflection), but by signals. Any logical connection calling for mental effort is painstakingly avoided.

[...]

In the culture industry the individual is an illusion not merely because of the standardization of the means of production. He is tolerated only so long as his complete identification with the generality is unquestioned. Pseudo individuality is rife: from the standardized jazz improvization to the exceptional film star whose hair curls over her eye to demonstrate her originality. What is individual is no more than the generality's power to stamp the accidental detail so firmly that it is accepted as such. The defiant reserve or elegant appearance of the individual on show is mass-produced like Yale locks, whose only difference can be measured in fractions of millimeters. The peculiarity of the self is a monopoly commodity determined by society; it is falsely represented as natural. It is no more than the moustache, the French accent, the deep voice of the woman of the world, the Lubitsch touch: finger prints on identity cards which are otherwise exactly the same, and into which the lives and faces of every single person are transformed by the power of the generality. Pseudo individuality is the prerequisite for comprehending tragedy and removing its poison: only because individuals have ceased to be themselves and are now merely centers where the general tendencies meet, it is possible to receive them again, whole and entire, into the generality. In this way mass culture discloses the fictitious character of the 'individual' in the bourgeois era, and is merely unjust in boasting on account of this dreary harmony of general and particular. The principle of individuality was always full of contradiction. Individuation has never really been achieved. Self-preservation in the shape of class has kept everyone at the stage of a mere species being. Every bourgeois characteristic, in spite of its deviation and indeed because of it, expressed the same thing: the harshness of the competitive society. The individual who supported society bore its disfiguring mark: seemingly free, he was actually the product of its economic and social apparatus. Power based itself on the prevailing conditions of power when it sought the approval of persons affected by it. As it progressed, bourgeois society did also develop the individual. Against the will of its leaders, technology has changed human beings from children into persons. However, every advance in individuation of this kind took place at the expense of the individuality in whose name it occurred, so that nothing was left but the resolve to pursue one's own particular purpose. The bourgeois whose existence is split into a business and a private life, whose private life is split into keeping up his public image and intimacy, whose intimacy is split into the surly partnership of marriage and the bitter comfort of being quite alone, at odds with himself and everybody else, is already virtually a Nazi, replete both with enthusiasm and abuse; or a modern city-dweller who can now only imagine friendship as a 'social contact': that is, as being in social contact with others with whom he has no inward contact. The only reason why the culture industry can deal so successfully with individuality is that the latter has always reproduced the fragility of society. On the faces of private individuals and movie heroes put together according to the patterns on magazine covers vanishes a pretense in which no one now believes; the popularity of the hero models comes partly from a secret satisfaction that the effort to achieve individuation has at last been replaced by the effort to imitate, which is admittedly more breathless. It is idle to hope that this self-contradictory, disintegrating 'person' will not last for generations, that the system must collapse because of such a psychological split, or that the deceitful substitution of the stereotype for the individual will of itself become unbearable for mankind. Since Shakespeare's *Hamlet*, the unity of the personality has been seen through as a pretense. Synthetically produced physiognomies show that the people of today have already forgotten that there was ever a notion of what human life was. For centuries society has been preparing for Victor Mature and Mickey Rooney. By destroying they come to fulfill.

The idolization of the cheap involves making the average the heroic. The highest-paid stars resemble pictures advertising unspecified proprietary articles. Not without good purpose are they often selected from the host of commercial models. The prevailing taste takes its ideal from advertising, the beauty in consumption. Hence the Socratic saying that the beautiful is the useful has now been fulfilled – ironically. The cinema makes propaganda for the culture combine as a whole; on radio, goods for whose sake the cultural commodity exists are also recommended individually. For a few coins one can see the film which cost millions, for even less one can buy the chewing gum whose manufacture involved immense riches – a hoard increased still further by sales. *In absentia*, but by universal suffrage, the treasure of armies is revealed, but prostitution is not allowed inside the country. The best orchestras in the world – clearly not so – are brought into your living room free of charge. It is all a parody of the never-never land, just as the national society is a parody of the human society. You name it, we supply it. A man up from the country remarked at the old Berlin Metropol theater that it was astonishing what they could do for the money; his comment has long since been adopted by the culture industry and made the very substance of production. This is always coupled with the triumph that it is possible; but this, in large measure, is the very triumph. Putting on a show means showing everybody what there is, and what can be achieved. Even today it is still a fair, but incurably sick with culture. Just as the people who had been attracted by the fairground barkers overcame their disappointment in the booths with a brave smile, because they really knew in advance what would happen, so the movie-goer sticks knowingly to the institution. With the cheapness of mass-produce luxury goods and its complement, the universal swindle, a change in the character of the art commodity itself is coming about. What is new is not that it is a commodity, but that today it deliberately admits it is one; that art renounces its own autonomy and proudly takes its place among consumption goods constitutes the charm of novelty. Art as a separate sphere was always possible only in a bourgeois society. Even as a negation of that social purposiveness which is spreading through the market, its freedom remains essentially bound up with the premise of a commodity economy. Pure works of art which deny the commodity society by the very fact that they obey their own law were always wares all the same. In so far as, until the eighteenth century, the buyer's patronage shielded the artist from the market, they were dependent on the buyer and his objectives. The purposelessness of the great modern work of art depends on the anonymity of the market. Its demands pass through so many intermediaries but admittedly only to a certain degree, for throughout the whole history of the bourgeoisie his autonomy was only tolerated, and thus contained an element of untruth which ultimately led to the social liquidation of art. When mortally sick, Beethoven hurled away a novel by Sir Walter Scott with the cry: 'Why, the fellow writes for money,' and yet proved a most experienced and stubborn businessman in disposing of the last quartets, which were a most extreme renunciation of the market; he is the most outstanding example of the unity of those opposites, market and independence, in bourgeois art. Those who succumb to the ideology are precisely those who cover up the contradiction instead of taking it into the consciousness of their own production as Beethoven did: he went on to express in music his anger at losing a few pence, and derived the metaphysical *Es Muss Sein* (which attempts an aesthetic banishment of the pressure of the world by taking it into itself) from the housekeeper's demand for her monthly wages. The principle of idealistic aesthetics – purposefulness without a purpose – reverses the scheme of things to which bourgeois art conforms socially: purposelessness for the purposes declared by the market. At last, in the demand for entertainment and relaxation, purpose has absorbed the realm of purposelessness. But as the insistence that art should be disposable in terms of money becomes absolute, a shift in the internal structure of cultural commodities begins to show itself. The use which men in this antagonistic society promise themselves from the work of art is itself, to a great extent, that very existence of the useless which is abolished by complete inclusion under use. The work of art, by completely assimilating itself to need, deceitfully deprives men of precisely that liberation from the principle of utility which it should inaugurate. What might be called use value in the reception of cultural commodities is replaced by exchange value; in place of enjoyment there are gallery-visiting and factual knowledge: the prestige seeker replaces the connoisseur. The consumer becomes the ideology of the pleasure industry, whose institutions he cannot escape. One simply 'has to' have seen *Mrs Miniver*, just as one 'has to' subscribe to *Life* and *Time*. Everything is looked at from only one aspect: that it can be used for something else, however vague the notion of this use may be. No object has an inherent value; it is valuable only to the extent that it can be exchanged. The use value of art, its mode of being, is treated as a fetish; and the fetish, the work's social rating (misinterpreted as its artistic status) becomes its use value – the only quality which is enjoyed. The commodity function of art disappears only to be wholly realized when art becomes a species of commodity instead, marketable and interchangeable like an industrial product. But art as a type of product which existed to be sold and yet to be unsaleable is wholly and hypocritically converted into 'unsaleability' as soon as the transaction ceases to be the mere intention and becomes its sole principle.

Source: Adorno and Horkheimer, 1979, pp. 120–4, 126–7, 135–9, 154–8.

READING B:
Bernard Gendron, 'Theodor Adorno meets the Cadillacs'

[...]

II

[In his 1941 essay 'On popular music'] Adorno attempted to expose the politically and aesthetically destructive ways in which the capitalist mode of production affects popular music. For him it all came down to one thing. 'A clear judgement concerning the relation of serious to popular music can be arrived at by strict attention to the fundamental characteristic of popular music: standardization. The whole structure of popular music is standardized even where the attempt is made to circumvent standardization' (Adorno, 1941, p. 17). Adorno was not speaking of all kinds of standardization, only of that kind which has emerged with the capitalist industrial system.

In the broadest sense of the term, standardization is an almost universal fact of human production. At any given time or place, because of prevailing techniques, artifacts of the same kind tend to be produced in the same way, or in only a small variety of different ways. For example, at the turn of the nineteenth century, before the industrial revolution reached the firearms industry, gunsmiths had at their disposal the techniques and resources for constructing a wide variety of gun locks: the match lock, the wheel lock, the flint lock, and the percussion lock. Once the percussion lock was perfected, however, there were no longer any good reasons for producing the highly awkward, unreliable, and inefficient match lock, or any of the other competing forms. The percussion lock became the standardized form. Such standardized uniformities of practice and technique inform pre-industrial music as well as manufacturing. It is sometimes said of Vivaldi that he composed the same concerto 500 times. Haydn was not averse to composing according to formula, nor were any of the anonymous contributors to the largely invariant tradition of the English folk ballad.

But what Adorno wanted to attack in the cultural sphere was not standardization in general. He was primarily concerned with two traits which only emerge in full force with industrial standardization: part interchangeability and pseudo-individualization, traits which are easily discerned in the large-scale manufacturing and marketing of such functional artifacts as the American automobile. For example, virtually any mechanical part from any 1956 Cadillac Eldorado (e.g., a carburetor) can be substituted for the corresponding part in any other 1956 Eldorado without disturbing the functional unity of the overall mechanism. Between the 1956 Eldorado and the 1956 Cadillac Sedan de Ville, the level of interchangeability is lower – the former was marketed as a classier car with greater horsepower – but most of the corresponding parts of these two cars are the same, as are the corresponding parts of lower-level Cadillacs and higher-level Oldsmobiles of later years. Interchangeability extends significantly, though not perfectly, beyond brand-name boundaries.

Interchangeable parts need not be qualitatively indistinguishable, though they usually are. All that is required is that the mechanism, after part substitution, continues to function in an integrated manner. For example, stereo speakers belonging to different systems may be interchanged, however much they may vary in design, size, and appearance, without disrupting these systems' ability to produce recorded sound. On the other hand, few parts of pre-industrially crafted products have interchangeable parts. In the eighteenth century, the odds were exceedingly low that the lock of one hand-crafted gun could be successfully replaced with that of another to effect a functional fit with the farmer's stock and barrel. Precision machinery can be used to produce interchangeable locks and barrels; skilled hands and tools cannot. The eighteenth century gunsmith had to spend considerable time filing each lock-barrel pair to bring about a proper fit; thus, no two locks had exactly the same kind of fit to their respective barrels.

Pseudo-individualization is the indispensable capitalist complement to part interchangeability. The latter has to do with the inner essential mechanisms of industrial products, the former with their external trappings. The latter accounts for their basic similarities, the former for their apparent (and illusory) differences. Part

interchangeability results from the drive to minimize the cost of production; pseudo-individualization results from the imperative to maximize sales. The system of advertising seduces us into believing that differences in packaging reflect differences in essence. Pseudo-individualization glamorizes style over the real inner content.

The 1956 Eldorado was the first Cadillac model to sport the famous tail-fin. To the mid-fifties consumer, all other Cadillac models paled in comparison, though their innards were virtually the same. Not surprisingly, the rest of the Cadillac fleet followed suit with wholly revamped tail-fin models in 1957, though mechanically they showed little improvement. In that brief period, pseudo-individuality within the Cadillac line operated both synchronically (for different models in the same year) and diachronically (for the same model in different years). For working-class youth, the fifties Cadillac was the most glamorous car on the American market, its body style standing for elegance, power, flash, adventure, movement – indeed, for having it all without drudgery or effort. The Cadillacs – the rock 'n' roll group – turned to General Motors for permission to bask in the glory of the name, and other groups had to content themselves with the names of particular models: the Fleetwoods, the Eldorados, the Sevilles.

Yet one who chose the more expensive Cadillac over the Oldsmobile was paying primarily for differences in style rather than mechanical quality. Even the Cadillac's equally expensive competitors outside of General Motors – the Lincoln Continental and the Chrysler Imperial–differed from it mainly in external wrapping, not engineering design. The fact that the Cadillac and the Chrysler and Lincoln had few if any interchangeable parts was more an artifact of marketing than of technology: the automobile corporations wanted to be the exclusive sellers of spare parts for their own models.

Pseudo-individualization tends not only to disguise part interchangeability but also to distort it, thus transforming it into near-interchangeability or pseudo-noninterchangeability. Thus, the minute design differences in Cadillac and Lincoln carburetors, by subtly undermining interchangeability, further enhance the illusion of essential qualitative differences between the two makes.

III

Adorno claimed that popular music is as constrained by capitalist industrial standardization as any mechanical product of the assembly line. Let us examine this analogy between text and mechanism.

Assuming that in each popular song it is possible to distinguish between the core (the musical skeleton) and the periphery (the musical embellishments), Adorno argued that in popular music the central core is either invariant or subject to part-interchangeability. The variant periphery is contrived either to appear like a variant central core or to disguise the invariance or interchangeability of the central core. 'In popular music, position is absolute. Every detail is substitutable; it serves its function only as a cog in a machine' (p.19). One may interchange rhythms, chord progressions, speeds of execution, melodic fragments, riffs, lyrical formulae, and various vocal and instrumental devices. Meanwhile songwriters search incessantly for the pseudo-individualizing 'hook' which will make the song appear unique and organically whole. The hook is to songs what the fin was to the 1956 Cadillac Eldorado. For Adorno the 'so-called improvisations' in jazz, provided the 'most drastic' (and deceptive) example of pseudo–individualization in popular music (p. 25).

Adorno believed that good 'serious' music does not suffer from this defect. 'To sum up the difference: in Beethoven and in good serious music in general ... the detail virtually contains the whole and leads to the exposition of the whole. In popular music the relationship is fortuitous. The detail has no bearing on a whole, which appears as an extraneous framework' (p.21). As an example, Adorno cited Beethoven's *Fifth Symphony*. One may get the superficial impression of interchangeable parts insofar as the symphony follows the four-movement formula, with the third movement being a scherzo in ABA form. Nonetheless, according to Adorno, one could not lift this scherzo out of the *Fifth Symphony* and place it, say, in a Haydn symphony without

dramatically altering its meaning, since it was constructed to lead subtly into the fourth movement. The meaning of the scherzo in this case is inextricably tied to its relation to the fourth movement (pp. 20-21). For Adorno it followed from this that while in popular music the mere recognition of the form virtually guarantees full understanding, in serious music one does not achieve full understanding until one has struggled with the concrete interconnections of the text – recognition of the form is merely the first step. Industrially standardized popular music is pre-digested, serious music is not (pp. 32–3). Adorno pushed his thesis of industrial standardization in popular music to the very limits of plausibility. Industrial standardization for him operated not only within genres but also between genres, diachronically as well as synchronically, in the long run as well as in the short run. He saw no significant differences between swing music and the sentimental ballads of the late thirties, no significant development from the 'hot' small combo jazz of the twenties to the cooler big band jazz of the thirties. In effect, he believed that nothing ever changes in popular music (pp. 26, 30).

According to Adorno, this dismal state of affairs in popular music reflects and reinforces the deterioration of consumer taste within advanced capitalist society. The assembly line that produces the standardized automobile also produces a bored, numbed, and passive worker. Workers are as customized by the capitalist production system as the commodities they are hired to produce (p.38). Industrial standardization in the culture industry both satisfies the consumption needs of bored, passive workers and contributes further to their passivity. Bored consumers need constant stimulation; therefore, the industry creates pseudo-individualized hooks in music and the constant illusion of novelty. Benumbed as they are, the workers have neither the inclination nor the capacity to struggle intellectually with the cultural products they consume. The products must come to them completely predigested. This need is met by musical homogeneity and part interchangeability; however, this uniformity must remain hidden if the illusion of novelty is to be sustained. But the stimulative power of each record palls very quickly, recreating the condition of boredom it was meant to relieve. The only antidote is the constant production of new recorded sounds (pp. 37–9).

In effect, 'there is a justification for speaking of a pre-established harmony today between production and consumption of popular music' (p.38). Industrial standardization reflects not only the requirements of production for the musical text but also the demands of consumption. It extends to the workers' leisure time the sort of control that capital has over their labor time.

IV

Adorno's extraordinary claims made considerable sense in 1941 when he published 'On Popular Music.' It is well known that the structure and musical content of Tin Pan Alley songs had hardly changed in the twenty years before the paper's publication. The over-whelming majority of these songs were composed in the 32-bar AABA format. Most songwriters never deviated from the simplistic harmonic paradigms in circulation, or from the 'June-moon-spoon' rhyming formulas. There were notable exceptions in the more unpredictable harmonic devices and clever lyrics of Cole Porter, George Gershwin, and Jerome Kern, though these were not sufficiently intricate and avant-garde to satisfy Adorno.

The rock 'n' roll revolution may have mercifully put Tin Pan Alley out of its misery, but it did not bring to an end the industrial standardization of music. This is especially clear in the work of the Cadillacs and other doo-wop groups.

Doo-wop is a vocal group style, rooted in the black gospel quartet tradition, that emerged on inner city street corners in the mid-fifties and established a major presence on the popular music charts between 1955 and 1959. Its most distinctive feature is the use of background vocals to take on the role of instrumental accompaniment for, and response to, the high tenor or falsetto calls of the lead singer. Typically, the backup vocalists create a harmonic, rhythmic, and contrapuntal substructure by voicing phonetic or nonsense syllables such as 'shoo-doo-be-doo-be-doo,' 'ooh-wah, ooh-wah,' 'sha-na-na,' and so on.

For structural and harmonic guidance, doo-wop musicians relied almost exclusively on the tried-and-true paradigms and formulas that had existed for decades in the Tin Pan Alley and rhythm and blues fields. This is clearly a case of diachronic standardization. About 75 percent of the doo-wop songs were structured in the 32-bar AABA fashion typical of Tin Pan Alley; the remaining 25 percent followed the 12-bar AAB fashion typical of rhythm and blues. The blues-derived doo-wop songs adhered for the most part to standard blues chord progressions: 1 (4 bars), IV (2 bars), I (2 bars), V (1 bar), IV (1 bar), I (2 bars). Those in the 32-bar format in most cases followed the simple chord progression so familiar to children who learn to play duet versions of songs like 'Heart and Soul' by ear: the I-vi-ii-V progression with two chord changes per measure. In 1955 the Moonglows, a doo-wop group, recorded 'Sincerely,' a song which is structurally and harmonically little different from Larry Clinton's 1938 recording of 'Heart and Soul'. For Adorno they shared the same standardized core. Similarly, the Silhouettes' 1958 doo-wop recording of 'Get a Job' incorporates the structural harmonic core of Big Joe Turner's 1944 blues classic 'Rebecca.'

It could be argued with equal plausibility that there is a high degree of synchronic standardization within the doo-wop genre itself. Most of the thousands of doo-wop songs composed during the late fifties closely resemble each other. But even their dissimilarities follow the principle of interchangeable parts. As an illustration, imagine a number of decks of cards, each of which represents a range of options within one doo-wop musical function. In one deck, the cards represent different doo-wop phonetic syllables, in another different call-and-response patterns, and so on; different melodic fragments for the lead voice, different counterpoint fragments for the background voices, different rhythms, speeds, vocal embellishments, lyrical fragments (e.g. 'Gimme some lovin', some turtle-dovin''), and gimmicks (a humorous bass voice, the sound of bells, a prepubescent singer). In most cases, one could create a credible doo-wop recording by simply picking one card from each deck. Thus, from any two doo-wop songs one could create two new songs by interchanging between them the strings of background vocal phonetic syllables (with proper adjustments in key signatures and rhythm). Imagine interchanging the 'Shoo-Doo-Be-Doo-Be-Doo's of the Five Satins 'In the Still of the Night' with 'Dum-Dum-Dum-Dum-

Dum-Dum-De-Doo-De-Dum' 's of the Dell-Vikings' 'Come Go With Me.' Where such interchanges are not immediately possible, certain amendations could make them work. But this only indicates that with certain doo-wop songs, interchangeability applies only proximally or is transformed into pseudo-noninterchangeability. Some doo-wop songs are as similar as two different Cadillac models; others are as unlike as a Cadillac and a Lincoln. Standardization and pseudo-individualization nonetheless prevail in both kinds of cases.

What is true for doo-wop also holds true for other rock 'n' roll genres: rockabilly, heavy metal, funk, etc. Consider how punk has standardized the musical sneer. There is also some standardization between rock 'n' roll genres (doo-wop and surf music, punk and rockabilly). So Adorno's analysis of popular music is not altogether implausible, and applies as well to the Cadillacs and the Sex Pistols as it does to Guy Lombardo and the Andrews Sisters.

V

I have tried to present Adorno's analysis of popular music in the best light, in order to eliminate the more facile and unfair objections usually leveled at it. Now I would like to discuss some of the failings of his theory. Adorno argued, successfully I think, that industrial standardization is an important feature of popular music, and must be taken seriously in any political assessment of the form. But he greatly exaggerated its presence, especially at the diachronic level. Secondly, he gave the wrong explanation for the music industry's predilection toward industrial standardization. This misconstruction of the role of the music industry affects the validity of his political critique, so I will discuss it first.

Adorno was not sufficiently sensitive to the crucial differences between the production of functional artifacts (e.g. the automobile) and the production of textual artifacts (e.g. the rock 'n' roll record). Thus he was too easily led to assume that, on the production side, the conditions which require industrial standardization in the culture industry are similar to those which require it in the rest of capitalist industry.

In functional artifacts, part interchangeability is largely a consequence of the technology of the assembly line. In this system of production, every whole (e.g. the automobile) is assembled out of qualitatively different parts, each of which is taken at random from qualitatively indistinguishable batches. Of course, different competitive brands (e.g., the Cadillac, the Lincoln) will emanate from qualitatively different assembly lines. But as long as state-of-the-art technology is allowed to flow freely, it will tend to prevail in all firms of a given industry, thus leading to a convergence of production techniques; assembly lines for Cadillacs and Lincolns will differ only marginally and contrivedly.

Technology does not put the same constraints on the production of recorded musical sounds. If anything, it greatly expands the possibilities for variation. For example, rather than supplanting the acoustic guitar, the electric guitar simply added to the rich variety of timbres obtainable with guitars. Nor do the technical constraints of production explain why doo-wop recordings typically use the saxophone for instrumental breaks, why doo-wop songs are usually cast in a 12- or 32-bar framework, or why doo-wop groups did not seize upon the potential of experimental tape editing, a technique which was later exploited by avant-garde composers (e.g. Stockhausen) and adventurous pop performers (e.g. the Beatles).

Adorno was aware that assembly line technology has little to do with the industrial standardization of popular music. He took this as a sign of the backwardness of the music industry, where 'the act of producing a song hit still remains in the handicraft stage' (p. 23). In order to locate the industrial source of musical standardization, he turned from the sphere of production technology to that of production and marketing organization, where the music industry had already reached an advanced level of 'industrialization', that is, oligopolistic concentration and cartelization. The story he tells is a rather familiar one. When the music industry was competitive and decentralized, many standards of popular song competed until one won out momentarily (synchronic standardization). But once the industry became concentrated and oligopolized, whichever form of music was dominant at the time was frozen permanently into place and 'rigidly enforced' (diachronic standardization). Presumably this is not unique to the music industry (p. 23). Great market concentration anywhere means greater standardization.

This explanation is altogether unsatisfactory. For one thing, the modern recording studio is not technologically backward – it is at least as sophisticated as the assembly line. Furthermore, Adorno greatly underrated the dynamic character of capitalism in its oligopolistic forms. One need only look at ATT's technologically innovative practices over the past few decades to see this. Although it may be true in the abstract that oligopolies and monopolies tend more toward rigidification than do competitive industries, we must not neglect the symbiosis existing between these two sectors. In the oil industry, the wildcatters take most of the risks in the search for new oil, and the major firms then buy up the proven wells. The personal computer was developed by small firms, and then the large firms moved in to consolidate. The music industry behaves similarly. Most of the early rock 'n' roll records were produced by the small record companies that emerged after World War II like the obscure Josie label – whose only claim to fame was that it recorded the music of the Cadillacs. Once rock 'n' roll was established, the major recording companies captured most of its markets, although small firms kept reappearing to clear the air, occasionally supported by the big companies.

Adorno came away empty-handed in his search for a general industrial model for standardization in popular music. His analysis ignored the inherent differences between text and functional artifact. A text (whether written or oral) is a universal, whereas a functional artifact is a particular. However, to be marketed and possessed, every universal text must be embodied in some functional artifact (paper, vinyl discs). There were two quite distinct products involved in the 1955 release of the Cadillacs' 'Down the Road' on the Josie label. The first – a universal – was the recorded sound resulting from the Cadillacs' studio performance and consequent re-mixing. The second was the moderately large batch of vinyl discs which, as particulars, embodied that sound. The processes used to produce the first are quite different from those used to produce the second. The vinyl discs of 'Down the Road' were produced in great numbers, and thus were amenable to the

disciplines of the assembly line, whereas Josie did at most only four or five recorded takes of the song, only one of which found its way onto wax. One simply doesn't mass produce universals. In 1955, Josie sold hundreds of thousands of discs, but generated only fifty to a hundred recordings – hardly a sufficient quantity to warrant the techniques of mass production. Even a large company like RCA, which may have sold over 50 million records that year produced no more than a few thousand recorded takes. Thus, whatever the technological state of the culture industry, the assembly line is simply an inappropriate model for the production of texts-as-universals. This is not to say that the production of musical texts (as compositions or as performances) cannot be technically rationalized to maximize the power of management – such rationalization occurred, for example, in the Brill Building 'song-writing' factory of the sixties. It does mean that it is and always will be a mistake to look to the techniques of mass production or the economics of market concentration for an explanation of industrial standardization in the culture industry. Whatever they are, the factors accounting for standardization in the production of musical texts must be significantly different from those which account for standardization in functional artifacts. Adorno's analysis is undermined by his failure to attend to these discontinuities.

[...]

IX

The central political question about rock 'n' roll today is: who creates the meaning of the rock 'n' roll record? Most rock critics, not surprisingly, fall under the sway of the *auteur* theory. According to them, rock 'n' roll meaning is created primarily by performers, songwriters, arrangers, and producers – that is, the artists most intimately involved in the production of recorded sound. The Birmingham School of Culture Theory in England has provided us with the only recent antidote to that approach. Dick Hebdige, for example, has argued that one cannot understand the meaning of any rock 'n' roll record without situating it within the youth cultures which most typically consume it. In effect, he is telling us that greasers, mods, hippies, and punks 'rewrite' the recorded text they consume by recontextualizing it within their practices and rituals (see for example, Hebdige, 1979). The doo-wop style was not, in terms of its sounds and lyrics, intrinsically threatening to the mid-fifties parent culture. But because it was an important element of the rock 'n' roll revolution along with the music of Little Richard and Elvis Presley, and because rock 'n' roll was first associated with youth under-classes (blacks, greasers, and delinquents), doo-wop acquired a mythical veneer of sex and rebellion.

The Birmingham approach is certainly a refreshing alternative to the reviewers' constant glorification of the artist. Yet it has the same political effect, which is to legitimize rock 'n' roll culture. If either the artist or the consuming community is the primary creator of its meaning, then rock 'n' roll does have the liberatory power so often claimed for it.

Meanwhile, no one is addressing directly the question of the industry's role in the creation of meaning in rock 'n' roll, perhaps because of the difficulties involved. The music industry is really an elaborate complex of many industries – radio, TV, records, publishing, publicity – whose integration is difficult to conceptualize. It is considerably more difficult to articulate theoretically how this convoluted system contributes to the creation of rock 'n' roll meaning – one must combine political economy and semiotics, and there is no established way of doing so. Rock 'n' roll theorists who attend to political economy – and they are few – don't attend to semiotics.

This is where Adorno's work can be of service. With his theory of industrial standardization in music, he combined concepts of both political economy and semiotics, drawing on analogies between the industrially-produced functional artifact and the industrially-produced cultural text. He failed, however, in not being sensitive to the limits of the industrial model. Thus he exaggerated the extent of the standardization in popular music, and arrived at the wrong explanations for its occurrence. He paid insufficient attention to sources of musical standardization lying outside the capitalist mode of production. His elitism led him to musical essentialism, and his modernism to a too uncritical stance toward the ideology of aesthetic rebellion and anti-standardization.

Nevertheless, we cannot let Adorno's intolerances and mistaken explanations deter us from attending to the important questions he has raised. No theorist who focuses on rock 'n' roll from the 'reception' side claims that youth cultures are capable of completely revamping the meaning of the records they consume. The rock 'n' roll record cannot function for them as an alien object which they may interpret altogether independently of the codes of the dominant culture. There is no doubt that some semantic contribution of the music industry survives the youthful consumers' final rewriting of the rock 'n' roll recorded text. What is at issue is how much survives and whether it undermines the youth subcultures' own political contributions. To use Barthesian terms, is the rock 'n' roll record primarily a 'readerly' or a 'writerly' text?

Perhaps nothing is as resistant to consumer reinterpretation as the standardized forms, sounds, and verbal devices operating at the conventionalized core of the popular song. Because of their intimate association with constant repetition, plugging, and self-advertisement, these standardized components probably evoke the entrenched codes of the dominant culture much more powerfully than do the non-standardized components. For example, most of the doo-wop songs that are clearly romantic and sentimental in the traditional Tin Pan Alley sense are usually cast in the 32-bar ballad form (with I-vi-ii-V harmony) so characteristic of Tin Pan Alley. The doo-wop songs cast in the blues AAB form are usually more upbeat, more ironic, or more lusty. Here certain standardized forms clearly call forth certain entrenched codes. Did the industrially-generated romantic and sentimental meaning of the doo-wop songs subvert or overcome the sexual and rebellious meaning produced by youth-cultural recontextualization?

There is in sum a constant struggle at the meeting point of production and consumption between the evocation of entrenched codes and the insinuation of alternative meanings. The tendency of the music industry is to employ in the production of musical texts devices, like standardization, that automatically call the dominant codes into play. Recent writers who have focused on reception in popular music have been insufficiently attentive to the power of these devices, and thus have tended to exaggerate the semantic creativity of the consuming subcultures. I believe that a reappraisal of Adorno's work can contribute significantly to the removal of these theoretical deficiencies. To further our understanding of the complex political stances of rock 'n' roll, we must now engage Adorno's productivist approach in a constructive dialogue with the more recent and fashionable reception approaches.

References

ADORNO, T.W. (1941) 'On popular music', *Studies in Philosophy and Social Sciences*, vol. IX, pp. 17–48.

HEBDIGE, D. (1979) *Subculture: the meaning of style,* London, Methuen.

Source: Gendron, 1986, pp. 18–36.

FASHION: UNPACKING A CULTURAL PRODUCTION

Peter Braham

Contents

1   Introduction

fashion

The word **fashion** is very often used as if it refers exclusively to apparel (and its associated adornments) and, above all, to women's clothes. Yet it is worth remembering that fashion operates in a wide variety of other fields as well. This is, of course, readily apparent in the decorative arts and branches of popular culture, for example, but it may be less evident in fields such as business management (on this subject, see Chapters 5 and 6), still less in the law and medicine. In these areas, though the idea that they are concerned about or involved with fashion would probably be derided, closer examination might reveal that what is explained not as fashion, but as 'best practice' or 'superior practice', often turns out to be no more than 'fashion' after all – and can be seen as such when that practice changes and the former practice is abandoned.

Nevertheless, the basic mechanism of fashion exists in a clear and highly visible form in women's clothing and in no other industry is the management of fashionability so central to its institutions and structures as it is in the design, manufacture, distribution, sale and consumption of women's clothing. The essence of fashion in clothes is that it compels us to discard a garment before it has outlived its usefulness – what Wark refers to as a condition of 'semiotic redundancy' (1991, p. 63) – though, oddly enough, this does not mean that fashion items are invariably sold without regard to durability.

The difference between fashion and other clothing is at the heart of this chapter. Though for much of the time it is the design, manufacturing, distribution and retailing of clothing and apparel that is being described and analysed, this is being done in order to illuminate fashion and fashionability: the emphasis is on, first, adopting and discarding fashion in clothing and, second, the problems that this poses for manufacturers and retailers.

It is perhaps only to be expected that in cultural studies fashion is treated as a cultural subject, in which most emphasis is on fashion as a badge or a means of identity. Yet fashion, as well as being a matter of creation, consumption and identity, is also a matter of production, distribution and retailing. It is therefore not just a cultural subject, but also a subject which has to do with apparently rather mundane matters of profit margins, response times, supply and demand, and so on. Accordingly, the assumption that fashion in clothes ought to be considered in terms of both its cultural aspects and its economic aspects is central to my approach, as is the contention that we must try to illuminate the connections between the production and consumption of fashion. It is the interplay between these different elements that will provide the main storyline of this chapter and it is this which allows us to raise 'external' as well as 'internal' questions about

cultural economy

fashion by treating it as an illustration of the notion of a **cultural economy** that Paul du Gay discusses both in the Introduction to this book and in his concluding remarks to Chapter 6. In the case of fashion this means that the question of whether or not 'fashion' is homogeneous – in the sense that there is a single, prevailing style of dress – cannot be treated simply as a cultural or aesthetic matter of why or how quickly one fashion replaces or remains alongside another, it also has material implications for manufacturing, distribution, ordering and selling.

This storyline should be seen as being firmly situated within the debates contained in the opening chapters of this book and Chapter 4 that follows. Thus in Chapter 2 Keith Negus argues that in studying the production of culture it is necessary to understand not only technical processes and arrangements for manufacture, distribution and so on, but also the 'culture' through which the products are given meaning. Though I put it the other way round, there is no disagreement between us about the need to attend to each of these aspects. The challenge for both of us is thus the same: to discover how products 'circulate', how they are given particular meanings in the context of a number of different production–consumption relationships. As far as this chapter is concerned, this means that what is being unpacked is not so much *fashion* as the *fashion industry* – and, most especially, fashion as it relates to clothing.

As you will have seen, a major part of both Chapters 1 and 2 is concerned with the issue of globalization, that is the extent to which the organization of production and the exploitation of markets has come to be conducted on a worldwide scale. This discussion is highly relevant for this chapter for several reasons: on the one hand, insofar as it exemplifies what is called the 'new international division of labour' or NIDL (which is discussed in section 4.3 below), the manufacture of clothing can indeed be regarded as global, in part at least.

On the other hand, many of the criticisms made in Chapters 1 and 2 of a supposed global culture are apposite here as well. First, the attack on the assumption that everyone within a global culture is equal has a special resonance in the context of clothing and fashion: the way in which migrants, for example, are on the 'receiving end' of things is surely nowhere better illustrated than in the extent to which inner-city clothing firms in developed countries depend on foreign migrants, many of whom are employed illegally, and who work long hours for little pay. Secondly, as you will have noted in Chapter 1, Kevin Robins pays particular attention to the idea of the global corporation. Such a corporation is said to operate not so much in different markets, as in a developing global market, within which global consumers with global tastes can be discerned. Here Benetton suggests itself as a prime example, not merely because the presence of Benetton – or United Colours of Benetton – in so many high streets indicates a measure of global consumption, but also because its advertising campaigns can be depicted as being predicated on the existence of a global culture, or at least as an attempt to create one (see section 4.3). However, the portrait of standardized production and passive consumption conveyed by the concept of globalization can be questioned on several grounds: in Chapter 1, for example, Kevin Robins criticizes the advocates of globalization for neglecting the national point of reference and underestimating cultural diversity; and in Chapter 2, Keith Negus further criticizes the concept for concentrating on how production determines consumption, without examining how it also *follows* consumption. Were consumption as uniform and as passive as is sometimes suggested, then the relocation of garment production to areas where labour is at its cheapest (which I discuss later) could be expected to continue without hindrance. That this has not happened alerts us to the degree to which the production of clothing and fashion has altered to take account of changes in consumer demand.

How and why these developments have occurred is of central concern in this chapter. This is why I devote so much attention to the role of retailers in the production and consumption of fashion, a subject that is developed further by Sean Nixon in the next chapter. As you will discover, the development of Electronic Point-Of-Sale (or EPOS) equipment provides a pivotal 'moment' in the circulation of capital in this area: prior to this retailers had used their dominant position in the market to persuade manufacturers to grasp the benefits of the economies of scale associated with mass manufacture. With this new technology, however, they were able to impose what is known as 'just-in-time' (or JIT) production on manufacturers in order to cater for a more diverse, fragmented and fast-changing consumer market – a market that could be nurtured by linking the design of shops to the identification of customers in terms of lifestyles, aspirations, preferred shopping experiences, and the like.

1.1   The consumption and production of fashion

The complex and uncertain relationship between the production and consumption of fashion may be illustrated by the following two stories. The first story concerns a major British retailer and the specifications they are said to have set for their suppliers of blue jeans. At the time, the prevailing fashion was for jeans to be faded: either they should be 'stone-washed' – resulting in a streaky pale blue colour – or they should be advertised to 'fade when washed'. The retailer was concerned about the implications of this for their reputation as a supplier of durable clothes of good quality. Should they maintain their preferred quality standards and risk losing out to their high street competitors in this lucrative market? They opted for insisting that their jeans should *not* fade. Later, this decision was criticized within the company for placing them outside the fashion market altogether – not just in relation to the sale of jeans.

The second story concerns a variant of a common nightmare that is said to haunt store buyers. It goes something like this: the buyer is in a hall which somehow combines elements of all the ready-to-wear collections held each year in Paris, Milan, New York and London. She is surrounded by jostling characters from the fashion circus who are holding out hundreds of dresses for her to inspect and, at the same time, waving order sheets in her face. Unable to resist such pressure she signs innumerable cheques and buys millions and millions of dollars worth of clothes. The scene then changes to the start of the next season: the buyer and the president of the store are standing just inside the store's main entrance. It is time for business. The doors are thrown open but no one comes in. An hour passes, then several hours, then a day, then a week – still the store is without customers. At the end of the week the president turns to the buyer and says, 'It is obvious that the public does not want your clothes. You have misread their taste. The best thing to do is pack all these strange garments and send them back' (adapted from Coleridge, 1988, p. 270).

ACTIVITY 1

Note down briefly what you think these stories tell us about fashion. Then compare your reactions with my comments.

Each of these stories offers a number of insights about fashion, though at first glance they seem to refer to very different worlds – indeed, while designer dresses are exclusive, produced on a small scale and appear to be the epitome of 'fashion', it seems more appropriate to see jeans, which are mass-produced for a market of millions, as mere 'clothes'. Yet there are good reasons for thinking that, perhaps, these differences are not so great after all.

Today, though jeans are no longer just the work clothes they once were, they still might be seen as a fairly standard item where style changes are limited

FIGURE 3.1   Fashion buyers, editors and others out in force around the catwalk at a Jean-Paul Gaultier show, Autumn 1994.

and, as such, it may be thought that they would be far removed from considerations of fashion. Yet retailers have discovered, sometimes to their cost, that demand is far from predictable:

> [Retail buyers have] to guess four or five months down the road what a consumer who is fifteen years old is going to want in jeans. During that time, a new movie can come out, and the trend goes from blue denim to black denim. And suddenly the inventory commitment is obsolete, causing costly mark-downs.
>
> (Howard, 1990, p. 136)

In addition, certain brands of jeans have been heavily promoted precisely to distinguish them from the other brands that were piled high and sold cheaply: 'We needed people to value a pair of Levi's. They had ... to become fashionable without becoming a fashion item, and to achieve a mystique' (Roy Edmondson, Managing Director, Levi Strauss UK, quoted in *The Sunday Times*, Culture Section, 26 November 1995).

The intriguing thing is that in order to become fashionable, jeans had not so much to overcome their firm identification with work, with the 'common man' and so on, as for it to become ambiguous as to whether what was now being emphasized was their original associations or their new-found hierarchical and distinctive aspects. We may see this particularly well in the case of faded jeans insofar as they make obvious reference to this original usage – the 'fashion' is that they must not look new, yet they do so in a way which reveals that *appearing* to be poor has really been a costly business for the wearer.

It took about one hundred years from the time that jeans had been devised by Levi Strauss in the American West as practical work clothes, to the moment that they became almost synonymous with youth – middle class, often rebellious youth especially. But what was most significant in transforming them into truly fashionable garments was the success of the fashion industry in extending the market for jeans far beyond both these old and new constituencies. This was achieved, above all, by the innovation of designer jeans, the first of which, by Calvin Klein, notched up 20,000 sales in their first week on the American market in 1978 – even though they were 50 per cent more expensive than Levi's – and by 1984 the sales of his jeans worldwide amounted to $400 million (Craik, 1994, p. 195). With Calvin Klein's success, other designers – not surprisingly – were quick to introduce their own variants and now we are quite familiar with jeans bearing none too discreet Calvin Klein, Donna Karen and Gloria Vanderbilt labels. And even though this practice of prominent labelling follows that of Levi Strauss, it seems to give a particular aura of conspicuous consumption to a garment of such humble origins, as well as suggesting to us that fashion does not just emanate from elite groups, but may also move 'upwards'. Yet perhaps the richest irony in this process of fashionability has been that, eventually, we find American consumers were prepared to pay much more for European designer jeans like Versace than for the original, quintessentially American garments that they imitated.

Our second story, centring on the store buyer's nightmare, also hinges on the unpredictability of fashion, but it has other elements too. For example, it suggests that fashion in the shops has its origins in what we might think of as the 'high fashion' (haute couture) of the catwalks of Paris and elsewhere; that it is the creation of experts (designers); that it is brought to the department store (or high street) by other experts (buyers). It is, therefore, a relatively conventional view of the fashion industry, except insofar as it suggests that the public may decide to refrain from consuming the selections of these experts, giving credence, perhaps, to the notion that there may be a considerable gulf between 'the look' that appears on the catwalks and what works in everyday situations.

These stories raise – implicitly or explicitly – several of the issues that I wish to explore and which, though important, may be regarded as being 'internal' to this chapter. For example, is fashion predictable or unpredictable? How does something become a fashion item and what is fashionable about it? Who shapes and influences fashion? Is it those within the industry – perhaps it is haute couture designers who proclaim that this year skirts will be so many inches shorter than last year, or perhaps it is previously unknown designers – or is fashion now created at 'street level'? And if there are different fashion 'worlds', what is the relationship between them?

To a degree, questions like these form much of the stock-in-trade of the fashion pages in our newspapers and magazines, where attention is focused on the latest trends and the 'hottest' designer or most sensational collection. Here, as you will know, fashion is generally portrayed in breathless and exaggerated language: at one moment a simple leather skirt costing several hundred pounds might be described as 'basic' or 'essential', and at another moment a certain designer dress will be described as 'to die for' (or, for that matter, 'to kill for'). And, in particular, the world of high fashion inhabited by designers and store buyers alike that is conveyed in these pages seems extremely pressured, not to say frenzied – just as it does in the store buyer's nightmare.

Now, it is undeniable that what is, at least at first glance, especially striking about fashion – whether near the catwalk or on the street – is the capacity it has to excite people, which it does by offering them the means to express their identity or the prospect of transforming themselves, and so on. Indeed, in some cases, the desire or compulsion to be fashionable may give rise to still more extreme action that is implied by the proverbial advice 'shop till you drop'. For example, where it is not enough for fashion-conscious youth to wear *any* trainers because what they *must* have is a particular model of a costly, high-status brand, but the money to buy them is not available (and cannot be begged or borrowed from a parent), then the pressure to resort to crime in order to possess them may be difficult to resist. That this is indeed so, is demonstrated by the frequency with which high school students in the USA are being robbed of expensive fashion items – like trainers and Levi jackets – a phenomenon that has given fresh impetus to campaigns in favour of making school uniform compulsory.

If the extensive coverage of fashion in newspapers and magazines invariably makes fashion seem exciting, it is also likely to be fairly superficial. How then are we to achieve a more incisive theorization of the sort suggested by Roche (1994) when he speaks of the study of clothing and fashion being at the 'heart of social history'? First, if we are to do more than reiterate common-sense assumptions and myths about fashion, if we are – in terms of this chapter – to succeed in 'unpacking' fashion, rather than simply disturbing its packaging, we need to begin by thinking carefully about what is the appropriate context within which our analysis should be conducted. To do this it is important not only to address both so-called 'internal' and 'external' questions about fashion, some of which have just been mentioned, but also to understand how, by exploring internal questions, we might illuminate more general ones. For example, whether fashion is best seen as basically homogeneous, created centrally by and for an elite and then transmitted downwards to the mass and outwards to a periphery, or whether the sources of fashion are now more diverse and 'polycentric' is an important issue for this chapter (see section 3.3). In order to discover if either of these perspectives is accurate, we need to focus on 'internal' matters – to examine, amongst other things, the power and influence of international fashion conglomerates and the intricate and long-standing relationship between haute couture designers and mass manufacturers of garments. But in so doing, we may be able to make a significant contribution to wider debates, such as those about the relationship between production and consumption and about globalization.

2   The study of fashion

2.1   The reliability of clothed appearance

It has been said that dress constitutes one of the most basic and reliable methods by which we are able to place ourselves and others in the social world. It is worth elaborating upon this a little.

In the fifteenth century, fashion constituted an important element of European society, and its significance in France was such that it is reported that Charles VII was petitioned to create a ministry of fashion (Foley, 1973, p. 167). In this period fashion was seen very much in terms of the type of attributes that clothing is said to reveal and this, in turn, involved an even more complicated issue, namely, whether or not apparelled appearance could be taken to be a reliable guide to the social world. It seems that most

people were predisposed to believe that those whom they encountered were dressed appropriately unless, that is, they had some specific grounds for doubting that this was so. That this was indeed the case is suggested by the large number of surviving texts, particularly those of the sixteenth century, in which numerous complaints are recorded to the effect that people had been dressed in a manner that gave a false impression of their real – that is to say 'proper' – station in society (Corrigan, 1993, p. 145).

FIGURE 3.2 Examples of fashionable dress in eighteenth-century France

This was not simply a question of those who were naïve or too trusting making the wrong interpretation of who or what someone was. It was also, and often, thought to be a consequence of those who were misleadingly dressed having been so quite deliberately. In any event, the outcome of this phenomenon was that such conduct was seen as disrupting the smooth and orderly running of society; the resulting confusion was a major factor in the imposition of the so-called **Sumptuary Laws** in various European countries in the fifteenth century. These laws were explicitly drawn up to protect the privileged by forbidding the less privileged from copying the fashions of their supposed betters or, indeed, of creating their own fashions. Yet these laws, as well as other attempts to regulate fashion – particularly those designed to maintain the exclusivity of the Royal Court by preventing those with 'new money' from displaying their wealth in what they wore – had the opposite effect to that which had been intended. That is to say, instead of 'confining people to their designated rank, the laws provoked an intense interest in fashion and a desire to transgress the codes, both in the process of prestigious emulation and as an act of rebellion' (Craik, 1994, p. 205). Moreover, the demand for fashionable clothes was by no means confined to the *nouveaux riches* (though socially suspect), but encompassed as well those who could not afford to buy from respectable or fashionable outlets. Thus the fashion-conscious poor resorted to a variety of means, such as

Sumptuary Laws

renting outfits, buying clothes which were second-hand, stealing clothes or wearing fakes – the last strategy providing an early example of the widespread and highly organized counterfeiting of much-prized designer clothes that exists today (see section 3.3 below).

The importance that was attached to fashion in earlier times is also clearly evident in the novel. Just as in the official documents referred to above, the question of the reliability of clothed appearance proves to be a central issue in the novel, though there the attitude displayed towards this question is more variable. We find, not unexpectedly, that characters are able to acquire a new identity by means of 'sartorial metamorphoses', but what seems a little more surprising, there gradually emerges a somewhat more positive attitude to the confusion of ranks that may arise from the borrowing of clothes:

> whether to restore everyone to his costume or to accept the disguises which correspond to new types of conduct was a dilemma which opposed two principles of society: that of the holistic and unequal world of families, guilds and states; that of individuals regulating their conduct by personal rather than collective imperatives.
>
> (Roche, 1994, p. 20)

Such a preoccupation with the competing tendencies of conformism (to assume a collective identity) and individuality (to assume a distinctive appearance) was and remains at the centre of fashion, a point that might be well illustrated if you consider how far a given fashion may resemble a uniform.

2.2 The fashion cycle

fashion cycle

There is a critical difference between a widely accepted clothing code – say, a man's business suit – and 'fashion' as such. The difference is best expressed by the apparent paradox that what is widely accepted is, for this very reason, no longer fashionable. This characteristic is at its sharpest and at its most interesting in the last stages of a particular **fashion cycle** – at the moment at which a style that has become part of what Davis calls 'the common visual parlance' confronts a new style that at first – and for a time thereafter – may seem odd, outlandish, misplaced (Davis, 1992, p. 14). Shortly after this confrontation there begins a process of conversion in which what was formerly not merely familiar, but also fashionable, is rendered not just dowdy, but also somehow 'wrong'. To put it bluntly, what was 'in' is now 'out'.

In the first instance, it is the wearers of the new fashion who appear conspicuous, but within a rather short time those who stand out are those who do not adopt the new fashion. As this transformation is generally perceived, the new fashion exerts a degree of conformity as retailers strive to satisfy the new-found, burgeoning demand and stock the new fashion – and variations upon it – and manufacturers seek to respond to and even anticipate orders from retailers. The result is that soon consumers find the shops have become saturated with the new fashion, and the more fashion-conscious among them begin to look urgently for fresh fashion: the once new fashion is then on the road to becoming old fashioned because as a fashion spreads it is on its way to destruction.

One long-term, though no doubt rather light-hearted, view of this process is provided by what is called Laver's Law. This suggests that the same 'costume', which is 'smart' now, will be:

Indecent	10 years ahead of its time
Shameless	5 years ahead of its time
Smart	now
Dowdy	1 year after its time
Hideous	10 years after its time
Amusing	20 years after its time
Quaint	50 years after its time
Charming	70 years after its time
Romantic	100 years after its time
Beautiful	150 years after its time

(quoted in Lurie, 1981, p. 6)

Up to relatively recent times the ability to indulge in fashion was confined to an affluent minority of the population. For the remainder, the purchase of clothes was likely to be more a matter of functionality: what was important for the majority was having sufficient changes of clean clothes or being able to cope with the vagaries of the climate; for many the chief object was to prolong the life of garments by repairing them or recycling them as 'hand-me-downs'. What happened was that those of high social status might advertise their position by their fashionability, a vital part of which was the cost and exclusivity of an item:

> The cotton printers produced patterns mostly on the more expensive type of fabric, that were calculated to attract well-to-do customers by the refinement and quality of the designs, as well as by their novelty. A constant succession of new designs was produced in small quantities for middle class women who wished to be dressed in patterns that they could be sure had not yet been reproduced on the cheaper fabrics worn by working class women [... M]any fashionable designs were subsequently reproduced by the manufacturers on cheap cotton, a practice which both attracted working class customers wanting to follow the fashion, and *caus[ed] the owners of dresses in the first, expensive printing of a pattern to discard them, because they had become 'common', and to buy new ones.*

(Forty, 1986, pp. 74–5, emphasis added)

Though there is general agreement that fashion in dress is cyclical, there is less agreement about the content of these cycles. In part, what we discover is that instead of there being a discrete, single fashion that runs its course, to be replaced by another discrete fashion, what we are likely to find is that a number of overlapping fashions are changing at different rates and to different degrees – changes that may be pronounced at one time and barely perceptible at another. For this reason alone, the semiotic redundancy referred to above, the 'in-ness' or 'out-ness' of fashion, may prove difficult to identify in practice.

On the other hand, there is widespread agreement that the *pace* of the fashion cycle has quickened very considerably since the nineteenth century, and that since 1945 it has become much faster still. The most important single factor in precipitating this profound change is said to be the emergence in Paris in the mid-nineteenth century of the independent couturier, the most notable of whom was Worth. It was the couturier who designed clothes mostly for upper middle-class women, a still small market it is true, yet a significantly wider one than the exclusive clientele belonging either to the aristocracy or to the haute-bourgeoisie who had formerly held undisputed sway in fashionable circles. Following the rise of the couturier, a new style would typically last no more than the best part of a decade, though sometimes longer – a vast time by present-day standards, of course, yet a sharp diminution from the previous position when a new fashion might well prevail for *several* decades before giving way to a new style.

Nowadays a new fashion may well have difficulty in surviving for a season, let alone for several seasons. A number of disparate factors are usually cited to explain why this is: for example, reference is made to the changing structure and apparatus of the garment industry; to increasing consumer affluence; to the weakening of class boundaries; and to the faster transmission of information in the mass media (Davis, 1992, p. 107).

In the view of some observers these forces – and others – have speeded up the pace of the fashion cycle so much that it threatens to collapse altogether:

> The cycles in fashion get shorter and shorter. How many times have the '60s been revived since the '60s? They're never out long enough to be completely out. Soon all the decades will overlap dangerously. Soon everything in will be simultaneously out.
>
> (Hochswender, 1991, quoted in Davis, 1992, p. 107)

Other observers have been more sanguine about these developments, remarking that 'the study of fads and fashions may serve the student of social change much as the study of fruit flies has served geneticists: neither has to wait long for a new generation to arrive' (Meyerson and Katz, 1973, p. 391).

2.3   The sociological study of fashion

Much of the treatment of fashion in the media is devoted to the latest collections of leading haute couture designers. Such coverage is not to be explained simply as a consequence of it being easy to cover a number of closely sequenced events in Paris or Milan, although this probably plays a part. What seems irresistible to the media is the tension between what is predicted to appear on the catwalk, what actually appears, and how what appears is received in the first instance by fashion editors, store buyers and others involved professionally, and then by the fashion-buying public at large. In all this the opinions of the designers themselves are made to occupy a pivotal position: their pronouncements that 'shoulders will stay wide' or 'skirts will be shorter' are often greeted with the sort of respect usually accorded to international statesmen. This may satisfy the immediate demands of the unfolding drama but, because the very unpredictability of fashion makes these pronouncements unreliable, the general effect is to attach an air of unreality and self-importance to the world of fashion – an effect which may be heightened where what is fashionable one year is the reverse of what was fashionable the year before.

All this helps to explain why it is that conventional sociology has tended to regard fashion as a phenomenon that belongs to the irrational and abnormal. More than this, the simple scarcity of sociological treatments of fashion seems to show that it is also seen as trivial, of peripheral importance. Of course, such apparent irrationality and triviality is far from being confined to fashion in clothes. For example, contrast the never-ending changes that fashion 'dictates' in the styling of cars, with the much less frequent changes that are made in the design of car engines. And, to pursue the transport analogy a step further, while it seems inconceivable that the stage-coach will replace the railway engine, in 'fashion' the equivalent of such a change is not merely not avoided, it is commonplace (Bigg, 1893, p. 35).

If we begin by thinking in terms of science and progress, it is easy to see why fashion appears retrogressive and why it is widely seen as little more than a constantly passing parade of inconsequentialities. This alone might be enough to explain why some modern dictionaries of sociology make no reference at all to fashion, a perception, it might be surmised, that owes something to the extent to which fashion in clothes is identified with *women's* fashions.

Yet the case in favour of undertaking serious sociological study of fashion on the grounds that dress is one of the most significant ways by which we locate ourselves and others in the social world, is surely a powerful one (Corrigan, 1993, p. 143). But this argument chiefly addresses one side of fashion and does not really overcome the problem that economic questions tend to be under-represented in cultural studies. In my view, it is much more compelling to try to consider fashion in terms of both its cultural and its economic aspects than to deal only with one aspect or the other, though it has to be recognized that this approach does not fit very well within established disciplinary boundaries. In taking this approach I am following the social theorist McKenzie Wark who draws our attention to the different aspects of fashion, notably the 'cultural temporality based on wilful forgetting', on the one hand, and, on the other, fashion as 'an interrelated cycle of production and consumption, culture and industry' (Wark, 1991, p. 61).

There are a number of ways in which sociology might approach fashion. For example, we might explore the role and meaning of fashion for societies, groups or individuals; we might try to examine the relationship between fashion in general or – more usually – a particular fashion trend or item and a climate of opinion in society; we might analyse the interrelationships between designers, manufacturers, retailers and consumers and, indeed, the implications that fashion has for modern economic life; or we might study the way an item becomes fashionable, how it moves from minority to majority acceptance and how it declines into a state of unfashionability.

None of these approaches is likely to be straightforward, nor is any of them necessarily discrete. For instance, if we seek to establish what a particular fashion item means to those who adopt it, a number of supplementary questions arise: for example, how do these meanings compare with the meanings of those who adopted the fashion before them, and of those who adopted it afterwards? Is the meaning altered by some modification to the 'basic' garment? In addition, it might be prudent to consider if the wearer is merely the 'mute carrier of trappings that scream out meanings to the passing socio-semiotician' (Corrigan, 1993, p. 145), as in the New Yorker cartoon (Figure 3.3), or whether we should seek to identify possible disjunctions of meaning between the wearer of an item and an observer.

ACTIVITY 2

You might try to apply these points to wearers of jeans – perhaps including yourself – referring back, if necessary, to my earlier discussion.

fashion code

Bear in mind that a **fashion code** is, with certain exceptions, a code which is much closer to an aesthetic code than it is to more reliable codes, such as traffic signals. In other words, meanings in dress are likely to be more ambiguous and more differentiated than they are in many other realms, a point that was touched on in my initial discussion of jeans. Aesthetic expression

> ... aims to communicate notions, subtleties, [and] complexities which have not yet been formulated and therefore, as soon as an aesthetic code comes to be generally perceived as a code (as a way of expressing notions which have already been articulated), then works of art will tend to move beyond it. They question, parody, and generally undermine it, while exploring its mutations and extensions. One might even say that much of the interest of works of art lies in the ways in which they explore and modify the codes which they seem to be using.

(Culler, 1976, p. 100)

FIGURE 3.3   Drawing by R. Chast; © 1988 The New Yorker Magazine, Inc.

When we try to apply this analysis to fashion codes many of these elements are immediately apparent – questioning, parodying and contradicting existing fashions is not merely rife, but probably *de rigeur*. But in emphasizing these aspects of fashion it is easy to overlook the extent to which new fashions strive to sustain some sort of connection to the most recent expressions of fashion.

What is particularly distinctive about the fashion code is that it must pass through the filter of the fashion industry. Thus the suggested code modifications displayed on the catwalks of Paris stand to be rejected, toned-down or embraced not only by a host of publicists, critics, journalists and fashion leaders, but also by garment manufacturers, retailers and store buyers. To say that 'the fashion industry in its totality is necessarily deeply implicated in the apprehension, definition, diffusion and dissipation of the collective moods and tensions that feed fashion' (Davis, 1992, p. 115) – whether by the construction of 'seasons', the choices of buyers, the contents of the fashion press or the merchandising strategies of major stores and chains, or by the structure of the garment industry – is therefore to realize that a new fashion does not merely stand in aesthetic relationship to previous fashions, it also has a material relationship to the cost and complexity of its design, manufacture and distribution.

This is not intended to reduce fashion simply to a matter of its economic apparatus. However, it needs to be recognized that fashion involves not just culture but also industry, and not just consumption but also production (and, by extension, the inter-connections between these different elements). So far from diminishing the importance of fashion, this approach serves to increase its importance for the same reason that Roche uses to support his problematizing of the history of clothing, that is to say that it is 'a way of penetrating to the heart of social history [by] posing the essential question: what should be produced? With its train of attendant questions: what should be consumed, what distributed?' (Roche, 1994, p. 5).

I would only wish to add to Roche's comment that we also need to ask whether changes in the consumption of fashion contribute to changes in the organization of production – but that is something that is explored later.

2.4   Classical views of fashion

Much sociological writing on the subject of fashion is aimed at developing, adapting or rebutting the classic work of the sociologist George Simmel, written in 1904. Simmel's analysis was based on the premise that the prerequisite for fashion's existence is a relatively open society, consisting of several classes in which an elite strives to separate itself from the bulk of the population by means of adopting observable signs, notably in dress. This adoption has the effect of encouraging those closest to the elite to embrace these same signs in order to gain the superior status that is associated with the elite and they, in turn, are copied by those inferior in status to them; and so the process is repeated down through the social strata. To the extent that through this sequence of events the elite class loses its distinct identity, it is persuaded to devise new signs of differentiation and this sets off the entire cycle of demarcation and emulation once again. In this way what ensues is a continual and arbitrary succession of fashions, each of which marches inexorably to its doom. (See also the discussion of Bourdieu on distinction and conspicuous consumption (**du Gay, Hall et al.**, 1997) and on distinction and the body (**Shilling**, 1997).)

As Blumer, another sociologist, says, Simmel's analysis is essentially very simple, yet though simple it has several significant virtues: for instance, it states that fashion requires a certain type of socio-cultural environment if it is to exist; it emphasizes the importance of prestige in the operation of fashion; and, of particular note, it is unequivocal that the essence of fashion lies in the process of change (Blumer, 1969, p. 278). To these conditions Blumer adds several conditions of his own which help to clarify our understanding further. Thus, Blumer states that for fashion to operate in a particular area it must be marked by a premium being placed on staying 'up to date' and, conversely, a penalty being placed on becoming outmoded;

models of fashions must be observable and their adoption must not be too severely constrained by absence of the means – such as wealth – necessary to acquire them; and the value of competing fashions cannot be established by means of objective tests, but is dependent on their being adopted or relinquished by significant numbers of those who, by common consent, are regarded as arbiters in matters of taste, an aspect on which Blumer places special emphasis, and to which further reference will be made (Blumer, 1969, pp. 286–7).

As has been said, of all these conditions, perhaps the most vital is *change*, for not only is it universally held to be central to fashion, but it is this which helps to distinguish fashion from several concepts (for example, style, custom and convention) that would otherwise seem to be closely and confusingly proximate, but where the emphasis is much more on what is customary, conventional, standardized or long-established. Indeed, it is the presence or absence of change that permits Simmel to draw a distinction between 'primitive' societies, where 'conditions of life favour correspondingly infrequent change of fashions', and 'civilized' societies, where 'whatever is exceptional, bizarre or conspicuous, or whatever departs from the customary norm, exercises a peculiar charm upon the man of culture' (Simmel, 1973/1904, p. 176).

The distinction between societies which are subject to change and societies which are relatively unchanging was usually employed to distinguish between western (modern) and non-western (traditional) societies, but to pursue this nowadays is to risk generating more heat than light. Nevertheless, we can focus on the nature of this change by looking instead at two simultaneous discourses that Roche finds in his examination of French society of the *ancien régime* (that is, France in the period before the revolution of 1789):

> ... one was of the stationary economy, in which everyone had their place and sought to consume according to their rank, where clothing revealed status. [In the other] in contrast the practitioners and interpreters of fashion exalted the desire of the privileged, true or false, to distinguish themselves from lesser mortals. Clothes became weapons in the battle of appearances. They were employed to erect a barrier, to stave off the pressure of imitators and followers who must be kept at a distance, and who always lagged behind in some nuance in the choice of colour or way of tying a ribbon or cravat. In a world ruled by the conventions of fashion, innumerable signs thus helped everyone to find their way.
>
> (Roche, 1994, pp. 4–5)

Thus we can see that change in fashion does not need to be extensive, but may involve nothing but slight modifications to the length of hem, the width of lapel – in other words, the smallest change may have the largest effect.

FIGURE 3.4
The Promenade
of the Palais
Royal Gallery,
Paris, 1787
(painting by
Debucourt,
detail).

2.5   Summary: fashion at the heart of social history

You will recall that earlier (p. 135) reference was made to Roche's argument that by providing a means of posing the essential question 'what should be produced?' – and its attendant questions relating to consumption and distribution – fashion lies at the heart of social history.

READING A

I want you now to read a short extract from Roche's book, *The Culture of Clothing*, entitled 'From crafts to customers: the Parisian clothing economy', provided as Reading A at the end of this chapter.

Before you do so, it is vital for you to understand that Roche argues that as far as the France of the *ancien régime* is concerned, economy and society in their entirety depended on fashion. By saying this he refers not simply to the manufacturers and merchants involved in the production and distribution of clothes, but also the development of new patterns and fabrics which were, in his view, 'both cause and consequence of sartorial competitiveness' (1994, p. 7). In other words, for Roche, the study of clothing involves not just examining the *real* (the structure of manufacturing clothes is the obvious example), but also the *imaginary* (what Roche refers to here as sartorial competitiveness) and, moreover, it demands that we treat these two elements as being closely connected and overlapping. For this reason he places particular emphasis on studying the relationship between the production of garments – the strategies and arrangements of manufacturers and merchants – and their consumption – via countless decisions of millions of consumers.

You should now read Reading A. As you read, you might find it helpful to make a note of what Roche has to say about the following matters:

1   What importance does Roche ascribe to the pressure of the consumer market?

2   What are the two types of production that Roche believes to be evident at this time and what is their significance?

3   Why was it said that new conditions rendered old regulations useless and, if true, what implications did this have?

4   According to Roche, how was the relationship between producers and consumers changing?

You will have noticed that the emphasis in Simmel's classic analysis of fashion is on change and up-to-datedness and also on the process by which the elite separates itself from the mass. You might think at first that this analysis has much more to do with fashion as consumption, than with fashion in terms of production. But as Roche helps to demonstrate, the consumption of fashion is closely related to its production. Thus given that fashion entails change and then more change, it follows that seemingly esoteric questions, such as the adoption of observable signs or the reliability of clothed appearance, may have important implications for the production of fashion. This is something which is pursued in more depth in later sections, but it is a theme that underlies this chapter.

3   The consumption of fashion

3.1   The sources of fashion

Despite the considerable merits of Simmel's analysis of fashion, which were discussed in section 2.4, Blumer (1969) considers it to be deficient in certain important respects. His first criticism is that though Simmel's treatment is quite appropriate to fashion in dress in seventeenth-century, eighteenth-century and nineteenth-century Europe, it fails to measure up to the operation of contemporary fashion, characterized as it is said to be by an emphasis on **modernity**. In this context, 'modernity' refers in particular to: modernity

1   the tremendous growth in complexity on the consumption side of fashion, and

2   the consequences that this complexity has had for the manufacture of clothes, particularly in terms of the arrangements of production and the organization of work.

In short, the variations in fashions and in styles have become much more complex whether viewed from the standpoint of consumption or from that of production – where, until recently, the order of the day was for there to be long runs of standardized garments on a scale sufficient to justify the costs of installing the requisite machinery. But this is to get ahead of an argument that is taken up in some detail in section 4.

Blumer was especially anxious to question one of Simmel's fundamental contentions: that a style comes into fashion because an elite gives its authority to that style. In Blumer's opinion, style comes into fashion only if it corresponds to what he terms 'the incipient taste of the fashion-consuming public'. Though the prestige of an elite may very well influence the direction of that taste, it does not control or determine it. In support of this argument, Blumer points out that there are plentiful examples of 'fashion' ignoring the taste of those of the highest prestige and so-called leaders of fashion: where fashion operates 'it assumes an imperative position'. By this he means that it sanctions what is to be done, that it is indifferent to criticism and that it bypasses those who do not accept it (Blumer, 1969, p. 276). For example, he mentions the failure of the well-financed campaign marshalled by clothing manufacturers in the period 1919–22, which enlisted the 'cooperation of the heads of fashion houses, fashion magazines, fashion commentators, actresses and acknowledged fashion leaders' to halt and reverse the trend towards shorter skirts. This campaign involved taking every opportunity that presented itself to declare that long dresses were returning – but these declarations were quite ineffective and the fashion for short skirts continued unabated (ibid., p. 281).

In Blumer's view, a fashion is born or dies not because a style is picked up or discarded by an elite, but because it is or is no longer in tune with developing taste. This, he contends, is a major departure from Simmel who depicted fashion as an outcome or process of class differentiation. Instead, fashion is treated by Blumer as an act of collective mood, taste and choice: 'the fact that this process of collective selection is mysterious – it is mysterious because we do not understand it – does not contradict in any way that it takes place' (ibid., p. 282). Nor does its mystery allow us to deny, Blumer argues, that the origin, formation and development of collective taste – for example, in the way fashion innovators may indicate the paths along which incipient taste may develop – constitutes 'the huge problematic area in fashion' and, moreover, constitutes the first aspect of modernity in fashion (ibid.).

Nevertheless, Blumer's study of the women's fashion industry in Paris helps us to begin to appreciate how this incipient taste emerges. What struck him included the following:

1 The setting of fashion involved an intense process of selection. For instance, of the hundred or more designs of women's evening wear presented by a major Parisian fashion house at its seasonal opening, the fashion house's management was able to indicate about thirty designs

from among which the assemblage of between one and two hundred store buyers would then choose no more than six or eight. But for some unexplained reason they were generally unable to predict which these six or eight chosen designs would be.

2   He discovered that the similarity of the choices that the buyers made could be explained in relation to their immersion in and preoccupation with a strikingly common world consisting of, *inter alia*, the diligent study of fashion publications, close observation of the lines stocked in the 'competitor' stores which their fellow buyers represented and, above all, a constant examination of prevailing and emerging tastes in the women's dress market. Just as was suggested in my introduction (see the store buyer's nightmare), 'their success, indeed their vocational fate, depended on their ability to sense the direction of taste in (the fashion) public' (ibid., p. 279).

3   Blumer discovered that the dress designers created their new styles – it should go without saying that this was with the hope of securing their adoption by the store buyers – by

a)   scouring plates of former fashions and of costumes of 'far-off' people;

FIGURE 3.5   Paris haute couture (Christian Lacroix, 1996).

FIGURE 3.6   A barrage of photographers at the end of the catwalk.

b) examining both current and recent fashions; and most significantly by

c) developing a deep familiarity with recent expressions of modernity –
whether they be manifest in the arts, literature, politics or elsewhere –
and translating the themes they uncovered thereby into dress designs
(though this is not to say that fashion should be seen, as some see it,
merely as a 'mirror' of a given moment or era).

From these observations, Blumer came to the conclusion that fashion was
being set:

> through a process of free selection from among a large number of competing
> models; that the creators of the models are seeking to catch and give
> expression to what we may call the direction of modernity; and that the
> buyers, who through their choices set the fashion, are acting as the
> unwitting agents of a fashion-consuming public whose incipient tastes the
> buyers are seeking to anticipate.
>
> (ibid., p. 280)

It can be argued that of all these complex elements, closely interconnected as
they clearly are, the most obvious is also the most important, namely the
way in which a new, would-be fashion relates to the fashion that is in mode.
That is to say, the new fashion seeks – inevitably – to extend, qualify,
comment on or contradict the existing fashion: in effect it stands in what
Davis calls a sort of 'dialectical relationship' with the prevailing fashion
(Davis, 1992, p. 130).

3.2 The diffusion of fashion

Broadly speaking, the first of the two aspects of modernity in fashion with
which I began section 3.1 can be equated with the consumption side of
fashion, while the second aspect is more closely related to its production
(though this demarcation should not be treated too rigidly). As I intend to
show later on, this second aspect is complex enough, but the first aspect,
which is examined next, is not only complex, it is also elusive.

As Blumer explains, because fashion is perennially modern it must keep up
with developments not just in its own field – the appearance on the market
of new fabrics would be an example – but also with those in related fields in
the fine arts, and in the wider social world – the emancipation of women
being an obvious example.

It should be quickly apparent to you that this portrait of modernity, to which
designers are said to be trying to respond and to give expression in each
season's collections, though it may be of great importance, is nevertheless

bound to be extremely difficult to specify and pin down – a problem of which Blumer and others of like mind are acutely aware.

Thus we can speak of designers somehow sensing 'currents of identity instability pervading a people and seek[ing] through the artful manipulation of the conventional visual symbols of clothing presentation to lend expression to them, or alternatively to contain, deflect or sublimate them' (Davis, 1992, p. 17). But it is altogether more demanding to begin to delineate the precise contents of this communication or to trace its operation.

There is much less mystery, however, if for one moment we accept Simmel's analysis of the matter, in forming an appreciation of what happens once the designers have produced their designs and the buyers have made their choices from among these designs. Indeed, if you recall the discussion of the fashion cycle (section 2.2) and of classical discussions of fashion (section 2.4), you should be able to anticipate what I am going to say. Here we have a straightforward scenario which commences with persons of social prestige taking up a new style, continues with a larger number following their example and ends with each individual (or at least with all but a small minority) feeling that she cannot afford to be different. This theory of **fashion diffusion**, which, as we have seen, is criticized by Blumer, is known technically as one of class differentiation, but it is known more popularly as the 'trickle-down' theory of fashion.

fashion diffusion

Suppose for a moment that we choose to distance ourselves from this view, which was, until recently, dominant, and opt instead for the view that fashion originates through designers identifying incipient collective tastes. What is far from clear is whether, if we do this, we must thereby abandon the idea that fashion – and here we are talking specifically about women's fashion – spreads from a 'creative centre' (usually thought of as a specific place – most often Paris – or places) to ever more remote fashion-consuming publics.

In other words, we may need to distinguish between the rather narrow conception that fashion is determined solely by the prestige of a social elite and the apparently more sophisticated view that fashion is generally determined by a relatively small number of 'players' who really count: a small group of fashion designers, a larger group of fashion buyers, those publicists and editors who inform the 'fashion conscious' about the direction that fashion is taking, as well as a small minority of fashionable consumers (whether we term them 'fashion innovators', 'fashion leaders' or call them by some other name).

Amongst these several types of 'player', as we might expect, most attention has been devoted to the power and influence of the designers – especially those producing haute couture in Paris (and, to a lesser extent, those working in New York, though British- and Italian-based designers have not been ignored). In this respect, the scholarly focus has, until recently at least, resembled popular beliefs about fashion which are encapsulated very well in George Bernard Shaw's remark that 'a fashion is nothing but an induced epidemic, proving that epidemics can be induced by tradesmen' (Auden and Kronenberger, 1962, p. 126, quoted in Davis, 1992, p. 109). Of course, which designers really count will depend in large measure on other key players, notably certain fashion editors and store buyers, so there is an element of circularity here.

ACTIVITY 3

Before you read on I would like you to jot down some brief notes about why you think that the concentrated focus on Parisian haute couture developed and why it may have come to be seen as outmoded by some students of fashion.

When you have done this, compare your thoughts on the latter question with my comments (in the remainder of this section and in the next section).

If we concentrate too much on who ought to be regarded as a key player or on which type of player has most influence on fashion, we may well neglect more important matters. We risk losing sight of the extent to which 'fashion' is these days an industry which not only employs millions of people, but also – and crucially – must *sell* to millions of people. In other words, our discussion of what is fashionable, and who it is that defines what is fashionable, might be thought to be incomplete if it did not take into account the size and nature of the market or markets for fashion and, by extension, the system of production for that market or markets.

In recent times the fashion industry has been transformed by a number of important developments. On the one hand we have the rise of mass production (see below, sections 4.2 and 4.3), but on the other hand there has been a growth in the diversity of products and a growth both in the number of markets and types of selling.

Probably the key development in fashion has been the growth in ready-to-wear clothes – whether displayed and sold in department stores and other retail outlets or by mail order. The American innovation of purchase by mail order is especially interesting in this context, not just because it enabled consumers in the most remote of locations to keep up with trends in fashion, but because it helped to establish the importance of what may be described as non-elite fashion. The size of this mail order market may be gauged by the statistic that in the early years of the twentieth century more than ten million Americans shopped in this way and by the fact that the bulk of the often enormous catalogues (in 1921 the Sears catalogue ran to 1,064 pages) was devoted to women's wear. Yet, as Craik points out, there has been little academic research into the mail order industry in general, and still less into the influence that the mail order industry has had in the formation of taste in clothing or fashion (Craik, 1994, pp. 207–9).

Despite these developments, even into the 1950s (and perhaps later still) many people would have accepted with little or no hesitation that 'fashion' had a distinct centre, namely Parisian haute couture. If this was indeed thought to be so, it was not, of course, meant in the sense that all who bought their clothes from, say, a Sears catalogue in America or a John Lewis department store in England, were buying one-off Parisian originals, but rather in the sense that it was Parisian couturiers who set the pace in the information landscape of fashion: in other words, it was they who decided whether an inch or two should come off skirts or whether shoulders should stay wide. As Wark puts it, it was 'they (who) dressed the fashion elites and sold each season's style to the mass manufacturers – or watched the latter simply steal the popular styles' (Wark, 1991, p. 62).

The taken for granted view of the diffusion of fashion was thus that it was created centrally and then transmitted towards the periphery. That is to say, the designs formulated by Parisian haute couturiers would move at varying pace not merely geographically outwards, but also socially downwards – probably losing a good deal in subtlety, quality and workmanship as they did so.

Davis aptly portrays this process as conveying a classic example of globalization, in that it contains 'the tacit assumption of a fashion-consuming public, international in scope, whose tastes and standards were located essentially within the vast shadow and penumbra of a Eurocentric culture' (Davis, 1992, p. 200).

In contrast to this picture, the increasingly heard contention is that in recent times – let us say from the 1960s or 1970s onwards – there has been an increase in what is variously termed 'polycentrism', 'polymorphism' and 'pluralism' in fashion. Thus, to use Wark's words once more, we now find ourselves confronted by 'new modes of fashionability in a far more widely dispersed information landscape' (1991, p. 62), by which he chiefly refers to increasing consumer affluence, the emergence of fashionable ready-to-wear clothes and, in particular, to the appearance of other sources and manifestations of fashion and style, notably those emanating from pop music and from youth culture. From this perspective, not only is it seen as pointless to turn to Paris or Milan to discover the direction of fashion – much less will there be a single fashion in play, such as, Dior's New Look – but in addition, it is said that fashion now originates from a diverse range of groups, sources *and* designers.

FIGURE 3.7
London fashion away from the catwalk, 1996: top down or bottom up?

What this entails is that a whole series of cultural and sub-cultural groups may create their own fashions, or make something fashionable by adopting it and, as we have seen in the case of jeans, by adopting a fashion they may cause it to move outward and upward to other groups and social strata – even to the point of such an item eventually becoming high fashion itself.

Whereas in the classic 'trickle-down' model there are regular seasons, there are no such seasons with these new sources of fashion, notably 'street fashion', 'pop culture' and 'ethnic cultures'. The chief result of this is that the supposedly orderly dissemination of couture copies and derivatives on which mass production is assumed to depend is no longer possible (Wark, 1991, pp. 64–5). On the one hand, so-called 'street fashion' very often takes no notice of designer innovations or merely adopts certain of their elements (Craik, 1994, p. ix); and, on the other hand, the constant search for inspiration by high-fashion designers to which Blumer refers (see section 2.6) is nowadays just as likely to be directed at appropriating or adapting street fashions in their own creations as they are to be scouring more traditional sources for ideas.

multiple fashion
systems

On the basis of these and other developments it seems perfectly reasonable to conclude that what we have now are **multiple fashion systems** in which fashion moves up, down and along from a variety of starting positions and in several directions, rather than a single system in which fashion only moves in one direction, 'trickling down' from the elite to the majority. If this is so, we should be looking for new fashions in the street, from students in colleges of fashion, from 'pop' designers, among ethnic minorities and so on, and not simply – or perhaps not at all – in haute couture. In other words, what was global in origin has become, to a considerable degree, local.

To summarize, changing views about fashion in clothes – from Simmel onwards – seem to present us with a number of distinct epochs, each of which is characterized by different systems of production and contrasting types of consumption: thus at one moment fashion is determined by an elite before 'trickling down' to the mass and the dominant form of manufacture is craft production; at the next moment fashion is dominated by mass production and mass consumption; and at a third moment the emphasis is on 'flexible production' (see below) and consumption becomes more diverse and segmented in line with the increasingly 'polycentric' origins of fashion.

3.3   Re-evaluating haute couture

The role of Parisian haute couture (and that of haute couture in other countries as well) in setting the new fashions in women's clothes has clearly changed in certain important respects. Nonetheless, this is certainly not to concede that its role has been so sharply diminished that we should ignore haute couture altogether and simply look elsewhere to see who or what sets the fashion agenda. In the light of the developments that have been described (and with which you may be familiar from your own observations), this may seem to be an odd or even obstinate stance to take. Despite this, I hope to persuade you that my position is at least tenable.

Taking this position does not mean that we have to completely reject this more open view of the sources of new fashions – indeed, it would be rather foolish to do so. However, there are a number of important qualifications that need to be made to it. In the first instance, the growing emphasis on identifying other sources of fashion inspiration and influence, notably the growing fascination with pop designers, has often had more to do with the excitement and novelty of the actual designs than it has with the extent – if any – to which these designs are or will be in production. Indeed in more than one case when an up-and-coming British designer has been telephoned by a fashion magazine and asked to send round one of their latest designs to be photographed for publication, it turns out that the design had never been produced at all – even as a prototype.

The question remains, however: should these developments cause us to desist from our traditional gaze on what is being worn on the catwalk and refocus our attention on the 'grassroots', on the 'street' itself? Or is it wiser to take account of these developments and use them as a reason for re-examining the relationship between high fashion and everyday fashion? Let me explain why the latter option has more to recommend it than the former.

First, it should be pointed out that because high fashion designers borrow from the 'street' this is, of itself, no reason to lose interest in high fashion; indeed, such borrowing does not necessarily diminish the ability of high-fashion designers to exploit their designs commercially and may actually enhance it by taking it in new directions.

Second, and more importantly, it is one thing to conclude that Paris is no longer the centre of fashion (in the sense that fashion should no longer be equated with haute couture), but it is quite another matter to overlook the extent to which the Parisian couturiers (and their counterparts elsewhere, notably in New York) have succeeded in becoming such major players that the designation 'pret-a-porter' may be not simply more pretentious sounding (which in Britain and the USA it is) than is the more down-to-earth phrase 'ready-to-wear', but is in fact somewhat more revealing about the sources of influence in fashion. Thus, the most compelling evidence of the continuing relevance of high fashion – and of the centre-to-periphery model – notwithstanding the developments that have been outlined, lies in 'the vast economic power and *global scope* of the international fashion conglomerates with their multi-billion dollar annual revenues: the St Laurents, Chanels, Armanis, Kleins, Laurens, Kawakubos etc.' (Davis, 1992, p. 203, emphasis added). These conglomerates, of course, encompass much more than just fashion in clothes, but deal as well in jewellery, cosmetics, accessories and, above all, in perfume.

Third, and equally important, rather than being replaced, the centre–periphery model of fashion has taken new and more complex forms – such that it is now profoundly changed. It is to some of these new forms that I now turn.

It is important to make clear that the relationship between high fashion and everyday fashion has in any case not been quite as straightforward as it might have seemed. For instance, this relationship had been significantly modified – long before any claims about growing polycentrism and the like were being made – in the late nineteenth and early twentieth centuries by the rapid rise of mass production. This allowed creditable facsimiles of clothes that for reasons of cost and complexity could previously only have been produced by the couturiers' own skilled workers (Davis, 1992, p. 139). Thereafter – despite the appearance of designs that the mass media are prone to highlight as demonstrating how far-removed high fashion is from everyday life – in practice, the artistic licence, creativity and fantasy of haute couture has been generally and seriously constrained by the presence of the mass manufacturers of garments and the vast orders that they may be prepared to place.

Davis provides a very interesting explanation of the effect that such constraints might have on the designers themselves and, more significantly, on their financial backers. What is said to happen is that the designers 'privilege' some of the offerings in their collections, namely those that are thought likely to prove popular with the fashion-buying public *and* which will not pose serious problems for the mass manufacturer, for example, in terms of the availability of fabric or because of threats to the integrity of the finished garment caused by too narrow cutting and joining tolerances:

> Thus, of the several dozen items of apparel presented on the (haute couture) runway, only a few are 'genuine entries'. The others are either sheer 'throwaways' meant to lend an aura of 'depth' to the show or, more strategically, purposefully exaggerated renditions of the more marketable items the design house hopes to cash in.
>
> (Davis, 1992, p. 152)

Not only are the 'privileged' items given favourable treatment when the collection is presented, but the fashion house is quite willing to provide toned-down versions of their designs that will be more suitable for the markets which the store buyers represent (ibid.). You might wish to compare this view with Blumer's findings on the same subject (see section 3.1 above).

In other words, the apparent distinction between elite designer fashion and high street fashion has been nowhere near as great as it is often assumed to be. Perhaps the best illustration of this has been the exponential growth in licensing agreements by and on behalf of the major fashion houses – not just for ready-to-wear clothes, but also for various fashion accessories and a range of consumer products. For example, Pierre Cardin has licensed his name and logo to more than eight hundred products (Milbank, 1990, p. 64), though this is not to say that this process is always smooth, witness Geoffrey Beene's complaint that, 'Sometimes they [the licensees] want your name and what you stand for, and then they don't want any input ... Sometimes I totally OK a collection and later I see in a store something with my name which I didn't even design. That gives me a cardiac arrest' (quoted in Coleridge, 1988, pp. 38–9).

This leaves open the possibility that even if we think we 'own' a designer label – after all, there it hangs in the wardrobe – our belief may be misplaced or at least open to question: leaving aside counterfeits (see below), is our prized garment really the creation of the designer whose name is on the label, did the designer merely approve a licensee's design, or did the designer even see it at all? And does this matter to us and if so, why? Is this comparable in some way to the differing reactions that we might have to possessing a work of art depending on whether it is an original (equivalent, perhaps, to haute couture), a limited edition, or simply an un-numbered print, and so on?

The cachet of the designer's name and logo is such that there has developed an extensive and sophisticated network to counterfeit designer items of all sorts. Indeed, as Craik says, counterfeiting amounts to an overt form of the practice of 'prestigious imitation' that constitutes the very foundation of the fashion industry, that is to say, the popularization of a style by means of modification and differentiation for different markets (Craik, 1994, p. 213). A good, and perhaps extreme, example of this is Katherine Hamnett's claim that thirty unlicensed manufacturers – from South America to South-east Asia – had between them produced half a million copies of her slogan T-shirts. In general, by the 1970s and 1980s counterfeiting had become so efficiently managed that the overnight couriering of catwalk photographs to pirate manufacturers was common. (As I write it is probably all done on the Internet.) The most bizarre aspect of counterfeiting may be that, apparently, in some cases 'the vogue is not to wear the genuine item but the fashionable facsimile' (Stead, 1991, p. 41).

If haute couture was simply a matter of attending to its exclusive clientele, who number no more than a few thousand world-wide – that is, those personal customers who actually attend the collections, or who, even more impressively, have items from the collections sent *to them* – we might be able to make little sense of the alliances formed between haute couture houses, fabric and garment manufacturers, and financial backers. Yet it is these alliances that reveal one of the most significant connections that exist, linking the individual workmanship of haute couture and the huge edifice of the mass production of ready-to-wear clothes. One of the most important of such alliances was the so-called High Fashion-Industry Accord signed in Italy in 1971, by which Italian couturiers received a subsidy if their new season's lines conformed to prior guidelines that they had agreed with the major garment manufacturers (Wark, 1991, p. 64). Since this pioneering agreement, these alliances have developed in Italy to the point at which the decision to launch a new designer label is often taken jointly by the designer, the garment manufacturer and the fabric firm. Moreover, the costs of the first few collections will, like as not, be borne by the manufacturer and the fabric house until the stage is reached that the label is sufficiently profitable to allow the designer to repay whatever debt has built up.

What should we conclude from all this? In my view, the present day situation of haute couture is perfectly and succinctly expressed in the remark of George Jolles, president of the huge French manufacturer of designer clothes, Biderman: 'It's time to stop deifying our creativity and think about how we can sell' (quoted in Coleridge, 1988, p. 182), hardly the attitude that we might have once expected.

4 The manufacturing and retailing of fashion

4.1 The role of major retailers

If we try to assess the relative contributions to what is produced and what is consumed in fashion, there is a good case for saying that (major) fashion retailers (and the store buyers who act for them) are more significant than manufacturers, designers and even, the fashion-consuming public itself. However, the inter-relationships between these categories are complex and, in addition, some of these categories are not as distinct as they might seem at first – thus we find in one important instance a so-called 'manufacturer without factories' (Marks and Spencer), and in another what has been termed a 'producer with shops' (Benetton). These complications help to explain (in this section and the following sections) why the discussion of the role and character of the retailing of fashion is not, nor should it be, treated wholly separately from that of the manufacturing of fashion.

Many of the changes in the nature and terrain of fashion can, nevertheless, be grasped by examining the power of leading clothing retailers and, in particular, the relationship that they have with fabric producers and garment manufacturers and their involvement with production and design issues.

What is very striking is that in the advanced industrial countries (AICs) there has been a growing trend in the retail clothing sector for sales to become concentrated in major retailing chains and in large buying groups. This trend is especially pronounced in the UK where Marks and Spencer and the Burton Group together account for approximately 25 per cent of all clothes sold. Such a concentration of retailing power has led to these and other major retailers becoming more and more concerned with matters such as product specification and design: a development that may be contrasted with an era when such issues were habitually regarded as more the province of those higher up the 'textile chain' and manufacturers might have seen themselves as producing 'for stock' rather than for their (eventual) customers, the retailers.

It might be expected that in the UK this concentration of retailing power would have led to less competition between retailers, but this was not how it turned out. Perhaps because, since the 1950s, householders have allocated a diminishing proportion of their income to clothing and footwear, retailers have found themselves in an increasingly competitive market. One of the chief consequences of this is that they discovered slowly but surely that there was a limit to the sales and profits that could be secured by their long-standing reliance on the 'economies of scale' associated with large-scale production. Instead, they began to comprehend that there was significant advantage to be derived by encouraging the development of diverse markets in clothing and fashion, in so far as 'consumer pursuit of individuality offers firms a seemingly endless potential to extend the levels of market segmentation *and to generate product redundancy*' (Rhodes, 1993, p. 162; emphasis added).

This is hardly to be wondered at, for nowhere, of course, is product redundancy more of the essence than it is in fashion in clothes (think of the message of Alexander McKendrick's film, *The Man in the White Suit*, which shows how jobs and investment are threatened at all levels of the clothing industry when an 'indestructible' garment is invented). And so, in these circumstances, retailers have sought to extend the designation 'fashion' to more and more of their products. The degree to which they have succeeded in this endeavour may be gathered from an official survey carried out in America – but which may, nevertheless, also serve to suggest the general position in the UK. According to this survey, 80 per cent of apparel products had in-shop 'lives' of twenty weeks *or less* and 35 per cent had lives of ten weeks *or less* (Rhodes, 1992, p. 30).

In order to fulfil these twin goals of increasing both market segmentation and product redundancy, retailers have been obliged to go beyond their traditional areas of expertise in distribution, display and selling. It is now in their interest to keep in close contact with manufacturers in order not only to provide detailed feedback on patterns of sales, but, even more significantly, to become involved in the design of both individual products and ranges of products.

We can see these developments very clearly if we look at Marks and Spencer:

> In order that this technological approach to retailing could be realized in practical terms, it was not only essential that Marks and Spencer technologists be consulted when a merchandiser detected a 'technical problem', but also that they should play an active part in the process of commercial decision taking.
>
> (Braham, 1985, p. 130)

In the case of Marks and Spencer the close inter-connection between the commercial and the technological is evident in several ways: in its expertise in technical matters and production technologies Marks and Spencer came to outstrip many of its suppliers; this, together with Marks and Spencer's pre-eminence as a retailer, enabled them to set technical standards for much of the UK garment industry; and these advantages also left Marks and Spencer well placed to persuade their suppliers to invest in new equipment – a form of 'pull-through technology' – which helped garment manufacturers to respond effectively to shorter lead times and to the improved data collection by **electronic point-of-sale (EPOS) systems** (Braham, 1985, pp. 135 and 140).

electronic point-of-sale (EPOS) systems

4.2   The growth of segmented markets in fashion

For many years it had come to be assumed that the manufacture of clothes was increasingly a matter of the high-volume production of a slowly changing range of garments and that, therefore, 'fashion' was of relatively marginal importance. In these circumstances, it is to be expected that retailers – particularly those retailers capable of placing orders in bulk – would wish to take advantage of the economies of scale associated with mass production.

To the extent that this is true, the outlook for the AIC-based garment industries was bound to be gloomy. This is because it appeared that they would sooner or later be undercut by the transfer of technology to manufacturers in less developed and newly industrializing countries (LDCs and NICs) who would enjoy a number of vital advantages: not only would they be able to train workers in the simple and repetitive skills required, they would not be constrained by the burden of social and welfare costs as would manufacturers operating in AICs and, crucially, they would need to pay their workers very little. Indeed, this prognosis seems to find confirmation in what happened in the 1960s and 1970s, during which time the AICs commanded a declining share of world trade in clothing and, in addition, there was a continuing loss of jobs among AIC clothing workers.

Yet if the mass market for clothes becomes fragmented in the way that was described in the previous section, and if fashion comes to occupy a higher priority, the balance of advantage between manufacturers in AICs and those in LDCs and NICs might begin to shift back again: the differentiation of markets and products now favoured by retailers, and the likelihood that this, in turn, would contribute to (as well as express) frequent and volatile changes in consumer demand, may have several significant consequences for both retailers and manufacturers. It means, for example, that the practice of retailers keeping large reserves of limited and little-changing lines would have to end, or be applied with much more discrimination, and that the advantage to manufacturers of long production runs of garments would, therefore, be severely eroded. And by the same token, there is likely to be a bigger premium placed on the ability of manufacturers to operate with lower inventories of stock and to rely on being able to respond quickly and flexibly to orders from retailers – which are, in turn, going to be based closely on fluctuations in sales of different garments, styles and colours. (The evolving relationship between retailers and manufacturers is discussed in more detail in the next section.)

It is worth pausing for a moment, however, to consider whether it is sensible to modify this picture of there having been quite such a dramatic swing away from mass production to flexible, small batch, production as is often claimed, and as the preceding remarks might suggest. For example, Leopold contends that the degree of difference that is supposed to separate the craft-based system of individual production of high fashion from the mass production of everyday fashion has been much exaggerated. He believes that 'the rapidly changing proliferation of style in women's clothes' distinguishes their production not only from production in other industries, but also from other (more predictable) branches of the clothing industry. And he goes on to argue that this has meant that though the industry has adopted the rhetoric of mass production, it has never fully adopted its techniques, relying instead on hand-finishing and on the individual sewing machine (Leopold, 1992, pp. 102 and 105, cited in Craik, 1994, p. 211). In my view, not only is there a good deal of truth in this analysis, but it goes to what are, perhaps, the central issues in the manufacture and selling of fashion clothing, namely, those of unpredictability and the response to unpredictability, the very issues that were central to the store buyer's nightmare with which this chapter began. And to the extent that it *is* a valid analysis, it is especially relevant to some of the recent developments that have taken place in the production of designer clothes in Italy in particular (discussed in section 4.3 below).

In any event, retailers have come to accept that to gain competitive advantage they have to place more emphasis on non-price factors, such as quality and design and that they have to extend the degree of **market segmentation** that exists – a segmentation that seems to have become especially pronounced in that sector of the market aimed specifically at women in the age-range 25 to 44. As has been remarked, it is precisely this form of 'market niching' that has become the slogan of the high street – not just in clothing, but in respect of a whole range of commodities. Thus market researchers now break down the market by age, income, occupation and the like, and analyse 'lifestyles' by correlating the consumption of one type of product with another (Murray, 1988, p. 11), a subject which is explored in more depth by Sean Nixon in the next chapter.

market segmentation

We can see this process particularly well in Burton's transformation from being a mass manufacturer of clothes with a large number of generalized retail outlets, to becoming, in the 1980s, 'a niche market retailer *with a team of anthropologists*, a group of segmented stores – Top Shop, Top Man, Dorothy Perkins, Principles and Burton's itself – with no manufacturing plants of its own' (Murray, 1988, p. 11; emphasis added).

One of the most striking examples of what may be thought of as 'the clothes shop as "lifestyle"' is provided by the design and ambience of Ralph Lauren's shops, a vivid impression of which is given in the following reading.

FIGURE 3.8 The exterior of Ralph Lauren's shop, 143 New Bond Street, London.

READING B

You should now read the short extract from *The Fashion Conspiracy* by the journalist and commentator on fashion, Nicholas Coleridge, provided as Reading B at the end of this chapter. As you read, think about the following issues:

1   What, according to Coleridge, constitutes the Lauren corporate image? How do you think it serves to sell the clothes? Consider the impression that the same ranges of clothes might make on potential purchasers if, instead of appearing in the settings Coleridge describes, they were displayed in relatively anonymous or much more functional surroundings.

2   Using your own knowledge or experience of a particular chain of fashion shops (or shops-within-shops) – or on a future visit – think about what sorts of images and impressions are being constructed to display the ranges of clothes that they carry? What means (lights, sound, furnishings, fabrics and so on) are being utilized to create these effects? What strikes you most: is it, for example, the decor, the room settings (if any), the music being played, the appearance of the staff? Is it the clothes themselves which are the centre of attention or is the main focus on the general ambience? What seems to be distinctive about that particular chain?

3   If it is the case that 'fashion' is truly at the heart of selling clothes – that is to say, that there is a rapid change of, and redundancy in, clothes, that the lives of clothing products are being shortened (both on the shelf and after they have been purchased), that there are now more retail 'seasons' than there once were, and hence more collections of new ranges are launched and sold – why then does it seem that fashion is often sold in a setting that conveys continuity, lack of change and, at least in the case of Ralph Lauren, tradition?

The new-found emphasis placed by retailers on 'fashion', and, therefore on variety and flexibility (which, as we saw in section 1, may apply to items like jeans that once might have been thought to exist in a relatively unchanging and predictable market), as well as the attention devoted to the design of their shops, has profound implications for the relationship that they have with their suppliers, some of which have been mentioned already. For example, it must raise questions about the surprisingly long cycle from design to production and delivery of garments that was often the norm. It is this general area that is addressed more fully in section 4.3.

4.3   Connections between the manufacturing and retailing of fashion

I have characterized the market for fashion in women's clothes as one in which styles change rapidly, in which product redundancy is high and shelf-life is low, and one in which market segmentation is well-established and growing. Not only are these factors intertwined, but they have become more pronounced in recent years. As has been suggested, this has important implications not just for retailers, but also for the relationship between retailers and their suppliers, a relationship which should be examined in the context of what is the most efficient form of production and where is the most desirable location for that production.

In this section these issues are further explored by outlining three models of garment production:

1   the relocation of production to LDCs or NICs where labour is both abundant and cheap;

2   subcontracting production within AICs to inner-city manufacturers who employ a mixture of cheap labour *in situ* and homeworkers who are cheaper still;

3   new forms of production and subcontracting (in particular, flexible specialization) that have been developed in some AICs, notably in parts of Italy.

As was suggested in section 4.2, it had come to be widely accepted in the 1960s and 1970s that manufacturers of garments in AICs would find it increasingly hard to fight off competition from LDCs and NICs. This belief found its most powerful expression in the idea which Frobel and his colleagues advanced: that a 'new international division of labour' had emerged (Frobel et al., 1980). Their thesis was that a number of developments had together permitted manufacturers to site their production facilities anywhere in the world depending on where the most profitable combination of capital and labour was to be found. These developments were that:

- the division and sub-division of manufacturing had gone so far that it now consisted largely of fragmented operations;

- advances in communications and transport meant that the location of production was much less constrained than it once was by technical, organizational and cost factors;

- these two factors enabled manufacturers to make use of the almost inexhaustible supplies of labour that were available in LDCs – thus operatives could be quickly trained in the minimal skills demanded by such fragmented operations and could be easily replaced by other suitable workers.

The chief consequence of these developments was the shutting down of certain types of manufacturing operations in AICs and the subsequent opening of these operations in LDCs or NICs – very often in the foreign subsidiaries of the same company. In Frobel et al.'s analysis, the garment and textile industries of the Federal Republic of Germany (as it still was at the time their work was published) provided one of the best exemplars of this process: 'Trousers for the Federal German market are no longer produced for example in Mönchengladbach, but in the Tunisian subsidiary of the same Federal company' (Frobel et al., 1980, p. 9).

Yet, as was explained earlier, the balance of advantage between manufacturing operations is not solely a matter of price, but may also be decided by factors such as flexibility and response time. Indeed, there has been a concerted attempt by manufacturers in AICs to counter the gains made by NICs and LDCs with a strategy that emphasizes their ability to provide variety in design, flexibility in production and, above all, 'quick response' – a slogan that is much heard in the garment industry today – to the changing orders from retailers and the fluctuations in consumer demand for different fashions, styles and designs (Mitter, 1991, p. 5).

In the second model, cost savings equivalent to those mentioned by Frobel et al., in certain cases and to some extent, are seen to have been obtained by subcontracting production to inner-city firms. Thus, it might be emphasized that though the overall production of clothing in the UK has fallen consistently (replaced by increased imports), production in women's fashionwear – where demand for individual lines is most variable – has not declined to anything like the same degree. In consequence, most orders in this sector of the UK clothing market continue to be supplied by British producers.

From this perspective, the 'survival' of fashionwear production in the UK is attributed to two main factors. The first is the nearness of local producers to this unpredictable market. In other words, any competitive advantage that they have depends in large measure on the flexibility of their output, in which a vital element is that it 'is heavily dependent upon the casualization of labour, particularly an increased use of homeworkers' (Phizacklea, 1990, p. 11). This brings us to the second factor, that is the extent to which production is subcontracted to firms that are run by ethnic minority entrepreneurs, and, more particularly, the extent to which such firms depend on ethnic minority labour – which is prepared or compelled to work long hours at low wages, giving them the ability to produce 'at prices competitive with so-called Third World countries'. The casualization of employment to which Phizacklea refers constitutes an important element in the way the UK clothing industry is depicted in this model. Thus a distinction can be drawn between (1) a stable sector of firms offering reasonably secure employment where firms can justify investment in new technology, perhaps because they have forged long-term relationships with major retailing chains, and (2) a multitude of precariously placed subcontractors which, given the abundance of cheap labour and the unpredictability of demand for their output, have little reason to invest in new capital equipment, and many of which are small independent producers employing less than ten workers (Phizacklea, 1990, p. 19). Thus we discover that the workers employed by 'local' manufacturers in the centre are sometimes indistinguishable from the workers in what we might think of as 'global' factories at the periphery.

The third model, usually referred to as **flexible specialization**, is the one I will discuss in the greatest detail. It must be conceded that the pattern that exists in the UK (outlined briefly in the second model, above) corresponds to *some* of the elements of flexible specialization, insofar as it relies on decentralizing production to small subcontractors who are capable of providing the diversity of output and the flexibility that the market demands. What is lacking in these instances, however, is the key aspect of extensive use being made of computer-controlled technology which, together with the flexible deployment and performance of the workforce, facilitates the establishment of close links between the point of production and the point of sale.

flexible specialization

The essence of flexible specialization is to utilize new technology to permit both economic production in small batches and what is known as **just-in-time (JIT) production**. JIT enables the manufacturer to operate with minimal levels of inventory – with components arriving as near as possible to the moment at which they are required – as well as allowing production to be undertaken and completed, as far as is possible, only on the basis of firm orders from retailers, which themselves are based on actual sales of individual lines.

just-in-time (JIT) production

It is important to comprehend that in this key aspect, flexible specialization goes against the conventional opinion that it was precisely rapid fluctuations in fashion which precluded costly investment in capital equipment. In fact, this conventional view has been undermined by the development of micro-electronically based technologies that can cope very well with short runs and frequent changes of style. In these circumstances, the need for a quick response to changing demand turns out to provide a compelling reason *for* investment in computer-aided design (CAD), computer-aided manufacturing (CAM) and the like, rather than a reason not to invest.

Perhaps the most interesting developments of flexible specialization are those that have taken place in what is often referred to as the 'Third Italy' – that is, the central and north-eastern regions of the country, which are thereby distinguished from the underdeveloped south and the more industrialized regions in and around Milan, for example, where what has been described as the most successful application of JIT on European soil has taken place (Mitter, 1991, p. 8). These developments should not be seen purely in technological terms however, important as these aspects have been. You may remember that in section 3.3, reference was made to the 1971 High Fashion-Industry Accord, the first of several such agreements that have been concluded in Italy. These agreements can be said to constitute a coherent policy for fashion, clothing and textiles, and one which 'combined both capital improvements and *cultural* capital development' (Wark, 1991, p. 71; original emphasis).

Possibly the ultimate expression of both these dimensions is provided by the creation and, much more to the point, the expansion of Benetton. All of those who have studied Benetton (e.g. Jones, 1987; Mahon, 1987; Mitter, 1991; Wark, 1991) seem to stress three inter-connected characteristics:

1   its awareness of trends in 'pop consumption' and its emphasis on quality and design;

2   its ability to respond to fluctuations in demand by producing in small batches, by utilizing state-of-the-art technology, for instance, to dye products at the last moment, and by developing a sophisticated computer network to integrate all stages of production, distribution and retailing;

3   its reliance on a plethora of small subcontractors, many of which have relatively few employees.

The system Benetton has developed offloads the less skilled and more variable parts of production onto these small subcontractors. This has the advantage of securing significant reductions in the cost of labour and minimizing the company's exposure to risk, while maintaining effective control of the entire process of production. But if this was all, though Benetton might well be judged to be more efficient than other subcontracting garment producers, it would not be radically dissimilar to them.

What *is* remarkable about Benetton is the way that it encompasses production, distribution, retailing and, in effect, consumption as well, and that it does so by combining a particular arrangement of production with a particular form of retailing. What is interesting about Benetton's production is that it relies on the utilization of advanced technology in its central operations while using more traditional methods of manufacture – including the employment of homeworkers – in its peripheral operations. What is interesting about the Benetton retailing format is that the majority of outlets are not owned by Benetton but run under what amounts to a form of franchising, and, although the franchise-holders pay no royalty to Benetton, they are obliged to sell only Benetton brand names and to conform strictly to Benetton's specifications on shop design and layout and the way the business is organized. And, again, what is distinctive about the enterprise as a whole is that:

> Benetton only produces goods in response to direct orders (that is from Benetton's retailers – both franchises and those that are directly owned) and both the pattern of sales and re-orders are continuously fed back to Ponzano headquarters by a private and exclusive information-technology network.
>
> (Phizacklea, 1990, p. 15)

Therefore, in assessing Benetton we might choose to stress, on the one hand, its character as a manufacturer and distributor of fashions – where cottage industry at the labour-intensive stage of production is linked to capital intensity in dyeing, packaging, warehousing and so on. On the other hand, we might emphasize the ingenuity with which Benetton has made available relatively cheap designer wear, the way it has developed the strong set of images and associations which mark its products and shops and which attract its consumers, and the success that it has had in selling its ranges, creating a global market. According to Luciano Benetton, co-founder of the Benetton company, 'If you are going to a country for the first time, you need to have a well-known brand, something that young people, even if they have not travelled, recognize' ('Profile of Luciano Benetton', *The Times*, 7 December 1996). To possess, as the company does, a name that is known throughout the world involves much more than the promotion of the clothes themselves in some 7,000 shop windows – important though that is. It is the result of advertising a brand and an image, and – more to the point, perhaps – of the publicity that this advertising regularly attracts because of its often controversial nature.

To neglect either of these dimensions – manufacturing/distribution and marketing/retailing –is unwise because what truly marks out the company is the manner in which both these dimensions have been developed deliberately and simultaneously.

READING C

I would now like you to look at extracts from Fiorenza Belussi's 1987 paper, 'Benetton: information technology and distribution: a case study of the innovative potential of traditional sectors', which is the third and final reading included with this chapter. As you read these extracts, think carefully about the following questions:

1   In what ways do information technology and JIT facilitate a quick response to changing demand?

2   How does Benetton make use of both its technological leadership and its retailing power to obtain a significant market share in sectors of the fashion industry traditionally dominated by small firms?

3   In what way does Benetton use subcontracting in production, advanced computer technology in its central operations and franchising in retailing to become 'a producer with shops'?

4   How and to what extent do the Benetton shops constitute the 'antennae' of Benetton's information system?

5   How would you assess the relative importance of, on the one hand, matters of image – whether discernible in the design of the products or the appearance of the shops – and, on the other hand, the information network that underlies the manufacture, delivery and replenishment of the Benetton ranges?

In a later article about Benetton, Belussi sought to situate discussion of Benetton's development in the context of the debate about *flexible specialization*. It is worth quoting from this subsequent analysis at some length because her argument questions the inevitability of key consequences that a more fragmented and less predictable demand is commonly thought to herald for the manufacturing of fashionable clothes and of other goods.

Belussi argues that flexible specialization had been regarded as a means of economic regeneration of certain traditional areas in the 'Third Italy':

> In these industrial districts, it is the small-scale units which produce a wide spectrum of industrial goods, from shoes, ceramics, textiles and garments on one side to motor-cycles, agricultural equipment, automotive parts and machine tools on the other. The firms perform an enormous variety of the operations usually associated with Fordist mass production. The average size of the unit varies from industry to industry, but it is generally extremely small. Ten workers or less in a unit are usual. A distinctive industrial structure based on small-batch production has been particularly successful in satisfying markedly differentiated consumer tastes in fashion and design of the 1970s and 1980s. The 'flexibility' offered by the small 'specialized' units catered ideally to a market where

'economies of scope' have gradually superseded the advantages associated with 'economies of scale'.

(Belussi, 1991, p. 74)

However, according to Belussi, what the Benetton case demonstrates is that:

information and computing technologies are now creating opportunities for change even in traditional and mature sectors such as the clothing and textile industry. Benetton's development is precisely the utilization of information technology in production and distribution.

On the one hand information technology has been widely applied within the production system, increasing the productivity of all factors and functions (capital, labour, energy, raw materials, inventory, buffer stocks, space, managerial coordination) enhancing the flexibility of the system as a whole, the quality control and product differentiation.

On the other hand, information technology has played a crucial role in the development of the distribution system. Here indeed lies the novelty of Benetton's model: the information system allows the linking up of a network of wholesalers and retailers with a *large constellation of producers*.

The analysis of the Benetton case shows clearly a shift towards JIT techniques. The increasing competitiveness of the Benetton model can be found in a particular form of 'system efficiency' of 'manufacturing' and 'selling'.

(ibid., pp. 75, 78; emphasis added)

Yet what Belussi discerns in the Benetton case is not what we might expect on the basis of flexible specialization, namely the glorification of the *small firm* model in which are stressed not only 'smallness' but also the flexibility associated with it. These qualities are depicted as being much better suited to a world characterized by segmented and niche markets, and by unpredictable and fickle consumer tastes, than is the large-scale enterprise, inhibited as it is by inflexibility, bureaucracy and the like. In Belussi's opinion, what a study of Benetton reveals is:

the evolutionary growth of a 'small firm network' and how small firms can turn into a 'big firm'. In other words, if we want to understand the tendency of the industrial dynamics of the more advanced system, be that Benetton or Japanese firms [...], the analysis has to be focused towards the emergence of new organizational 'concentrate regimes' and towards new forms of oligopolistic power concealed within a structure formed by small (often apparently independent) firms.

In Italy, and in other countries, one of the characteristics specific to the fashion industry is the dominance of small firms, due mainly to volatility of demand, low entry barriers and lack of economies of scale. The Benetton strategy has been aimed specifically at reducing the potential competitive advantages of small firms in expanding its market share. Benetton's dominance over the peripheral network of subcontracting firms thus comes through its technological leadership and its retailing power. The effects of Benetton's organizational revolution, matched with a high propensity to innovate, have deeply modified the pre-existing market structure.

(ibid., p. 78; original emphasis)

Apart from such rapid and continuing trends towards concentration of production, it can be seen that Benetton also offers several important lessons for the retailing side of the fashion industry: for instance, a number of new clothing chains have attempted to emulate Benetton's approach to franchising, style and marketing; while well-established retailers like Marks and Spencer began to instruct their suppliers to pay more attention to the 'fashionability' of the clothes they produced (Belussi, 1987, p. 61).

The Benetton system viewed in its entirety may rely more strongly on the 'antennae' of its shops than other, less formally integrated, major production-to-retailing fashion chains. Nonetheless, we may expect to find the same, or similar, elements at work in all these cases. Both manufacturers and retailers tend to rely on a number of sources to provide guidance and information about the direction of fashion: for example, the sensitivity of their designers; developments in the fashion industry and in the fashion press at large; and the feedback provided by EPOS – which, as you will have appreciated, is regarded as being of increasing importance.

Without EPOS, just-in-time production of garments in response to fluctuations in consumer demand would be quite impractical. Should we then conclude that EPOS and, in turn, JIT results in the production and retailing of clothes coming simply to 'mirror' the public's demand for fashion as it changes from time to time and moment to moment? In these circumstances what was described as the 'art of retailing' becomes more of a 'science', being much less dependent than it once was on the store buyer choosing from the wholesaler's stock, which itself reflected what the manufacturer had decided to produce (Rees, 1973, pp. 97–8). Or to put the point more graphically, by reducing a store's dependence on the sensitivity of their buyers, does this mean that the 'store buyer's nightmare', which I mentioned in the Introduction, need never become a reality?

5   Conclusion

The comments that were made at the end of section 3.3 about the increasing sensitivity of production to changes in consumption ought not to be interpreted to mean that in dissecting fashion we are concerned solely or even primarily with questions of consumption or only with cultural questions more generally. As I have argued, if we are to arrive at a comprehensive understanding of fashion in clothes, we are obliged to explore the rhythms and constituents of production and those of consumption with equal vigour and attention. And in the main body of this chapter I have tried to give practical expression to this view by looking at a variety of cultural questions and by examining various structures of production, as well as by trying to relate the two. In particular, I have looked at: the role of haute couture in elite and non-elite fashion; the role that key retailers have played both in increasing the presence of 'fashion' in clothing and in developing diverse or segmented markets in fashion; and the significance of changing links that exist between the point of production and the point of sale for fashionable garments – a relationship that is technological as well as cultural insofar as it involves production, distribution and retailing on the one hand, and image, advertising, lifestyle and consumption on the other, a relationship that is especially well illustrated by the case of Benetton.

Given the changing nature of the subject matter, you will appreciate that my investigation of fashion is merely provisional: it would certainly have been significantly different had it been undertaken, say, 30 or 40 years ago. This is not because fashion must, by definition, involve change, but rather because both the organization of the production of fashion and the interconnections between the production, distribution and consumption of fashion have undergone such profound modifications, as has been described; and it is not too fanciful to suggest that the production and consumption of fashion and the relationship between the two might be further transformed if an investigation was to be undertaken some years in the future. In addition, and of necessity, my investigation has been selective. This is largely because the world of fashion in clothes includes many very different 'worlds': from the catwalk to the inner-city sweatshop, to the so-called world factory situated in an LDC but supplying the fashionable designer shops of London or New York, and from the judgement of the buyers or designers to the technology of CAD, CAM and EPOS. Not one of these scenes is typical of the whole.

Nonetheless, a few scenes might reveal key aspects of fashion: one might be the store buyer's nightmare, with which I began; another is the dry cleaner's shop in Kuwait which Coleridge visited. It seems to me that there is a strong connection between the two scenes, though one is troubled and frenetic, the other tranquillity itself.

On his visit Coleridge was told that some of the clothes had not been collected for four or five years. A rail of such clothes was wheeled out for him to inspect (the reasons for non-collection are too complex to enter into here, otherwise than to say that in Kuwait dry cleaners were not permitted to dispose of uncollected items after only a few months – as they are, for example, in the UK). What he saw, which he calls an 'elephant's graveyard' of discarded clothing, seemed to him to provide, if only for a fleeting moment, a singularly appropriate vantage point from which to grasp what the fashion industry was about:

> ... four dozen dresses, half of them couture, sparkled under the neon strip light of the cleaner's. There were chrome yellow and fuschia Ungaro skirts, Saint Laurent suits, white Chanel coats with their shining gold buttons, cashmere jersey dresses from Valentino and Hanao Mori, heavily beaded cocktail outfits by Jean-Louis Scherrer. I saw Ted Lapidus, Carven, a monstrous Nina Ricci, Louis Feraud and Philippe Vernet. There were American designers too, though fewer in number: suede Calvin Klein skirts, Norma Kamali fun-fur coats and ripe Bill Blass. As each outfit was unwrapped, the treasure house grew in scale. Italian designers were represented: Gianfranco Ferre, Per Uno, a grey suede suit with zips from Basile. Altogether in the cleaner's there must have been six full rails – of orphaned clothes, worth about £400,000.
>
> (Coleridge, 1988, p. 308)

Could there be a better evocation or illustration than this of Barthes's pronouncement that if a person purchases more than he wears, then there exists 'fashion' and that the more the rhythm of buying exceeds that of dilapidation then the greater the submission to fashion (Barthes, 1983, p. 298)? There may be, but I doubt it.

References

AUDEN, W. and KRONENBERGER, L. (1962) *The Viking Book of Aphorisms*, New York, Dorset.

BARTHES, R. (1983) *The Fashion System*, New York, Hill and Wang.

BELUSSI, F. (1987) 'Benetton: information technology in production and distribution: a case study of the innovative potential of traditional sectors', Occasional Papers No. 25, Science Policy Research Unit, University of Sussex.

BELUSSI, F. (1991) 'Benetton Italy: beyond Fordism and flexible specialization. The evolution of the network firm model' in Mitter, S. (ed.) pp. 73–91.

BIGG, A. (1973) 'The evils of "fashion" ' in Wills and Midgley (eds) pp. 35–46. First published 1893 in *Nineteenth Century*, Vol. 3, No. 3.

BLUMER, H. (1969) 'Fashion: from class differentiation to collective selection', *Sociological Quarterly*, Vol. 10, pp. 275–91.

BRAHAM, P. (1985) 'Marks and Spencer: a technological approach to retailing' in Rhodes, E. and Wield, D. (eds), *Implementing New Technologies*, Oxford, Blackwell.

COLERIDGE, N. (1988) *The Fashion Conspiracy*, Oxford, Heinemann.

CORRIGAN, P. (1993) 'The clothes-horse rodeo; or, How the sociology of clothing and fashion throws its (w)Reiters', *Theory, Culture and Society*, Vol.10, No. 4, pp. 143–55.

CRAIK, J. (1994) *The Face of Fashion*, London, Routledge.

CULLER, J. (1976) *Ferdinand De Saussure*, Glasgow, Collins.

DAVIS, F. (1992) *Fashion, Culture and Identity*, Chicago, University of Chicago Press.

FOLEY, C. (1973) 'Consumer fashion' in Wills and Midgley (eds) pp. 157–70.

FORTY, A. (1986) *Objects and Desire: design and society, 1750–1980*, London, Thames and Hudson.

FROBEL, F., HEINRICHS, J. and DREY, O. (1980) *The New International Division of Labour*, Cambridge, Cambridge University Press.

HOCHSWENDER, W. (1991) 'Patterns', *New York Times*, 1 January.

HOWARD, R. (1990) 'Values make the company: an interview with Robert Haas' (Chairman of Levi Strauss), *Harvard Business Review*, September–October.

JONES, T. (1987) 'Mr Fiorucci: 20 years of global pollination', *i-D, 51*, September.

LURIE, A. (1981) *The Language of Clothes*, Oxford, Heinemann.

LEOPOLD, E. (1992) 'The manufacture of the fashion system' in Ash, J. and Wilson, E. (eds) *Chic Thrills*, London, Pandora Press.

MAHON, R. (1987) 'From Fordism to ?: new technology, labour markets and unions', *Economic and Industrial Democracy*, Vol. 8, No. 1, pp. 5–60.

MEYERSON, R. and KATZ, E. (1973) 'The natural history of fads' in Wills and Midgley (eds) pp. 391–400.

MILBANK, C. (1990) 'When your own initials are not enough', *Avenue*, October.

MITTER, S. (ed.) (1991) *Computer-Aided Manufacturing and Women's Employment: the clothing industry in four European countries*, London, Springer-Verlag.

MURRAY, R. (1988) 'Life after Henry (Ford)', *Marxism Today*, October, pp. 8–13.

PHIZACKLEA, A. (1990) *Unpacking The Fashion Industry: gender, racism and class in production*, London, Routledge.

REES, G. (1973) *St Michael: a history of Marks and Spencer*, London, Pan.

RHODES, E. (1992) *A Review of Design, Principles and Practice*, T264, Milton Keynes, The Open University.

RHODES, E. (1993) 'The interaction of markets and supply: a case study of textiles', McCormick, R. et al. (eds.) *Technology for Technology Education*, Wokingham, Addison-Wesley.

ROCHE, D. (1994) *The Culture of Clothing: dress and fashion in the 'ancien régime'*, Cambridge, Cambridge University Press.

SHILLING, C. (1997) 'The body and difference' in Woodward, K. (ed.) *Identity and Difference*, London, Sage/The Open University.

SIMMEL, G. (1973) 'Fashion' in Wills and Midgley (eds) pp. 171–91. First published 1904 in *International Quarterly*, Vol. 10, October.

STEAD, K. (1991) 'Heists of fashion', *Australian Magazine*, 22 June.

WARK, M. (1991) 'Fashioning the future: fashion, clothing, and the manufacturing of post-Fordist culture', *Cultural Studies*, Vol. 5, No. 1, pp. 61–76.

WILLS, G. and MIDGLEY, D. (eds) (1973) *Fashion Marketing*, London, Allen and Unwin.

READING A:
Daniel Roche, 'From crafts to customers: the Parisian clothing economy'

Voltaire souriait à toutes les créations de luxe.

(Louis Sébastien Mercier)

Cloth and clothing create a code, as Descartes was aware, since the successive processes, from the production of fabrics to the making of garments, have such far-reaching implications. But fashion and regional variations confuse the social signs. Philosophers since Plato have found in the orderly manufacture of fabrics and in their materiality a model for understanding thought in the face of reality; praise of the weaver and the lace-maker are its symbols. Historians, meanwhile, have traced the fortunes of an exemplary industry and described the economy of production. It is undoubtedly one of the best-known aspects of the history of the industrial development of France, indeed of Europe. Through it, we have begun to rewrite the history of the industrial revolution and discovered the complexity of the proto-industrialization which disseminated among rural and urban families the textile culture; that is, the technical, economic and social principles of an industry without entrepreneur when the market was organized by the initiative of the merchant. Spinning and weaving generalized the habits, skills and ways of the early modern textile industry. Their expansion in the countryside helped to destroy the power of the urban textile corporations and guilds.

The development of new technologies led to new social relations, different types of behaviour and even a politics of artisans, journeymen, merchants and industrialists. Between the seventeenth and the eighteenth centuries, the increase in the production of broadcloths and linens, cottons and silks is visible in every graph. New spatial distributions appear on every map recording the creation of new establishments and the dynamism of profits. A growth rate of one per cent between 1730 and 1790 seems likely for the broadcloth industry, which retained a leading role, though it was eventually overtaken by the new textiles: printed linens, cottons and silks. During the Enlightenment, the France of broadcloths and linens, the textile

kingdom of the west, from Flanders to Brittany, lost ground to Languedoc, the east and the south-east. In brief, the cloth industry was on the move.

It was a process which involved chemists, dyers and engineers. Réaumur dreamed of liberating man from the vegetable and the animal by creating artificial fabric; the production of 'indiennes' promoted improved mechanization in the printing of fabrics; Hallot, Macquer and Chaptal – whose *Chimie Appliqué aux Arts* dates from 1806 – strove to discover new processes and new colours. The urban clothing revolution reflects the successive stages of these transformations, in which a different materiality helped to transform social and cultural relations.

The production of textiles and textile culture

To recognize this is to admit the pressure of the consumer market. Throughout France, a greater volume of trade responded to a more diversified internal demand. Only this could stimulate the merchant and the artisan to produce more, cheaper and less undifferentiated fabrics. We have observed in the case of Paris the major developments which encouraged the manufacture of more elaborate textiles. The taste of the public stimulated an industrial production and a commercial élan which then grew through exports. French textiles and French fashions progressed hand in hand.

Though no historical economist or economic historian questions the increase in demand, none has so far studied the intermediate stages by which a piece of cloth is turned into a garment, or a length of linen into an item of underwear. It is as if the mechanisms of luxury consumption and the increase in popular demand acted without mediation to regulate the market. It is no part of our project to write this history, but it seems necessary to open the dossier the better to understand the modalities of a profound transformation in which the material facts – the production and commercialization of the raw materials, wool, cotton, linen, natural silk and hemp, and the economic and social factors – the production and commercialization of yarns and fabrics, accompanied and stimulated needs. Cloth was thus at the interface between two worlds, the old and the new, its manufacture transformed by the application of intellect. Its formidable materiality influenced behaviour and altered sensibilities.

For perhaps the first time in history we see so clearly outlined two systems of production, two economies and two types of consumption. On the one hand, mass manufacture, rapid, dominated by a concern for productivity and profit, strongly influenced by financial and technical imperatives; cottons and printed indiennes were its characteristic products. On the other, high-quality production, dependent on long hours of toil, protected from competition by privilege, sheltered by guild regulation; the traditional textile products typify its stability, security, even routine. The two economic conceptions and the two models of activity were not entirely separate, the two types of conducts and the two outlooks interacting through response and exchange as tastes and needs evolved.

The originality of the innovations of the eighteenth century lies in this ambivalence. It is visible in the work of the inspectors of manufactories, torn between strengthening defences and protecting tradition, and the ideas of economists aware of changes in taste and changes in the market. 'The new conditions,' said an inspector in Picardy, 'render the old regulations useless. Everybody knows that when people dress today they intend to replace [their clothes] as soon as their means allow. Trade itself and the sale of these fabrics used to proceed only gradually; today things happen more quickly; we need to seek out and attract the consumer throughout the whole of Europe.' 'The people love the novelties,' wrote Pradier to the Bureau du Commerce, 'they find them cheap, durable and clean.' To understand these imperatives, we need to examine the crucial contribution of the garment makers and linen merchants to the formation of new material and mental structures. In their way, they helped to disseminate the consumer revolution, when increasing needs coincided with the possibility of increased production. In France as in England, incomes and wages responded, though with both social and geographical disparities.

Paris is central to our project for two principal reasons: in spite of its economic complexity and historiographical lacunae, the capital is ideal for the analysis of the commercialization of needs and tastes, since it combines all the problems; second, because of the size and nature of its population, we are able to observe in action the imbrication of causalities and the action of supply and demand through their various circuits. Here, producers and consumers, in the commercial relationship, shaped the new manners.

Source: Roche, 1994, pp. 259–62.

READING B:
Nicholas Coleridge, 'The fashion conspiracy'

It is a game of mine, whenever I am in a Ralph Lauren shop, to inspect the cloth-covered books arranged in the evocative room settings. Whether you are in the Lauren department in Bergdorf Goodman or Harvey Nichols, or the Lauren shop in New Bond Street or the Place de la Madeleine or Stamford, Connecticut, or the Lauren store in the Rhinelander Building on 72nd and Madison, there they are – the waterstained cloth-covered volumes – strategically stacked on a bedside table, or higgledy-piggledy on a marble washstand, or leant up on their sides above the fireplace. The covers are carefully chosen, mature but not too scruffy, worn and distinguished but never dog-eared. Often they have faded in sunlight, or seem to have run slightly, as thought they were left outside overnight on dewy grass by a tennis court. I tried but failed to discover where they are bought centrally. Perhaps there is an employee of the Ralph Lauren Company who does nothing except trawl country-house auctions in Inverness-shire or car-boot sales in Iowa, equipped with swatches of the new spring colours and a mandate to choose matching folios for the shops. Clearly the books are not bought to be read. Their titles are so abstruse, so bizarre, that if they are intended to reflect the lifestyle of the Ralph Lauren customer then the Ralph Lauren customer is a multi-disciplined mastermind. In the Ralph Lauren corner of Bergdorf Goodman these books are scattered amidst the merchandise: *Cognition, Personality and Clinical Psychology* by Jessor and Feshbach, *Abortion and the Law* by Professor David T. Smith, *Public Issues in Ohio* by John L. Gargun in a muted blue, fawn and white binding to blend with the lily-coloured slacks ($160) and pink chintz sweatshirts (reduced, $50).

In the London shop in New Bond Street, in the old Savory and Moore building, the reading list is largely in Latin and medieval English, or else they are Greek myths translated into French or theological tracts: *The Well of the Saints* by J. M. Synge and *Persi et Juvenalis* by Saturae.

The Lauren library is the only discordant note in a corporate image so integrated and holistic that it can truly be said to have created a world apart. It is a requirement of any department store selling Ralph Lauren's clothes in volume that they build a separate Lauren kiosk with its own mahogany shelves, fireplace, framed Victorian Spy caricatures, polo sticks, umbrella stands, carriage clocks, shaving mirrors, and a host of similar bric-à-brac. It is a look that is usually described as English, though it draws on related nostalgias too: stalking parties in Scottish baronial lodges at which the men come down from the hill with a twelve-point stag lashed to a Highland pony; safari expeditions in Kenya; picnics on the prairie eaten off Navaho blankets; fishing trips from Long Island; colonial hotels at Nuwara Eliya in Ceylon; croquet in a Surrey vicarage; high-goal polo in Palm Beach. Seven disparate cinematic dreams synthesised into a single billion-dollar fashion empire. 'In essence,' wrote *Time* magazine, 'Lauren dangles old-money prestige in front of new-money clientele.' That is only half true. It has been Ralph Lauren's cleverness to tap a submerged global yearning; a yearning for open space and stability and an elusive quality dimly heard of, but never experienced, called Absolute Values. The marketing of Ralph Lauren, the advertisements, the shops, the faded cloth-covered books, all propagate the same myth that somewhere in the world, somewhere else, there are Absolute Values of probity and continuity. It is a compelling myth that has made one man from the Bronx rather rich. By January 1988, Ralph Lauren's personal fortune was estimated at $350 million. Five foot five inches tall in his stockinged feet, five foot seven in his cowboy boots, with a thatch of thick grey hair, he is probably the richest designer in the world and among the most content; he shuttles by private Hawker Siddeley jet with his family between homes on Fifth Avenue, Montego Bay in Jamaica, their ranch near Tellride in Colorado with its 1,600 head of cattle, a house on the tip of Long Island, and a hundred-acre property in Pound Ridge, New York.

Source: Coleridge, 1988, pp. 39–41.

READING C:
Fiorenza Belussi, 'Benetton: information technology in production and distribution: a case study of the innovative potential of traditional sectors'

Introduction

[...]

In recent years the international (and Italian) press have frequently remarked upon the striking performance of the Benetton Group. Why does the Benetton case attract such wide attention? Several reasons are worth noting. Firstly, Benetton's growth represents one of the most striking success stories of Italian industry and marketing in the last few years. Secondly, and more importantly, the development of the firm has taken place in the 'transient world of fashion'; in a traditional sector characterized by uncertainty and, in the 1970s, by a low (even negative) expansion of market demand. Thirdly, in comparison with the 'textile decline' (of total output and employment) observed in nearly all industrialized countries – due to the competitiveness of products from Third World industry in international trade (Hoffman and Rush, 1984) – Benetton's performance represents an impressive counter-tendency worthy of analysis.

This paper attempts to gain a better understanding of the main factors associated with Benetton's expansion; in particular the crucial role played by innovation as a major determinant of the sustained growth of the firm.

Since the influential works of Schumpeter, the importance of technological change and innovative activity for industrial dynamics and for economic growth have been widely discussed. Our Benetton case study is conducted within a Schumpeterian perspective. As in all Schumpeter's analyses, technological progress is not treated in isolation from the business milieu in which it occurred. In this respect the discussion focuses on the entrepreneurial function and on the successful sequence of 'acts of innovations' (Schumpeter, 1928).

[...]

Within the analysis the concept of *firm strategy* plays a fundamental role. Using the seminal contribution of Porter (1980), the paper refers to his idea of a competitive strategy. In terms of this analytical framework Benetton's competitive advantages over its rivals were gained by being a highly innovative firm which maintained a cumulative leadership over time.

The relationship between the market structure, the firm's conduct and its performance (Bain, 1967; Caves, 1964) are also analysed, describing the induced process towards an increasing domination of the market by the firm. The Chandler (1972) strategy-structure model, and some recent comments by Williamson (1985; 1986), have also indirectly inspired some considerations of the advantages of the Benetton organizational structure which extends its boundaries, incorporating strong linkages among the agents involved in the production and distribution systems (suppliers, subcontractors, agents, retailers).

A further element, which is a major focus of analysis, is the impact of new technologies on the firm's pattern of growth. The approaches adopted by Freeman and Perez (1986), and by Freeman and Soete (1987), regarding information technology, have been considered in order to describe the more recent evolution of Benetton. The paper will illustrate the finding that it is the utilization of information technology that appears to be the real motor sustaining the latest (and more intensive) phase of Benetton's development. On the one hand, it is widely applied within the production-system, increasing the *productivity* of all productive factors and production functions (capital, labour, space, raw material, inventory, buffer stock, energy, managerial coordination), the *flexibility* of the system as a whole, the *quality control* and *product differentiation*. On the other hand, information technology played a crucial role in the development of the distribution system. Here lies the novelty of Benetton's model: the information system allows the linking up of a network of wholesalers and retailers with a large constellation of producers.

[...] *Close relations with demand* and the creation of a novel retailing system [...] allows a better understanding of consumer preferences. In other words, thanks to the flexibility of the system and the use of information technology, the firm is producing in interaction with its outlets and its purchases. Second, this 'incorporation' of the selling system is a new way for the firm of *reducing uncertainty and risk*. As a direct consequence, through the planned expansion of its outlets, through an accurate strategy on price policies and through the marketing and advertising strategy, the firm was able to establish sovereignty over its market.

[...]

To summarize, the increasing competitiveness of Benetton's model can be found in a particular form of 'system efficiency' of 'manufacturing' and 'selling'. In other words, this model works as a combined strategy of 'just-in-time' systems in production and distribution.

[...]

The growth of the firm

[...]

Benetton's story began with Luciano Benetton and his sister Giuliana. A difficult domestic situation obliged both to work while still very young: Luciano was a shop assistant in a textile shop in Treviso and his sister was working in an artisanal knitwear producing factory. Luciano was also moonlighting as a salesman of a knitwear firm from Carpi (Carpi is a specialized ancient Italian area of knitwear producers). In the 1950s the production in this sector was highly decentralized (and focused on the role of the commissioning buyer, who on the basis of a sample collection made by the company, collected orders from shops and subcontracted work to the home workers). In 1957 they decided to work together. Giuliana had discovered a talent for designing and making knitwear; Luciano would collect orders and Giuliana would produce them at home. So, the origin of Benetton's organizational structure lies with the ancient local putting-out system, which was never fully superseded by the factory mode of production. In 1965 they established a small factory in Ponzano (in the Veneto region of North-East Italy) with 60 employees.

At that time the other two brothers (Gilberto and Carlo) joined the company. The division of labour among the family was clear-cut and it is the same

nowadays: Luciano deals with the marketing, Giuliana with the design function, Gilberto with administration and finance and Carlo is in charge of production.

The creation of the retailing system

Benetton was the first firm in Italy, and possibly in the world, to introduce a system of franchising[1] in the textile and clothing industry[2]. This system must be considered a special form of franchising which is informally regulated. Retailers which sell Benetton's products do not pay any royalties, but have rigid controlling terms. No other make of clothing can be sold in the shop.

The first shop was opened directly by Benetton, with other financial partners in 1968 in Belluno, a small city near Treviso (in the Alps). During the 1970s the chain of Benetton shops grew rapidly, first of all in Veneto (the region where Benetton is based) and later throughout Italy. The financial resources to develop such an imposing structure were found outside the firm, through partnerships with several commercial partners. Benetton moved from jerseys, cardigans and other knitted clothes, to denim jeans in time for the great jeans boom of 1975–6, and then started to make cotton clothes and T-shirts.

By 1975 it had about 200 shops in Italy and was opening more at the rate of 100 or so a year. Throughout this period of growth Benetton ensured that it kept direct control of its outlet markets.

Benetton's exports are 'pushed' by the creation of shops with the Benetton name. In Italy, as well as abroad, Benetton does not sell its products to other outlets. In essence they export the entire selling strategy: not only their products but also the Benetton style, the shop organization and the marketing strategy – in other words, 'product with shops' (Rullani and Zanfei, 1984). With respect to the competitors in the fashion industry, this represented a point of strength for Benetton: it was an organizational innovation of great significance.

[...]

In 1978 Benetton was already considered an important firm in the textile/knitwear sector with around 1,000 employees and with an export market which amounted to 26% of total sales [...] The crucial years of fast growth were between 1978 and

1981; in this period total sales increased from 55 to 322 billion lire. The increase in exports was clearly the leading mechanism in the growth of sales. In only four years the export share rose to 40% of total output.

The second take-off began when Benetton started operating abroad on a large scale and when it filled the remaining gaps in its coverage of the Italian market. Three main factors can explain this new phase: (a) Benetton's leadership on costs which made its products very competitive with respect to its competitors; (b) the rapid expansion in the market for informal clothes; (c) the existence of a protectionist policy implemented by the industrialized countries to stop (or at least to reduce) the competitive pressure of commodities from Newly Industrializing Countries (NICs), formally concluded with the Multi-fibre Agreement [in 1974 and 1977].

Over the same period a very low increase in Benetton's employees can be observed, with even a decrease in 1982. The existence of this asymmetry, between high growth of sales and very low increase in employment, can be explained by the organizational structure of the firm.

[Subcontracting]

Benetton chose from the beginning to create a 'subcontracting system', so a consistent part of the total value-added, which is estimated to be at least 70%, is made by small artisan firms [...] which are located near the Benetton plants.

This strategy of 'decentralization' of some productive phases to subcontractors is not at all specific to Benetton firms, but had been a widespread phenomenon of reorganization in many Italian companies in the 1970s. What is specific to the Benetton case is the combination of this productive strategy with [its] commercial strategy, and with technological innovations.

As we have mentioned, it is only since 1978 that the attention of the firm shifted to foreign markets. The first Benetton shop outside Italy was opened in Paris in 1969 when Benetton was still a small firm (Racchah, 1983). Since that date the number of Benetton shops in France gradually increased. In 1974, French sales were already 500 million lire. Three years later (in 1977) Benetton's exports to

France exceeded seven billion lire. By 1983 [...] the French market represented 17.6% of total production and the number of Benetton shops in France had increased to 387. After conquering the French fashion market, Benetton turned to others in Europe, in particular Germany, Benelux and the UK.

The initial strategy was gradually to penetrate those foreign markets whose culture, tastes and retailing system most closely resembled those of Italy. Subsequently most of the effort was concentrated on the US, Canadian and Japanese markets. Growth potential lies in export markets; in the last five years the growth of the Benetton chain shops in Italy has reached saturation point: one Benetton shop for every 50,000–55,000 inhabitants.

[...]

Conversely, the company has made very little direct foreign investment in the productive sector. [...]

[...]

Benetton shows that the introduction of new technology with a new organizational view of relations with the market strongly influences the pattern of costs [...] of firms in sectors which until now were regarded as mature and standardized. So, contrary to expectations [...], the shift in the location of production of so-called mature industry (and among those par excellence textile/clothing firms) towards less-developed countries, typically abundant in low cost labour, does not appear a fixed route. The Benetton case shows that given the possibility of the accumulation of technological and organizational know-how, firms can exist in the high wage economies of industralized countries. [...]

[...]

Subcontractors are involved in all the labour-intensive phases of production: assembly, ironing, finishing. [...] The subcontracting firms can be divided into four main categories: (a) those under the financial control of the Benetton family (through various financial companies); (b) 'affiliate' firms; (c) independent firms; (d) homeworkers. 'Affiliate' firms are those belonging either to former employees or to actual Benetton managers or clerks. Benetton has directly promoted the creation of such firms with the guarantee of orders in the start-up phase.

This subcontracting system has two main advantages for Benetton: (i) the use of external managerial resources, and (ii) a significant reduction in labour costs (one can estimate that in terms of unit labour cost the saving is about 40%). Subcontractors agree to work exclusively for Benetton because of the stability of demand and the guarantee of 10% profit margin on their sales [...]

The typical subcontracting firm is small (20–40 employees), but there are also firms with 80–100 employees. Workers are not unionized but there is an agreement signed by local trade unions and Benetton about the observance of the same pay conditions between Benetton workers and subcontracted workers. [...] Benetton is very advanced in its estimates of industrial costs: for every phase that is decentralized a detailed cost analysis is made. Benetton also provides product standardization and process optimization procedures, so that satellite firms can increase their productivity.

Labour productivity in subcontracting firms is estimated to be 10% higher than that which could be achieved through in-house manufacturing (this is due essentially to management's greater control over the workforce and their ability to enforce a faster working pace).

[...]

Innovative activity

[...]

Notwithstanding the common belief that Benetton is an innovative firm, there has been an inadequate conceptualization of the specific features of its innovative process. [...] According to the traditional distinctions in innovation literature (Freeman, 1982), innovation can be oriented to:

(a)   product changes;

(b)   process changes;

(c)   organizational changes.

[...] Benetton's expansion is characterized by the systematic coordination and complementarity of innovative efforts in each of these dimensions (product-innovation; process innovation;

organizational innovation). [...] we can distinguish four major phases in terms of the shifting focus of innovative and adaptation efforts.

In the first phase, from 1965 to 1970, three dominant features can be observed; namely (a) the introduction of in-house incremental innovations in machinery through minor but effective changes in ordinary second-hand machines bought in the market and adapted by the firm itself, (b) the building up of Benetton's particular retailing system [...] which made available a major resource for the general growth of the firm, and (c) special attention towards a product differentiation strategy with the introduction of light colours (e.g. 'pastello') in casual and sports fashion.

During this period specific entrepreneurial skills are revealed in the ability to utilize already existing resources and knowledge, for example, in the adaptation of second-hand machines which were originally used to manufacture women's seamed stockings (at the time out of fashion) to produce knitwear. These machines, which at the time provided 90% of Benetton's knitting capacity, were purchased for approximately $1,000 per machine, converted for an additional $4,000 each: the same machines were valued at roughly $470,000 each in 1982 (Harvard Business School, 1985).

Another example is the adaptation of a very old and well-known system of 'beating' and dyeing wool in the final manufacturing phase. This process was adopted by Benetton after a trip by Luciano Benetton to Scotland, where this process is used in artisan shops. However, Benetton was the first in the world to transform this into an industrial process, and allowed Benetton to follow more closely the variability of demand.

Using the concept of a technological trajectory (Dosi, 1982) Benetton's case appears to be a very complex process in which a significant role is played by:

(a)   tacit knowledge about the productive process;

(b)   the capacity to link innovations to a systematic 'vision' linking production and distribution (that is, an integrated innovative entrepreneurial strategy);

(c)   the cumulative advantage coming from an innovative lead.

Many researchers have explored the diversity of patterns of technological change (see in particular Pavitt, 1984). Clothing firms are considered 'supplier dominated' with only a weak tendency towards innovation activity. According to Pavitt, in such firms: (a) technological change comes (exogenously) from suppliers' equipment and materials; (b) the technological trajectories are defined in terms of cutting costs. However, in Benetton we can observe two phenomena. First, there are 'non-technological' innovations directly linked to design, trademarks, advertising and so on. Secondly, one observes process-related innovative activities, which are complementary to purchases of equipment from outside.

This last aspect appears to be linked to a specific knowledge about the production process, and is based on the engineering capabilities of the entrepreneur. (Giuliana Benetton even now goes daily to the factory, controlling and making minor modifications to the looms.)

It is important to observe that this technical know-how precedes the constitution of the firm (and in fact it can be considered a condition, necessary if not sufficient, to explain the creation of the firm and its success). Historically, Treviso is an important area for textiles in Italy. The young Benetton brothers worked in the textile industry as blue-collar workers (they came from a poor family and were forced to leave school because of economic circumstances). Their knowledge of the production cycle came directly from the shop floor.

In the intermediate period, in the 1970s, Benetton's growth was not characterized by the introduction of major innovations: the firm was in a process of learning by doing, learning by using, and learning by failing.

In a third phase (approximately between 1977 and 1982), the distinguishing element is the introduction of process innovation aimed at a higher level of automation in some production processes (cutting, knitting and dyeing). This phase is characterized by acquisition of external new technology supplied by the machinery producers. The rate of growth in the internal and foreign markets required (and allows for) an increase in the scale of production, and relatedly, an acceleration in the rate of adoption of new and expensive automated machinery. More than in the first period,

the introduction of innovations were pushed by outside technological opportunities and based on the use of micro-electronics in the industrial machinery.

Certainly, this technological 'leap' appears to be a consequence of (or at least allowed by) the expansion of the firm. However, right at the origin of Benetton's technological trajectory there are some incremental improvements of machinery and some 'innovative' procedures and behaviour.

The most recent phase is characterized by a wider use of new information technologies, involving: the building up of an information network, connecting productive and commercial activities, the first application of CAD and a new automated warehouse.

[...]

Getting closer to demand

[...]

The shops, which conform to an image and style of management decreed by the company, are called by various brand names, such as Jeans West, Sisley, Tomato, 012 (for children) and increasingly only Benetton. Benetton or its agents choose the sites for the shops with great care, looking for the more prestigious locations, and often ending up with four or five Benetton shops in the same street.

The typical Benetton shop is standardized. This allows for a centrally determined 'optimized' lay-out for the display of goods and the selling system. In a Benetton shop it is the colours, the window displays and the open shelves that strike you most, as they are designed to do by the now famous architects Afra and Tobia Scarpa. The organizational and labour costs [...] are much lower than in other typical clothing shops.

Another advantage, also in terms of space, is the absence of warehousing: indeed all the items are displayed on the sets of shelves. The absence of warehousing is linked to the use of information technology and to the flexibility of the whole productive cycle. Benetton's commercial strategy is to stay ahead of competitors in costs, and thus on prices; both in Italy and abroad Benetton imposes the price of each item on the retailers. (This does not imply a reduction of the profit rate compared to

FIGURE 3.9   The interior of a United Colours of Benetton store.

other retailers, because the shop organization turns out to be less expensive.)

[...]

The shops are the antennae of Benetton's information system. [...] The pattern of sales and extent of re-orders are regularly fed back from the shops to Benetton, and in this way the time required for the final decision of distribution among subcontractors is markedly reduced. This allows for an optimization of the total production cycle and a better utilization of capital equipment of the whole system. Notably, 'real time' planning of production based directly on shops' orders has the effect of reducing the typical seasonal peaks which characterize this industry. Moreover, a large reduction is obtained in the size of inventory and in the average length of time that a single item spends in the warehouse. The specific use of such

a private and exclusive information network was supported by a very particular organization of production. These characteristics represented the heart of the system. Unlike other firms in the fashion sector Benetton only produces goods in response to direct orders. This has an enormous influence on total costs, and on the ability of the firm to follow market trends.

[...]

A source of strength for Benetton since the 1970s has been its capacity to adapt quickly to new and changing markets. It discovered an unsatisfied 'potential demand' – 'casual' fashion for young people. [...] Benetton has been able to anticipate the direction of such market segments by intervening and reacting speedily to changing demand. Benetton's products [...] are concentrated precisely in the areas of fastest growth of demand. The whole structure of the firm (information system, retailing system, etc.) is orientated towards something similar to a 'just-in-time' system of response to consumer demand.

[...] Benetton is able to reach the market 6–8 weeks before its competitors, and, thanks to the flexibility of the system, it is able to respond within a very short time (about ten days) to the re-orders of domestic and foreign shops. In this way, it almost directly 'interacts' with its consumers.

[...]

[...] The novelty of Benetton can be seen in the creation of its own retailing system; building up a chain of shops using franchising. These enormously improved the firm's competitive position over its rivals. The main advantages realized were: (i) direct knowledge of consumer's preference; (ii) the use of shops for advertising and marketing; (iii) guaranteeing outlets for production; (iv) easier planning and co-ordination of the production process; (v) finally, and very importantly, reducing uncertainty and risk in the market.

[...] Benetton's system became more and more flexible: ready to capture minor changes of demand identified by shops, and ready to distribute new orders within the network of subcontracting. [...] Information technology was the enabling tool for sustaining such an impressive performance, and the organizational model, shaping every production and distribution stage, can be described as an integrated just-in-time system.

Notes

1 The system of franchising was well known and had been established in the US for some time (e.g. MacDonald's fast food chain) but the traditional system and relationship between franchiser and franchisee was radically modified by Benetton.

2 With regard to the UK, for example, there is a famous forerunner, Marks and Spencer (Tse, 1985), a chain of large 'high-street' shops which established a close relationship between retailing and production through subcontracting since 1930. However, this set-up is considerably different from the Benetton system because the emphasis is placed on quality control of the products through a high control of new materials realized directly by the technologists employed by the company (Rees, 1969). Benetton, by contrast, emphasized the colour coordination and design of their garments, based on an innovative system which narrows the gap between producer and consumer. In addition, Benetton began as a producer (and only later entered retailing); Marks and Spencer, on the other hand, began as retailer and only later took an interest in production.

References

BAIN, J.S. (1967) *Industrial organization*, New York, J. Wiley.

CAVES, R. (1964) *American Industry: structure, conduct, performance*, Englewood Cliffs, NJ, Prentice Hall.

CHANDLER, A.D. (1972) *Strategy and Structure*, Cambridge, MIT Press.

DOSI, G. (1982) 'Technological paradigms and technological trajectories. A suggested interpretation of the determinants and direction of technological change', *Research Policy*, Vol. 11, No. 3.

FREEMAN, C. (1982) *Economics of Industrial Innovation*, London, Frances Pinter (first edition 1974).

FREEMAN, C. and PEREZ, C. (1986) 'The diffusion of technical innovations and changes of techno-economic paradigm', paper presented at the Venice Conference on Innovation Diffusion, March.

FREEMAN, C. and SOETE, L. (1987) *Technological Change and Full Employment*, (forthcoming).

HARVARD BUSINESS SCHOOL (1985) 'Instituto studi direzionali: the Benetton case-study', mimeo.

HOFFMAN, K. and RUSH, H. (1984) *Microelectronics and Technological Transformation of the Clothing Industry*, Geneva, ILO.

PAVITT, K. (1984) 'Sectoral patterns of technical change: towards a taxonomy and a theory', *Research Policy*, Vol. 13, No. 6.

PORTER, M.E. (1980) *Competitive Strategy*, New York, Free Press.

RACCHAH, H. (1983) 'Irresistiblement emporté par se croissance Benetton se transforme en multi nationale', *Journal du Textile*, No. 1.

REES, G. (1969) *St Michael: a history of Marks and Spencer*, London, Wedengteld and Hudson.

RULLANI, E. and ZANFEI, A. (1984) 'Benetton: invenzione e consolidamento di un sistema internazionale', *Bolletino Ospri*, No. 1.

SCHUMPETER, J. (1928) 'The instability of capitalism', *Economic Journal*, September. Republished in Rosenberg, H. (ed.) (1971) *The Economics of Technological Change*, Harmondsworth, Penguin.

TSE, K.K. (1985) *Marks and Spencer*, Oxford, Pergamon Press.

WILLIAMSON, O.E. (1985) *The Economic Institutions of Capitalism: firms, markets, relational contracting*, New York, Free Press.

WILLIAMSON, O.E. (1986) *Economic Organization: firms, market and policy control*, Brighton, Wheatsheaf Books.

Source: Belussi, 1987, pp. 1–4, 10–12, 14–16, 28, 31, 40, 43–6, 34, 49, 61, 65, 71, 80–1.

CIRCULATING CULTURE

Sean Nixon

Contents

1   Introduction

In September 1987 the advertising agency D'Arcy Masius Benton and Bowles (DMBB) produced a series of press advertisements for the Royal Mail. These advertisements, which ran initially in a range of women's magazines, aimed to promote the activity of letter-writing. More specifically, in fact, DMBB's brief was to promote letter-writing as 'an acceptable and contemporary activity amongst a young female audience'. Embedded in the brief, however, was an additional concern to shift – as the advertising trade magazine *Campaign* put it – the Post Office's 'stuffy image' (*Campaign*, 25 September 1987, p. 14). We shall begin by considering the advertisements which DMBB produced in response to this brief.

Look at Figure 4.1. The first thing to note about this advertisement is that it draws strongly on the visual codes of fashion photography. This is clear from the casting of the model in the advertisement and from the way she is posed. The mobilization of these codes is also clear from the decision to style the model wearing high fashion clothing and accessories. The status of this image as a fashion photograph is further underscored by the studio backdrop placed behind the model, by its stylized use of lighting and by the quality of its reproduction.

The graphic design of the advertisement is the second key element in shaping its overall look and feel. Central to its design is the use of a full-bleed image. By this I mean that the fashion photograph is reproduced on the page of the magazine without a framing border, instead 'bleeding' off the edges of the page. In addition, the advertisement follows the conventions of fashion features in listing the garments being worn by the model and related information alongside the image. The text or copy relating the clothes worn, the names of the photographer, stylist and designer and the advertising copy – 'By Air, By Land, By Hand' – is then placed directly onto the image. This layout, together with the size and choice of typeface, draws upon the clean lines and understated approach associated with the most innovative graphic design idioms of this period. In particular, the spacing of the type and the graphic motif which constitutes the corporate logo – 'Royal Mail' – are characteristic of what Catherine McDermott has called 'new wave graphics' (McDermott, 1987).

I have dwelt upon these visual codes because it is through them that the advertisement works to signify a particular set of cultural meanings. These are meanings which are centrally to do with style, fashionability and exclusivity. It is precisely the coding of these values and meanings in relation to the activity of letter-writing and the image of the Post Office as an organization, however, which is so striking about the advertisement. In fact, the mobilization of these codes in relation to this client is, on first impression, extraordinary. Isn't it deeply incongruous to bring together the apparently distinct universes of high fashion and stamps? It is this apparent

Photography by Marc Roger

Styling by Tracey Jacobs

Hair and Make-up by Kenny Campbell

Ebony Beads by Dinny Hall for Ozbek £150

Bronze Leather Gloves by Ozbek Not For Sale

Dark Pink Body Suit by Ozbek £276

Letter by Royal Mail 19p

By Air, By Land, By Hand

incongruity built into the DMBB advertisements, however, which is so instructive for the argument I want to develop in this chapter.

What the advertisements vividly illustrate is the increasing importance of advertising, design and the wider processes of consumer marketing to the selling of goods and services. There are two distinct aspects to this process evident in the DMBB advertisement. The first concerns the application of the most contemporary techniques in advertising, market research and design to a greater range of goods and services – including public services and public sector organizations. The second concerns the more intense aestheticization of the representations which accompany the circulation of these goods and services. By this I mean that an attention to the qualities of taste and beauty have become more important in the production of these representations.

The aim of this chapter, then, is to explore the practices associated with advertising and to consider the ways in which they work to add cultural values and meanings to goods and services. As such, a good deal of this chapter (section 4) is necessarily concerned with setting out an account of a particular set of advertising practices. In doing so, however, I want to reprise the arguments about the significance of advertising and design and how these practices are situated in the circuit of culture (see the Introduction to this volume). In their study of the Sony Walkman, **du Gay, Hall et al.** (1997) argue that the meaning of the Walkman as a cultural artefact was produced through the coding of its physical design (the styling of the casing, the positioning of the switches, the choice of colour and finish) and through press advertising. In the latter instance the advertising attempted to establish and fix a set of meanings around the Walkman. Du Gay, Hall et al. suggest that at the heart of the processes of advertising and design is a concern not only to associate the product with particular cultural meanings, but also to address these values to prospective buyers. In other words, the advertising and design attempted to create an identification between the consumer and the Walkman. In doing this, they argue, the practices of advertising and design play a key role in the cultural circuit – linking the worlds of engineers and technicians with that of consumers. Specifically, it is argued that advertising and design practitioners – those individuals who perform the advertising and design work – play a pivotal role as *cultural intermediaries* in articulating production with consumption. This articulation of production and consumption itself constitutes a determinant moment in the circuit of culture: the moment of circulation. What is important about the moment of circulation is that it both articulates production with consumption, and draws consumption back into the process of production. Thus, novel or unforeseen uses of the Walkman by groups of consumers were picked up on by Sony or its advertising agency and incorporated back into the design and advertising of the Walkman. Market research represents the most formalized way in which this monitoring of consumers' uses takes place and represents an important set of practices through which wider social and cultural shifts affecting the product can be registered by the producers of that product.

FIGURE 4.1
DMBB's advertisment
for Royal Mail.

Alongside the concern to detail the way in which the practices of advertising add cultural meanings to goods and services, this chapter is also concerned to reflect on why advertising and associated forms of promotion should have come to acquire a more intensified role in the process of circulation. Given that advertising techniques have a long history, I want to ask what is new about the way contemporary advertising works to add cultural values and meanings. As a way of doing this, I shall consider two contributions – those of the French critic Jean Baudrillard and of the Canadian sociologist Andrew Wernick. Both Baudrillard and Wernick invoke the notion of a widespread cultural transformation associated with the emergence of consumer society and privilege marketing (which includes the practices of advertising, market research and design) as a central engine in this process of cultural change. Reflecting on their work allows us to clarify a number of issues about the novelty of contemporary developments in advertising practice. I shall then consider another set of arguments – derived principally from studies in political economy – which offer us a different way of conceptualizing the shifts in advertising practice as part and parcel of a wider process of economic restructuring. At the heart of this work is an argument about the transition from one socio-economic formation to another – namely, the transition from mass production to flexible specialization.

The final section of this chapter will focus on the individuals who work in advertising. The reason for this is straightforward. Given the increasing importance of advertising as a cultural intermediary occupation, cultural critics have become interested in both the characteristics of the individuals who occupy such key positions in the circulation of culture and the way in which their cultural preferences and dispositions shape the processes of symbolic production in which they are involved.

The aims of this chapter can thus be summarized as follows:

- To explore the usefulness of debates about 'consumer society' and 'promotional culture' in interpreting the contemporary centrality of techniques of advertising to the selling of goods and services.

- To explore the relationship between advertising and the wider economic structures associated with mass production and flexible specialization.

- To develop an account of recent developments in advertising practices in relation to the strategy of market segmentation.

- To consider the make-up of advertising and design practitioners as cultural intermediaries and to reflect upon their cultural preferences.

2   The engines of consumer culture

The essay entitled 'Consumer society' by the French critic Jean Baudrillard (1988) and the book *Promotional Culture* by the Canadian sociologist Andrew Wernick (1991) are a useful place to start our reflections on the contemporary role of advertising in the circulation of goods and services. Both writers identify the new importance of the moment of circulation, and of **consumer marketing** in particular, as central to the deep-seated transformations in western societies associated with the expansion of consumer culture. For them, as for a number of other writers, the development of modern consumer marketing represents the engine of this consumer revolution – both expanding consumer demand and transforming the very nature of commodities.

consumer marketing

Baudrillard begins his essay by conjuring up an image of a society dominated by an abundance of consumer goods, services and messages and advances two initial observations. Firstly, he suggests – in a formulation which echoes Marx's arguments about commodification and reification – that the new explosion of consumer goods and services produces (in his words) 'a fundamental mutation of the ecology of the human species' in which individuals' principal relationships have become those with consumer objects and their associated messages rather than with other people. Secondly, Baudrillard argues that in the new profusion of commodities, consumers relate not to the utility of particular consumer objects (such as the capacity of a washing machine to wash clothes), but to a new calculus of consumption in which individual consumer objects refer to a wider network of objects and lifestyles. In other words, for Baudrillard, the decision to buy is now based upon the cultural meanings and values associated with particular objects (such as the type or brand of washing-machine) and the consumer lifestyle invoked through these.

For Baudrillard, both these characteristics of **consumer society** find their fullest expression in the shopping mall. In offering the consumer both a wider range of shops under one roof and by providing a range of other services (such as places to eat and leisure facilities), the mall

consumer society

> ... practises an amalgamation of signs where all categories of goods are considered a partial field in the general consumerism of signs. The cultural centre becomes an integral part of the shopping mall. This is not to say that culture is here 'prostituted'; that is too simple. It is culturalized. Consequently, the commodity (clothing, food, restaurants etc.) is also culturalized, since it is transformed into a distinctive and idle substance, a luxury, and an item, amongst others, in the general display of consumables.
>
> (Baudrillard, 1988, p. 32)

For Baudrillard the mall is, in this sense, paradigmatic of a more general process in which everyday life has become totally dominated by the logic of consumerism. The central consequence of this, he argues, is a deep cultural homogeneity. As he puts it:

> Work, leisure, nature and culture, all previously dispersed, separate, and more or less irreducible activities that produced anxiety and complexity in our real life ... have finally become mixed, massaged, climate-controlled, and domesticated into the simple activity of perpetual shopping. All these activities have finally become desexed into a single hermaphroditic ambience of style.
>
> (Baudrillard, 1988, p. 34)

Having characterized consumer society in this way, Baudrillard attempts to develop his argument further by reflecting on the transformation of material objects brought about by the emergence of consumer society and the system of human needs which he sees as being conditioned by these developments. Drawing upon his assertion about the centrality of the sign-value of commodities to contemporary consumption, Baudrillard suggests that one principal effect of this 'play of signs' is to constitute a new dominant form of social communication. As he argues,

> Marketing, purchasing, sales, the acquisition of differentiated commodities and object/signs – all of these presently constitute our language, a code in which our entire society communicates and speaks of and to itself.
>
> (Baudrillard, 1988, p. 48)

In addition, Baudrillard argues that it is this logic of signs which now dominates consumption and not the putative needs of consumers. What he means by this is that advertising, packaging and design all work to mark out new desires and pleasures for the consumer which have very little to do with the utility of goods or their ability to satisfy biological needs. He suggests that not only are human needs reconditioned by the system of consumption, but that this system imposes new injunctions on consumers to consume. This compunction or duty to consume is not accidently associated with consumption. For Baudrillard it is central to modern consumption because it is precisely through consumption that capitalist social relations are reproduced. Thus:

> We don't realize how much the current indoctrination into systematic and organized consumption is the equivalent and the extension, in the twentieth century, of the great indoctrination of rural populations into industrial labour, which occurred throughout the nineteenth century ... Production and consumption are one and the same grand logical process in the expanded reproduction of the productive forces and of their control.
>
> (Baudrillard, 1988, p. 50)

Baudrillard's argument in his essay, 'Consumer society', represents a very emphatic characterization of contemporary western societies. What is most noteworthy for us, as I have suggested, is his assertion about the centrality of marketing to the ascendancy of consumer culture. In establishing a new dominant form of social communication in which it is the sign value of commodities which dominates, and in 'indoctrinating' consumers into a compulsion to consume, Baudrillard's account privileges the role of marketing in the cultural transformation associated with consumer society. This is a theme even more explicitly developed in Andrew Wernick's book, *Promotional Culture.*

READING A

Now turn to Reading A, an extract from Andrew Wernick's book, *Promotional Culture: advertising, ideology and symbolic expression.* As you read Wernick's essay, consider the following questions:

1   What does Wernick mean by promotional culture?

2   What is Wernick trying to illustrate with his example of the Paradise myth?

3   What is new about the relationship between circulation and production for Wernick?

promotional culture

As you have seen from Reading A, *Promotional Culture* presents a picture of contemporary western consumer societies characterized by cultural homogeneity amidst the apparent diversity of commodity spectacle and consumer choice in terms reminiscent of Baudrillard. For Wernick it is the spread of **promotional culture** which has brought about this situation.

Thus, while promotion generates what Wernick calls *semiological complexity*, in so doing it also produces a symbolic universe 'boringly void of deeper content' and one in which the distinctions between different domains of symbolic production have been flattened. Wernick's example of the Paradise myth makes this point particularly clearly. He even reads the consequences of promotional culture in the expansion of a culture of self-promotion. Thus, individuals are tied into promotional culture via the forms of promotionally-based, public representations in circulation – from, as Wernick notes, dating and clothes-shopping to attending a job interview.

At the heart of promotional culture are the techniques of promotion associated with modern marketing: specifically, for Wernick, advertising, packaging and design. As you have seen, he argues that these techniques have come to dominate all forms of contemporary communication. Underpinning this spread of the rhetoric of promotion is an intensification of commodity production symptomatic of what he calls 'late capitalism'. For Wernick this more intensive commodification of social life produces not just more commodities, but a new type of commodity. This is a commodity itself transfigured by the impact upon it of the techniques of advertising, packaging and design which either 'transfer cultural associations onto

products propagandistically … [or] by inscribing them into their actual body'
(Wernick, 1991, p. 18). Wernick suggests that this transfiguring of the
commodity through the techniques of promotion has significant effects.
Firstly, he argues that it blurs the line between an object and its promotion.
For Wernick, the consequence of this is to produce objects which are
explicitly designed to circulate. In other words, the moment of circulation
begins to inform the production of an object. Secondly, and following on
from this, 'promotional culture' establishes a new relationship between
culture and economy. On the one hand, Wernick argues, developments in
promotion associated with the circulation of goods become as important to
profitability as technical developments in the product. On the other hand,
the work of adding cultural values and meanings to products is more firmly
drawn into the operation of commodity production. In fact, for Wernick, as
you have seen, 'through commodity imaging the circulation and production
processes have come to overlap'.

Wernick's comments, like Baudrillard's, are suggestive in the way they
attempt to think through the cultural implications of the increased
commodification associated with the expansion of mass consumption and
the image-driven forms of marketing linked with the broadening of modern
consumption's social base. In particular, the way in which both writers
highlight the insinuation of commercial marketing techniques into a wider
field of public representation and the associated 'culturalizing' of the objects
being promoted have some immediate explanatory power in relation to the
Royal Mail advertisement with which I began this chapter. I want to suggest,
however, that there are some real limitations to the approaches developed by
Baudrillard and Wernick in terms of accounting for the role played by
advertising and design in contemporary circulation. Although their accounts
appear to offer some descriptive fit, at root the problem concerns the
overgeneralized account of consumer culture which they advance, and their
inattentiveness to periodizing the developments in marketing to which they
refer. Let us take the question of periodization first. This is important
because it is central to our understanding of cultural processes that it is
possible to locate distinct moments or periods which are characterized by a
degree of stability and continuity in cultural formations.

2.1   Periodizing consumer culture

Baudrillard is particularly cavalier about periodizing the impact of marketing
techniques on the circulation of goods and services and simply invokes the
twentieth century in general as marking the take-off of these developments.
Wernick does recognize the need to specify more carefully the novelty of
'promotional culture', but in the end is equally slippery on the issue of
periodization. He gestures towards a series of evolutionary stages – beginning
in the eighteenth century and proceeding through the 'radio/film age, coca-
colonization and the electronic malls of commercial television' (Wernick,
1991, p. 185) – in which consumer marketing implicitly becomes

increasingly central to (in his terms) 'late capitalist' culture. In sketching out the evolution of promotion, however, Wernick discusses the work of the economic historian Neil McKendrick. (This is in the introduction to *Promotional Culture* and not in the extract you have just read – don't panic if you thought you had missed it!) In fact, it is McKendrick's work on the business practices of the English pottery manufacturer Josiah Wedgwood, and his arguments about the emergence of recognizably modern forms of marketing with Wedgwood, which informs Wernick's decision to locate the beginnings of modern promotion in the eighteenth century. McKendrick's work, however, in contrast to Wernick, precisely offers a tighter periodization of the formation of modern techniques of marketing and their relationship to mass production in setting in motion the birth of consumer society. One reading of McKendrick's work, then, would suggest that there is very little new about the centrality of marketing to the culture of mass consumption. Wedgwood's use of showrooms, exhibitions, trademarks, displays and advertisements suggests continuities over the last two centuries and undercuts claims about the novelty of contemporary consumer culture. In particular, the contention shared by both Baudrillard and Wernick that contemporary consumption is characterized by the dominance of the sign-values of objects (or their cultural meanings) over their 'use-value' is problematized by Wedgwood's strong imaging of his commodities: a manufacturer who named his factory – together with leading lines of his pottery – *Etruria* knew a thing or two about the symbolic dimensions of commodities.

The general terms of Baudrillard's and Wernick's respective accounts of 'consumer society' and 'promotional culture' present further problems. In setting up a picture of a deep-rooted transition to consumer society, both Wernick and Baudrillard follow what Paul Glennie has identified as a familiar theme in work on 'consumer revolutions': a sharp distinction between 'pre-modern consumption, in which people were "users of things"' and modern consumption in which they are the 'consumers of commodities' (Glennie, 1995, p. 165). What such a formulation tends to downplay, Glennie suggests, is the complex use of objects – or **cultures of consumption** – which predate more systematic developments in commercial culture (ibid., p. 177). In addition, both Wernick's and Baudrillard's work, again in line with much of the work on the birth of modern consumer culture (including McKendrick's), tend to conflate a number of distinct developments related to the size of markets, the emergence of new consumption practices, the range of commodities and sectors involved, the levels of investment in production and distribution of consumer goods and the expansion of related economic and cultural institutions. It is precisely by collapsing together these distinct developments within their invocation of a general transition to consumer society, that marketing can emerge as the driving force of these complex economic and cultural changes.

cultures of
consumption

In charting historically both the development of modern marketing and its role within the formation and expansion of consumer culture, we need more grounded accounts of the economic and cultural developments within which shifts in marketing practices are themselves located. Such accounts allow us both to be alert to the continuities over time in the role of marketing in the circulation of goods and services and to recognize the changes associated with the consolidation of new economic and cultural formations. It is through such an approach that we can begin to open up the novelty of contemporary developments in advertising and design.

Recent work in economic and political theory and business history has something to offer in this regard. Taken as a piece, the debates within these fields of enquiry about developments this century during the inter-war and post-war years, in particular, are instructive. This work allows us to consider the interrelationship between developments in production techniques and the distributive trades, in business practices and organizations, in the make-up of the workforce and occupations, in real wages and consumer expenditure, in credit provision and in marketing techniques themselves. In other words, it allows us to consider the relationship between marketing and wider economic processes. These point to the emergence of a decisive new economic formation which took root in western societies during the first half of the twentieth century. It is in debates about Fordism and mass production where this economic formation has been most fully conceptualized.

3   Mass production, mass consumption and the role of consumer marketing

At the heart of debates about **mass production** within political and economic theory is a conception of an economic era dominated by the influence of the technological innovations of mass production. Exemplified by the innovations in motor car manufacture pioneered by Henry Ford, mass production is characterized by the production of standardized units using special-purpose machinery. The drive in production is towards volume output and the pursuit of economies of scale, with each piece of machinery mass-producing a specific component or part of a standardized product. These developments in the production process were, significantly, applied to the mass production of a standardized consumer durable – initially, of course, the Model T Ford. It was the development of this link between mass production and the consumer goods sections that was seminal to the impact of mass production.

As mass production was applied in modified and uneven forms in the inter-war and post-war years across sectors such as clothing and footwear, consumer electronics, white goods production and industries supplying consumer durables production (plate glass, rubber, plastics and steel) (Cutler et al., 1987), western economies were significantly restructured. For a

mass production

number of writers (Murray, 1987; Lipietz, 1982; Jessop et al., 1988) it was the ability of mass production to transform key consumer sectors and to subject a whole range of products and services to the logic of mass production (of scale and standardization with limited differentiation) that allows them to speak of a distinct economic formation that dominated western economies, especially in the period after 1945: that of Fordism or mass production.

This economic formation was additionally characterized by its distinctive regulatory institutions and practices that provided effective conditions for economic growth. In the UK the institutional complex of the Keynesian welfare state established many of these conditions. These included, importantly, the state benefits system and policies aimed at securing full employment, regularized collective bargaining, and the availability of public and private credit (Jessop et al., 1988, p. 129). All these regulatory institutions were shaped by a concern to balance mass production (or supply) with **mass consumption** (or demand).

mass consumption

3.1   Retailing and marketing

Economic and business historians have also noted the way in which the advances in mass production in the consumer goods sectors were linked with developments in wholesaling and retailing. In particular, it was the development of 'economies of scale' in trading through the expansion of the size of retail outlets and, more importantly, the concentration of retailing with the emergence of high-street multiples which were significant features of the inter-war years. In Britain the process of retail concentration was particularly marked. As Scott (1994) has shown, it was in these years that some of the best-known multiple retailers in Britain emerged as dominant players on the high street: Marks and Spencer, Burton, Woolworth, J. Sainsbury, Boots, Tesco, Great Universal Stores and British Home Stores. Together with other forms of large-scale retailing (notably, the Co-operative societies and department stores), multiple retailers expanded rapidly at the expense of independent retailers and accounted for a third of all retail sales by 1939. By the end of the 1930s, as Scott notes, 'there were very few good High Street shopping pitches which were not occupied by multiple retailers, department stores or Co-operative societies' (ibid., p. 2).

In certain retailing markets the emergence of high-street multiples had significant consequences for the manufacturers in these sectors. In the clothing sector, most strikingly, the concentration of sales placed the retailers in a position of dominance over what were – in effect – dependent manufacturers. As you will see in the next chapter, this dominance was important for the development of mass production techniques in clothing production as it was multiple retailers who provided the major impetus towards the introduction of more standardized, long-run clothing manufacture.

Retail concentration in the inter-war years was also assisted by the growth of nationally advertised, branded goods (Scott, 1994). The importance of national advertising, and the mobilization of consumer marketing more generally, represented another significant feature of the consolidation of mass production. They were central to balancing the expansion of supply generated by the productivity gains of mass production with consumer demand for the new mass-produced products. In considering the relationship between marketing and mass production in the UK, however, it is important to recognize the particular ways in which this relationship developed. This means being alert to the developments in consumer marketing in distinct product markets and even companies within these markets.

In his survey of consumer marketing in the UK between 1914 and 1960, Corley (1987) suggests that many British consumer goods manufacturers remained throughout this period more interested in the products their companies produced and in developments in production techniques, than in being what he calls 'marketing-orientated'. Reflecting on the state of consumer marketing at the beginning of World War I, in fact, Corley suggests that marketing had become less skilful and effective than it had been during the industrial revolution. With organizations becoming more complex and bureaucratized, there was no space for what Wilson calls the 'personal hunch' or intuitive 'commercial flair' characteristic of the early commercial entrepreneurs (such as Wedgwood). Corley quotes Kindleberger's emphatic summary of this situation: 'The commercial ability [which had been] so crucial to the innovator – more important than technical capacity – was downgraded as firms grew and became bureaucratic' (ibid., p. 66).

Corley suggests, however, that the picture was far from uniform. In the private car market, both William Morris and Herbert Austin realized the potential of mass marketing and, in the case of Morris, established a network of retail agents and, in the case of Austin, built showrooms and promoted the models through a regular journal. In the area of medicines and toiletries, Beecham was also a strong user of marketing in the period after 1914, making use of the new popular press and poster sites as vehicles for its frequently changing advertising (see Figure 4.2). Another company notable for its marketing strategy was Rowntree. For its Elect cocoa, the company used advertisements in halfpenny newspapers, as well as free promotions sent in the form of postcards to housewives. This latter use of an early form of direct marketing drew upon information gained about its customers from the return of newspaper coupons. This information formed part of Rowntree's interest in market research, an interest which drew its methodology, as Corley notes, from the social surveys carried out by one of the family's own grandees, Seebohm Rowntree.

Rowntree's interest in market research formed part of wider interest in collecting more systematic data on consumers in the inter-war period. The attempt to systematize these procedures went hand in hand with the contiguous ambition of advertising practitioners to formalize advertising

FIGURE 4.2
Magazine advertisement for Beecham, 1915.

techniques and the whole rationale of the process of advertising. Corley refers to the manuals produced by S.H. Benson and the work of the advertising consultant Thomas Russell during this period. Perhaps the most significant development affecting marketing and its relationship to mass-produced consumer goods, however, was the impact of US commercial techniques. This process begins in the inter-war years, but it was in the post-war years of the late 1940s and through the 1950s and early 1960s that these US techniques had their biggest impact on UK marketing. At the heart of this was the so-called 'American invasion': the arrival in London of some of the big players of the US advertising industry, such as J. Walter Thompson and Ted Bates. Their impact was most visible with the arrival of commercial television in 1955 and the influence of techniques of television advertising developed in America. These techniques of selling played an important role in the expanding mass markets for consumer durables which were so central to the cultural transformations – especially in working-class culture – which were noted by commentators at the time in debates about affluence (Pearson and Turner, 1965; Hall et al., 1978; Laing, 1986).

3.2   Articulating mass production with mass consumption

The work on developments in marketing techniques associated with business historians like Corley usefully fills in the picture of the role played by consumer marketing in the consolidation of Fordism in the inter-war and post-war period in the UK. In doing so, it also directs us towards the differentiated use of mass marketing techniques across different sectors.

More importantly, however, the work on Fordism, as I suggested earlier, allows us to conceptualize developments in marketing in relation to wider economic processes. Thus, it was with the expansion of mass production into modern consumer durable sectors that distinctive forms of mass advertising developed. It is therefore impossible to understand the developments in advertising – particularly in the post-war years – without recourse to the consolidation of mass production in these key consumer goods sectors.

Distinctive promotional techniques were developed within advertising in order to reach particular groups of mass consumers with messages about these products. There is, however, another pay-off from considering the work on Fordism produced within economic and political theory. This concerns the more recent work on the crisis of mass production and the arguments about the transition to a new economic era dominated by flexible manufacturing techniques and novel forms of economic regulation. What is significant for us is that this work on **flexible specialization** – or post-Fordism – again has quite a lot to say about the role of consumer marketing. What looms large in the analysis of this form of production is the way in which it is, in contrast to mass production, marketing-led.

flexible
specialization

3.3   Market differentiation, flexible production and the role of marketing

The debates about post-Fordism concern wide-ranging arguments relating to structural changes in both western economies and the wider global economy throughout the 1970s and '80s. A number of processes loom large in these accounts: the increasing globalization of production, the emergence of a new international division of labour, and a new financial order. What has attracted most attention, however, has been the development of new flexible forms of manufacturing within western economies. Peter Braham has set out in Chapter 3 the key innovations associated with flexible manufacturing techniques. As you will recall, he emphasized the way in which these techniques were geared around short-run production for segmented markets rather than being driven by the principle of long-run production of standardized products for mass markets which characterized mass production. He also noted the way in which flexible manufacturing techniques are more directly marketing-led than mass production, with a tighter integration of the stages from design and production to distribution or circulation.

Alongside the developments in manufacturing techniques, the work on flexible specialization has also emphasized the consolidation of new ways of regulating economic activity. One strand of this has been the language of enterprise and enterprise culture. As Paul du Gay argues in Chapter 6, the language of enterprise proposed a new way of regulating economic and organizational activity and was shaped by arguments developed within new wave management theory. A central aspect of this thinking was the emphasis on the need to focus the organizational structure of the firm and its practices upon the consumer in new ways: that is, to develop what Rodney Fitch of the design company Fitch-Rs termed 'an end-user culture' in which the activity of the organization is marketing-led (Gardner and Sheppard, 1989, p. 4). What was meant by this was a greater concern with picking up on shifts in patterns of consumer spending or consumer tastes. Rather than being driven by its own internal priorities, the aim was for organizations to be highly responsive to the demands of its customers or consumers.

This more self-conscious focus on the consumer within organizational theory often took the form of representing the market-place as more diverse in its consumer constituents and faster-changing than the relatively stable formations of mass markets and mass consumers. This conception of consumer markets drew upon an expanding body of new consumer research produced during this period, a body of research itself connected to significant developments in both the advertising and marketing industries. It is to a consideration of these developments that the next section is devoted. In reflecting on these shifts in commercial practices, however, it will be necessary to move from a discussion of structural economic questions to a micro-level analysis of concrete practices and forms of expertise. The aim in doing this is to set out in detail the ways in which these practices work to add cultural values and meanings to goods. The link between the two levels of analysis is, however, key. It is my argument that the shifts in advertising practices associated with the development of a culture of flexible specialization offer us a way of situating the new centrality of advertising and related forms of marketing to the process of circulation. In other words, it is the articulation of new advertising and marketing practices with this wider process of economic restructuring which accounts for the intensification of their role. There is an important conceptual point to draw out from this. Rather than seeing developments in advertising as simply reflective of an already settled reorganization of production processes, I want to suggest that they are playing a leading role in developing wider economic restructuring. Thus, it is the development of a culture of flexible specialization within these service industries which is helping to forge the introduction of flexible manufacturing techniques within production.

3.4   Summary of section 3

I have covered a lot of ground in these first two sections and it is worth briefly taking stock of what has been argued. This is particularly important given the shift to a new level of analysis which I shall undertake in section 4.

1   Arguments about the increasing importance of advertising to the circulation of goods and services are not helped by situating them within accounts of a general transition to 'consumer society' or a 'promotional

culture'. These accounts – notably Baudrillard's – tend to cast as wholly new the role played by contemporary marketing or else – as in the case of Wernick – present a general evolutionary account of its increasing importance.

2   We need to be able to periodize developments in the practices of advertising and to see these developments in relation to wider economic processes. To this end, the increasing importance of advertising can be usefully understood in relation to the transition from an economic era dominated by mass production to an emergent era of flexible specialization.

3   In exploring the articulation between the more intensified role of advertising and marketing and new forms of production, it is important not to see the developments in marketing as merely *reflective* of more fundamental shifts in manufacturing techniques. My contention is that these shifts in manufacturing techniques are, in important ways, driven by developments in marketing practices. The emergent system of flexible specialization is also more clearly marketing-led than is mass production.

4   UK advertising and design practices

In this section, I want to open out for you some of the key developments in advertising practice which were forged during the 1980s and which continue to be influential in shaping the development of advertising campaigns. Figuring prominently in this account is an attention to the so-called 'creative revolution' within UK advertising and a consideration of the way in which the rubric of creativity became key to the articulation of a new vision of advertising. This new vision of advertising itself drew upon developments in consumer research, in account planning and media buying. In reflecting on these forms of advertising knowledge and expertise, I want to suggest that it was their alignment in the language of creative advertising which was central to the creation of a more 'image-led' style of advertising. It is this shift which offers us one way of explaining the intensified aestheticization of advertising representations with which I began this chapter.

4.1   'Creative advertising'

The advocacy of **creative advertising** was most strongly associated with a   creative advertising
group of new agencies which opened in the UK in the late 1970s and early 1980s. These so-called 'second wave' agencies – agencies such as Gold Greenlees Trott (GGT) and Bartle Bogle Hegarty (BBH) – developed a strong emphasis on 'creativity' in part to signal their distance from the large (typically USA-owned) agencies which dominated the industry in the 1970s. The concern to produce creative advertising – advertising which was

BODDINGTONS. THE CREAM OF MANCHESTER.

FIGURE 4.3

One advertisement from an award-winning campaign for the Whitbread Beer Company by Bartle Bogle Hegarty, 1993.

innovative and provocative – was therefore established in opposition to what was represented as the boring and unimaginative advertising produced by the large multinational agencies. At the root of the advocacy of creative advertising was a concern to shift the terms of what constituted an effective advertisement, how consumers should be addressed, and the image of the market-place which underpinned campaign development. For John Hegarty, whose work with BBH was closely associated with the advocacy of creative advertising, the strategy behind developing a successful campaign was centrally based upon the construction for consumers of 'a vision they can aspire to' (*Marketing Week*, 3 March 1989, p. 42). What this meant was producing advertisements which worked directly at the level of identity and desire. BBH's company maxim underlined this commitment to a creative style of advertising: 'We don't sell,' it claimed, 'we make people want to buy' (ibid., p. 44). It was about, in other words, constructing an advertisement around the *emotional selling-point* of the product.

This concern to construct for consumers an elaborated imaginary landscape within which the 'emotional' values of the product were signified, took issue with the styles of (particularly television) advertising which had been enshrined in the textbooks of advertising practitioners in the post-war years. One figure had best articulated this established form of advertising practice and was the implicit target of the new formation of practitioners. This was Rosser Reeves. Reeves, the Chairman of Ted Bates through the 1960s, had expounded what he termed the 'USP' method of advertising in his highly influential book, *Reality in Advertising*, published in 1961. For Reeves, good advertising sprang from the effective identification of a product's *unique selling proposition*: that is, the product's distinctive features or qualities – usually features and qualities associated with what the product could *do* – which distinguished it from competing products. Once these had been identified, they could be hammered home in the campaign. In doing so, USP centre-staged the written copy or verbal statements in delivering the advertising message. In other words, it was a copy-led form of advertising. This technique underlay the classic genre of fast-moving consumer goods advertising which included products such as foods and household goods. The immortal piece of copy – this product 'washes whiter' – said it all.

Heineken. Refreshes the parts other beers cannot reach.

The creative ambitions of advertising associated with the so-called creative agencies in the 1980s were not, however, entirely new. Television advertising – where USP styles were most aggressively mobilized – had from the early to mid-1960s begun to use strong narrative elements, musical scores instead of jingles and a more dynamic combination of picture editing and sound to signify a particular 'way of life', mood or emotional feel in relation to the product. The language of creative advertising had also been mobilized at earlier points in the post-war period. Collett Dickenson Pearce – responsible for Heineken advertising – had made a name for itself as a creative agency during the 1970s, whilst the top London agencies S. H. Benson and the London Press Exchange had reputations as 'creative' agencies in the early 1960s (Pearson and Turner, 1965).

FIGURE 4.4
An example of the innovative campaign for Heineken beer in the 1970s.

This is not to suggest, however, that the advertising produced by the 'creative agencies' of the 1980s did nothing new. What was distinctive about many of the advertisements produced under their rubric was the specific representational techniques and conventions mobilized in the making of advertisements based upon an emotional selling-point strategy. The development of more elaborated forms of story-telling, the turn to forms of pastiche in appropriating retro-imagery, the self-conscious use of black-and-white film stock, cinematic forms of lighting, very fast editing and jump cuts, and the use of new typefaces for the accompanying copy on television advertising were just some of the shifts in the construction of representations which extended the ambition of emotional selling-point advertising in the work of widely respected agencies such as BBH, Yellowhammer and GGT. Similarly, in press advertising, as we saw from the Royal Mail advertisement by DMBB, a more stylized approach to photography, layout and graphic design was evident.

The turn to these representational techniques was dependent on a number of factors. What interests me here are some of the institutional reasons for these shifts. Firstly, they were underpinned in part by the change in the relative mix of clients serviced by agencies. In the 1980s a marked feature of advertising expenditure was the relative decline in the advertising of fast-moving consumer goods and the expansion in the advertising of financial services, government services and information, cars as well as corporate advertising (Jordons, 1989). These clients and product fields were not only less rooted in the tradition of copy-based, USP advertising, but also more open to new approaches. In particular, the marketing managers of these clients tended to be free from the legendary conservatism which characterized the marketing managers of companies such as Unilever and Procter & Gamble – the big-spending advertisers of fast-moving consumer goods.

Secondly, and more importantly, three related elements impacted upon the drive towards creative advertising in the 1980s. These were the influence of new forms of consumer research, the rise to prominence of account planning and the perception by advertising practitioners of media pluralization and a concomitant fragmentation of mass audiences and readerships. These were crucial dependencies within which the arguments advanced by groups of practitioners about creative advertising were rooted. They laid the institutional basis for the deployment of new representational languages within creative advertising. Let us look at the practices and forms of expertise associated with planning.

4.2   Planning advertising

Account planning has a history within UK advertising which extended beyond the emergence of the 'creative agencies' towards the end of the 1970s. Two individuals – Stephen King at J. Walter Thompson and Stanley Pollitt at BMP – were generally credited with having formulated the principles of planning in the late 1960s. Behind both men's formulation of planning was a concern to improve the way in which market research information fed into and – in their terms – helped to improve the production of advertisements and the running of campaigns. For many advocates of this approach, this was represented in terms of planning (and specifically, the planner) acting as the voice of the consumer in the advertising process.

Reflecting on the role of planning in 1987, Kay Scorah, former head of planning at Ted Bates, identified three aspects of the way in which planning intervened in the process of advertising production: via planners' relationship to clients; via planners' relationship to consumers; and via planners' relationship to art directors and writers within the agency's creative department. Let us consider Scorah's arguments.

In reflecting on the first of these relationships – with clients – Scorah suggested that the aim of the planner should be to formulate a clear sense of the product and the client's own marketing ideas. This included the planner being attentive, as she suggested, to informal company knowledge about the product which could reveal fresh information about it and which in turn would help to contribute to an innovative campaign.

The planner's relationship to the consumer was the second key relationship which structured the planning process. Scorah saw this relationship as being built up through a number of procedures. Firstly, it involved a clear specification of at whom the product was being aimed; as Scorah put it, 'Who is the target audience, and what are they like?' (Cowley, 1987, p. 3). In fact, a number of distinct moments came into play in the specification of the target consumer. These involved the planner moving from a representation of the consumer drawn from the consumer research to extended discussions with groups of consumers. The use of these discussions – known as *focus groups* – itself represented an important shift in how researchers attempted to understand consumer behaviour. They displaced the forms of scientific laboratory testing (such as the measurement of consumer responses to advertisements using machines for measuring pupil dilation or blink rates) which had previously been the stock-in-trade of behavioural consumer research. Qualitative consumer research through focus groups enabled the planner to develop a more effective strategy for the advertising, one which could 'present those aspects of [the] product or service most motivating or appealing to our target audience, and in a way which is both interesting and sympathetic' (Cowley, 1987, p. 9).

The third dimension of planning's input into the development of advertising, for Scorah, was the relationship between planners and advertising creatives. This was a crucial relationship, since advocates of planning made significant claims for planning in improving creative execution. Scorah outlined the process as follows:

> The creative team should see the planner as a source of clear briefs, telling them exactly what aspect of the product is most motivating to the target audience and why. They should also see the planner as an objective sounding board for ideas, representing the likely consumer response but also going beyond that to analyse and develop embryonic creative routes.
>
> (Cowley, 1987, p. 5)

The relationship between planners and creatives – as Scorah articulated it – was organized through a number of briefings. These included early strategy formulation and further conversations between creatives and planners which followed the planner-led consumer-group discussions of the proposed advertisements. The creative brief was a key document in this process. This was a succinct statement, usually only one side in length, which consisted of a number of elements:

1   a characterization of the target consumers;

2   a list of the explicit objectives of the advertising and its role in the marketing process;

3   a 'proposition' or 'positioning statement';

4   detailed supporting reasons for the proposition;

5   a list of creative guidelines or what was generally called 'tone of voice';

6   finally, any mandatory requirements or practical considerations.

I can illustrate what these looked like in concrete terms by using the example of a brief produced for one of the more famous campaigns of the last decade – BBH's television advertisements for Levi Strauss 501 jeans (see Box 4.1 overleaf).

For the advocates of planning, developing a good brief lay behind the production of effective and focused advertising. Planning, however, was not without its critics within the industry. Its detractors often saw it as imposing mechanical constraints on the creativity of art directors and writers. A celebrated attack on planning, attributed to Dave Trott, then creative director at GGT, captured this feeling. Likening planners to parrots, he is supposed to have suggested, 'They sit on your shoulders while you're working and crap down your back. And when you've finished, they crap on your work' (*Campaign*, 18 March 1988, p. 20).

Trott's (alleged) use of the parrot analogy was particularly pointed. Don Cowley of the Account Planning Group, a loose grouping of practitioners concerned to advance the cause of planning within the industry, had used the analogy to convey the way in which the planner could help to stimulate the creative development process by providing good briefs for writers and art directors. As Trott's reworking of it suggested, however, Cowley's conception of planning had not, perhaps, deployed the happiest of analogies.

The clash between Cowley and Trott alerts us to the contested nature of planning within the industry. It is clear, however, that despite these public controversies and, importantly, the local variation in the way in which planning was practised within different agency cultures, planning as a function was well established within a large proportion of agencies by the late 1980s. In fact, by the time planning celebrated its twentieth anniversary in 1988, twenty-five of the top thirty agencies had account planning departments. In addition, it was a strong presence in some of the most self-consciously creative agencies. Thus, John Bartle, for example, one of the industry's most thoughtful and respected planners, was a co-founder of BBH – the so-called 'style agency' (*Marketing Week*, 3 March 1989).

BOX 4.1 CLIENT: LEVI STRAUSS, PRODUCT: 501s

1   Why are we advertising?

In order to make *501s from Levis* compulsory equipment, establishing them as the definitive, classic jean.

2   Who are we talking to?

15–19-year-old male jeans-wearers, who care about the way they look, and are in the opinion-forming and early adopter fashion take-up categories.

3   What must the advertising say?

501s from Levis are the right look, and the only label.

And why should they believe it?

Because they represent the way jeans should be worn today; and because they are the original jean, indelibly associated with the birth of teenage culture in the fifties, and its finest expression since.

4   What tone of voice?

Heroic

Highly charged

American ('but period')

5   What practical considerations?

The 501 'look' must be conveyed (product focus).

The international usage argues against dependence on words.

Time length: 30 through 60.

2 × TV

Source: drawn from Feldwick, 1991, p. 186.

4.3   Media buying

In pushing for the value of planning, its supporters argued that developments in the world in which advertising operated – particularly in advertising media – made planning increasingly important through the 1980s. These were developments related to the pluralization of media and the associated fragmentation of television and press audiences. Gary Betts, writing in *Campaign* in 1982, suggested that:

PROCESSION

The action follows the progress of an informal, New Orleans-style procession through a town in the deep south.

A young man carries a battered bag at the centre of a loose association of people, proceeding down a street. Reactions of onlookers are variously quizzical and indifferent.

The man stops briefly by the window of a girl, and their eyes meet. A clumsy cop dropping a cup of coffee breaks the moment.

Moving on, the crowd assembles on top of a hill as the young man pulls a pair of 501s from his bag so worn, they are beyond wearing. He buries them in a hole, marking the spot with the patch.

Pulling back we see many other similarly marked burial sites.

We close with a caption:

SOME THINGS LIVE FOR EVER

FIGURE 4.5 One of the television advertisements produced by BBH for Levi Strauss 501 jeans.

Today's mass circulation newspapers face increasing competition from a plethora of mini-circulation weeklies, shoppers' guides and local government newsheets ... The development of alternative TV channels, satellites, video records, personal computers, TV games and fibre optic cable systems will accelerate the demassification of the media.

(*Campaign*, 23 July 1982, p. 19)

Richard Eyre, media director of *Aspect Advertising*, also identified the erosion of mass audiences as the key to characterizing the shifts which were taking place in advertising media. Periodizing these shifts from the end of the 1960s (the high water-mark, for him, when the 'media was genuinely mass'), Eyre suggested that: 'The media environment has changed. Society has shown a shift away from homogeneity ... towards greater individualism' (*Campaign*, 15 February 1985, p. 47).

The emergence of a more segmented media universe – one in which, in trade terms, there were more media, each with a more tightly defined audience or readership – posed a serious challenge to some of the established conventions of media buying (the practice of buying media space for an advertisement). Central to this challenge was the sense that audience or readership profiles based upon social class categories were insufficiently flexible to grasp the new media audiences being organized within this more diverse market-place. In particular, there was the sense that new ways of categorizing audiences and readerships were needed which could grasp these shifts amongst media consumers. For Richard Eyre, information about the *attitudinal* nature of audiences was required. As he put it, referring to magazines:

> Though age, and to a lesser extent class, may be a discriminator of sorts in identifying the readership of a particular magazine, attitude is always going to be vital when it comes to the actual business of identifying those people who are most likely to buy.
>
> (*Campaign*, 15 February 1985, p. 46)

These attitudinal descriptions of consumers were taken from psychographic and lifestyle segmentations of consumers. First developed in the USA in the early 1960s, **psychographics** used theories of motivation from social psychology to segment consumers into broad motivational groups. **Lifestyles research**, on the other hand, was based upon more descriptive accounts of attitudes, opinions and beliefs. Let me give you some examples of what these segmentations might look like.

psychographics

lifestyles research

READING B

Turn now to Reading B, 'A breakthrough in the study of women' by Christine Restall, planning director of McCanns. When you are reading this extract, make sure you are clear about how the groupings are built up from the attitude statements given by the consumer sample in response to the McCann questionnaire. You might also want to consider what you think the value is of 'personifying' the clusters of responses in this way.

The McCann-Erickson lifestyle study presents an infuriatingly catchy set of consumer types. You may have recognized yourself in them or alternatively perhaps you simply found them crude and patronizing (particularly the categories like 'The Blinkered' and 'The Down-trodden'). What is striking about classifications of this sort, however, is the way they are explicitly counterposed by many market research companies to demographic segmentations. Demographics uses a social class classification of consumers based on occupation (and ranked from A to E). Thus, social class A includes higher managerial and professional occupations, while social class E includes casual workers, labourers and those on Benefit. In research documents these class classifications are clustered to produce more meaningful target groups of consumers. In addition, they are supplemented by the factors of age and gender. Thus, for example, a classic demographic segmentation is 'ABC1 housewives with kids'. For one of the more doctrinaire advocates of attitudinal and motivational segmentations, Liz Nelson of Taylor-Nelson, lifestyles and psychographic profiles made these demographic segmentations redundant. She argued:

> I mean social class is just so [inadequate]. We do a tremendous amount of interviews among doctors. They are all the same demographic group but – crumbs! – you can differentiate between them perfectly in their attitudes towards technology, patients, their attitude to the profession. You can actually have a perfect way of discriminating.
>
> (Nelson, 1989)

For Nelson, then, lifestyles and psychographics could deliver an account of the most pertinent differences between groups of consumers which cut across social class and which were, importantly, the significant factors when it came to understanding consumer behaviour – whether this was in relation to media consumption habits or other purchasing preferences. What is so striking about these segmentations, however, is the way they produced a very different representation of consumers from that formalized within demographics. This stemmed from the way in which lifestyles and psychographics tended to produce both a more intensive individualization of consumers than demographics and emphasized the differences between groups of consumers in more explicitly cultural terms. It is worth examining these processes in greater detail.

Let us take the question of individualization first. You have seen from the McCann-Erickson's 'Woman Study' that it classified eight different types of consumer. Five of these lifestyle types included groups of consumers likely to have been grouped within a demographic segmentation such as 'ABC1 females'. Thus, instead of this singular category, the McCann study identified 'The Avant Guardian', 'The Lady Righteous', 'The Lively Lady', 'The New Unromantic' and 'The Hopeful Seeker'. In other words, it produced a new set of individual types in place of the identity of the mass market housewife ('ABC1 females'). In addition, the study represented the differences between each of its lifestyle types in cultural – rather than occupational – terms. Thus, the differences between 'Lively Lady' and 'Avant Guardian' were represented in terms of the latter's preference for healthy food in relation to food purchases and the former's emphasis on the sensuality of food and the pleasure in eating. This way of segmenting consumers, then, marked out differences between consumers more or less invisible within a demographic segmentation. Both these characteristics of attitudinal and motivational classifications are absolutely key, as we will see later, to their impact on the creative execution of advertisements.

For media buyers like Eyre, being able to employ these attitudinal and motivational segmentations of readerships or audiences was central to the more intensive forms of targeting needed within a more diverse market-place. This concern to target more tightly had implications for the way in which advertising agencies went about buying media space for any particular advertisement. Specifically, it meant that the dominant calculation shifted away from questions of cost and circulation or readership figures, towards questions of what was called 'environment'. In other words, getting value for money in buying advertising space was not simply about buying the cheapest media or (in the case of press or television) the one with the largest viewing or circulation figures (known as achieving 'coverage'). It was about ensuring that the advertisement was appropriately placed so that it could reach the maximum number of its (attitudinally defined) target audience and that this space reinforced or confirmed the values which the advertisement was promoting. In relation to new, declining or relatively small media sectors these were particularly important media-buying criteria. Such an exercise clearly depended upon a good knowledge of the media universe – in particular, the qualities and characteristics of different media. It was in relation to the garnering of this kind of knowledge that planning was again put forward by its advocates as germane to producing an appropriate creative strategy. Thus, for John Bartle of BBH, the planner could furnish the creative team not only with information about the attitudinal characteristics of the most important target consumers, but they could also provide information on the media consumption habits of these consumers (what they read or watched) and offer an analysis and assessment of that media. In this sense, the relationship between the planner and the media buyer was the fourth key relationship through which planning intervened in the process of making advertisements and running campaigns.

ACTIVITY I

If you wanted to target the innovators and early adopters for the Levis advertisement on television, where would be the premium site you would place the advertisement? In *Coronation Street* or *Brookside*, *Eurotrash* or *Inspector Morse*? ITV or Channel 4? UK Gold, Sky Sport or MTV?

Or where might you place an advertisement if you were targeting St Ivel Gold to 'Lively Ladies'?

4.4   The impact on creative execution: IWS and 'new Europeans'

There were important consequences for the creative execution of advertisements pursued by art directors and writers in these shifts in the priorities of media buying and in the impact of planning more generally on the creative development process. Advertising to more segmented media audiences and readerships meant that not only was the choice of media important in terms of targeting, but also that advertising representations had to be appropriate for the media space selected. Putting it bluntly, the advertisement had not only to be in the right place, but it had also to look right in that place to the target consumers. One way in which this concern impacted upon the execution of the advertisements was for the creative team to draw upon (in the case of press advertising) the visual style of the publication in which the advertisement was placed. The DMBB advertisement with which I began this chapter does precisely this.

More important, however, was the new centrality given to attitudinal and motivational consumer classifications within the advertising process. In representing the consumer marketplace as more diverse in terms of groups of consumers and in foregrounding the cultural differences between groups of consumers, these classifications drove a more intensive logic of differentiation and cultural distinction into the heart of advertising production. What this meant for art directors and writers was that their practices were now governed much more by a concern to work upon these distinctions to deliver effective advertising. We can see these processes at work in CLM/BBDO's advertisement for the International Wool Secretariat (see Figure 4.6).

Based in London, the International Wool Secretariat (IWS) is the international marketing arm of the wool producers in the Southern hemisphere and is responsible for promoting wool through the 'Woolmark' label. In 1989 IWS decided to review its apparel advertising with a view to systematizing its European advertising. Previously a number of agencies had promoted the 'Woolmark' in Europe; the IWS has long-term relationships with agencies in three of the four major European markets – Publicis in France, HDM in Germany and Davidson Pearce in the UK. The decision of IWS to review its marketing – particularly its ambition to address a single pan-European market simultaneously – was strongly informed by market research being generated by the Research Institute on Social Change (RISC) and its 'Anticipating Change in Europe' (ACE) programme.

RISC/ACE was a research programme which drew upon psychographic segmentations of consumers. In the UK Taylor-Nelson were one of the best known proponents of this type of research. Derived from an American system called the Yankelovitch Monitor, Taylor-Nelson's psychographic research segmented consumers into three broad motivational groups on the

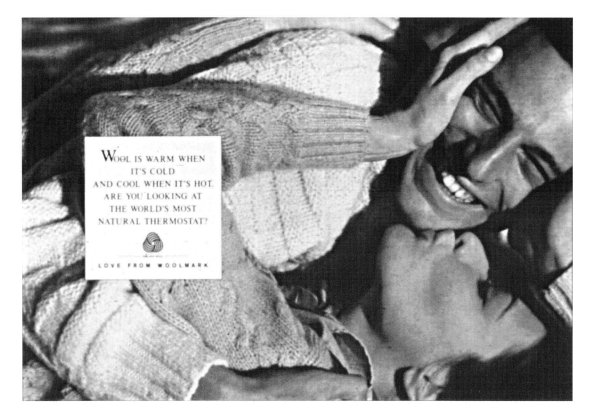

basis of analysing responses to a wide spread of questions – about the environment, technology, big business, women's rights and drug abuse. The segmentations derived from this produced three motivational groups: the 'sustenance-motivated'; 'outer-directed'; and 'inner-directed'. Taylor-Nelson's work was particularly concerned with charting the relative balance over time of these three motivational categories. A good deal of this concern was focused through the terms of reference of RISC/ACE: that is, by the concern to analyse social trends and the movement of these motivational categories on a pan-European stage. In carrying out this work, Taylor-Nelson were concerned to explore the motivations of what they saw as individuals 'at the forefront of social trends'. To do this Taylor-Nelson charted the movements of values along a graph of 'traditional norms and values' to 'new values'. For Taylor-Nelson, the key motivations amongst the 'social innovators' were fivefold:

FIGURE 4.6
CLM/BBDO's advertisement for the International Wool Secretariat.

1 'desire for emotional experience'
2 'polysensuality'
3 'risk-taking'
4 'networking'
5 'exploring new mental frontiers'.

Let me give you a flavour of a couple of these terms. *Polysensuality* identifies and charts the increasing importance to the consumer of 'smelling, tasting, touching, as well as seeing and hearing and being in touch with his [*sic*] affectivity ... To the consumer this means the joy of smelling fresh bread and newly ground coffee, feeling silk next to one's skin or the texture of ripe Brie'; while the '*desire for emotional experience*' homes in on the way 'people have the need to feel their body in new and different, intensive ways, the desire for frequent emotional experiences and the enjoyment of doing something which is just a little dangerous or forbidden.'

The significance of this research for IWS was that it also pointed to strong continuities across different European countries within this group of 'social innovators'. As IWS put it, 'our target customers aged between 20–35 years old were becoming increasingly similar across Europe.' IWS elaborated, suggesting 'it is especially true of clothes – if you go to an airport now you can't tell where young people come from by their clothes.' IWS's decision to focus its marketing upon this pan-European market segment had major consequences for the three big agencies which had run previous campaigns in the UK, France and Germany. IWS invited each of these agencies to pitch for the new pan-European campaign in an open review of the account. In the end the French agency CLM/BBDO emerged as the successful agency. In developing their campaign, CLM/BBDO drew heavily on the RISC/ACE findings and put together a campaign which attempted to speak directly and in the appropriate 'tone of voice' to this group of consumers. This meant attempting to produce an identification between the target consumers and the cultural meanings coded in the advertisement. One of the striking features of the advertisements was the way in which they broke with many of the established limitations of pan-European advertising. In trade terms these limitations were that such advertising – because it had to address different national markets with the same advertisements – was typically bland and uncreative. As *Campaign* put it, 'in pan-European advertising the highest common factor is not all that far removed from the lowest common denominator'. It was precisely by drawing upon the RISC/ACE research that CLM/BBDO could develop a campaign targeted specifically at this segment of 'style-conscious 20–35 year-olds' or 'social innovators' and produce an advertisement with a high creative content. At the heart of its creative strategy was an emotional appeal to the qualities of wool and a linking of it with notions of sensuality and heterosexual complementarity. As CLM/BBDO put it:

> [We] wanted a very strong emotional platform which would set wool apart from synthetics. But then that had to be reinforced by rational benefits: our target audience hadn't necessarily grown up thinking wool was wonderful. All that had to be summed up by a consistent and universal motif – an ongoing relationship between a couple. One of the things that came out of the research is that people could identify with the couple.
>
> (*Campaign*, 3 February 1989, p. 25)

The campaign was run in twelve languages across sixteen countries and was placed as a double-page spread in fashion magazines (*Vogue, Elle, Marie Claire*) and men's style magazines (*Arena, GQ*), together with Sunday colour supplements. The creative strategy pursued by CLM/BBDO was formed in relation to these priorities: to speak to a specific consumer segment, to reach them via the most appropriate media and to give the advertisements a 'look' which was sympathetic to the media environment chosen. Each of these priorities required the foregrounding of questions of cultural distinction – the ways in which this group of consumers was differentiated from other lifestyle or attitudinal groups – and in doing so it produced a trenchantly image-led style of advertising.

4.5 Some concluding thoughts on advertising practices

Let me pull together the threads of the argument which I have been developing in this section and link these up with the more general arguments about economic change which were introduced in section 3. I have detailed a number of practices and their associated forms of knowledge and expertise central to the development of 'creative advertising'. In doing this, the main aim has been to demonstrate the ways in which these practices worked to add cultural values and meanings to goods and services. Alongside this, though, there has been a more specific insistence about the way in which recent shifts in these creative practices marked an intensification of the process of adding cultural meanings. I suggested there were a number of dimensions to this intensification. We saw how the aim to develop a more image-led style of advertising by groups of advertising practitioners formed one part of this. Most importantly, however, the ambition to target a more differentiated set of consumer markets led advertising practitioners to place greater emphasis on a more stylized or aestheticized set of visual codes. The reason for this was that these codes were mobilized in order to produce an identification between the product and a specific segment of consumers. Playing a key role in this shift was the influence of attitudinal and motivational forms of consumer research. As we have seen, these classifications were critical in terms of the way in which advertising practitioners and their clients approached what they saw as shifts in consumer lifestyles and tastes and how they reorganized their practices in order to capitalize on these shifts.

I framed my account of these developments in advertising practices by indicating the importance of being aware of their connections to wider economic processes. In fact, you will remember that I ended section 3 by arguing that shifts towards more flexible forms of production needed to form part of our understanding of the emergence of new advertising and marketing techniques, and that we could account for the more intensive role played by advertising and design in terms of the way in which these practices were articulated with the emergent forms of production. In reflecting on this articulation, however, I suggested that service-providers (within advertising, design, market research and retailing) – through the institution of a more segmented view of mass markets – were leading the way in establishing a new attention to product differentiation, diversity and consumer choice.

The examples I have set out in section 4 underline this establishment of a culture of flexible specialization within these creative industries. While reaffirming this link between the new techniques of advertising and the wider economic restructuring, however, I would also point out that it is important not to overplay these developments. Whilst I have emphasized the emergence of advertising techniques geared towards segmenting mass markets, mass marketing techniques have remained an important part of the commercial practices of these industries. In relation to product fields such as soap powders, for example, mass advertising techniques are still trenchantly deployed. In addition, where techniques geared towards market segmentation have been used, they have often been combined with practices associated with mass marketing. In the IWS advertisement discussed in section 4.4, for example, the concern to reach the target consumers through segmented or niche publications – like the men's magazine market and the style press – sat alongside the placing of the advertisement in the Sunday supplements (offering access to a large but undifferentiated market of consumers). The important point here is that the transformation of commercial cultures does not occur in neat homogeneous blocks. It is a process of uneven development. This is even more important when the processes we are discussing are themselves part of a wider, on-going transformation in economic formations.

5   Situating advertising practitioners

In setting out an account of the practices of 'creative advertising' in section 4, I have made use of accounts drawn from the practitioners who were themselves involved in these processes. As I hope emerged from these accounts, a good deal can be learnt from such an analysis. It provides us with a route into the broader cultural analysis of the way in which advertising practitioners add cultural values and meanings to goods and services. In insisting on the value of these accounts, however, it is worth underlining that they only offer us a partial view and need to be carefully handled. Why qualify in this way what we can take from the practitioners' reflections on their own practices? You might argue that their accounts of the advertising process simply reflect what is going on. My feeling is that rather than reading them as true accounts of the processes in which they are involved, we need to be aware that in producing these accounts the practitioners are also representing the process to themselves: that is, they are attempting to organize their own understanding of what they do. Their accounts are, in addition, shaped by the context of their formulation –

namely, by the business or commercial culture of their respective industries; in other words, their accounts are formulated with particular audiences in mind. This will include colleagues, competitors and clients. This context will often mean that their accounts are informed by an attempt to argue for the value of the practices they describe (or conversely, by a concern to rubbish them). The account of planning which I gave in section 4 particularly needs to be seen in these terms, but the principle applies more generally.

Insisting that we need to read critically the accounts given by practitioners as particular representations of the practices of advertising (and not as simplistically 'true') has specific consequences. It means that we need to be alert to the ways in which they represent these practices through specific codes and consider how these codes prevent certain things being said. We need to develop a sense of these absences and blind-spots, in particular, in order to develop a fuller account of the practices of advertising. Let me suggest four areas about which we might want to know more in order to produce a fuller account of these processes.

The first concerns the way in which informal knowledge enters into the development of advertising. A good example of this would be the way in which information about the target consumers, not evident in the consumer research or brief but known to the creative team or designers as part of their general cultural knowledge, would shape the execution of the work. This is particularly important if the practitioners are culturally close to the target audience. Secondly, the kinds of education and training received by the practitioners will shape the volume and quality of cultural resources – or **cultural capital** – on which they can draw and will, therefore, shape the   cultural capital
final work. Thirdly, the kinds of cultural languages and representational practices in circulation in the wider culture will both help to generate and also set limits on what the practitioners can represent. The innovations in design and pop video which emerged from the late 1970s, for example, were important influences on advertising creatives working in the 1980s discussed above. Fourthly, and perhaps most elusively, the cultural identifications of the practitioners themselves will influence their creative work. By this, I mean their cultural preferences and tastes. Opening out this last category means considering further the individuals who are employed in this occupation. It means asking: Who are they? What are their backgrounds and lifestyles? It is to an exploration of these questions that the remainder of this chapter is devoted.

5.1 Dealing in culture: the new bourgeoisie and the new petite bourgeoisie

Perhaps the most immediately striking feature about exploring the make-up of advertising practitioners as an occupational group is the paucity of scholarly work on them. Compared with the amount of work on occupational groups in other sectors, they remain under-researched. What this means is that there are very few good accounts from which to begin to develop a picture of the social make-up of these creative practitioners and their lifestyles and cultural preferences. One book, however, which does have something suggestive to say about cultural occupations is *Distinction* (1984) by the French sociologist, Pierre Bourdieu (see the discussion of Bourdieu in **du Gay, Hall et al.**, 1997).

Distinction is a rich, dense and often obtuse book which is principally concerned to offer a sociological analysis of taste. Bourdieu's central aim in *Distinction* is to challenge what he calls the 'ideology of charisma'. This regards what is typically seen as good taste (in legitimate or high culture) as an innate disposition – something which some people have and which others (conspicuously) do not. In contradiction to this, Bourdieu argues that taste, in fact, has specific social conditions of existence (principally structured, he argues, according to access to formal educational qualifications) and operates, in addition, as a classificatory system through which different social classes both establish their own class identity and at the same time mark distinctions between themselves and other classes. Based on research conducted in France in the 1960s and '70s, *Distinction* is, to this end, dominated by an analysis of the particular dispositions and structures of taste through which fractions of the French middle class (the bourgeoisie), the lower middle class (the petite bourgeoisie) and the working class signify their class position or identity. Bourdieu charts these dispositions and tastes by looking at the consumption preferences of these social groups. It is through exploring these patterns of consumption – particularly the consumption of literature and music, but also food and clothing – that Bourdieu is able to identify distinctive sets of dispositions and cultural preferences, or distinctive structures of taste.

Within this dense empirical analysis it is Bourdieu's comments on the new petite bourgeoisie and the new bourgeoisie which stand out in relation to our concerns in this section. It is in his comments on both these class fractions (and in particular the new petite bourgeoisie) that Bourdieu explicitly addresses the social make-up of **cultural intermediaries**. Thus, in an oft-quoted passage, Bourdieu suggests:

cultural intermediaries

> The new petite bourgeoisie comes into its own in all the occupations involving presentation and representation (sales, marketing, advertising, public relations, fashion, decoration and so forth) and in all the institutions

providing symbolic goods and services. These include the various jobs in medical and social assistance [...] and in cultural production and organization which have expanded considerably in recent years.

(Bourdieu, 1984, p. 359)

The new petite bourgeoisie represents, for Bourdieu, a distinctive grouping within the lower middle class as a whole. They are differentiated by their lifestyles and cultural preferences from the two better documented fractions of the lower middle class: the declining petite bourgeoisie (made up of shop-keepers and master artisans) and the executant petite bourgeoisie (white-collar employees). In exploring the distinctive cultural dispositions of this group, Bourdieu places much emphasis on the diverse social background of the individuals who make up the new petite bourgeoisie and on the relatively open nature of cultural intermediary occupations (open in terms of formal entry requirements and career paths). Bourdieu makes much of what he calls the 'heterogeneity of the agents' trajectories' who make up the intermediary occupations. By this he means the variety of social class backgrounds of the individuals who constitute the new petite bourgeoisie. Bourdieu suggests that an 'ambivalent relationship to the educational system' is shared by those individuals originating in particular from the middle class or working class and entering into intermediary occupations. As he puts it:

The new occupations are the natural refuge for all those who have not obtained from the educational system qualifications that would have enabled them to claim the established position their original social position promised them; and also those who have not obtained from their qualifications all they felt entitled to expect by reference to an earlier state of the relationship between qualifications and jobs.

(Bourdieu, 1984, p. 357)

In place of recognized educational qualifications, Bourdieu suggests that these individuals (especially from the middle class) often possess high levels of cultural capital (most usually associated with knowledge of legitimate culture, though it might also include other cultural knowledges). This fact, combined with their ambivalence towards the formal educational system, induces:

A sense of complicity with every form of symbolic defiance, inclines them to welcome all the forms of culture which are [...] on the (lower) boundaries of legitimate culture – jazz, cinema, strip-cartoons, science fiction – and to flaunt (for example) American fashions and models – jazz, jeans, rock or the avant-garde underground [...] as a challenge to legitimate culture; but they also often bring into these regions [...] an erudite, even 'academic' disposition which is inspired by a clear intention of rehabilitation, the cultural equivalent of the restoration strategies which define their occupational project.

(Bourdieu, 1984, p. 360)

It is worth reflecting on the cultural choices of the new petite bourgeoisie outlined by Bourdieu in this quotation. They amount to the carving out of a distinctive structure of taste and lifestyle through the appropriation and 'rehabilitation' of specific cultural forms and practices. A strong feature of this – as Bourdieu's comments make clear – is the mixing of high and popular cultural forms. Although Bourdieu's example draws on French sources, it is possible to identify equivalent cultural forms within the UK which evidence the impact of this new petite bourgeois structure of taste – in particular, its mixing of legitimate and popular culture and its preference for retro-imagery or the recycling of cultural forms. One good example would be the Biff cartoons which run (most notably) in the *Weekend Guardian* (see Figure 4.7). The rehabilitation to the television schedules of 1960s' popular programmes such as *The Munsters*, *The Avengers* and *Captain Scarlet* also suggests the concern of broadcasters to explicitly address these new tastes.

FIGURE 4.7

A Biff cartoon – typifying the taste of the new petite bourgeoisie?

What is clear – certainly if we follow Bourdieu's argument – is that the appropriation of these cultural forms is associated with two strategies of distinction amongst the new petite bourgeoisie. The first concerns the ambition of the new petite bourgeoisie to establish areas of expertise or cultural authority over the provision of symbolic goods and services. The advertising and design industries offer good examples of the importance of

this strategy. Both areas of service remain weakly professionalized and the knowledge which they mobilize is poorly formalized as bodies of expertise. This is in marked contrast to successfully professionalized occupations such as the law or medicine. Advertising folk and designers, then, can *de facto* lay claim to a monopoly of expertise over their respective areas of symbolic production by these more explicitly cultural forms of occupational closure.

The second strategy of distinction relates to the differentiation of the new petite bourgeoisie from the structure of traditional petite bourgeoisie taste. For Bourdieu this traditional form of lower middle-class taste (which he calls middle-brow taste) is characterized by an anxious cultural pretension and a reverence for – combined with a lack of knowledge of – legitimate culture. Bourdieu identifies in this petite bourgeois relation to (legitimate) culture a disposition which he calls *cultural goodwill*. By this he means an ambition on the part of the petite bourgeoisie to aspire to the same ease with which the bourgeoisie relate to legitimate culture. This ambition, however, is undermined by the lack of adequate knowledge of these cultural forms amongst the petite bourgeoisie and leaves them open to what he calls *cultural allodoxia*, or 'the mistaken identifications and false recognitions which betray the gap between acknowledgement and knowledge ...' (Bourdieu, 1984, p. 323). This cultural allodoxia, however, generates its own distinctive cultural forms: middle-brow culture. For Bourdieu, middle-brow culture is petite bourgeois culture par excellence in that it represents a form of popularized legitimate culture. He thus describes it as, 'accessible versions of avant garde experiments, ... film adaptations of classic drama and literature, popular arrangements of classical music or orchestral versions of popular tunes. ... in short, everything which goes to make up "quality weeklies" and "quality" shows' (ibid., p. 323). It also includes new cultural forms which represent 'genres half-way between legitimate culture and mass production'.

ACTIVITY 2

> Are Bourdieu's comments useful for thinking about the decisions made by TV producers and executives concerning programming policy and commissioning in relation to 'quality' television? Can you think of recent examples of middle-brow culture on television? Classic serials, science programmes (like *Tomorrow's World*)?

The choices that the new petite bourgeoisie make concerning their own cultural consumption and lifestyles are thus strongly shaped by an overriding concern to differentiate themselves from the cultural goodwill typical of petite bourgeoisie taste. Bourdieu suggests that this differentiation is clearest amongst the metropolitan new petite bourgeoisie. In fact, he goes so far as to argue that the dispositions of the new petite bourgeoisie find their fullest expression in Paris – nearest the centre of cultural values and closest to the most 'intense supply of cultural products'. This is a particularly suggestive point for us in reflecting on the cultural dispositions of advertising practitioners.

One of the striking features of this industry is the location of the offices of the leading companies at the heart of metropolitan life. In the 1980s many agencies were clustered in Soho and Covent Garden in London. Bartle Bogle Hegarty had their offices in Great Pulteney Street in Soho, whilst Saatchi and Saatchi's main offices were in Charlotte Street, just north of Soho behind Tottenham Court Road. This geographical clustering of the industry within the London West End and Soho has a long history, with J. Walter Thompson being the first agency to occupy offices in the West End in the 1930s with its move to Berkeley Square (Mayfair). The decision to locate in these places carried particular cultural associations. At the heart of these was an association of the agencies with modernity and urban sophistication, together with – in the case of the agencies based in Soho – a set of references to bohemia and sexual transgression (cf., Okin, 1991; Mort, 1995). The self-representation of advertising practitioners – particularly advertising men – has, since at least the 1960s, made extensive use of metropolitan scripts. Looming large in this has been the take-up of the most contemporary signs of modern consumption – notably in terms of dress (Nixon, 1996b).

Bourdieu also suggests that the influence of a post-1968 counterculture represents a key component of the formation of the metropolitan new petite bourgeoisie. He sees this latter influence as manifesting itself as a concern to experiment with new lifestyles and values. Prominent amongst these are attempts to develop new forms of child-rearing, sexual expression and the experience of the body and pleasure (Bourdieu, 1984, pp. 366–71). Bourdieu sees in these dispositions a new 'art of living' characterized at root by its opposition to older notions of duty, sobriety, modesty and deferred gratification. In their place it embodies a commitment to a 'morality of pleasure as duty' (Bourdieu, 1984, p. 367). We can see in this characterization an echo of the values identified by Taylor-Nelson's RISC research amongst the 'new Europeans', particularly the notion of 'desire for emotional experience'. This is quite appropriate. Bourdieu sees in this new morality or ethic rooted in pleasure a more intensive form of individualism which, he suggests, fits with the demands of a consumer-driven economy. It is an individualism best represented, he suggests, precisely in the language of pleasure and desire associated with advertising research; an individualism which undercuts the older anti-market values embedded in the collective structures associated with extended family forms and the networks of spatially embedded communities. Bourdieu concludes his comments on the new petite bourgeoisie, then, by locating them as part of the 'ethical avant garde' of consumer capitalism and its new form of 'enlightened conservatism'. For Bourdieu, this is an ethic which the new petite bourgeoisie both embodies in its own values and lifestyle and articulates through its role in cultural circulation. It is this ethic and these values and lifestyles which also, for Bourdieu, draw the new petite bourgeoisie into a close cultural alliance with the new bourgeoisie, who share the same anti-puritan values and lifestyle. The new bourgeoisie occupy similarly key roles in the modern consumer-based economy as executives and directors in the cultural intermediary industries (tourism and journalism, publishing and the cinema, fashion and advertising, decoration and property development) (Bourdieu, 1984, pp. 310–11).

Significantly for us, one of the case studies which Bourdieu offers in *Distinction* to flesh out his conception of the cultural preferences and dispositions of the new bourgeoisie is that of a young advertising executive.

> READING C
>
> Now turn to Reading C, Pierre Bourdieu's 'A young executive who "knows how to live"'. While you are reading the extract, try to pull out the general qualities which Bourdieu identifies in Michel R.'s and Isabelle's choices of food, clothing, home decoration, car and leisure activity.

5.2   Advertising practitioners as cultural intermediaries

Where do Bourdieu's comments on the new petite bourgeoisie and the new bourgeoisie leave our attempts to reflect upon the dispositions and make-up of advertising and design practitioners? Positively, Bourdieu presents us with a suggestive general picture of the lifestyles, dispositions and cultural preferences of these cultural intermediary social groupings. These are dispositions and cultural preferences shaped by the wider dynamics of class, taste and cultural distinction which, for Bourdieu, structure social space. This approach, as I have tried to suggest, gives a certain depth to thinking about the role played by advertising and design folk as creative practitioners dealing in symbolic goods and services. We can see this role as being shaped by the ambition to establish authority over particular areas of symbolic production stemming from the relatively open nature of these occupations. The concern of the new petite bourgeoisie to promote new tastes and values in this process further stems from its attempts to differentiate itself as a class fraction from the other sections of the lower middle class. Bourdieu's suggestive comments still leave us with much work to do, however, in terms of grounding his insights in relation to the cultural intermediaries who have figured in this chapter. A number of immediate qualifications to Bourdieu's arguments become necessary once we try to do this.

Firstly, Bourdieu offers a too homogeneous picture of these creative practitioners. We need a more differentiated picture of these occupational groupings. This would mean attending to the differences marked by educational background and training and by the particular organizational function performed by practitioners. Within UK advertising agencies, for example, planners will typically have university degrees (in a diverse range of subjects), whilst art directors and writers are increasingly likely to have been through art school or the former polytechnic art and design courses. The differences between advertising practitioners in this respect and other cultural intermediaries – such as television producers – also need to be explored.

The organizational cultures of the businesses which make up the advertising and design industries represent a second area where we need to add to Bourdieu's analysis. This would mean looking at the particular workplace cultures which develop within advertising agencies. Such an approach would include attending to their formal management practices as well as the more informal dynamics of advertising workplaces. Exploring these questions would also direct us towards the kinds of gender, 'racial' and ethnic identities or scripts that are sanctioned within these creative industries. I have already hinted at how particular masculine scripts were privileged within the culture of advertising. In addition we might note how the arguments about 'creativity' in advertising during the 1980s were often coded in relation to questions of ethnicity/national identity. Thus, the high creative content of UK advertising was explicitly set against the less creative techniques of USA advertising. This was seen as stemming from an inherently British reserve about the dirty business of selling: emphasizing the creativity of advertising was a way of finessing its underlying commercial imperatives. Whatever we might think of this analysis, it points to the way in which the conduct of the business of advertising might be closely linked with representations of national or ethnic characteristics.

Opening up the gender, ethnic and 'racial' scripts privileged within these commercial cultures leads me onto my final point. Whilst Bourdieu emphatically reads the values and lifestyles of the new petite bourgeoisie and the new bourgeoisie as being highly conservative, it is possible to read them in other ways. Certainly if we consider gender and sexual scripts, we get at the very least a more complicated picture. Thus, for example, the strong investment by groups of advertising men in the new, more stylized forms of masculinity associated with the 'new man' during the mid to late 1980s (see **Nixon**, 1997) points to progressive currents within the values and lifestyles promoted by these intermediary players.

6   Conclusion

Let me draw together the key themes which have been developed through this chapter. I have devoted a good deal of it to detailing a set of practices associated with the production of advertising campaigns. A central aim in doing this has been to draw out the way in which advertising practitioners as cultural intermediaries articulate two key moments in the circuit of culture: the domains of production and consumption. We saw this process at work very clearly in the IWS advertisement. The advertising agency CLM/BBDO mediated between the IWS (representing the wool producers) and the group of consumers which they were attempting to reach. This process involved the mobilization of some specific kinds of advertising knowledge and expertise. I foregrounded the importance of debates about creative advertising and the role of planning, consumer research and media buying in shaping the development of campaigns. Each of these elements impacted upon the creative execution of the advertisements, shaping the kinds of cultural values and meanings added to the goods being promoted. In the case of the IWS advertisement, these were meanings to do with the sensuality of wearing wool and the emotional and physical intensity of a young couple.

The IWS advertisement also made clear the way in which the process of adding cultural values and meanings not only attempted to fix the meanings of goods and services, but was also concerned with producing an identification between these meanings and the target consumers. The latter ambition was dependent upon particular ways of talking about or representing the target consumers. In the case of the IWS advertisement both the client and the agency conceived of the target consumers as a particular market segment – 20–35 year-old 'social innovators'. In specifying the target market in this way, they drew heavily upon psychographic consumer research. It was this research (and the associated forms of lifestyles research) which emerged as a key concern of the chapter. As I suggest in section 4, what was significant about both psychographics and lifestyles research was the way they produced a very different representation of consumer markets from that formalized within demographics. Lifestyles and psychographic research placed a greater emphasis on the mobility of markets and threw up a more tightly individualized set of consumer types. Most importantly, however, they foregrounded the cultural differences between groups of consumers. I suggested that this aspect of psychographics and lifestyles research played an important role in driving a more intensive logic of cultural distinction into the process of advertising. It was this logic which partly underpinned the emphasis on a more stylized or aestheticized set of visual codes in advertising representations.

The mobilization of psychographics and lifestyles research was also central to the institution of a more segmented view of mass markets within important areas of the business of advertising. It was the currency of this research in the creative development process, then, which represented the way in which what I called a culture of flexible specialization was established within the commercial practices of advertising. Emphasizing this link with flexible specialization was important to the more general model of advertising advanced in the chapter. Against those interpretations which tended to produce overgeneralized accounts of the centrality of advertising (and associated forms of marketing) to the expansion of consumer culture, the chapter has insisted on linking advertising practices to wider economic and cultural processes in a more tightly periodized way. In particular, the articulation between developments in advertising and marketing and the restructuring of the consumer sectors of the economy have been emphasized.

The men and women of the advertising industry – the cultural intermediaries themselves – have also loomed large in this chapter. In detailing the way they mediated between the world of production and the activities of consumers I not only emphasized the formal practices through which they shaped the circulation of goods and services, but also suggested that their cultural preferences and tastes impacted upon the production of advertisements. Developing this assertion led me to explore the make-up of this occupational group in the latter part of the chapter. To this end, I drew upon Bourdieu's work and attempted to develop an account of the cultural preferences and tastes of advertising practitioners by making use of his analysis of the lifestyles and tastes of the new bourgeoisie and the new petite bourgeoisie. The strength of Bourdieu's work was to offer an account of the dispositions and cultural preferences of cultural intermediaries grounded in the wider dynamics of class, taste and cultural distinction. Bourdieu's work in itself, however, could not provide a sufficient picture of the cultural preferences of advertising practitioners. The insights which can be drawn from his study require further work in order to produce an adequate account of these cultural intermediaries. Given the importance of the role they play in the circulation of culture – a role which this chapter has detailed – developing this work is a pressing intellectual concern. The value of doing such work is underscored by Graeme Salaman in the next chapter where he considers another symbolic intermediary occupation – that of management consultants – and the role of this grouping in 'culturalizing' organizational life.

References

BAUDRILLARD, J. (1988) 'Consumer society' in *Selected Writings* (ed. M. Poster), Cambridge, Polity Press.

BOURDIEU, P. (1984) *Distinction: a critique of the judgement of taste*, London, Routledge.

CORLEY, T. A. B. (1987) 'Consumer marketing in Britain 1914–60', *Business History,* Vol. 29, No. 4, pp. 65–83.

COWLEY, D. (ed.) (1987) *How to Plan Advertising*, London, Cassell.

CUTLER, T., HASLAM, C., WILLIAMS, J. and WILLIAMS, K. (1987) 'The end of mass production', *Economy and Society*, Vol. 16, No. 3.

DU GAY, P., HALL, S., JANES, L., MACKAY, H. and NEGUS, K. (1997) *Doing Cultural Studies: the story of the Sony Walkman*, London, Sage/The Open University (Book 1 in this series).

FEATHERSTONE, M. (1991) *Consumer Culture and Postmodernism*, London, Sage.

FELDWICK, P. (ed.) (1991) *Advertising Works 5*, Institute of Practitioners in Advertising.

GARDNER, C. and SHEPPARD, J. (1989) *Consuming Passion: the rise of retail culture*, London, Unwin Hyman.

GLENNIE, P. (1995) 'Consumption within historical studies' in Miller, D. (ed.) *Acknowledging Consumption*, London, Routledge.

HALL, S. et al. (1978) *Policing the Crisis*, Basingstoke, Macmillan.

JESSOP, B., BONNETT, K., LING, T. and BROMLEY, S. (1988) *Thatcherism*, Cambridge, Polity Press.

JORDONS (1989) *Britain's Advertising Industry*, Bristol, Jordons & Son Ltd.

KINDLEBERGER, C. P. (1964) *Economic Growth in France and Britain 1851–1950*, Cambridge, MA, Harvard University Press.

LAING, S. (1986) *Representations of Working-class Life 1957–1964*, Basingstoke, Macmillan.

LASH, S. and URRY, J. (1987) *The End of Organized Capitalism*, Cambridge, Polity Press.

LIPIETZ, A. (1982) 'Towards global Fordism', *New Left Review*, No. 132, pp. 33–47.

MCDERMOTT, C. (1987) *Street Style: British design in the 1980s*, London, Design Council.

MCKENDRICK, N. (1982) 'Josiah Wedgwood and the commercialization of the potteries' in McKendrick, N., Brewer, J. and Plumb, J. H. (eds) *The Birth of a Consumer Society: the commercialization of eighteenth-century England*, Bloomington, IN, Indiana University Press.

MORT, F. (1995) 'Archaeologies of city life: commercial culture, masculinity and spatial relations in 1980s London', *Environment and Planning D: Society and Space*, Vol. 13, pp. 573–90.

MURRAY, R. (1987) 'Ownership, control and the market', *New Left Review*, No. 164, pp. 87–112.

NELSON, E. (1989) Interview with author.

NIXON, S. (1996a) *Hard Looks: masculinities, spectatorship and contemporary consumption*, London, UCL Press.

NIXON, S. (1996b) 'Advertising executives as modern men: masculinity and the UK advertising industry in the 1980s' in Blake, A. et al. (eds) *Buy This Book: studies in advertising and consumption*, London, Routledge.

NIXON, S. (1997) 'Exhibiting masculinity' in Hall, S. (ed.) *Representation: cultural representations and signifying practices*, London, Sage/The Open University (Book 2 in this series).

OKIN, C. (1991) 'Why move out?', *Campaign*, 13 December, pp. 22–3.

PEARSON, J. and TURNER, G. (1965) *The Persuasion Industry*, London, Eyre and Spottiswoode.

RESTALL, C. (1985) 'A breakthrough in the study of women', *Campaign*, 22 November, pp. 26–8.

SCORAH, K. (1987) 'The planning context' in Cowley, D. (ed.).

SCOTT, P. (1994) 'Learning to multiply', in *Business History*, Vol. 36, No. 3.

WERNICK, A. (1991) *Promotional Culture: advertising, ideology and symbolic expression*, London, Sage.

READING A:
Andrew Wernick, 'The promotional condition of contemporary culture'

Advertising is commonly taken to mean *advertisements*, paid for and recognizable as such, together with the process of their production and dissemination. In that restricted sense, however vast and ubiquitous a phenomenon, advertising is certainly only one aspect of a wider process of cultural commodification: institutionally, a subsector of the culture industry; textually, a delimited sub-field within the larger field of commercially produced signs. At the same time, the word has a more general meaning. Originally, to animadvert to something was just to draw attention to it; whence to advertise came to mean to publicize, especially in a favourable light. By extension, then, the word refers us not only to a type of message but to a type of speech and, beyond that, to a whole communicative function which is associated with a much broader range of signifying materials than just advertisements *stricto sensu*. Whether as senders, receivers, or analysts of cultural messages we all recognize that advertising in this second, generic, sense exceeds advertising in the first. But it is hard to grasp the full significance of advertising for contemporary culture unless these meanings are clearly separated. A starting-point for the present study, then, has been to give the functional or expanded sense of advertising a name of its own: *promotion*.

The term has two semantic advantages. The first, reflecting its colloquial usage, is its generality, which directs our attention to the way in which all manner of communicative acts have, as one of their dimensions, and often only tacitly, the function of advancing some kind of self-advantaging exchange. *Promotion* crosses the line between advertising, packaging, and design, and is applicable, as well, to activities beyond the immediately commercial. It can even (as in 'promoting public health') be used in a way which takes us beyond the domain of competitive exchange altogether. For current purposes, though, I have confined it to cases where something, though not necessarily for money, is being promoted for sale – while recognizing that the metaphorical diffusion of the word, wherein it has come to mean any kind of propagation (including that of ideas, causes, and programmes), reflects a real historical tendency for all such discourse to acquire an advertising character. The second advantage stems from the word's derivation. Promotion (as a noun) is a type of sign, and the promoted entity is its referent. From this angle, the triple meaning of the Latin prefix 'pro' usefully highlights the compound and dynamic character of the relationship between promotion and what it promotes. A promotional message is a complex of significations which at once represents (moves in place of), advocates (moves on behalf of), and anticipates (moves ahead of) the circulating entity or entities to which it refers.

Given the definition, the thesis I have been exploring can be simply stated: that the range of cultural phenomena which, at least as one of their functions, serve to communicate a promotional message has become, today, virtually co-extensive with our produced symbolic world.

This may seem hyperbolic, until we start to enumerate the sorts of promotional message, and, associated with them, the circuits of competitive exchange, which are actually swirling about. As we have seen, these include not only advertising in the specific and restricted sense, that of clearly posted 'promotional signs'. They also include the whole universe of commercially manufactured objects (and services), in so far as these are imaged to sell, and are thus constructed as advertisements for themselves. A special case of the latter (in my terminology: 'commodity-signs') is cultural goods. These, indeed, are typically cast in a doubly promotional role. For not only are cultural goods peculiarly freighted with the need and capacity to promote themselves. Wherever they are distributed by a commercial medium whose profitability depends on selling audiences to advertisers they are also designed to function as attractors of audiences towards the advertising material with which they are intercut. In the organs of print and broadcasting, information and entertainment are the flowers which attract the bee. In this sense, too, the non-advertising content of such media can be considered, even semiotically, as an extension of their ads.

But this is not all. The multiply promotional communicative organs constituted by the commercial mass media (and even, via sports sponsorships and the like, by the organs of 'public broadcasting') are also transmissive vehicles for public information and discussion in general. Through that common siting, non-promotional discourses, including those surrounding the political process, have become linked (Bush in Disneyland on prime time news) to promotional ones. It is this complex of promotional media, too, which mediates the communicative activity of all secondary public institutions – aesthetic, intellectual, educational, religious, etc. – to what used to be called 'the general public'. Furthermore, even if not directly commercial themselves, these secondary institutions also generate their own forms of promotional discourse, whether, as in the case of university recruitment campaigns, because they have become indirectly commodified, or, as in the case of electoral politics, because they have a market form which is analogous to the one which operates in the money economy.

There are several respects, finally, in which competition at the level of individuals generates yet a further complex of promotional practices. In part this is an outgrowth of the commodification of labour power, and more particularly, in the professional and quasi-professional sectors of the labour market, of the way in which differentially qualified labour power commands a differential price. Hence the dramaturgical aspects of careers and careerism. In addition, however, as Veblen and many others have described, the promotionalization of the individual also extends into the sphere of consumption, both through fashion and more generally through the way in which status competition is conducted through the private theatre of projected style. At a quite different level of social practice (though, as in the TV ads for Towers department stores, 'everything connects'), the entry, on increasingly symmetrical terms, of (unattached) women and men into free (or non-parentally supervised) socio-sexual circulation has also created a mate/companion/friendship market which generates its own forms of competitive self-presentation. Lastly, when any instance of individual self-promotion spills over from the private realm to become a topic of public communication, whether unintentionally, as a personal drama that makes the news, or deliberately, as the amplified staging of a career (sporting, political, artistic, intellectual, etc), inter-individual competition gives rise to yet a further

form of promotional practice: the construction of celebrityhood. This itself enters into the realm of public promotion not just as self-advertising, but as an exchangeable (and promotable) promotional resource both for the individual involved and for other advertisers.

[...]

What the rise of promotion as a cultural force signals, in fact, is not simply a shift to a new mode of producing and circulating signs (cultural commodification), but an alteration in the very relation between culture and economy. Baudrillard (1981), following Debord (1977), has depicted his movement ('the union of sign and commodity')[1] as a merger, although it might be more accurate to depict it as a takeover, since culture has lost its autonomy thereby, while the (market) economy has hypostatized into an all engulfing dynamic. The result is a mutation: still capitalism, but a capitalism transformed. In effect, during the course of advanced capitalist development the globalization and intensification of commodity production have led to a crucial economic modification in which (a) with mass production and mass marketing the moments of distribution, circulation, and exchange have become as strategic as technical improvements in production for profitability and growth and (b) through commodity imaging the circulation and production processes have come to overlap. In which context (with disturbing implications for even an updated Marxism) it has further come about that the ('superstructural') domain of expressive communication has been more and more absorbed, not just as an industry but as a direct aspect of the sale of everything, into the integral workings of the commodified economic 'base'.

[...]

This has been a complex transformation, and it evidently did not occur all at once. There have been many phases and stages: from industrialism and the first consumer-oriented urban centres to the radio/film age, coca-colonization and the electronic malls of commercial TV.[2] Whence a further caveat. Besides eschewing an expressionist view of its object, any thesis about the changed weight of promotion within 'late' capitalist culture must also be careful to avoid too sharp a sense of periodization.

[...]

[...] It is not just that such diverse vehicles of symbolic expression as pop records, political candidates, philosophical texts, art galleries, news magazines, and sporting events, are all intensively advertised, and that this draws attention to what, as promotables, they all share: the de-sacralized status of publicly circulating, and privately appropriable, items of commercial exchange. The marketing imperative feeds back into their actual construction; so that, for example, the use and build-up of promotional names and the adoption of majoritarian entertainment values have become a common feature of all marketed discourse, regardless of whether its manifest function is to inform, inspire, solidarize or just to entertain. Moreover, this homologous proliferation of self-promotional forms goes beyond the cultural sphere. Not only are the same forms – imaged commodities as advertisements for themselves – to be found throughout the whole world of commercially produced goods. From the clothes we wear, to the parties we vote for at election time, wherever in fact a market of some kind operates, everything mirrors back the same basic signifying mode.

Thus, and this is my first point, we can say that the extension of promotion through all the circuits of social life is indeed a force for cultural homogenization, but only if we add the rider that the outcome is not a mere repetition everywhere of the same. For it brings into being a vast web of discourse which is at once continuous from one part to the next, yet asymmetrical with regard to what (and how many) purchasable entities are being aided thereby in their competitive circulation. Overall, then, the sameness of rhetorical form which promotion everywhere installs is counter-balanced by a semiological complexity which makes every point in the flow as intriguing in its formal construction as it is boringly void of deeper content. [...]

[...]

[...] In promotion, these second-order meanings themselves fade in the extrinsic (and profaning) use to which they were put. The Paradise myth evidently packs less of a spiritual punch in a cigarette ad than in an act of worship. In turn, because of the associative responses which advertising itself engenders, this cheapening of the symbolic currency becomes general and feeds back. Even in a church, it is hard to hear 'paradise' without thinking of the multitude of goods – starting with song and film titles – to which that idea, and the many ways of rendering it, have been promotionally linked.

Such devaluation applies, moreover, not only to the plane of the signified, but also to that of the signifier. When Billie Holiday's poignant rendition of 'Summertime' is played as the voice-over for a VW ad, its own mystique as a 'classic' performance, which is inextricable from her own as a tragic figure, is diminished in the very act wherein that of the car is associatively enhanced. Fear of a similar effect has led to the banning in British commercials of direct references to royalty. Paradoxically, then, while the vast apparatus of selling uses established social and psychological values to move the merchandise, and thus incidentally serves as an ideological transmitter as well, that very linkage, which makes the rhetoric of ideology itself rhetorical, dis-cathects the moral, political, etc., categories and symbologies of ideological discourse as such.

[...]

To this catalogue, I would add only one further point. It concerns not the psychology or anthropology of consumption but the impact on individual consciousness of promotional culture as a whole. If we accept that the symbolic universe reconstituted by the rise of promotion has been dereferentialized – a quality which stems, on the one hand, from promotion's instrumentalization of values and symbols, and on the other from its perpetual deferral of the promoted object, together with any closure of the gap of desire which that object's final arrival might bring – then the promotionally addressed subject has been placed in a novel cultural predicament: how to build an identity and an orientation from the materials of a culture whose meanings were unstable and behind which, for all the personalized manner in which its multitudinous messages are delivered, no genuinely expressive intention can be read. Schizophrenic disintegration and the consumerized conformism of the Pepsi Generation are only the most extreme poles of a possible response. More common is a sensibility which oscillates between a playful willingness to be temporarily seduced and a hardened scepticism about every kind of communication in view of the selling job it is probably doing. In that light, cynical privatism and mass apathy – an index of which is the falling participation rate in American elections – can even be construed as a sign of resistance: for Baudrillard (1983), the only form of resistance still open to the media-bombarded 'silent majority'.

But the envelopment of the individual by promotion must be grasped from both sides of the promotional sign. It is not enough to look at this question only from the side of reception, that is to look at subjects only as readers/listeners addressed by a certain kind of speech. We must also take account of the way in which the contemporary subject has become implicated in promotional culture as a writer/performer of its texts.

Of course, only a minority play a directly authorial role in the imaging and marketing of commercial produce. Fewer still are the named creators or performers of cultural goods, though these have an exemplary importance since media stars are our equivalent of mythic heroes, providing the most salient paradigms of how individual praxis contributes to the shaping of our world. But the list grows if we also include all those playing a more specialist or subordinate role in commercial promotion, as well as those engaged in non- or quasi-commercial forms of promotional practice like electoral politics, or the public relations side of hospitals, schools, and churches. In any case, from dating and clothes shopping to attending a job interview, virtually everyone is involved in the self-promotionalism which overlays such practices in the micro-sphere of everyday life.

Notes

1   For Baudrillard, however, the crux of the sign-commodity conjunction lies in the totemic and status-differential 'system of objects' which mass-produced consumer goods represent at the point of consumption. Sign-exchange-value doubles exchange-value in the constitution of commodity, constituting a new term (the sign-commodity) within an expanded, and infinitely commutable, field of 'general exchange'. This model is elaborated throughout Baudrillard's early writings, and receives its most formal treatment in 1981, especially pp. 123–9 and 143–63.

2   To which we might now add the promotional conquest of outer space. In saying this I am not just referring to the superpower boosterism of outer space, but to its actual commercialization as a spectacle (logos on spaceships etc.) which the post-Cold War Soviet programme, suddenly starved for cash, has pioneered.

References

BAUDRILLARD, J. (1981) *Towards a Critique of the Political Economy of the Sign* (tr. C. Levin and A. Younger), St. Louis, MO, Telos.

BAUDRILLARD, J. (1983) *In the Shadow of the Silent Majority*, New York, Semiotext(e).

DEBORD, G. (1977) *The Society of the Spectacle*, Detroit, IL, Black and Red.

Source: Wernick, 1991, pp. 181–3, 185, 187, 188, 189, 192.

READING B:
Christine Restall, 'A breakthrough in the study of women'

Following its comprehensive study of UK men in 1984, McCann-Erickson has now turned its sights on the British female. Woman Study, published this week, throws new light on the complex make-up of women, and uncovers two new groups. Christine Restall, planning director of McCanns, describes how the study was compiled and its implications for the advertising industry.

So much has been written and researched about women over the past decade that a question must be raised by anyone coming fresh to the McCann-Erickson Woman Study: why another study about women? We have had women at work, women in business, women in middle age, women and the home, women and beauty, and a host of others. Why add to the list?

The answer is threefold: first, the precedent was created for this new study by the McCanns Man Study of 1984 – the first comprehensive study of the UK male, looking at his attitudes, beliefs, wants and needs as well as his personality and his behaviour, both general and product related. We wanted to take a similar look at women, to explore the whole issue of whether the sexes really are different in attitude and psychological make-up, and what those differences might be. With the two studies we would have an unprecedented opportunity to look at British life today, from both male and female viewpoints.

Second, many of the studies about women in the past have concentrated on one particular aspect of their lives or interests. We wanted to look at the whole woman, and in particular look at how attitudes, personalities and behaviour are clustered together in a complex modern society. It is a truism that the rate of change is increasing – yet it *is* still true that data becomes obsolete quicker than ever. At the end of the European Decade of the Woman (1975–1985), we wanted to record a definitive and full account of women in the UK without preconceptions or prejudgement.

Third, we would be able to examine many marketing and advertising concepts. Is there anything real in the idea of the feminist? Or the

Sloane? Or the Yuppie? And if there is, are there sufficient of them to make a real marketing target – or an aspirational target for advertising? The study was designed to cover as many of the varied aspects of life as we could think of in order to arrive at an empirical series of groupings of women. Finally, all this would have been of little practical value if we had not also recorded a great deal of behavioural and purchasing data.

Our initial stance was, of course, that modern markets are segmented, another truism but one still often ignored. And the results of both Man Study and Woman Study confirm that British society is indeed highly complex and highly segmented – by personality, by beliefs and attitudes, by lifestyle and finally by demographics, all in interaction: no one kind of measurement today is enough to comprehend large groups of people.

The study was a big one: not only a good-sized sample (1,000) but using a questionnaire lasting one-and-a-half hours. Marplan conducted fieldwork and analysis, as it did for Man Study, and Youth Study before it, and there was extensive pilot work and follow-up research. Much of the study is sociologically interesting, especially the comparisons between the sexes, and much is specific to product fields and brands, and a summary like this cannot hope to cover these issues. But some marketing and advertising generalisations can be made.

The first finding is that in real life the mentalities of men and women differ only slightly. The Man Study revealed eight psychological and lifestyle clusters, and so does the Woman Study. Significantly, using the same questions, six out of eight clusters are almost identical from one study to the other.

Such a close parallel in the results was something of a surprise – but perhaps it should not have been, since much classic personality and psychological research, does not find the sex differences pronounced. Of course the six similar clusters were of slightly different sizes as between men and women, and different demographics, too, to a limited extent – but the personality and lifestyle groupings were almost the same.

Two female groups were different, and one of them – the New Unromantic – we believe to be explicitly described for the first time in this study.

We chose an illustrator to draw the stereotypes because finding exact parallels in life or entertainment proved to be difficult: they do exist but usually in an over-simple or parodied form, which is limiting. And we chose to illustrate the clusters through gentle and witty drawings of animals – again to avoid pre-conceptions. It is particularly difficult to comment on women (even for a female commentator) without falling into a morass of prejudice and latent sexism.

However, at least it is nowadays possible to laugh over the female condition – as advertisers such as *Cosmopolitan* have noticed – and we wanted as vivid and direct a way as possible of personifying our clusters. To the planning professional they may leap from the page of print-out, but marketers and others prefer a more approachable portrait.

The eight clusters divide broadly into four pairs: two motivated primarily by ideals or opinions, two identified by their self-awareness and independence of spirit, two driven by a questing or seeking personality, and two marked principally by their lack of involvement. And out of the eight clusters we have four who are "their own person", leaders of opinion in their separate ways, and four who are followers.

Taking the first pair of clusters primarily motivated by ideas or opinions, we find two diametrically opposed types: the Avant Guardian and the Lady Righteous. Both are medium-sized segments. The Avant Guardian is, as her name suggests, of a liberal left persuasion – and she does in fact read the *Guardian*. She agrees with many concepts favoured by SDP/Labour right, and the women's movement – but not to the detriment of men. She enjoys her career, she likes men and expects equal treatment and equal shares. She believes in 'fairness' and emancipation all round. She is likely to be young, upmarket, highly educated and single, but if married has children, a nanny or baby-minder, and probably keeps cats. Predictably, she is thoroughly up-to-date in her attitudes to health and cares about exercise and her diet; actually doing something about it. The Avant Guardian, like some other groups, favours Sainsburys and some Boots brands. She is much more likely than other clusters

to watch Channel Four and likes documentaries, particularly on wildlife. She has an exact counterpart in the Man Study.

The Lady Righteous, conversely, represents the broad right-wing establishment – the backbone of Tory England. A pillar of the church and local committees, her attitudes on moral issues are traditional – though she believes herself to be tolerant. The Lady Righteous is in fact the oldest of all eight clusters, a considerable proportion having grown-up children or husbands retired. Upmarket, like the Avant Guardian, she believes in hearth and home and is highly contented in her role as a housewife provider. She knits, cooks, gardens and, naturally, is keener on flower arranging than are the other segments. Like the Avant Guardian, she considers health and diet of great importance, but tends to favour more traditional brands and products such as All Bran (she has probably used it all along). She has quite wide tastes in television programmes but more than any other group prefers the BBC news, backed by the *Daily Telegraph*.

Our second pair, identified by a certain self-awareness and independence, are again rather different from one another. One is the Lively Lady, and the other, the New Unromantic. The Lively Lady is not actually a 'Yuppie' in demographic terms at all, but comes the closest to that concept in attitudes – but even then it is not a perfect fit. The Lively Ladies are a medium-sized group and have been observed before (including her counterpart in the Man Study, the Self-Admirer). Outgoing, sociable and self-aware, she is deeply involved with her job and juggles her work, her social life and her family with flair. She takes her appearance and her health seriously, and enjoys all aspects of her modern female role, including coping with motherhood. She likes male company and knows how to handle success. She relishes the trappings of such a life – the credit cards, the car, the sports club – and watches less television than other groups; probably because she is out, or has people round.

The New Unromantic is, we believe, a new group to be identified. Certainly there is no exact male equivalent, and certainly the group is stereotypically young and single. It is also the smallest cluster in the Woman study. Like many new discoveries, once observed we now see the

The Avant Guardian

Key Attitude Statements
- There has not been a general decline in morals.
- I'm in favour of demonstrations . . . for a sensible society.
- It's not important my home is clean and tidy.
- I don't adapt to circumstances.
- I don't agree that most men know nothing about women.
- Abortion should be available on demand.

What Is She Like?
- Young, up-scale, working — single *or* married with children.
- Outgoing, strong "liberal-left" opinions.
- Into many modern trends (health foods and so on).
- Likes own life, own career, sexual freedom and so on.
- Emancipated — sees men as equals, as people.
- Has exact male counterpart — The Avant Guardian.

Typical Brands
- *Guardian*
- *Daily Mail*
- Pear's Soap
- National Westminster
- John Player's Special
- Soft and Gentle

The Lady Righteous

Key Attitude Statements
- The most important thing is believing in God.
- I'd rather look after the home than go to work.
- It's a pity the . . . church is in decline.
- I'm not often bored.
- You need high standards to judge yourself by.
- Abortion should not be available on demand.

What Is She Like?
- Upper middle class, older, married, housewife.
- Strong traditional ideas and beliefs.
- Happy with life, complacent over attitudes.
- Protective of family, believes women should be at home.
- Has exact male counterpart — The Pontificator.

Typical Brands
- *Telegraph*
- Elizabeth Arden
- Mum
- Avon Conditioner
- TSB
- All Bran

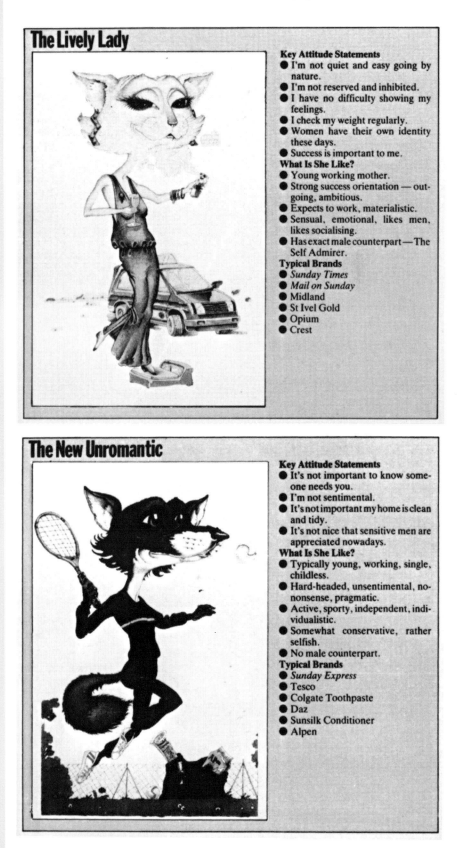

The Lively Lady

Key Attitude Statements
- I'm not quiet and easy going by nature.
- I'm not reserved and inhibited.
- I have no difficulty showing my feelings.
- I check my weight regularly.
- Women have their own identity these days.
- Success is important to me.

What Is She Like?
- Young working mother.
- Strong success orientation — outgoing, ambitious.
- Expects to work, materialistic.
- Sensual, emotional, likes men, likes socialising.
- Has exact male counterpart — The Self Admirer.

Typical Brands
- *Sunday Times*
- *Mail on Sunday*
- Midland
- St Ivel Gold
- Opium
- Crest

The New Unromantic

Key Attitude Statements
- It's not important to know someone needs you.
- I'm not sentimental.
- It's not important my home is clean and tidy.
- It's not nice that sensitive men are appreciated nowadays.

What Is She Like?
- Typically young, working, single, childless.
- Hard-headed, unsentimental, no-nonsense, pragmatic.
- Active, sporty, independent, individualistic.
- Somewhat conservative, rather selfish.
- No male counterpart.

Typical Brands
- *Sunday Express*
- Tesco
- Colgate Toothpaste
- Daz
- Sunsilk Conditioner
- Alpen

The Hopeful Seeker

Key Attitude Statements
- I like to try new products.
- I wish I had more independence.
- I am often under pressure . . . to achieve self-fulfilment.
- You only get on in life if you're lucky.
- I adapt to circumstances and try to attract little attention.
- It's natural for men to cry in public if upset.

What Is She Like?
- Middle-aged mother, keeping up with the times.
- Likes to be trendy, socially acceptable.
- Somewhat anxious, needs to be liked, to do "right".
- Gentle and pleasant, believes in luck.
- Admires effective people, tries to mirror their attitudes.
- Has male near-counterpart — The Chameleon.

Typical Brands
- *Star*
- *News of the World*
- *Woman's Own*
- Wella Conditioner
- Coca-Cola
- Harvey's Bristol Cream

The Lack-A-Daisy

Key Attitude Statements
- You don't need high standards to judge yourself by.
- I'm one of those people who can't cope with life.
- Success is not a question of hard work . . . and energy.
- Women do not have a separate identity these days.
- I'm often bored.
- I'm not very tolerant.

What Is She Like?
- Young working class mother with young children.
- Little money, rather worn-down by life (unemployed).
- Tries to cope but often fails, or feels a failure.
- Easy going, self-forgiving, unassertive, evades pressures.
- Traditional views, life drifts over them.
- Has exact male counterpart — The Token Trier.

Typical Brands
- *Sun*
- Silvikrin Conditioner
- Wimpy
- Kwik Save
- Gateway
- Kellogg's Cornflakes

The Blinkered

Key Attitude Statements
- Success is not very important to me.
- I'm not under any pressure.
- I'm not ambitious.
- Ideals don't make life meaningful for me.
- I wouldn't like to go on holiday on my own more.
- I don't care to buy new products.

What Is She Like?
- Married, with children, part-time work.
- Self-contained, doesn't care about life outside self.
- Conservative, traditional.
- Uses TV and video as escape.
- Has male near-counterpart—The Sleep Walker.

Typical Brands
- Barclays
- Knights Castille
- Charlie
- Ready Brek
- Littlewoods

The Down-Trodden

Key Attitude Statements
- Married with children, no longer young, part-time job.
- Shy, negative, timid, indecisive, put-upon.
- Unhappy, pressured by life and personal relationships.
- Would like to do better.
- No male counterpart.

What Is She Like?
- I'm not happy with life.
- I'm not very optimistic.
- I find it difficult to show my feelings.
- I'm always under pressure.

Typical Brands
- *Woman's Weekly*
- Fine Fare
- National Giro
- Palmolive Soap
- Players No. 6
- Maxwell House

type around us everywhere. The New Unromantic is a working girl – not a career woman – independent, tough-minded and very unsentimental. Self-aware and rather self-centred, she is not turned on by traditional female values such as being needed or wanting an ultra-clean and tidy home, nor is she professionally ambitious. Of all the clusters she is the most active and sporty, and enjoys going out with her friends, male and female. She does not centre her life around a man, and expects her mate to be a fairly traditional type; in fact many may not want to relate particularly to the opposite sex: men are just there. The New Unromantic has many spare-time pursuits, including sewing and reading, and her preferred television entertainment is straight ITV and BBC1 – *Coronation Street*, sitcoms like *Just Good Friends*, and quizzes like *3-2-1*.

The pair of questors in the Woman Study are again somewhat different from each other. The Hopeful Seekers are a substantial cluster (and matched with a Man Study group, the Chameleons). Their principal characteristic is to agree – with people around them, and with a variety of sometimes contradictory trendy views. Gentle, pleasant, likeable people, the stereotype is a middle-aged mum keeping up with the times. She gets a lot of pleasure out of trying new products and new ideas, like putting on a new set of clothes, and she seeks approval. A *Woman's Own* reader, she watches a lot of television, particularly soap operas and documentaries which tell her what's going on out there.

The other seeking type is less successful and happy, perhaps because she has a lot on her hands actually coping with children and home, with a little money and a part-time job. She is christened Lack-a-Daisy because she tries intermittently to keep up, but often does not quite make it. She would like to be more successful and is neither completely happy nor optimistic; but she is easy-going and unassertive, and thereby is not actually unhappy. She is less likely to have use of a car than other groups are, and watches a lot of television – *Coronation Street* or *Crossroads*.

Our final two clusters are characterised by being uninvolved; one, the Blinkered, is relatively happy, and the other, the Down-Trodden, is depressed and somewhat embittered. The Blinkered is not at all

idealistic or motivated by ambition. She is not interested in anything new, and her views and habits are deeply traditional. There is an air of unawakened anger about the male type which is less obvious in the female, but for both there are few outlets and few outside interests, although the Blinkered is a heavy reader. They watch quite a lot of television, particularly thrillers and over half of them have a VCR machine.

The Down-Trodden has no male equivalent, probably because of her somewhat traditional door-mat-like attitudes, which have been seen as typically female. No longer young and with a family and a part-time job, she is timid and easily put-upon.

While the clusters in the Woman Study have been simplified here, the critical issue is whether such segmentation has any meaning for marketing and advertising purposes. Some examples of 'trigger' brands are shown below each segmentation and the product and brand usage data across the board some extremely marked usage differences between the segments. But what does it all mean?

If we analyse the principal 'trigger' brands that differentiate between the clusters and attempt to understand the brand positionings, via their advertising messages, that appeal to different segments we can begin to find some patterns.

Essentially, we can take the Avant Guardians and tease out the main appeal of their brands as a lifestyle argument: 'for men', talking about individualism, health, naturalness, or contemporaneity using Avant Guardian ideals and 'triggers'. For the Lively Ladies, we find that exotic, glamorous appeals give their brands an aspirational benefit, and that they also respond to clever and witty argument. For the Down-Trodden, the main brand messages are security and homeliness. And for the Blinkered, conventional escapist messages often identify their brands. Having understood the arguments that could address each cluster, we can then analyse each product field and look for positioning gaps; quite aside from raising the even more important issue of whether we really are reaching the right women.

Not every brand can or should aspire to appeal to the Avant Guardian, the New Unromantic or the Lively Lady. The 'follower' segments represent big business and have large and distinct brand franchises, even though their constituents do not represent 'leadership' attitude groups. Making the best of what you are, as so often, is the message from the study for advertisers, but a small step forward has been taken in understanding the nature of the message that appeals to each target sub-group; and in understanding that target in the round, as a segment of womanhood in the UK in 1985.

Source: Restall, 1985, pp. 26–8.

READING C:
Pierre Bourdieu, 'A young executive who "knows how to live"'

Michel R., an advertising executive working in a Paris agency, the son of the managing director of the French subsidiary of a leading multinational corporation, studied in a private Catholic secondary school in the 17th arrondissement and then at the Paris Political Science Institute; his wife, Isabelle, the daughter of a provincial industrialist, also went to Sciences Po and works for a weekly news-magazine. He is 30, she is 28; they have two children. They live in Paris, in a modern five-roomed apartment in the 15th arrondissement. They like things to be 'snug and cosy'. They have no interest in 'home-improvement' and have kept their apartment as they found it. 'The decoration is all the work of our predecessor. I didn't much like the green in the dining-room, it was rather gloomy, but we got used to it, and I get bored working on the place I live in.' 'I hate that beading on the doors. I'd like to get rid of it. The pseudo 16th- or 18th-century veneering or whatever it is all over this modern apartment is ghastly; I put up with it but it gets on my nerves,' says Michel, who has removed some of it but 'couldn't face the rest'.

'The world of my grandparents'

Their flat 'is partly the world of my grandparents, my great-grandparents, who were *grands bourgeois*': pictures by Michel's grandfather, 'who spent his whole life painting and never did a day's work'; other pictures which they have been given – a Boudin, a Bissière, and a Folon. But Michel, who 'adores the Impressionists in general and especially Bonnard, and Monet or Manet, the one who does a lot of landscapes, and Pissarro', does not like them.

Nor does he like still lifes, or 'problem pictures': 'Fernand Léger, and stuff like that, is horrible, it's thick and heavy ... two or three Braques can be interesting to look at, but when you see two hundred of them, all done the same way, it gets a bit repetitive, a bit nightmarish ... I tend to go for landscapes ... My grandmother's got a Bonnard in her apartment, the one really valuable picture she owns. *We* won't inherit it because there are lots of relatives. But it would be wonderful to own it. I go for things that are outside fashion, sort of timeless.'

Isabelle doesn't entirely agree with her husband: 'There are some things I like a lot in modern art, but that's because I like the colours ... For example, Vieira da Silva (she hesitates over the name), Boudin, who is behind you, I like a lot.' They both occasionally visit galleries, and exhibitions two or three times a year. They went to the Braque exhibition and expect to see the Impressionists at Durand-Ruel.

'We'd seen a lot of mediocre stuff'

The dining-room tables and chairs, mahogany, 18th-century English style, were bought in London as soon as they were married. 'I don't know if we'd do the same thing today ... I can't remember why we bought them, but from a bourgeois point of view they must be a good investment.' After visiting many antique shops, they 'finally chose something very expensive. It would have cost twice as much in Paris. We'd see a lot of mediocre stuff and decided we didn't like it. Importing the furniture 'was no problem. It's exempt from customs duties. You just have to pay VAT [value-added-tax].' In the living-room they have some modern and some old furniture, a bookcase from Roche-Bobois, a sofa from a shop in Le village suisse ...

Michel's car is 'only an old Peugeot 404', whereas his bosses 'have got Jaguars, the director of the agency has an Alfa-Romeo, a Lancia'. 'From time to time, they say "So you aren't trading it in?" They'd be relieved if I got a new car. They're afraid I'll visit clients in my car.'

'The right sort of clothes for people in advertising'

Though at weekends, at home, he wears 'a filthy pair of trousers', for work he dresses with great care and elegance. He buys his suits at Barnes, the advertising man's tailor, in the rue Victor Hugo in Paris. 'They're the right sort of clothes for people who make it in advertising – English cloth, Prince of Wales checks with a touch of luxury. Not the sort of thing civil servants could wear, and bank managers couldn't get away with it either. In banking you need a plain shirt; banking isn't showy, whereas in advertising, people put every

penny they earn into clothes ... In my business we're constantly classifying people, there are social classes, castes, and it's a matter of fitting a product to the right caste. When someone new comes to the agency, we size them up at a glance ... A guy with a velvet suit and big lapels is compensating for something, he's not very sure of himself, he wants to make an impression.' For a while, the agency had 'a finance manager from a very modest background; when he arrived he was so badly dressed that it was bad for business [...] he was dressed like a junior clerk.' 'Wearing a suit with narrow lapels, narrow bottoms, a bit short, in a loud colour with a shirt that doesn't match and a narrow tie, for example, by our standards, that's grotty.'

'Not the way some secretaries do it'

'On the other hand, being too fashionable is not much better,' adds Isabelle, who dresses their children 'in fairly classic style', paying particular attention to the colours. 'I like a pretty smocked dress from time to time, and English overcoats. Of course it's done with an eye to fashion, but not in the silly way some secretaries at *L'Express* do it, dressing their children in the new kiddy-boutiques, Mini-this and Mini-that, with things that cost a fortune and are a miniature copy of the parents' clothes.' These secretaries 'are all well-dressed, by my standards, they have perfect colour sense ... There were some girls who arrived, who dressed with terrible taste, it was vulgar, cheap, tacky, just awful ... and then, after four years, they finally got it right.' Isabelle has a friend who is 'always exquisitely dressed ... the effect is always stunning, I mean, it's chic, it's got real class ... She pays attention to every little detail.' Michel's father is also 'very well-dressed, nothing is ever over-done, his colours are always perfect. Refinement without the slightest ostentation. He has a tailor in London.' Michel's mother is 'equally restrained. Always a beautifully cut fur coat.' She, too, often buys her clothes in London.

'Provincial clerks who fill their gardens with gnomes'

'The *petits bourgeois* have no taste, it's a phrase we often use, though we're well aware it's racist.' (Michel and Isabelle constantly indicate in this way their 'distance' from the ways of the older generation of the *grande bourgeoisie* – perhaps especially when speaking to a sociologist, albeit a friend's sister.) Isabelle's parents, provincial industrialists, are more severe or less tolerant: 'About the *petit bourgeois* phenomenon – provincial clerks who fill their gardens with gnomes, windmills and similar rubbish, Mummy used to say, "It's outrageous; making things like that ought to be banned." It was terribly authoritarian, really fascist, whereas we spoke up for everyone's right to have their own tastes.'

A very light meal, a vegetable dish and some cheese'

In cooking, as in clothing and furnishing, they manifest the same refusal of pretension, of 'excess', the same sense of 'distinction'. Without being 'a wine-buff who can tell one year from another', Michel is 'something of an expert'. His father-in-law, who has a huge cellar, has slowly initiated them. When they visit him, they drink 'Margaux 1926, amazing things that they don't stock in restaurants any more ... With colleagues, for example, I'm the one who chooses the wine. They can see I know what I'm doing. I don't go for some miserable Cahors, for example. I know it doesn't taste the same as a Saint-Estèphe or a Saint-Emilion ... Hardly anyone knows how to choose wine, so as soon as you know a little bit about it, you look like someone who knows how to live.' At home, they have a few magnums of Veuve Clicquot 1926 which they bought: 'good-quality things; we drink some two or three times a month and then there are the Christmas presents ... If it's whisky, we drink Chivas, we're rather demanding.' They buy their claret direct from the producer 'at fifteen or eighteen francs a bottle, forty francs in the shops, a very good wine.' In the evening, when they are alone, they eat 'a very light meal, a vegetable dish and some cheese.' They like to invite friends for *'escalopes à la crème, sauté de veau*, curry, salmon that we buy occasionally.' Michel is particularly partial to *'foie de canard frais aux raisins* cooked in the coals, and *confit d'oie.'* He has eaten in 30 of the 100 best restaurants in Paris listed in the *Gault et Millau* guide, often business lunches ('I only paid for ten of them'). He also likes traditional French food ('plain home cooking, in other words')

but is not keen on little local restaurants or 'foreign dishes, Italian or Chinese cooking.'

'Healthy exercise'

Michel and Isabelle are members of a golf club: 'it's marvellous, but the people aren't. They're mostly gaga. In France it's always a certain type of people, whereas in Japan 30 per cent of the population belong to a golf club.' Their initial subscription cost them 10,000 francs; they no longer go, because of the children, but they have kept up their membership. Michel no longer plays tennis: 'It's very stressful ... you have to keep moving all the time, running up to the net. It gives me backache ... Golf is less hard on the muscles.' 'Victims of fashion, everyone's talking about it this year,' they are going to go cross-country skiing. They have also bought second-hand racing bicycles and last summer they went for long rides: 'It's healthy exercise.'

When he was a student, Michel used to go to the TNP (Théâtre National Populaire) in Aubervilliers, to see Gombrowicz or Brecht, but he no longer goes; they have recently been to the Cartoucherie de Vincennes and the Paris Opera: they go to the cinema fairly often. They have a hi-fi system and a tape-recorder; they listen to the classical record reviews on France-Musique. Michel particularly likes Mozart (*The Marriage of Figaro*), Schubert Quartets, Bach, and the Beethoven Quartets. 'I haven't learnt to appreciate purely modern stuff, Webern and so on.' Michel does not read many novels but intends to read Tony Duvert (he likes books that are 'a bit stimulating': he read Robbe-Grillet's *Les Gommes* but 'couldn't get into it'). He mainly reads 'anything in social studies' – psychology, economics.

Source: Bourdieu, 1984, pp. 298–301.

CULTURING PRODUCTION

Graeme Salaman

Contents

1 Introduction

Earlier chapters in this book – for example, Sean Nixon's Chapter 4 – have looked at the ways in which organizations work to produce meanings for outsiders – consumers and audiences. In this chapter the focus shifts. Here we are looking at the ways in which – and reasons why – organizations seek to structure meanings *internally*, for their employees. We continue the book's interest in the ways in which the economy and the economic are inherently cultural phenomena: not only are goods and services increasingly culturalized, but the processes of organization and production themselves are the subject of cultural change and reconstruction.

In this chapter, we analyse the ways in which senior managers of organizations increasingly attempt to define, for their employees, the meaning of employment, and the relationship these employees should have with their employing organization. They attempt do this because they are convinced that changing the 'culture' of an organization is an effective way of improving its performance – in terms of their own objectives. This approach – referred to here by the term **Corporate Culture** – arises from, and is encouraged by, a body of current management thinking which offers a way of conceiving and understanding how organizations work, what affects their performance, and how performance can be improved.

Corporate Culture

A second core theme of the chapter is that these efforts to define what employees should believe, how they should behave, value, think, relate to their employer and so forth, demonstrate a close connection between knowledge and power. Corporate Culture projects – defined and discussed more fully below – are achieved and buttressed through a variety of managerial practices. Of particular importance are:

- training courses where the appropriate attitudes and beliefs are defined and developed;
- assessment centres where employees are assessed against the new virtues - which are often in stark contrast to the previous ones, such as initiative instead of obedience, innovation against caution;
- newly defined management competences which describe the qualities which distinguish the successful manager (and which supply a bench-mark for performance against which managers are measured, often by their peers and subordinates);
- reward and appraisal systems which reward the new virtues and penalize the old; and
- counselling procedures which handle the recalcitrant and delinquent (in terms of the new corporate values) and help them come to terms with, and overcome, their confusion or resistance.

The management literature which asserts the role and implications of Corporate Cultures in organizational restructuring and organizational performance is supported and sponsored by senior managers' authority and their priorities and assumptions. While Corporate Culture discourse insists on the essential reality of consensus and harmony within the organization, this conception of the organization is often at odds with the existing conceptions and experiences of many employees. As with all such efforts to define reality for others, those at whom these efforts are aimed interpret and react to them in the light of their existing views and experiences, often 'consuming' these representations in ways which differ significantly from senior managers' intentions. Attempts by senior managers and their advisers to establish Corporate Cultures thus represent authoritative efforts to *constitute* the meaning of certain key aspects of organizational structure, process and membership.

The chapter is structured as follows. First, in section 2, the role of culture in economic organizations is discussed in general terms. This is followed by an introduction to the Corporate Culture approach, and its promises. In section 3, the internal logics of this approach are discussed, with particular reference to the ways in which the approach insists on a form of diagnosis of corporate ills which leads inexorably to a cultural solution. In section 4, some of the organizational narratives which re-imagine the corporation and role of the executive are described. In section 5, some grounds for the appeal of these logics to senior managers are identified; specifically, the ways they celebrate the role of corporate leaders. In section 6, some critiques of Corporate Culture projects are assessed, and section 7 rounds off the discussion with some concluding comments concerning the production of Corporate Culture.

2   The culturing of organizations and work

It is not just products and artefacts that are 'cultured' but also economic activity. Work itself is 'represented' in distinctive ways such that its meaning can vary, and be experienced in different ways.

Our understanding and knowledge of things, events, processes, relationships, is structured through meanings we share, which organize, define and locate our experience. Our heads are full of knowledge, ideas and images, not only about our society but also about our work – and these ideas, images and values provide us with shared frameworks, assumptions and moralities which we use to define and make sense of our work and employment.

These shared meanings (or *culture*) – which differentiate work from non-work, and which define the precise significance of work activities and relationships – vary over time, space and cultural context. They are variable and contingent. For example, the same activity – cooking a meal, digging the earth, cleaning a car, using a word processor – can have very different significance for the people involved, depending on the circumstances. Who are you doing the activity for: yourself, an employer, your children? Have you chosen to do it? Are you in some sense forced to do it?

2.1   The meaning of work

The history of work in industrial societies shows that, depending on the circumstances and management regimes prevailing, every aspect of work – as well as work itself – takes on particular meanings. But one feature of the meanings associated with work is that those who initiate the work of others – who own the productive process, the site of production, the means of production and who in some way employ staff to work for them – consistently show an interest in defining the meanings associated with work and employment. Sometimes the meanings introduced by new management regimes are in stark contrast to previously prevailing systems of representation of work and they are all the more obvious for this contrast or difference. These meanings address various key aspects of work – work activities themselves, work rhythms, schedules and time discipline, workers' relations with each other, with their employers, even with their own physical activity.

Two examples may illustrate this.

First, consider how, with the onset of industrialization, working time itself was redefined. Owners of capital were concerned to ensure that workers' sense of time – the meaning associated with the 'passing' of time – changed drastically. Whereas time had been measured in terms of seasons, agricultural work rhythms and feast days, henceforth working time was clock time. The working day was now measured mechanically; workers were assigned different working time periods and paid in terms of time units. Workers' performance was a function of, and was indicated by, their self-discipline and accuracy in 'time-keeping' and was regulated by the factory clock, the time card, 'clocking in'. Time now mattered in a new way – meant something new. Now time was money.

In the early industrial period, production was organized through the 'putting out' system under which an entrepreneur had no way of compelling the workers to do a given number of hours of labour; the domestic weaver or craftsman was master of his/her time, able to start or stop as desired. The employer could *try* to control behaviour through sanctions or incentives, but this often *reduced* output because the worker preferred leisure to income after a certain point. Workers had not yet developed a 'proper' work orientation.

Changing this attitude to time was one reason for the development of the factory system, and was one of a number of prerequisite disciplines on which the effectiveness of the factory system depended. Compliance with the requirements of factory discipline and factory time, furthermore, was seen by employers as an essential feature of the good worker: 'A man [sic] who has no care for the morrow, and who lives for the passing moment, cannot bring his mind to indulge the severe discipline, and to make the patient and toilsome exertions which are required to form a good mechanic' (quoted in Pollard, 1965, p. 269).

The onset of the factory system brought with it, indeed depended on, a new culture, a new structure of meanings governing time, attitude to work, discipline, preparedness to accept regulation, and so on: 'men [sic] who were non-accumulative, non-acquisitive, accustomed to work for subsistence, not for maximization of income, had to be made obedient in such a way as to react precisely to the stimuli provided' (Pollard, 1965, p. 254).

Second, during the industrial period, the physical actions of work have been persistently redefined under changing management regimes. For example, under an approach to work called Taylorism, in the early part of this century, the activities associated with production within the factory system were broken down into a series of minutely defined units or acts. Activities which had previously occurred together as part of the total and integrated process of production – making a shoe, butchering a carcass, tailoring clothes – were now fragmented, and then re-constituted into 'jobs' so that workers' activity became precisely and minutely defined – the position of the body, the movement of a hand or arm, the frequency and nature of movement. Furthermore, with action thus fragmented, dis-assembled and re-assembled by management, the workers' authority was replaced by that of managers and the workers' skill replaced by, and relocated in, the role and functions of management.

Under this new regime of work organization, the meaning of the work activities changed fundamentally. What was once integrated became disintegrated; what was part of the workers' skill became de-skilled, with skill located elsewhere; what was under the workers' authority now fell under the managers'; what was done in the workers' time according to the workers' schedules, became dominated by the factory clock. And what was previously subject to the workers' standards and demands now fell under the scrutiny of the supervisor and the quality inspector. The actions themselves remained, but the meaning changed totally.

2.2   The culturing of work

Today such specification of work is more likely to focus on the employees' relationship not with the product or the productive process, but with the client purchasing the service – hence current concern with 'customer care' programmes and with training in customer skills. Previously, factory regimes defined the meanings of the workers' physical actions; now they seek to define the workers' emotions and relationships – or at least their physical manifestations.

Staff, for example, may be exhorted to:

> smile to make initial welcome contact ... smile warmly with direct eye
> contact ... watch customer reactions ... note customer's embarrassment by
> lack of eye contact ... keep eye contact with customer, nod when customer
> makes valid point ... give customer full attention ... smile ... avoid too much
> eye contact to allow customer to relax.
>
>   (Kenney et al., 1981, p. 82, quoted in Townley, 1993, p. 533)

What is new about recent interest in the meaning of work is not simply that
it now attracts a huge amount of management time and effort but also that
the management of the meaning of work is now seen as a major management
priority and responsibility, and is theorized as a major innovation in the
achievement of superior work performance. The management of culture
involves deliberate attempts to structure the meanings employees attribute to
their employer, the organization, and their work, and this is presented by
popular management writers as the major method of achieving a new and
necessary form of organization and control which will produce great benefits
in organizational performance.

Managers' attempts to define a culture of work for employees – to define
what work and organizational membership *really* mean – thus represent an
attempt to achieve an internalization of regulation. Those who advocate such
programmes are quite clear on this:

> The guiding aim and abiding concern of Corporate Culture ... is to win the
> 'hearts and minds' of employees: to define their purposes by managing
> what they think and feel, and not just how they behave. The strengthening
> of Corporate Cultures, it is claimed, provides the key to securing 'unusual
> effort on the part of apparently ordinary employees'.
>
>   (Peters and Waterman, 1982, p. xvii)

Corporate Culture initiatives thus form a part – the most recent expression –
of a long-term management interest in managing the meaning of work for
employees. As the examples given earlier suggest, while management has
always been concerned to ensure the 'morality' and discipline of the work
force – to ensure that workers had the appropriate attitudes and values –
Corporate Culture projects represent this interest in a particular energetic
and self-conscious form. This is largely as a result of the writing of Corporate
Culture consultants – for example, Peters and Waterman, Deal and Kennedy
– who supply some sort of theoretical support for this concern, by arguing
that organizational success depends on managers' manipulation of
organizations' cultures and by basing these arguments on a 'theoretical'
understanding of organizational functioning.

2.3   Corporate Culture: the promise

Senior managements' concern with organizational culture has been fuelled by the insistence of management writers that Corporate Cultures offer an effective means of managing organizations and the organizational employee. It is the power and appeal of this claim that is responsible for the enormous management interest in Corporate Culture projects.

> READING A
>
> 'Values: the core of the culture' is an extract from a book by two popular management writers, Terence E. Deal and Allen A. Kennedy, provided as Reading A at the end of this chapter. In this reading, the authors neatly summarize the core elements of the Corporate Culture approach. Try to identify these ideas.

Fundamental to any consideration of organizational cultures is the argument that such cultures play a major part in determining organizational performance.

More specifically the argument of the Corporate Culture school as a whole is that:

1   All organizations have cultures.

2   An organization's culture has an effect on corporate performance.

3   Organizations become more effective when they develop the right cultures.

4   These cultures create consensus and unity and motivate staff.

5   When necessary, cultures can be – and should be – changed.

6   It is the responsibility of senior managers to change them.

The Corporate Culture approach thus presumes that organizational cultures can be assessed, managed, constructed and manipulated in the pursuit of enhanced organizational effectiveness. Employees' norms, beliefs and values can (and, when necessary, *should*) be changed so that they contribute appropriate behaviour, commit themselves to the organization and support management strategy. This view holds that the norms and values shared by members of the organization create consensus and unity.

The claims made for 'cultural change' are enormous: Corporate Culture is considered 'the managerial formula for success' (Jaggi, 1985). When cultures are strengthened, organizational performance will be enhanced and greater commitment, involvement and flexibility from staff will be forthcoming (Deal and Kennedy, 1982).

The 'right' culture may 'reap a return on investment that averages nearly twice as high as those firms with less efficient cultures' (Denison, 1984). 'Sustained competitive advantage' (Barney, 1986) is expected from the 'right' culture, which is also characterized as 'strong' (Bleicher, 1983, p. 495), 'rich'

(Deal and Kennedy, 1982, p.14), 'healthy, blooming' (Ulrich, 1984, p. 313), and 'consistent' (Hinterhuber, 1986). Improvements in performance, quality, productivity, innovation, customer-focus are claimed to flow from Corporate Cultures where individual employees identify their personal purposes and values with those of the organization.

This argument is most frequently associated with the writings of Tom Peters and the 'Excellence' approach. Peters and Waterman (1982) argue that in 'excellent' companies employees are committed to their organization and to its goals, and that this offers a firmer basis for achieving competitive excellence than the traditional determinants of behaviour – structures, procedures and rules. These writers argue that there is a growing international consensus that, for western societies, economic renaissance is dependent upon the cultural transformation of large-scale business; in particular, on the extent to which decaying bureaucracies can be replaced with dynamic, organic, organizational cultures.

To summarize where we have got to so far: like all activities, work has always been associated with, and defined and experienced in terms of, structures of meaning. Recently something has changed: senior managers, persuaded by management writers and consultants acting as 'cultural intermediaries' (see Chapter 4 of this book), have begun to try to manage the culture of the organization – to influence how staff relate to the organization, its structure and purpose, and their employment.

Rose (1995) has offered a simple and useful framework for analysing attempts to construct meanings for others. He notes that such an analysis should address the languages of 'personhood' that define, in our case, the nature and constituent skills, attributes, values, beliefs and personality of the ideal employee, and the norms, techniques and relations of authority within which these languages circulate in organizational contexts and practices and thus act upon the conduct and constitution of employees (Rose, 1995, p. 6). Such an evaluation requires analysis of five issues:

> *Problematization* – where, how and by whom are aspects of the organization, work and the employee rendered problematic, according to what organizational systems of judgement and in relation to what concerns?

> *Technologies* – what organizational means have been invented to govern the employee, to shape or fashion conduct in desired directions, and how have organizational programmes sought to embody these in certain technical forms?

> *Authorities* – which members of the organization have been accorded the capacity and authority to speak truthfully about the organization and its staff?

Teleologies – what organizational attitudes, values and attributes are the aims, ideals or exemplars for these different practices for working upon organizational employees?

Strategies – how are these procedures for regulating the capacities of employees linked into wider moral, social, political – and organizational – objectives concerning the desirable and undesirable features of the workforce?

(adapted from Rose, 1996, pp. 7–9)

Try to keep Rose's framework in mind when working through this chapter. On a number of occasions there will be explicit reference to one or more of the five issues, and at the end of the chapter we will return to his model.

In terms of what has already been said about the early entrepreneurs' concern for the time-keeping of the factory workers, such a concern would, in these terms, be a clear example of *problematization* – time-keeping was defined as a moral issue. These days 'customer handling skills' (the smile) and the pursuit of quality are becoming similarly problematized – a matter for management concern – and a measure of worker performance and suitability.

Corporate Culture projects can be fruitfully analysed in terms of these five issues. For example, the Hilton chain of hotels has made vigorous attempts to ensure that staff commit themselves to certain core 'service' ideals – a classic Corporate Culture project. This takes the form of a set of explicit and widely publicized rules or ideals. These rules are communicated energetically; staff are encouraged – and rewarded – for showing compliance; those who fail to accept them are subject to remedial counselling support. The rules are enshrined in training programmes and displayed on notices and leaflets; line managers are encouraged to instil them in subordinates; appraisal processes refer to evidence of compliance. These practices display the *technologies* of the project.

Also in terms of Rose's categories, this initiative *problematizes* the compliance and commitment of the employee, and his/her willingness to abide by - indeed, enthusiastically to accept – the rules and the inherent value of customer service. *Authority* for the initiative is vested in senior management – who speak glowingly of the Corporate Culture initiative and its impact – and their expert advisers and implementers, the Human Resources specialists. The scheme also reveals its inherent *teleologies:* an obsessive commitment to customer service – to ensuring that staff, even when not under direct control or surveillance, have internalized high standards of customer service. And finally the underlying *strategies* of the scheme are two-fold: that all organizations depend on their capacity to satisfy customers, and that this capacity at both macro (organizational) and micro (individual employee) level is the determinant of organizational (market) success.

FIGURE 5.1
An employee of
the Cairo Hilton
receives a reward
for commitment
to customer
service.

As in the Hilton example, inherent within all Corporate Culture initiatives is the *authority* of management, for management claims the right to speak truthfully, expertly and authoritatively about what organizations are like and what employees should be like. But this does not mean that this voice drowns all others, or is compliantly received.

There are indeed occasions when the literature produced by those consultants and writers who recommend that senior managers manipulate Corporate Cultures, gives the impression of an organization 'split between the privileged actor whose will counted and the rest of the world [or organization] whose will did not count – having been denied or disregarded' (Bauman, 1992, p. xi). But in practice efforts to define organizational realities by senior management are rarely wholly successful, largely because they collide with alternative views of organization and organizational membership.

3   Corporate Culture: diagnosis and treatment

Those who represent and argue the case for organizational 'culture change' base their case on the assertion that the appropriate manipulation of an organization's culture is an effective organizational solution to certain defined corporate problems and corporate threats. These threats are themselves defined in cultural terms, in that the success or failure of economies or organizations is attributed to the extent to which organizations are dominated by cultural consensus or bureaucratic rigidity. Within the logic of Corporate Culture, organizations are seen as vulnerable, or dominant, according to the qualities of their cultures – the values, attitudes and knowledge shared (or not shared) by their members. Poor performance is a result of poor cultures. Thus Corporate Culture offers *culture* as a solution to organizational problems which are seen to stem from the organization's failure to constitute its cultural dynamics properly.

However, while Corporate Culture solutions focus on the organization's culture, the factors underlying organizational failure are often defined in terms of aspects of *national* cultures which are seen to have an impact on organizational cultures. Interest in organizational cultures is therefore situated within and arises from a conception of national threat from the 'other', and offers a solution that claims patriotic authenticity and integrity by countering the power of the 'other' through revitalizing indigenous virtues. Specifically, in organizational terms, Corporate Culture offers to save America (or the West) from the dangers posed by foreign threat by rediscovering the real values of America and enabling these to be reasserted in the workplace. Interestingly, the Corporate Culture movement, which originated in the USA, has had considerable impact in the USA and UK but very much less in other European countries, and relatively none within Japan.

The 'Corporate Culture' argument contains three key inter-related elements:

1   The claim that foreign (Asian, specifically Japanese) organizations pose a serious threat to US/western companies. The Japanese companies' performance is accounted for in terms of (a) their superior cultures; and (b) their recognition of the role of culture as the source of commitment, focus and cohesion in the workforce.

2   Concern about the claimed internal decay, poor performance, failing standards and weakness of US/western organizations. This is seen as a result of their inability to understand and manage their organizational cultures.

3   The claim that current competitive and environmental conditions – not least the threat from Japan and the 'Asian Tigers', but also new technology, globalization and de-regulation – necessitate new forms of organization, not dominated by bureaucratic forms of control and principles of work design, but governed by strong, shared cultures. The way forward, say the Corporate Culture writers, is through culture change.

We will look at each of these elements in more detail.

3.1   The threat from the 'other'

The emphasis on Corporate Culture as a basis for organizational transformation occurred in the 1980s as a response to the much-discussed decline in US economic performance which was attributed to the failure of US companies to attend to, and manage, the cultural aspects of organization, a failure that was seen to be in direct contrast to Japanese companies. For while the United States had recently experienced a long period of low or non–existent productivity improvements overall, Japanese projections showed annual growth of five per cent or more. Yet Japan is a small, crowded, resource-poor country.

The report of the President's Commission on Industrial Competitiveness in 1985, as well as a number of other studies by the US Commerce Department, argued that America had lost its competitiveness in a range of industries including steel, motor vehicles, textiles, electronics, robotics, and telecommunications. One particularly severe setback was the declining performance of the American auto industry. Between 1979 and 1981 the US share of the world car market declined from 35 per cent to 27 per cent. Japanese labour costs were only 65 per cent of US costs, but at the same time Japanese car quality was considerably better than that of American vehicles. In 1980 Japan overtook the USA as the world's leading producer of cars. Similarly, in the computer industry, in 1981 the Japanese Government launched a ten-year programme to build a fifth-generation computer system, thereby becoming the world's leading supplier of advanced computer systems. For US business people, something was going wrong.

For the Corporate Culture writers, this situation was seen as a consequence of the deficiencies of the American way of managing, organizing and producing, and of the virtues of the Japanese approach and their attributed cultural characteristics – commitment, loyalty, deference, obedience, shared values. Best-selling management texts on American failure and Japanese success – *Theory Z* (Ouchi, 1981), *The Art of Japanese Management* (Pascale and Athos, 1981), for example – had the same message: that the key to organizational performance is 'trust, subtlety and intimacy', described as essentially Japanese qualities. The Japanese, it was claimed, knew better than the West how to 'manage ambiguity, uncertainty and interdependence in organizations'. In these texts the strength of Japanese companies was attributed to the features of 'Japanese culture', and to the importance placed on ensuring cultural consensus as a form of control; this was in contrast to the dependence of US corporations on bureaucratic or assembly-line control and discipline, which was represented as destroying commitment. The crisis concerning national economic performance was thus defined in terms of aspects of national culture, and of the failure to exploit, or develop, cultural forces within organizations. The culture of the organization was defined as the central variable in determining organizational performance.

This view generated two types of research: a concern to identify the inherently 'Japanese' cultural qualities of the nation as a whole, and analysis of the specific organizational arrangements of Japanese organizations.

The first is represented in the work of writers on organizations like Geert Hofstede who attempt to map the specific cultural features of nations and to relate these to organizational performance. The second analysis, more organizationally focused, is represented in the work of management writers such as Ouchi and Pascale, which argues for the superiority of Japanese organizational cultures and the need for American organizations to learn from, or borrow from, the practices of their Japanese competitors.

At the broadest level, work such as Hofstede's attempts to systematically plot national cultural dimensions and variations by identifying and analysing culturally-based variations in management practice and organizational process across countries. This research defines organizational culture as an outcome of the organization's location within a host society and culture. So the cultural values, distinctive to the host society, are revealed in the behaviours of organizational members. Furthermore, this type of research seeks to map and classify differences in cultural variables and relate these national differences to organizational performance.

As McMillan notes, 'Of all the approaches to the analysis of Japan, the cultural thesis has been the most enduring. Evident differences in language, history, race, religion, and social etiquette have provided the starting point for culturalist explanations' (McMillan, 1985, p. 34). The conventional focus of such analyses is: Westerners are individualistic, mobile, heterogeneous, with short-term horizons; Japanese are strong on collective consensus, highly stable, homogeneous and disciplined with long-term horizons.

You may well have some objections to this kind of argument, and few serious students of Japan or Japanese organizations would attribute the staggering performance of Japanese organizations solely to cultural factors, cautioning against placing too much weight on culturalist explanations of Japanese success. A major problem in the use of national culture as an explanatory variable is the ill-defined concept of culture, which is used as an indiscriminate, general explanation to account for differences that cannot otherwise be accounted for: 'the concept of national culture is a sort of explanatory dustbin in which is deposited everything that cannot otherwise be explained' (Child, 1981, p. 306).

Another objection you might have against culturalist explanations is that they underestimate the importance of non-cultural explanations of Japanese economic success. These might include organizational and managerial factors (flexible labour utilization, close managerial involvement in production, close relations between large corporations and suppliers), business–government relations and finance–business relations. Culturalist explanations also seriously underestimate the role and importance of state intervention and support in Japan, with the Japanese state historically playing an active part in shaping domestic markets, overseeing the supply of long-term cheap credit and supporting technological development.

But all these criticisms in a sense are by the way: despite these flaws, the culturalist approach to organizational and societal economic performance holds enormous influence. This is the important point. Consultants and management writers have been hugely successful in presenting Japanese success as a result of the role and nature of specific cultural factors in work organizations which created commitment, obedience, focus etc. The management consultant Kenichi Ohmae's insistence is widely accepted:

> Japanese management keeps telling the workers that those at the frontier know best ... A well-run company relies heavily on individual or group initiative for innovation and creative energy. The individual employee is utilized to the fullest extent of his [sic] creative and productive capacity ... The full organization ... looks 'organic' and 'entrepreneurial' as opposed to 'mechanical' and 'bureaucratic'.
>
> (Ohmae, 1982, p. 11)

The culturalist explanation of Japanese success is undoubtedly one-sided and partial. But it is enormously influential, and it has helped to give birth to the Corporate Culture movement.

3.2   The costs of denial of the affective: internal decay and weakness

The second factor contributing to the development of interest in culture as a source of competitive advantage lay not with Japanese success, but with American failure – a failure directly attributed to American managers' inability to recognize the importance of organizational cultures and to manage them effectively.

This literature argues that American failure is due to the historic dominance of methods and principles of organization which deny the affective: which stifle innovation and initiative, are insensitive to the needs of the client, and destroy worker commitment – in other words, something termed 'bureaucracy'. According to the authors of this school, bureaucratic organizations must be replaced by an approach based on the Japanese recognition of the importance of shared culture as the foundation of a successful organization. The contrast is starkly presented. Within bureaucracies staff are required to be compliant, obedient; but within organizations based around shared culture, performance will be achieved through employees' enterprise. This key issue is explored further in Chapter 6.

A hugely influential literature thus argues that American methods are failing – and failing because the role of Corporate Culture was not understood as a source of organizational cohesion; American industries were being (mis)managed into failure.

> As the list of industries – textiles, consumer electronics, steel, autos – that have been conquered or need government protection to survive has grown, it has become increasingly obvious that something is systematically wrong with American management. Not long ago General Motors was commonly referred to as the 'best-managed firm in America'. Why couldn't the best-managed firm in America see the Japanese challenge coming and defeat it? ... Why can't the best-managed firm in America compete with Japanese-made products?
>
> (Thurow, 1984)

Traditional American success recipes had betrayed American virtues, and the American worker.

This analysis of American decay *problematizes* the organization and employee by insisting that bureaucratic, Taylorite organization and work principles render problematic the commitment, attitude, involvement, energy, enthusiasm of the employee. Ouchi, for example, author of *Theory Z*, in his comparison of Japanese and American firms, explains American failure by the negative impact of American hierarchical work structures on workers' attitudes: 'involved workers are the key to productivity' (Ouchi, 1981, p. 4).

Thurow and other commentators argued for a moralistic, back-to-basics approach for American management: a form of corporate cultural fundamentalism. But while they diagnosed the problem, they had to wait for Peters and Waterman to supply the answer. Their *In Search of Excellence* (1982) appeals to American pride – and to American values. It argues that Americans know – or *knew* – how to manage, but that they had forgotten.

Grint (1994, p. 180) in his analysis of another recent management fad – Business Process Re-engineering (BPR) – notes the role of national cultural factors in the success of BPR presentations. BPR is presented in terms of its appeal to, and connections with, *American-ness*. It claims to sweep away the dangerous practices and beliefs of recent years and to connect with real, fundamental American values that had been overlaid by dangerously irrelevant errors and confusions.

Furthermore, this appeal to American fundamentalism is necessary because of the threats of foreign-ness: the threat from the 'other' – Japan and the 'Asian Tigers'. Corporate Culture scapegoats a national past and recommends salvation through a rediscovered national authenticity: salvation means a clean slate, a fresh start. 'This isn't tinkering; it is all or nothing. A total reversal of history is required; and total conversion – "Don't automate, obliterate."' (Hammer, 1990).

The critics of traditional American business methods, and the proponents of new organizational forms, have to strike a delicate balance. They are happy to use Japan (*the other*) as a comparison to demonstrate the extent and causes of American business failure. But there are problems with then insisting that the solution is for America to become like this stereotyped 'other'. The solution is to insist that while there is a need for 'radical' change in American attitudes as a result of the threat of the 'other' – the superior Japanese – the solution is not for Americans to become *like* the 'other' (for the whole point of the notion of the 'other' is to use it to maintain – and justify – your distinctiveness). The solution is for America to become *more* American – to rediscover its roots. The originators of BPR claim:

> The alternative is for corporate America to close its doors ... Reengineering isn't another imported idea from Japan ... Reengineering capitalizes on the same characteristics that made Americans such great business innovators: individualism, self-reliance, a willingness to accept risk and a propensity for change. Business Process Reengineering, unlike management philosophies that would have 'us' like 'them', doesn't try to change the behaviour of American workers and managers. Instead it takes advantage of American talents and unleashes American ingenuity.
>
> (Hammer and Champy, 1993, pp. 1–3)

Corporate Culture seeks to defend and emphasize 'fundamental' American values in the face of dangers from the 'other'. American inefficiencies are not due to fundamental weaknesses, but to America's recent complacency and inertia. The Corporate Culture gurus offer salvation: to show the way back to true values and proper practices, enabling American managers to recognize how they have gone astray.

> The language ... renders opaque developments clear, not by providing a more objective analysis of the situation and the solution, but by providing a persuasive rendering of these. Moreover, part of the persuasive essence lies in the resonance that it 'reveals' between American past glories and future conquests ... 'American industry is weak now *because*, rather than despite the fact that, it was so strong before; and American industry will be strong again *because* of, rather than despite, American culture.'
>
> (Grint, 1994, p. 194)

In the narrative of Corporate Culture, the organization is presented as having slipped into a dangerous state of torpor. Although besieged by wily and opportunistic enemies, proper vigilance has not been maintained; the people are stupefied, indifferent, their natural enthusiasms wasted and dulled; the castle walls are crumbling, for the competition have artfully and surreptitiously removed and loosened key bricks; standards and morale have slipped. The enemy is at the gates, and while there is yet time, senior management – with the help of the Corporate Culture consultant – must rediscover the values and practices that will re-invigorate the garrison, motivate 'the troops', awaken and alert them – the values and practices that once made America great. 'The rhetoric ... is deployed in a way that certainly captures and displays again the American Dream: the way organizations can model themselves on individual qualities that first led the USA to dominate the world by a process of mass boot-strapping' (Grint, 1994, p. 195).

This literature achieves a *strategic* connection between wider national cultural issues (Japanese success, US failure) and organizational cultures, and indeed individual attitudes and values. The significance of the literature lies in the asserted connections between these levels (societal culture – organizational culture – individual values and behaviour), and in the implication that managers are, in Rose's terms, the *authority* that has responsibility for heeding the warnings and transforming the cultures of US organizations.

3.3   The way forward? New times, new organizations

A third dimension in the rise of interest in Corporate Culture is related to the gradual emergence of a conviction of the importance of 'soft' aspects of organizational structure and process, in contrast to rational systems and structures, in achieving superior levels of organizational performance.

The Corporate Culture writers claim that the traditional organizational form was obsessed with order and with attempts to achieve it. But organizational order could only be achieved through rigorous, comprehensive and exhaustive control. The dream of order, attempts to achieve order, and the practice of ordering, constituted the bureacratic organization. Management fear of uncertainty, unreliability and variability prompted an obsessively legislating, defining, structuring, segregating, classifying, recording and universalizing organization which was inefficient (Bauman, 1992, p. xiv).

Corporate Culture writers point to the inefficiencies of these rational, bureaucratic, ways of achieving order and offer to replace them with forms of organization that allow for – and take advantage of – the 'emotional, the primitive side of human nature' (Peters and Waterman, 1982, p. 60). They advocate a return to cultural basics, an undoing of history: the rediscovery of the role and power of meaning. They quote Nietzsche with approval – 'he who has a *why* to live for can bear almost any *how*' (p. 76).

These Corporate Culture writers argue that under modern forms of rational organization workers were stripped of their humanity; they became mere objects, instruments. Rational, bureaucratic forms of organization robbed them of the possibility of meaning at work. Corporate Culture writers claim to regain worker commitment through the management of meaning. Peters and Waterman are quite specific about this: 'What our framework has done is to remind the world of professional managers that "soft is hard" ... It has enabled us to say, in effect, "All that stuff you have been dismissing for so long as the intractable, irrational, intuitive, informal organization can be managed" ' (Peters and Waterman, 1982, p. 11).

The dream that the Corporate Culture books and consultants promise to realize has long been a dream of managers; to be able to manage staff without their knowing or resenting this control; to get workers to accept managerial goals, authority and decisions so that they don't need managing or controlling – in fact, so that they see the organization and their work as their managers see it. The Corporate Culture approach offers to 'colonize the affective domain ... (by) ... promoting employee commitment to a monolithic structure of feeling and thought' (Willmott, 1993, p. 517). Peters sees this, and emphasizes the new role for managers: 'These devices – vision, symbolic action, recognition – are a control system in the truest sense of the term. The manager's task is to conceive of them as such, and to consciously use them' (Peters, 1988, p. 486).

One of the distinctive features of this approach is the claim that it is possible for employees to want, on their own, to do what their managers want them to do. Employees can safely be autonomous because they will 'own' responsibility for doing, to high standards, what they are required to do.

> Corporate culturism expects and requires employees to internalize the new values of 'quality', 'flexibility' and 'value-added' – to adopt and cherish them as their own – so that in principle, their uniquely human powers of judgement and discretion are directed unequivocally towards working methods that will deliver capital accumulation.
>
> (Willmott, 1993, p. 519)

No wonder the culture literature is powerful and popular. But:

> like the 'philosopher's stone' of medieval alchemy, the genre of organiza- tional interpretation [Corporate Culture writing and consultancy] has *appeared* to provide a medium through which the theoretical and empirical 'base metal' of organization could become transformed into the 'golden glow' of ordered success.
>
> (Jeffcutt, 1994, p. 233)

It promises to increase workers' co-operation and commitment, encouraging them to direct their intelligence and creativity towards the goals and standards set by management by managing not simply the distribution of rewards and privileges within the organization, but the normative framework within which they are employed and within which they work.

In Rose's terms, Corporate Culture is seen, not least by its authors and by some of its critics, as a *technology* – a means to govern organizational life.

4   Re-inventing the corporation: Corporate Culture narratives

Analysis of Corporate Culture projects shows that they centre around one or more of three core cultural narratives which offer a re-imagining of the organization. Each narrative has major implications for a view of what organizations are like and how they work, and for the employer–employee relationship. All Corporate Culture narratives establish the essential *teleologies* of the organizational regime: they describe the ideal, the exemplars, the heroic, virtuous employee, and how s/he must relate, and contribute to, the employer.

Corporate Culture narratives are less a form of control or a source of consensus than a medium of understanding which contributes to, but does not determine, the construction of organizational realities. Such narratives *make natural* prevailing organizational structures and political conditions – they define them as 'facts of life' – they prepare employees for the way they will participate in organizations and for how they will be treated. Organizational employees do not experience their work, organization and employment 'transparently' but through structures of meaning, and these narratives supply frameworks of meaning. Cultural narratives play a role in defining limits of our expectations, constructing parameters for the tolerable, locating us within particular organizational spaces, supplying ways of thinking about things.

As indicated above, Corporate Culture narratives centre around three common themes.

The first narrative theme focuses on the collective aspect of the corporation and asserts its existence, primacy and power. It insists that organizations are harmonious, consensual, unitary; that employees share key values and purposes. It defines the individual employee in terms of the organization, in terms of collective, shared and consensual values. Employees are defined as members of an organizational or corporate community, with all that this entails: they are sharers of a value system.

The second theme is the enterprising nature of the organization as a whole and the relationship of individual employees to the total, collective organization. It defines these shared values in terms of a market focus and market values. This theme focuses on the individual as defined by, and embodying, these collective organizational, market values. Employees are constructed and defined by these shared values, as enterprising, market- and customer-focused individuals, as microcosmic organizations, with individualized organizational qualities. (The notion of enterprise is taken up again in Chapter 6.)

The third theme imagines the organization as if it were an individual, attributing to the organization the capacities, needs and responses of the human organism. It represents the organization in terms of the attributed qualities of an intelligent, responsive, adaptive individual.

4.1   The organization as an 'imagined community'

In this narrative, the organization is seen as characterized by consensus, harmony, co-operation, lack of division, high levels of commitment, etc. These qualities are emphasized in discussions of Japan for they are seen as peculiarly characteristic of Japanese society and its organizations. But interestingly they are also seen as fundamentally American values, if only they could be re-discovered.

In this element of Corporate Culture the organization is presented as an idealized community, and its employees as members of this community – members who are compliant, consensual and committed. These qualities may or may not be overtly asserted, as in references to 'we at IBM ...' or to 'the BA way', for example. But even when the community is not directly invoked it is clearly assumed as the basis for detailed exhortations which would be ludicrous unless employees shared values and purposes. None of the more detailed recommendations would make any sense unless the first precondition of commitment, consensus and co-operation were achieved.

The important thing about imagined communities in the context of Corporate Culture activities is, as Bauman notes, that **imagined communities** – and this is particularly true of imagined *corporate* communities – exist only because people believe they exist, or insist they exist. Corporate Culture activity can be seen as an effort to make sure that imagined communities exist 'through their manifestations: through occasional spectacular outbursts of togetherness (demonstrations, marches, festivals, riots)' or, one could add, corporate presentation sessions, video displays, etc. (Bauman, 1992, p. xix).

imagined communities

However, while Bauman notes the importance of public attention and support – however fickle – in sustaining imagined communities, the point about Corporate Culture's imagined communities is that *they are imagined for us* – by powerful members of the organization who struggle to gain employees' attention in order to make the imagined community – the organization itself – authoritative.

This element of Corporate Culture narratives borrows heavily from a particular tradition within anthropology and sociology – structural functionalism – but borrows selectively, stressing some aspects and ignoring others. Structural functionalism has been criticized:

> ... for its insistence that social order is created and maintained through individuals internalizing dominant social norms and values, for its treatment of people holding alternative norms and values as being socially

deviant, and for its assumption that the parts of a society exist in a natural state of equilibrium, functioning effectively so as to maintain the effectiveness of the total social structure.

(Meek, 1992, p. 195)

This narrative of the imagined community is revealed in the Corporate Culture argument that culture is a unifying force; that it reflects the collective will of the organization; that it is consistent with, or derives from, the wishes of senior management; that deviants must be dealt with. Thus, as a result of the borrowing of structural-functionalist assumptions, Corporate Culture approaches tend to ignore the possibility of conflicts within the organization, ignore structures of power and interest, ignore structures of hierarchy and inequality, and ignore difference and differentiation of groups and of cultures. As a result culture is viewed '... as a product of consensus rather than as the precarious outcome of continuous processes of contestation and struggle' (Knights and Willmott, 1987, p. 41).

Within this Corporate Culture theme, the quest for the 'imagined community' takes the form of an heroic search in which the heroes (the senior managers led by the consultant) recreate a state of organizational harmony and unity that has been lost, sacrificed or neglected through the imposition of previous organizational regimes. The objective is an harmonious and integrated organization, with the Corporate Culture approach as both the means of achieving unity and the expression of the discovered unity.

The view of the organization as a community defines the role of senior managers as community builders: upholders and representatives of core values, of tradition and continuity. Like the young King Henry V on the eve of Agincourt, the manager modestly moves amongst the people, disclaiming the panoplies of rank, a leader in touch with the people, who manages by 'walking the talk', by being accessible, staying in touch. Middle managers are exhorted to become team builders, managing through consensus, working *with* subordinates, who should be encouraged to become empowered – for as a consequence of the shared community of values and purpose within the imagined community narrative, employees are both free to make their 'empowered' decisions, and can safely be relied upon to execute their new authority judiciously.

Thus, within the imagined community of the organization, employees are required to behave according to their shared values, their shared purposes, their commitment to organizational objectives and directives. Yet this commitment to the collective is seen as permitting employees considerable individual discretion within the confines of shared goals and purposes. The values employees are exhorted to hold in common, collectively, are values that require them to behave individualistically and autonomously. Because of their shared belief and values they can be charged to take seriously the objectives and requirements of the organization and to internalize them as if they were their own.

A task-oriented, traditional company hires people and expects them to follow rules. Companies that have been reengineered don't want employees who can follow rules: they want people who will make their own rules ... Within the boundaries of their obligation to the organization – agreed-upon deadlines, productivity goals, quality standards, and so forth – they decide how and when work will get done.

(Hammer and Champy, 1993, p. 10)

4.2   The enterprising organization

If in the first narrative the organization is defined as an idealized family or community, in this second narrative it is defined as a market place – a competitive, potentially hostile milieu where employees must constantly maintain standards in order to meet, if not exceed, the standards (quality, speed, service standards, cost) of competitors. If the organization is in the public sector – universities, hospitals – then the narrative construction of the organization (and individual employees) as market agents will be associated with technologies of performance measurement which allow inter-organizational performance comparisons, and thus supply a base for enforced competition where the 'winners' receive larger shares of governmental resources.

This narrative means not simply that the organization as a whole must behave competitively, but more fundamentally that *within* the organization employees must behave *as if* they were operating within a market where competitive standards are constantly applied. The employees must act *as if* (thinking and feeling *as if*) they were microcosms of the organization as a whole; *as if* they have internalized and adopted the objectives of the organization; *as if* they were small-business entrepreneurs within the larger organization. Employees become miniaturized enterprises – individually embodying the necessary functions and activities of the successful corporate enterprise. Just as corporations must market products and services, maintain customer relations, manage clients, ensure standards and quality, achieve profit and manage costs, so individual employees must also show mastery of these functions on an individual basis. They must be commercially sensitive, quality-focused, customer-focused, pro-active, cost-sensitive and responsible, capable of doing what is best and necessary without having to be told what this is; capable of acting without detailed regulation and instruction but in accordance with internalized demands and standards. Each employee in effect becomes his/her own firm.

Thus the narrative of enterprise not only allocates 'paradigmatic status' to the commercial enterprise as the preferred model for all forms of organizational conduct and all internal organizational relationships, it also celebrates and demands enterprising qualities and behaviour from all employees. And, of course, it insists on a causal relationship between organizational demands and employee behaviour (du Gay, 1994, p. 133).

Within this element of Corporate Culture narratives, the individual is defined in aggressively individualistic terms: '... governing the business organization in an enterprising manner involves cultivating enterprising subjects – autonomous, self-regulating, productive, responsible individuals' (du Gay and Salaman, 1992, p. 626).

This narrative typically focuses on the senior manager as an epic hero/ine, who, recognizing the slothful, complacent ways into which the organization has sunk, through personal energy and valour, and with commitment to standards and vigour, confronts the internal dangers, and enables the organization to awaken to its perils and overwhelm them (through quality and excellence). The enterprise of the heroic leader is matched and supported by their 'transformative' abilities; these managers are revolutionaries; they carry a heavy burden (and take high rewards); they 'turn the corporation around'; they are 'pace setters', 'benchmarking' performance, obsessed with quality standards, highly committed to the 'bottom line', ruthless when necessary, endlessly focused on the achievement of higher and higher standards.

In this narrative, the organization has been seduced by inertia and sloth; it has slipped into torpor induced by dysfunctional traditional working practices and wickedly distracted and complacent managers. The role of senior managers (inspired by the consultant) is to identify these threats, and to warn of the dangers – the 'corruptive spectre of failure'. Redemption is 'through the heroic struggle with these limitations (e.g. radical restructuring, transformations in employee and managerial effectiveness) ... which culminates in the organization's assertive rebirth and subsequent burgeoning ... With vision, charisma and belief identified as the special qualities that enable the successful attainment of this quest' (Jeffcutt, 1994, p. 229).

4.3   The learning organization

In the third Corporate Culture narrative, the organization is defined as if it were an individual or organism within a competitive and hostile environment. The focus here is not primarily on enterprise and quality (although these are certainly *outcomes*) but on the necessary process of growth, development, adaptation and learning that are seen to underlie intelligent survival within the competitive world. The objective of these versions of the Corporate Culture approach is the achievement of a 'learning organization'. The healthy organization, like the healthy individual, must be alert, in touch with the world, well-adjusted to what is happening around it.

As one major culture consultant argues:

> Our prevailing system of management has destroyed our people. People are born with intrinsic motivation, self-esteem, dignity, curiosity to learn, joy in learning. The forces of destruction begin with toddlers – a prize for the best Halloween costume, grades in school, gold stars, and on up through

the university. On the job, people, teams, divisions are ranked – reward for the one at the top, punishment at the bottom. MBO (Management by Objectives), quotas, incentive pay, business plans, put together separately, division by division, cause further loss, unknown and unknowable.

(Deming, quoted in Senge, 1990, p. 7)

Superior performance, argues Senge, depends on superior learning: '... the most successful corporation of the 1990s will be something called a learning organization, a consummately adaptive enterprise' (Fortune, quoted in Senge, 1990, p. 8).

This is a common consultancy view. Much recent management literature stresses the value of organizational 'flexibility', or 'responsiveness', and these qualities are seen as related to environmental developments, particularly changes in the business environment – the increasingly competitive global nature of product markets. Under these circumstances, commentators claim, competitive advantage accrues to those businesses that '... promote continuous learning, teamwork, participation and flexibility' (Dertouzos et al., 1989, p. 118).

But what is a learning organization? Senge defines his view of the learning organization as follows: 'Organizations where people continually expand their capacity to create the results they desire, where new and expansive patterns of thinking are nurtured, where collective aspiration is set free, and where people are continually learning how to learn' (Senge, 1990, p. 8).

It is increasingly common for business consultants, academics and managers to argue that to achieve competitive edge in a highly competitive business environment it is necessary to unleash and tap the energy, intelligence, creativity and enthusiasm of staff.

Bureaucracy is giving way to new approaches that require people to exercise discretion, take initiatives, and assume a much greater responsibility for their own organization and management. The need to remain open and flexible demands creative responses from every quarter, and many leading organizations recognize that human intelligence and the ability to unleash and direct that intelligence are critical resources.

(Morgan, 1988, p. 56)

But it is apparently easier to say this than to achieve it. Despite the widespread acceptance of this requirement, Morgan notes, 'Many of our organizations have difficulty doing their best. Though they show considerable promise (or promises?), they fall short in their action' (Morgan, 1988, p. 54).

Culture consultants claim that learning in organizations is blocked in the same way, and for the same reasons, that it is obstructed in individuals. For example, learning cultures are antithetical to hierarchy – for hierarchy, routine and conformity are all anti-learning, since they encourage compliance, deference and denial. Similarly in times of rapid change these defensive processes are often intensified, because of anxiety and insecurity.

It is claimed that another important source of 'resistance' to learning can derive from organizational cultures. Some organizational cultures may predispose against learning by discouraging any one of the key elements that learning requires.

They do this by trapping employees in a 'single loop' model of learning whereby they are unable to see, or question, the basic assumptions on which their thinking rests. Employees are seen subconsciously to collude in a set of beliefs and mental categories that limit possibilities, and restrict fundamental analysis.

> The [organizational] culture, once established, prescribes for its creators and inheritors certain ways of believing, thinking and acting which in some circumstances can prevent meaningful interaction and induce a situation of 'learned helplessness' – that is, a psychological state in which people are unable to conceptualize their problems in such a way as to be able to resolve them. In short, attempts at problem-solving may become culture-bound.
>
> (Bate, 1992, p. 214)

Some contributors to the debate about the learning organization see, predictably, a major role for national cultures in determining the willingness or capacity of organizations to learn. Steele (1977) identifies certain UK cultural factors that inhibit organizational learning:

1 the value of security and stability;

2 the value of avoiding embarrassing and 'unsuitable' topics;

3 the sense of the legitimacy of hierarchical authority;

4 the emphasis on tradition and continuity;

5 a strong strain of fatalism;

6 an emphasis on rationality which leads to the rejection of new methods which are untested.

And, predictably, the British failure is contrasted with the Japanese cultural supremacy at achieving learning. For central to the Japanese organizational structure is the notion of *kaizen* – or continuous improvement – which results from particular organizational forms which encourage discussion and learning, principally team working with a core of flexible workers.

And once again, it is the job of managers to manage the learning (performance improvement) of their staff and to adjust the organization's culture so that it is pro-learning, to identify and overcome blockages to learning – in themselves, their staff and even their superiors. For, as Kolb et al. have noted, the '... organization's ability to survive and thrive in a complex dynamic environment is constrained by the capabilities of managers who must learn to manage both this greater environmental complexity and the complex organizational forms developed to cope with the environment' (Kolb et al., 1986, p. 14).

The manager in this narrative is defined as a teacher, therapist, coach, developer and mentor. The role of managers is to develop and guide their staff, to improve their performance, to help them grow, to offer feedback skilfully, to overcome 'organizational defences', to confront 'defensive routines' and 'single-loop learning'. These managerial responsibilities are seen as critical. For:

> the ability of a company to learn should be under regular scrutiny. In other words, the ability of an organization to reconstruct and adapt its knowledge base (made up of skills, structures and values ...) should be a key task for managers. They should also be able to apply the 'unlearning' test. In other words, is the organization capable of mounting the creative destruction necessary to breaking down outmoded attitudes and practices, while at the same time building up new, more appropriate competences? [The] ... ability to learn faster than competitors may be the only sustainable advantage.
>
> (Pettigrew and Whipp, 1991, p. 290)

The implications of these narratives – especially the narrative of enterprise – for the identities of employees will be considered in Chapter 6.

FIGURE 5.2 Getting the message across: introducing the corporate culture at the Cairo Hilton.

5 Marketing the message: Corporate Culture's appeal to managers

There are major reasons to question the efficacy of Corporate Culture writers' ideas. One exhaustive study of the performance of the Peters and Waterman 'excellent' companies notes that the research 'cast doubts on the excellence of several firms in Peters and Waterman's sample ... Further, the results cast doubt on the importance of several of the excellence principles' (Hitt and Ireland, 1987, p. 95). These authors conclude that Peters and Waterman's work '... may be one of advocacy rather than science' (p. 96). Burrell notes of the same literature that '... it is little more than a "tattered web" of assertions, some of which are self contradictory' (Burrell, 1989, p. 308). (We shall look at these critiques in more detail in section 6.)

Yet these writings have been hugely influential and have great appeal to managers. So why is this? Part of the appeal lies in the attractiveness of what is promised:

> *In Search of Excellence* succeeded because it brought welcome balm for America's battered self image. Here was a better, wholly indigenous solution to declining productivity and industrial decline and Peters' and Waterman's argument is put in terms that most people could immediately grasp.
>
> (Keisling, 1984, p. 40)

But there are three other bases to this appeal.

First, these projects resonate with managers' own values; what they emphasize, and what they ignore or deny strikes a chord with managers. They are not only about the importance of values and feelings in organizations, they also cleverly tap into, and appeal to, the values and feelings of managers. Furthermore, the suggestion that organizational cultures matter and can be manipulated to managers' advantage is consistent with managers' values and beliefs and with their conception of themselves and their role.

The literature strikes a chord with managers because it accesses fears about the *other* while appealing to American values of enterprise, commitment, energy, consensus.

> Corporate Culture is positive. It appeals to American pride. It says Americans – at least some Americans – know how to manage. The secret Japanese potion is available at the corner drugstore, not just in Kyoto. This message is just what the doctor ordered for a nation which is questioning its ability to compete in an economically restructured world.
>
> (Maidique, 1983, p. 155)

Corporate Culture may also appeal because of what is *not* said. These analyses studiously ignore certain uncomfortable elements of organizational structure and process – the nature and role of power, of conflicts, or exploitation, of difference. Some of the basic assumptions and taken-for-granted 'realities' of organization are left unquestioned and unanalysed by the gurus of organizational culture. Corporate Culture programmes with their focus on performance and commitment, their lack of interest in, or attention to, divisive, exploitative aspects of organization, are from a managerial point of view quite 'natural', 'neutral' and necessary.

The second aspect of the appeal of the Corporate Culture project lies in the *form* in which the ideas are presented – the style and performance of culture consultants whose work brims with optimism, energy, enthusiasm. '... They are enthusiastic about the business world, about the possibility of organizational transformation, about the new culture of management ... the authors often eschew the syntax of reservation and qualification common to academic prose.' (Freeman, 1985, p. 347).

The ways in which Corporate Culture writers publicly present their ideas and themselves mirror the nature and quality of their ideas. Clark and Salaman (1996) have compared the performance of management gurus to witchdoctors, seeing similarities in the power of the presentation, the intensity of commitment and passion; the implicit, occasionally explicit, element of threat and confrontation; the total conviction and commitment of the performer (no doubts here); the presence of riddles, dilemmas, mysteriously gained insights that confuse and surprise the audience, leaving the impression that somehow the performer 'knows' them, their problems, disguises and subterfuges (Clark and Salaman, 1996, p. 88).

They describe the powerfully manipulative elements of culture consultants' presentations:

> ... the strenuous efforts ... to awaken; to generate fundamentally transformed 'consciousness' of self, organization and priorities; to see new patterns and new possibilities, which ordinary life, before the perform-ance, had not made available or obvious. The focus on the emotional and irrational, with all the fear and anxiety that this occasions for audience and performer ... There is also risk for the audience ... No one is safe. Those who hope they can remain immune and detached as observers soon find that by a variety of devices they are drawn into the session, become the focus of the session in which strange things happen to them – to be exposed to combative questions, publicly posed with riddles, forced to reveal their ignorance which is then immediately exposed, required to participate in role plays – a battery of de-stabilizing techniques are used which move the content of the event from a safe, cerebral level to the level of 'here and now' with egos, identities and pride at stake ... As Goffman put it (1990, p. 135): 'reality is being performed'.

(Clark and Salaman, 1996, pp. 103–4)

Culture consultants show impressive mastery of the management of symbols and occasions – skills they assert are crucial to *managers'* performances.

> Consultants like Rosabeth Moss Kanter and Tom Peters have recognized the new *Zeitgeist* and its emphasis on appearance, image and superficiality ... Their writings and TV appearances are all showbiz and presentation skills blending enthusiasm, fear, sweat and humour in ways reminiscent of vaudeville. In a society where the manager has become a hero, where the dominant metaphors are military ones, where the enemy is Japanese and corporate leaders resort to rhetoric it is less clear than it might be that it is only the content that is missing from their books and videos.
>
> (Burrell, 1989, p. 310)

Thus culture consultants' performances govern management identification.

FIGURE 5.3
Rosabeth Moss Kanter,
Professor of Business
Administration at
Harvard Business School.

But finally, and probably most significantly, the Corporate Culture message is attractive to managers because it offers them a dramatic and heroic status. It defines the nature and importance of the senior management role and function, celebrating and glorifying senior management by placing them in a central position as 'transformative leaders'. The manipulation of cultures and the symbols of which they consist becomes, according to culture consultants, the primary task for managers. In Rose's terms *authority* rests with senior managers who require, and in turn claim, the capacity to speak about employees and organizations and the relations between them.

Managers are thus similar to the 'cultural intermediaries' (discussed in Chapter 4), people who play an active part in attaching particular meanings to the world of work. Their role is to manage culture. As Peter has argued: '... symbols are the very stuff of management behaviour. Executives, after all, do not synthesize chemicals or operate fork lift trucks; they deal in symbols' (Peters, 1978, p. 10).

Peters and Waterman address the issue of corporate leadership directly. Initially, they confess, they were tempted to discount the role and practice of leadership; but in due course they found that 'associated with almost every excellent company was a strong leader' (Peters and Waterman, 1982, p. 26). In fact they claim not only that senior managers are directly responsible, through vision and strength, for the quality of corporate performance but that they are also responsible for leading ('championing') the process of change ('turnaround') through the management of meaning. The senior manager, as leader, is the hero/ine of the Corporate Culture narrative.

The appeal of Corporate Culture for senior managers is not simply the emphasis – and value – placed on the leadership function by writers such as Peters and Waterman. It also lies in the *nature* of this emphasis. For writers in this area, the job of senior managers is precisely *to define reality* for their staff.

Not surprisingly, managers welcome consultants who offer this flattering view of their responsibilities. Within the Corporate Culture project, senior managers are defined as 'transformative leaders – that is, people who can build 'on man's *(sic)* need for meaning, leadership that creates institutional purpose' (Peters and Waterman, 1982, p. 83). Strong cultures, argue these authors, are impossible without the energy and intervention of the heroic transforming leader.

6 Critiques of Corporate Culture programmes

There have been a number of different critiques of the nature and impact of Corporate Culture projects.

First, there are those writers who criticize the way Corporate Culture gurus define and employ the concept of 'culture', arguing, for example, that in its passage from anthropology to organizational analysis the concept has been systematically distorted and misused. The sociologist Lynn Meek, for example, condemns the 'pop cultural magicians', who make their living 'by convincing North American and European corporate executives that they can equal the productivity of Japanese industry through the mechanical manipulation of organizational symbols, myths and customs' (Meek, 1992, p. 194). She castigates these writers on a number of counts.

1   She argues that they ignore the multiplicity of theories of culture and draw excessively from one tradition – structural functionalism – a tradition that relies on biological metaphors which stress the role of shared and internalized social values in the achievement of social order.

2   She criticizes the argument that cultures can be created by senior managers. 'Most anthropologists would find the idea that leaders create culture preposterous: leaders do not create cultures' (Meek, 1992, p. 198).

3   She argues that, because of this structural-functionalist legacy, Corporate Culture writers tend to gloss over inherent conflicts within the organization, and the role of power and structured inequalities; the political contexts within which organizational cultures develop, and

with which they engage, are ignored. She notes that they tend to assume that the norms, values and beliefs of organizational employees are factors which create consensus and unity, and argues instead that organizations are not consensual, and that they have a variety of cultures, often conflicting.

Critical commentators such as Meek have also argued that the concept of culture deployed by consultants is excessively focused on managerial preoccupations – with emphasizing those values within the organization which are seen to promote employee commitment and compliance. At the same time, the consultants are insufficiently concerned with exploring (or even acknowledging) core aspects of managerial culture which (1) might be inimical or damaging to consensus and cultural unity, and (2) might undermine employee commitment and obedience; aspects such as hierarchy, control, instrumental values and racism are not discussed (Alvesson, 1987).

The focus on 'culture change' for example, is often an attempt to impose a consensual, unitarist conception of the organization on all employees, and thus to gain their commitment. Organizational attempts to achieve homogeneous, unitary cultures contrast, and possibly conflict, with employees' conceptions and experiences of organizations as arenas of conflicting interests and values. Even Wickens, an enthusiast for the Corporate Culture approach, acknowledges this: 'We spend vast amounts of time talking and negotiating about employee involvement and very little time actually involving employees. As with many of these ideas – the flavour of the month that will be our managerial salvation – we construct an edifice which simply invites opposition' (Wickens, 1987, p. 85).

A second group of writers, while agreeing that the conception of culture employed by Corporate Culture writers is partial and unitary, focus more attention on the uses and purposes to which cultural change is put, and on the processes of organizational control. For these writers, Corporate Culture is an ideological project, in the sense that it is committed to the maximization of organizational, managerial control for the achievement of productive, reliable, compliant behaviour, supportive of the existing organizational power structure. Many of these writers analyse Corporate Culture in terms of the managerial benefits (under current turbulent conditions) of controlling culture, assuming that knowledge about the role of meanings in organizations, and how to manage meanings to change Corporate Cultures, provides management with a powerful means for improving the efficiency and scope of management control. For example, Knights and Wilmott emphasize the role of Corporate Culture in supporting the exploitative character of working arrangements. They stress, '... the role of symbols and the expression of culture in the reproduction of labour processes through which the fundamentally exploitative character of production relations, involving the pumping out of surplus from employees, is routinely secured as it is concealed' (Knights and Wilmott, 1987, p. 43).

These writers explain the appeal of Corporate Culture by its power as an improved means of organizational control, better fitted to the challenges of an increasingly complex and dislocated global environment: '... a central element in the corporate strategies for gaining competitive advantage ... corporate culturism can be seen to form an ideological element within a global restructuring of capital' (Wilmott, 1993, pp. 517–9).

There is a tension between these two positions – on the one hand that Corporate Culture misuses or distorts the concept of culture (Meek), and on the other that it represents a powerful and effective means of management control (Wilmott). Corporate Culture regimes may be criticized for their 'misuse' of the concept of culture but they are also seen as highly effective; a paradox some authors find difficult to resolve. The first position suggests that it is all ill-founded nonsense – 'smoke and mirrors' – achieving its impact through its appeal to senior managers' conceptions of organization. But the second position argues that Corporate Culture is real and important, contributing significantly to new processes of organizational control.

Two further implications of the second approach are that Corporate Culture projects are elements of widespread programmes of organizational restructuring in *response* to changes in organizations' environments, and are central to new, insidious and dangerous programmes of managerial control.

There are three problems with this.

Firstly, it ignores the extent to which conceptions of the business environment, or of new organizational forms, have themselves been developed by Corporate Culture writers and are inherent elements of their analyses and prescriptions. It also overlooks how conceptions of the relationship between these elements (environment – organization – Corporate Culture) are defined by the Corporate Culture approach itself, which defines how environments are changing and how organizations must change. The world of the organization and its environment is the world as represented by Corporate Culture approaches. Corporate Culture is therefore a 'solution' to problems which it itself constitutes.

For example, within contemporary management discourse (including Corporate Culture) the case against bureaucracy and for the new sorts of 'organic' and 'flexible' organizational forms is directly associated with changes in the 'external environment' (du Gay, 1994, p. 131).

The second problem is the conceptualization of the ways in which environmental 'imperatives' 'cause' or 'require' organizational responses. Management consultants may refer to this sort of causal determination in order to persuade managers of the need for change, but in fact this mechanical form of explanation whereby organizations 'respond' to environmental stimuli is flawed, since it fails to recognize or acknowledge the role of organizational members making choices about processes of change in terms of how they see and understand and value the organization, its structure and purposes. In short, this sort of model of causation totally ignores managers' structures of meaning.

Thirdly, this model simplifies and distorts the impact of Corporate Culture programmes on targeted employees. Within the Corporate Culture approach itself, this impact is largely unproblematic: it is assumed that staff will relish the opportunity to commit themselves to the liberating, autonomous, empowering, flexible, consensual, entrepreneurial culture of the organization.

And we have noted that Corporate Culture projects appeal to senior managers because they:

- appeal to their understanding of organizations and employees;
- seem to resolve problems of organizational restructuring;
- resonate sympathetically with senior managers' understanding of the cultural bases of well-performing and poorly-performing organizations (and national economies);
- supply culture as an answer to problems which are themselves posed in cultural terms and which stress values that senior managers hold dear.

However, if we can understand the appeal of these ideas to senior managers, we should not overestimate their appeal to other employees, at whom culture change programmes are directed. The impact of any structure of meanings cannot be assumed or simply 'read off', but must be empirically investigated, in order to see how meanings are constructed, mediated, neglected and subverted.

READING B

> In his article 'Strength is ignorance; slavery is freedom', Hugh Willmott analyses the Corporate Culture literature. In the extract, 'Symptoms of resistance', provided as Reading B at the end of this chapter, he explores the possibility that employees may react to culture change initiatives in terms of their existing convictions and values.

Willmott's argument strongly suggests that management programmes of culture change do not succeed in radically transforming employees' values and beliefs. Similarly, the academic Emmuel Ogbonna concludes his assessment of Corporate Culture change with the comment that 'management was only able to generate behavioural compliance from an indifferent workforce ... changes in the visible manifestation of culture were observable while values and assumptions remained intact' (Ogbonna, 1992, p. 94).

7   Conclusion

It might be concluded that the Corporate Culture project is of no great importance – simply a fad encouraged by management consultants, appealing to senior managers because of its implied celebration of their role and status but of no significance to the management of organizations – the 'smoke and mirrors' mentioned earlier. This conclusion would be too hasty, however. If Corporate Culture programmes cannot be seen simply as an effective new form of control – at least in the terms claimed by their proponents – they can nevertheless be seen in general terms as key aspects of the government of organizational life in that they represent a new way in which management thinks about, calculates and acts on, the structuring of organizations and the behaviour of employees. One way of seeing this 'government' of organizations is as a form of activity aiming to shape, guide or affect the conduct of some person or persons. Government as an activity can concern the relation between self and self, private interpersonal relations involving some form of control or guidance, and relations within social institutions (du Gay, 1996, p. 54). As du Gay remarks,

> forms of government rely upon a particular mode of representation: the development of a language for delineating and depicting a certain domain that claims both to capture the nature of the 'reality' represented and, literally, to 're-present' it in a form suitable for deliberation, argumentation, scheming and intervention.
>
> (du Gay, 1996, p. 54)

In these terms the narratives of Corporate Culture are associated with contemporary programmes of organizational restructuring – quality programmes, new methods of payment, restructuring, performance assessment systems, customer focus programmes, etc. – which have radically and systematically transformed earlier conceptions of the employee/ organization relationship. While Corporate Culture programmes may not have created the docile, enthusiastic employee extolled in the consultants' texts, willingly accepting the values and beliefs inherent in Corporate Culture narratives, they have succeeded in re-engineering the psychological contract between employee and employer, through the processes by which sense-making and the construction of meaning are structured in and by the employing organization.

7.1   Postscript

At the beginning of this chapter, it was noted that culture change initiatives in modern organizations supply a powerful example of the interplay of power and knowledge as senior managers seek to define the meaning of work and employment. We suggested that Rose's five dimensions of the process of subjectivization – *problematization, technologies, authorities, teleologies, strategies* – can usefully be applied to an analysis of Corporate Cultures. By way of a brief overall summary, let us now apply these dimensions to the narratives to assess their use and relevance.

In Corporate Culture activities, senior managers, and the consultants who guide them, try to define specific aspects of the employee's existence and his/her relationship to the corporation as important and *problematic* – i.e. employees' commitment to management values and purposes; their 'enterprise' and willingness to adapt and change, to be flexible. (This issue is discussed in more detail in the next chapter.)

Secondly, Corporate Culture programmes are associated with specific *technologies*, which seek to shape and fashion employees' behaviour. (These have only been touched on, in the Introduction to this chapter.) You may be able to think of examples from your own experience where culture projects are associated with new means (or criteria) of staff recruitment or appraisal, new means of monitoring performance, or new management competences. These too are further discussed in the next chapter. The process of government of an organization involves more than matters of representation. It also involves processes of intervention. These interventions – or 'technologies' – are the 'mechanisms through which managements seek to shape, normalize and instrumentalize the conduct, thought, decisions and aspirations of others in order to achieve the objectives they consider desirable' (Miller and Rose, 1993, p. 82).

Thirdly, within Corporate Culture projects, despite the possibility that a variety of diverse and competing systems of meaning exist within the organization, senior management clearly claim the *authority* to speak truthfully and expertly on behalf of the organization as a whole and its purpose and direction, about and for employees, their nature, attributes and attitudes. Indeed as discussed in section 5, one of the main reasons for the appeal of these projects is that they not only offer a way of thinking about and acting upon problems but they do so in a way that is inherently attractive to managers, by simultaneously legitimating and celebrating their role and status, and offering a conception of the organization (in the three core narratives) which they find highly congenial. These narratives may not square with everyone's experience but they square with how managers see themselves and with how they would like their employees to think about the organization for which they work.

Furthermore, we have noted that Corporate Culture projects clearly stipulate the *teleologies*, or forms of life that are or should be the aims, ideals or exemplars for employees. This is one of the main points that emerged in the discussion of the three cultural narratives in section 4.

Finally, the analysis in this chapter has demonstrated some of the *strategies* inherent within the Corporate Culture approach, by identifying the grounds for the appeal of these projects through the links between Corporate Culture activities and wider moral, social or political objectives.

References

ALVESSON, M. (1987) 'Organizations, culture and ideology', *International Studies of Management and Organization*, Vol. XVII, No. 3. pp. 4–18.

BARNEY, J. B. (1986) 'Organizational culture: can it be a sustained source of competitive advantage?', *Academy of Management Review*, Vol. 11, No. 3, pp. 656–65.

BATE, P. (1992) 'The impact of organizational culture on approaches to organizational problem-solving' in Salaman, G. et al. (eds) *Human Resource Strategies*, London, Sage, pp. 213–36.

BAUMAN, Z. (1992) *Intimations of Postmodernity*, London, Routledge.

BEICHER, K. (1983) 'Organizationskulturen und Fuhrungsphilosophien in Bettewerb', *Zeitschrift fuer Betriebswirtschaftliche Forschung*, Vol. 35, pp. 135–46.

BURRELL, G. (1989) 'The absent centre: the neglect of philosophy in Anglo-American management theory', *Human Systems Management*, Vol. 8, pp. 307–12.

CHILD, J. (1981) 'Culture, contingency and capitalism in the cross-national study of organizations' in Cummings, L. L. and Staw, B. M. (eds) *Research in Organizational Behaviour*, Vol. 3, Greenwich, CT, JAI Press, pp. 303–56.

CLARK, T. and SALAMAN, G. (1996) 'The management guru as organizational witchdoctor', *Organization*, Vol. 3, No. 1, pp. 85–107.

CONRAD, C. (1985) 'Review of *A Passion for Excellence*', *Administrative Science Quarterly*, Vol. 30, No. 3, pp. 426–8.

DEAL, T. E. and KENNEDY, A. A. (1982) *Corporate Cultures: the rites and rituals of corporate life*, Reading, MA, Addison–Wesley.

DEAL, T. E. and KENNEDY, A. A. (1991) *Corporate Cultures*, Harmondsworth, Penguin.

DENISON, D. R. (1984) 'Bringing Corporate Culture to the bottom line', *Organizational Dynamics*, Vol. 12, pp. 5–22.

DERTOUZOS, M., LESTER, R. and SOLOW, R. (1989) *Made in America: regaining the competitive edge*, Cambridge, MA, MIT Press.

DU GAY, P. (1994) 'Colossal immodesties and hopeful monsters: pluralism and organizational conduct', *Organization*, Vol. 1, No. 1, pp. 125–48.

DU GAY, P. (1996) *Consumption and Identity at Work,* London, Sage.

DU GAY, P. and SALAMAN, G. (1992) 'The culture of the customer', *Journal of Management Studies*, Vol. 29, No. 5, pp. 615–33.

FREEMAN, F. H. (1985) 'Books that mean business: the management best seller', *Academy of Management Review*, pp. 345–50.

GOFFMAN, E. (1990) *The Presentation of Self in Everyday Life*, Harmondsworth, Penguin.

GRINT, K. (1994) 'Reengineering history: social resonances and Business Process Reengineering', *Organization*, Vol. 1, No. 1, pp. 179–201.

HAMMER, M. (1990) 'Reengineering work: don't automate, obliterate'. *Harvard Business Review* (July–August).

HAMMER, M. and CHAMPY, J. (1993) *Reengineering the Corporation: a manifesto for business revolution*, London, Nicholas Brealey.

HITT, M. and IRELAND, D. (1987) 'Peters and Waterman revisited: the unending quest for Excellence', *Academy of Management Executive*, Vol. 1, No. 2, pp. 91–8.

HINTERHUBER, H. H. (1986) 'Strategie, Innovation und Unternehmenskultur', *Blick durch die Wirtschaft*, Vol. 20, No. 10.

HOFSTEDE, G. F. (1980) *Culture's Consequences*, London, Sage.

JAGGI, D. (1985) 'Corporate Identity als Unternehmerische Erfolgsformel', paper presented at the Second WEMAR – Tagung.

JEFFCUTT, P. (1994) 'The interpretation of organization: a contemporary analysis and critique', *Journal of Management Studies*, Vol. 31, No. 2, pp. 225–50.

KEISLING, P. (1984) 'Economics without numbers: review of *In Search of Excellence*', Washington Monthly , March, pp. 40–46.

KENNEY, J., DONNELLY, E. and REID, M. (1981) *Manpower Training and Development*, London, Institute of Personnel Management.

KNIGHTS, D. and WILLMOTT, H. (1987) 'Organizational culture as a management strategy', *International Studies of Management and Organization*, Vol. XVII, No. 3.

KOLB, D., LUBLIN, S., SPOTH, S. and BAKER, R. (1986) 'Strategic management development', *Journal of Management Development*, Vol. 5, No. 3, pp. 13–24.

LORENZ, C. (1992) 'A drama behind closed doors'; 'Re-appraising the power base'; and 'A cultural revolution' in *B884 Human Resource Strategies*, Supplementary Readings 1, Milton Keynes, The Open University, pp. 5–12.

MAIDIQUE, M. A. (1983) 'Point of view: the new management thinkers', *California Management Review*, Vol. 26, No. 1, pp. 151–62.

McMILLAN, C. (1985) *The Japanese Industrial System*, Berlin, de Gruyter.

MEEK, L. (1992) 'Organizational culture: origins and weaknesses' in Salaman, G. (ed.) *Human Resource Strategies*, London, Sage, pp. 192–212.

MILLER, P. and ROSE, N. (1993) 'Governing economic life' in Gane, M. and Johnson, T. (eds) *Foucault's New Domains*, London, Routledge, pp. 75–105.

MORGAN, G. (1988) *Images of Organization,* London, Sage.

MORGAN, G. (1988) *Riding the Waves of Change*, San Fransisco, CA, Jossey Bass.

OGBONNA, E. (1992) 'Organizational culture and human resources management: dilemmas and contradictions' in Blyton, P. and Turnbull, P. (eds) *Reassessing Human Resource Management*, London, Sage, pp. 74–96.

OHMAE, K. (1982) *The Mind of the Strategist: the art of Japanese business*, New York, McGraw-Hill.

OUCHI, W. G. (1981) *Theory Z: how American business can meet the Japanese challenge,* Reading, MA, Addison-Wesley.

PASCALE, R. and ATHOS, A.G. (1981) *The Art of Japanese Management*, New York, Simon and Schuster.

PETERS, T. and WATERMAN, R. (1982) *In Search of Excellence*, New York, Harper and Row.

PETERS, T. (1978) 'Symbols, patterns and settings', *Organizational Dynamics*, Vol. 9, No. 2, pp. 3–23.

PETERS, T. (1988) *Thriving on Chaos*, London, Pan.

PETTIGREW, A. and WHIPP, R. (1991) *Managing Change for Competitive Success*, Oxford, Blackwell.

POLLARD, S. (1965) *The Genesis of Modern Management*, London, Edward Arnold.

ROSE, N. (1996) 'Identity, genealogy, history' in Hall, S. and du Gay, P. (eds) *Questions of Cultural Identity*, London, Sage.

SENGE, P. (1990) 'The leader's new work', *Sloan Management Review*, Vol. 32, No. 1, pp. 7–23.

STEELE, F. (1977) 'Is the culture hostile to organization development?' in Minis, P.M. and Berg, D.N. (eds) *Failures in Organization Development and Change*, New York, Wiley.

THUROW, L. (1984) 'Revitalizing American industry: managing in a competitive world economy', *Californian Management Review,* Vol. 27, No. 1, pp. 9–40.

TOWNLEY, B. (1993) 'Foucault, power/knowledge, and its relevance for human resource management', *Academy of Management Review*, Vol. 18, No. 3, pp. 518–45.

TOWNLEY, B. (1994) *Reframing Human Resource Management*, London, Sage.

ULRICH, P. (1984) 'Systemsteuerung und Kulturentwicklung', *Die Unternehmung*, Vol. 38, pp. 303–25.

WICKENS, P. (1987) *The Road to Nissan*, Basingstoke, Macmillan.

WILLMOTT, H. (1993) 'Strength is ignorance; slavery is freedom: managing culture in modern organizations', *Journal of Management Studies*, Vol. 30, No.4, pp. 515–52.

READING A:
Terrence E. Deal and Allan A. Kennedy, 'Values: the core of the culture'

Values are the bedrock of any corporate culture.[*] As the essence of a company's philosophy for achieving success, values provide a sense of common direction for all employees and guidelines for their day-to-day behaviour. These formulas for success determine (and occasionally arise from) the types of corporate heroes, and the myths, rituals, and ceremonies of the culture. In fact, we think that often companies succeed because their employees can identify, embrace, and act on the values of the organization.

These values may be grand in scope ('Progress is our most important product'), or narrowly focused ('Underwriting excellence'). They can capture the imagination ('The first Irish multinational'). They can tell people how to work together ('It takes two to Tandem'). Or they can simply drive ('15 percent period-to-period sales and earnings growth'). If they are strong, they command everyone's attention: 'What people really care about around here is quality.' If they are weak, they may often be ignored: 'It's not the same company since the old man stepped down. Nowadays everyone around here is just more or less doing his own thing.'

'Rational' managers rarely pay much attention to the value system of an organization. Values are not 'hard,' like organizational structures, policies and procedures, strategies, or budgets. Often they are not even written down. And when someone does try to set them down in a formal statement of corporate philosophy, the product often bears an uncomfortable resemblance to the Biblical beatitudes – good and true and broadly constructive, but not all that relevant to Monday morning.

We think that society today suffers from a pervasive uncertainty about values, a relativism that undermines leadership and commitment alike. After all, in this fast-paced world, who really *does* know what's right? On the philosophical level, we find ourselves without convincing responses. But the everyday business environment is quite different. Even if ultimate values are chimerical, particular values clearly make sense for specific organizations operating in specific economic circumstances. Perhaps because ultimate values seem so elusive, people respond positively to practical ones. Choices must be made, and values are an indispensable guide in making them.

Moreover, it is clear that organizations have, in fact, gained great strength from shared values – with emphasis on the 'shared'. If employees know what their company stands for, if they know what standards they are to uphold, then they are much more likely to make decisions that will support those standards. They are also more likely to feel as if they are an important part of the organization. They are motivated because life in the company has meaning for them.

Since organizational values can powerfully influence what people actually do, we think that values ought to be a matter of great concern to managers. In fact, shaping and enhancing values can become the most important job a manager can do. In our work and study, we have found that successful companies place a great deal of emphasis on values. In general, these companies shared three characteristics:

- They stand for something – that is, they have a clear and explicit philosophy about how they aim to conduct their business.

- Management pays a great deal of attention to shaping and fine-tuning these values to conform to the economic and business environment of the company and to communicating them to the organization.

- These values are known and shared by all the people who work for the company – from the lowliest production worker right through to the ranks of senior management.

What are these values that hold a company and its workforce together? Where do they come from? And more important, how do they influence the successful operation of an organization?

[*] Much of the original work on the ideas expressed in this chapter was done by McKinsey consultant Julien Phillips.

The corporate character

For those who hold them, shared values define the fundamental character of their organization, the attitude that distinguishes it from all others. In this way, they create a sense of identity for those in the organization, making employees feel special. Moreover, values are a reality in the minds of most people throughout the company, not just the senior executives. It is this sense of pulling together that makes shared values so effective. Let's look at a few:

- *Caterpillar*: '24-hour parts service anywhere in the world' – symbolizing an extraordinary commitment to meeting customers' needs.

- *Leo Burnett Advertising Agency*: 'Make great ads' – commitment to a particular concept of excellence.

- *American Telephone Telegraph*: 'Universal service' – an historical orientation toward standardized, highly reliable service to all possible users, now being reshaped into values more relevant to a newly competitive marketplace.

- *DuPont*: 'Better things for better living through chemistry' – a belief that product innovation, arising out of chemical engineering, is DuPont's most distinctive value.

- *Sears, Roebuck*: 'Quality at a good price' – the mass merchandiser for middle America.

- *Rouse Company*: 'Create the best environment for people' – a dominating concern to develop healthy and pleasant residential communities, not just to build subdivisions.

- *Continental Bank*: 'We'll find a way' (to meet customer needs).

- *Dana Corporation*: 'Productivity through people' – enlisting the ideas and commitment of employees at every level in support of Dana's strategy of competing largely on cost and dependability rather than product differentiation.

- *Chubb Insurance Company*: 'Underwriting excellence' – an overriding commitment to excellence in a critical function.

- *Price Waterhouse Company*: 'Strive for technical perfection' (in accounting).

Most of these phrases sound utterly platitudinous to the outsider. Indeed, many of them are little more than slogans that might be (and often were) used in advertising campaigns. What makes them more than slogans is the degree to which these phrases capture something people in the organization deeply believe in. Within each of these corporations, these words take on rich and concrete meaning.

We call these phrases 'core values' because they become the essence of the organization's philosophy. These slogan-like themes are only the most visible parts of a complex system that includes a whole range of beliefs about how the organization should achieve success. These values and beliefs are closely linked to the basic concept of the business and provide guidelines for employees to follow in their work.

For example, if you are in the business of selling cars – as is Joe Girard, the world's most successful car salesman – and if your experience in the marketplace leads you to think that taking care of your customers is *the key way* to get them to come back again, then you will put this philosophy to work. Girard's core value is 'customer service'. From this basic concept, Girard has developed a number of beliefs – that you should studiously respond to all customer complaints, make sure their service problems are handled, even send them cards at Christmas and on their birthdays. In some months Girard sends out more than 13,000 cards to customers. He puts his values and beliefs into action, and he sells more automobiles every year than any single car salesman in the world.

In the case of one person, it is easy to see how one basic value backed by enormous energy can make for success. What is harder to understand is how this same principle applies in a larger corporation. Companies are, after all, only collections of individuals. If they all believe and behave as Joe Girard does, they will undoubtedly succeed at what they set out to do. And that is the real challenge for management: to make thousands and thousands of people Joe Girard-like figures who have a strongly ingrained sense of the company's value.

The Pepsi-Cola Company seems to have met this challenge by fostering the values of competition. As *Business Week* recently reported, 'Once the company was content in its No. 2 spot, offering Pepsi as a cheaper alternative to Coca-Cola. But today, a new employee at PepsiCo quickly learns that beating the competition, whether outside or

inside the company, is the surest path to success
[...]. Because winning is the key value at Pepsi,
losing has its penalties. Consistent runners-up find
their jobs gone. Employees know that they must
win merely to stay in place – and must devastate
the competition to get ahead.'

Dana Corporation, on the other hand, has a very
different, but still successful, set of values. As a
competitor in the long-established automobile-parts
manufacturing business, it has virtually doubled its
productivity over the past seven years, a period
when the overall growth of American productivity
has been slowing. Dana did not accomplish this
record with massive capital investment, with
sophisticated industrial-engineering studies, or
with management-imposed speed-up measures.
Instead, it relied on its people, right down to the
shop-floor level. Management continually stressed
the value of productivity to company success. It
put this value into action by creating a multitude of
task forces and other special activities; by giving its
people practical opportunities to generate
productivity; by listening to ideas and then
implementing them; and by consistently, visibly,
and frequently rewarding success. 'Productivity
through people' is no mere advertising phrase to
the employees of Dana Corporation.

Procter & Gamble: forging a value system

Although a value system may be most visible in the
few words that make up an advertising slogan,
many successful companies have a very rich
tradition of values, beliefs, and themes that have
developed over the years. Where do these values
come from? They mostly come from experience,
from testing what does and doesn't work in the
economic environment. But individual people
within an organization also have strong influence
in shaping the standards and beliefs of the
organization.

[...] let's look at a [...] corporation [...] that has been
able to sustain its strong philosophy – and its
success – over 150 years of growth.

By almost any measure, the Procter & Gamble
Company of Cincinnati, Ohio, is one of the best
models of persistent long-term attention to building
a strong culture company, particularly in its

emphasis on values. First, let's look at a brief
history:

In 1837, upon the suggestion of their father-in-law,
William Procter and James Gamble joined forces in
a partnership. The candle and soap industry they
entered that year was a highly competitive one;
there were eighteen direct competitors in the
Cincinnati market alone and many more across the
burgeoning country. In P&G's early years, candles
were the company's principle source of income,
and the company enjoyed a modest success. By the
1870s, however, the growing popularity of oil
lamps for illumination left Procter and Gamble
justifiably worried about the future of their candle-
making business. To protect their future, they
redoubled their efforts to become a leader in the
soap market. In 1878, James N. Gamble, son of the
founder and a chemist by education, perfected the
formula for a new, white soap.

It was cousin Harley Procter's job to sell the soap.
He sensed it could be a good product, so he spent
weeks trying to come up with the right name. In
church one Sunday it came to him while reciting
Psalms 45:8 – 'All thy garments smell of myrrh and
aloe, and cassia, out of the ivory palaces whereby
they have made thee glad.' Ivory soap was born.

Realizing the opportunity this invention offered the
company, Harley employed the creative use of the
new medium of display advertising to turn Ivory
into the first nationally branded soap product. The
company's major growth had begun.

The initial success with Ivory soap was followed
up some thirty-three years later by the introduction
of Crisco shortening; as a substitute for lard, it was
a radically new product at the time. Then came
Camay (1923), Tide and Prell (1946), Joy (1949),
Cheer (1950), then Crest and Comet (1956), Head &
Shoulders (1960), Pampers (1961), Safeguard
(1963), and, more recently, Downy, Mr. Clean, and
Top Job. As any consumer can attest, to this day
these products are leaders in the market segments
they serve.

What was it that made this company so strong in
the field of consumer packaged goods? What is it
about P&G that has allowed it to sustain its
enviable track record so long and so consistently
through good economic times and bad? Was it
being first to the market with a new product?

Perhaps true in the early days but certainly not relevant for products like Tide and Charmin. Was it an absence of competition in its main markets? Certainly never true in any of the markets P&G served. Was it a better strategy than Colgate or others? We doubt there are that many degrees of strategic freedom available to allow P&G to differentiate itself in all the diverse markets it serves.

We believe P&G's success can be traced most directly back to a very strong culture, founded on a set of beliefs and values. The first and most basic of these values is 'do what is right.' As William Cooper Procter said at the time he handed the reins of management to Richard R. Deupree, the first non-Procter or Gamble to run the company: 'Always try to do what's right. If you do that, nobody can really find fault.' This rule has lived to this day, being passed on to every head of P&G since Cooper – and every new employee as well.

Where did this and other beliefs and values come from? There was no visionary among the early Procters and Gambles to codify the value system and drum it into the heads of employees. Rather these values evolved over years and years of trial and error as many people worked to figure out just how such a business should be run. Let's see how a few of these key values evolved.

'The consumer is important'

From the earliest days of P&G, its founding fathers always had an eye clearly fixed on what might be important to customers. One morning in 1851, William Procter noticed that a wharfhand was painting black crosses on P&G's candle boxes. Asking why this was done, Procter learned that the crosses allowed illiterate wharfhands to distinguish the candle boxes from the soap boxes. Another artistic wharfhand soon changed the black cross to a circled star. Another replaced the single star with a cluster of stars. And then a quarter moon was added with a human profile. Finally, P&G painted the moon and stars emblem on all boxes of their candles.

At some later date, P&G decided that the 'man in the moon' was unnecessary so they dropped it from their boxes. Immediately P&G received a message from New Orleans that a jobber had refused delivery of an entire shipment of P&G candles.

Since these boxes lacked the full 'moon and stars' design, the jobber thought they were imitations. P&G quickly recognized the value of the 'moon and stars' emblem and brought it back into use by registering it as a trademark. It was the beginning of brand name identification for P&G and the first of many times that P&G listened to its customers.

P&G paid attention to customers because over the years they learned that the more they did so, the greater the payback to the company. Certainly, the customers discovered and launched Ivory soap. Soon after it was introduced, P&G learned from its customers that Ivory floated. Initially, P&G managers were so surprised by this they assumed it was an accident in the mixing of the soap. So it was, but customers kept asking for the 'floating soap' so P&G incorporated the 'mistake' into their regular production.

P&G continued listening to customers, who helped them develop all of their major products. Their experience through the years has taught them step-by-step that such attention always pays off. P&G calls this mania 'consumerism: a response, after comprehensive market research, to what consumers need and want.' Over the company's history, consumerism has taken many forms, from testing kitchens for Crisco in 1912; to hiring housewives to provide consumer feedback on liquid dish detergents in 1922; to large-scale, door-to-door sampling efforts for Camay in the 1920s. Today, P&G conducts over 1.5 million telephone interviews annually. That's the equivalent of 1,000 Gallup polls each year.

In short, P&G is a culture that glories in listening and listening well to consumers. Furthermore, they have developed more ways to listen to customers than anyone else. And why wouldn't they, they've spent years learning how.

'Things don't just happen, you have to make them happen'

P&G is the largest consistent advertiser among the giant consumer-products companies. For the last century, managers at P&G have believed that advertising works and they bet their company's future on it. How did they develop this trust in the media's efficacy? Again the answer did not come easily, but through years and years of hard work.

It all started with Harley Procter and his Ivory soap. For several years, Harley had been arguing with his relatives–colleagues in the company to convince them that media advertising could sell more soap. Finally, he convinced them to take the first step and allocate $11,000 to this new and unproven medium.

Harley decided to emphasize the purity of Ivory in his first advertising effort. To do this he hired a science consultant from New York who both defined purity and went on to determine that, given this definition, Ivory was 99.44 percent pure. Armed with this statistic, Harley began advertising Ivory. The results of this brilliant innovation were twofold: booming sales for P&G and the birth of modern advertising. Like listening to consumers, it worked.

But getting hooked on advertising in a company like P&G does not mean standing still. When P&G begins to believe in something like advertising, given such bedrock cultural values as 'make it happen', they keep testing, keep trying new ideas, keep evolving the basic idea year by year. In 1923, P&G was first to capitalize on the use of what was then a brand-new advertising medium – radio. Staring with informational radio spots, P&G went on to invent the daytime soap opera. Thirty years later, P&G did the same for television.

'We want to make employee interests our own'

Even as early as the late 1880s, and with a hot, new product in Ivory, William Cooper Procter had a problem: how to keep P&Gers not just productive but loyal, too, and how to express the company's sense of responsibility to its people.

In 1883, Procter started working for P&G at the lowest level of menial factory labor – loading the soap mixers, a job that wasn't just for show. At work, Procter lived the life of a laborer to its fullest, even eating lunch with the other workers while sitting on the factory floor. During this early work, Procter developed a first-hand understanding of the perspectives and concerns of the P&G workers. This understanding was to serve as a foundation for his insistence on improved labor relations.

In 1884, Procter finally persuaded his father and uncle to give workers Saturday afternoons off without loss of pay, a radical proposal at the time.

However, growing labor unrest across the country quickly proved Procter's plan to be grossly inadequate. He wrestled with this problem for two years, then suggested that profit-sharing might develop greater loyalty and respect among P&G workers. Again failure – Procter's profit-sharing plan realized no gains in productivity and loyalty; workers simply viewed the payments they received as extra salary. Undaunted, he tinkered with it over several years, and in 1903 devised a scheme to couple profit-sharing with the purchase of P&G stock – the company would add $1 for every $1 invested by a worker up to an amount equal to the worker's annual salary. Its success emboldened Procter to establish ongoing two-way communications between management and workers by instituting the Employee Conference Plan (1918) and creating one seat for a worker representative from each domestic plant on P&G's board of directors (1919). Then he shortened the workday from ten to eight hours. Still not content in his efforts to improve worker relations and realizing his action would benefit all involved, Procter singlehandedly abolished job uncertainty at P&G by guaranteeing employment for workers. To do this he took the enormous risk of developing direct distribution (in other words, a sales force), thus bypassing the distributors who previously had created highly uneven demand. The risk succeeded and, even during the Depression, P&G was able to keep its workers on the payrolls.

So Procter & Gamble has a long history of working hard on the 'right' things: James Gamble perfecting his soap, Harley Procter forging a new field of advertising, and William Cooper Procter establishing the principle that the interests of the company and those of its employees were inseparable. All along, P&G paid scrupulous attention to its customers. These values were formed and refined by years of experience in the marketplace. They didn't just appear overnight. Although P&G is a highly successful company, it has had its share of problems; Rely tampons are only the most recent example. Still, its continuing experiences in the marketplace have evolved into a rich and varied culture that has sustained it through difficult times.

The evolution of a value structure like P&G's is the core element in all the strong culture companies we studied. The stronger the culture, the richer and more complex the value system, the longer the chain of evidence that these values really do produce results.

The influence of corporate values

As we've seen with P&G, a corporation's values will affect all aspects of the company – from what products get manufactured to how workers are treated. Companies that are guided by strong shared values tend to reflect those values in the design of their formal organization. The most readily recognizable case is the company that believes that the way to put its values to work is to control costs tightly. Generally, its financial vice president and controller will be leading members of the top-management group, and very frequently the divisional controllers will report directly to the corporate controller rather than to the division head. Almost always, its dominant management systems will be those for budget development and operation control, and even its longer-range planning will be geared to the needs of financial control.

A company with values geared primarily to the external marketplace, like P&G, will probably have several very senior marketing vice presidents in its top-management structure, and it is likely to rely on some version of product managers or brand managers to handle product marketing. It will surely have rather elaborate systems for gathering and sifting data on customer tastes, customer response to its products, and initiatives by its competitors.

The values and beliefs of an organization indicate what matters are to be attended to most assiduously – for instance, current operations in one company, external relations in a second, longer-term strategy in a third. They suggest what kind of information is taken most seriously for decision-making purposes – experienced judgment of 'old hands' in one organization, detailed 'number-crunching' in another. They define what kind of people are most respected – engineers versus marketing men versus financial types.

Values also play a very important role in determining how far one can rise within an organization. If product development is the company's overriding ethic, the best people will want to work in the company's research and development laboratories. If customer service is the important value, the go-getters won't want to be in finance but in a sales or field service function. The company will tend to reinforce the primacy of that value by promoting a disproportionate share of the people in these jobs.

Shared values and beliefs also play an important role in communicating to the outside world what to expect of a company. The philosophy at Sears, for instance, marks its corporate personality consistently to suppliers and customers alike: the Sears value – 'Quality at a good price' – encourages buyers to become crusaders in driving down the cost of products. Many companies depend on Sears for most of their business, yet these companies often live in fear of the giant retailer. 'That price isn't good enough,' Sears buyers will say. 'We want to sell a muffler for $19.95 and buy it from you for $9.95 and that's it.' The producer can argue that the steel costs $7.14 and that something in addition must be charged to manufacture the muffler, but then Sears will only threaten to take their business someplace else. After all, Sears sell more mufflers then anyone in the world. So the producer huffs and puffs and figures how to make a muffler for $9.95. That's the way Sears does its purchasing and it's infamous for it. Yet that's part of its image for its customers: Sears gets the lowest prices for quality products.

Delta Airlines' value as 'the people company' is expressed in its slogan, 'The Delta Family Feeling.' As only a caring family would, Delta pays higher salaries than the industry average and thus attracts the best employees – people whom the company works very hard to get and to whom it gives significant responsibilities for delivering quality service. It was only natural, therefore, that when Delta braced itself for the last recession, senior management, in effect, told shareholders and the financial community, 'Now that times are tough, you'll have to pay. We're not going to earn what we could over the long term if we let go of people now; our people are very important to our long-term performance; they're what makes this place work. So, shareholders, it's your time to give a pint of blood; until this recession is over, our earnings and maybe even our dividends are going to be down because we are not going to lay our people off.' Such a move was acceptable only because Delta had communicated the sanctity of this value of 'family' over a long period of time. Shared values are what has made Delta great.

In 1982, while other carriers made cutbacks of 15,000 workers, Delta held firm. As a result, the company gained considerable loyalty from its employees. In the past, non-unionized employees have carried luggage and handled the ticket counters to help the airline get through the slumps so that regular employees would not be laid off.

Delta points up the importance of a company's living by its values, even in a difficult situation. Yet the example also underlines the all-or-nothing stakes involved. Once a company tries to shape values, the company is often locked in – the actions of management must be consistent, because the inconsistencies will be noticed and magnified out of proportion. In creating values that will work, managers are forced to live life as they say they would ... whatever the circumstances.

How do shared values affect organizational performance? In broad terms, they act as an informal control system that tell people what is expected of them. More specifically, shared values affect performance in three main ways:

> **Managers and others throughout the organization give extraordinary attention to whatever matters are stressed in the corporate value system** – and this in turn tends to produce extraordinary results. An oil company produces crude and petroleum products much more efficiently than others because efficient operation is what it values and what its managers concentrate on. One of this company's principal competitors values trading and financial management most highly. Accordingly, its managers worry less about production operations and concentrate instead on squeezing every cent of potential revenue from their sales.

> **Down-the-line managers make marginally better decisions, on average, because they are guided by their perception of the shared values.** When a manager at Dana is confronted by a close question – like making a particular investment in increased productivity versus one in new product development – the manager is likely to opt for productivity.

> **People simply work a little harder because they are dedicated to the cause.** 'I'm sorry I'm so late getting home, but the customer had a problem and we never leave a customer with a problem.'

Source: Deal and Kennedy, 1991, pp. 21–33.

Symptoms of resistance

Especially in cases where insecure, fashion-conscious management strives to 'modernize' its practices, aided and abetted by consultants who prey upon managers' vulnerability, a paradoxical consequence of culture-strengthening programmes is a further degradation and distortion of communication as employees instrumentally adapt their behaviour to conform with the relevant corporate code (Anthony, 1989; Knights and Willmott, 1987). Associated with this instrumentality is a scepticism, often expressed as cynicism, about the 'genuineness' of corporate culturist values and ideals. Instead of the promised gain in commitment, there can be an unwelcome loss in credibility. As one of the respondents told Hope (1991, p.14) in her study of a cultural change programme at a large insurance company,

> There are a lot of contradictions in this new culture thing and I haven't come to terms with this open style being great for everybody ... I think it can start to be patronising ... there's normal suspicion.

Instead of a deep identification with corporate values, there can be selective, calculative compliance. In which case, employee behaviour is (minimally) congruent with 'realizing' the values of the corporation, but only insofar as it is calculated that material and/or symbolic advantage can be gained from managing the appearance of consent. Where calculative compliance is substituted for the desired commitment to corporate values, employee behaviour may be successfully modified by schedules of reinforcement that, for example, reduce the irksomeness and boredom of work, which formally permits no exercise of discretion (Wilkinson et al., 1991). However, corporate culture programmes strive to achieve more than the operant conditioning of behaviour. Their aspiration is to secure 'commitment' by treating staff as dedicated enactors of the prescribed organizational reality. Mere compliance is insufficient since it signals a failure to mobilize the emotional energies

of staff in ways that inspire them to embody and live out the corporate values.

Indeed, the gurus of corporate culture construe reluctance to suspend disbelief in the prescribed corporate values as self-defeating, both materially and symbolically, for employees. Materially, because lack of commitment is deemed to weaken the competitiveness of the company and thus the security of their jobs; but also symbolically because the reward of commitment is presented as an opportunity for each individual to gain more discretion and raise self-esteem. That is the theory. However, from the standpoint of the individual, the distancing of self from corporate values may be the preferred means of preserving and asserting self-identity.

This response to the demands of corporate culture can be further elucidated by reference to Berger and Luckmann's (1966) concept of 'cool alternation'. As a mode of (dis)engagement associated with the life-world of advanced industrial societies, Berger and Luckmann (1966, p. 192) note how individuals contrive to distance themselves from the roles that they play (cf. Goffman, 1959). So, instead of experiencing the social world as reality, it is regarded as 'a reality to be used for specific purposes' (Berger and Luckmann, 1966, p. 192). A sense of subjective detachment *vis-à-vis* the roles is achieved as the individual '"puts them on" deliberately and purposefully'. In this way, the modern individual contrives to enjoy the material and symbolic benefits of occupying the role without feeling that his/her identity is defined by it. Moreover, by playing the role at a psychological distance from what is deemed to be the 'real self' (Goffman, 1959), the individual feels little existential responsibility for its consequences. However, this dramaturgical 'game play' is not without its costs. For the individual is inescapably constituted in the process of playing the role, and often in ways that escape his or her conscious monitoring (Giddens, 1984). The 'real' self is a construction of the enacted self; it does not exist independently of the moment of its constitution.

The dynamics of entrapment

A dramaturgical orientation to life is seductive because it feeds the (humanist) idea that the player is in control as s/he calculates which role s/he will elect to play, whilst of course preserving a sense of subjective detachment from the reality of the role's demands. What is obscured, if not lost, from such consciousness is a capacity to reflect critically upon the sense and impact of 'being in control', and, in particular, the extent to which dramaturgical action systematically excludes the players from involvement in the (re)design of the institutions from which these roles are derived (cf. Habermas, 1987). This argument can be expanded by considering Kunda's (1991) study of 'Tech.', a company strongly committed to corporate culturism.

Kunda (1991) reports a widespread distancing of self amongst Tech. middle managers. Principally, this distancing was expressed in cynical comments about the purpose of the culture and a deft parodying of its demands. Amongst many Tech. staff, Kunda found that displays of 'controlled self-consciousness' were highly regarded as expressions of personal skill and elegance. This 'distanced' orientation to the Tech. culture enabled employees to retain a sense of independence and control. It allowed them to resist naive seduction by the corporate culture. However, a less obvious and perverse effect of playing the game of cool alternation was an undermining or numbing of a capacity directly to criticize or resist the cultural logic. Why so? Because *the very possibility of engaging in the playful ironicizing of the Culture was widely interpreted as evidence of Tech.'s commitment to openness, freedom of expression etc.* (Kunda, 1991, p. 22). The most insidious effect of Tech. culture, Kunda reports, was its promotion of almost universal, undiscriminating cynicism. Employees were inclined to 'question the authenticity of all beliefs and emotions', and were thereby disarmed of a critical standpoint from which to evaluate the relative merits of competing value-standpoints. As a consequence, they lacked any basis for refusing to play out any scripts they are handed. Commenting upon this entrapment, Kunda concludes,

> Under these circumstances, many employees may find that their work lives are enmeshed in an ever-accelerating vicious cycle (*sic*). The race to meet corporate standards of accomplishment, get corporate approval, and procure the pecuniary and personal rewards the culture promises becomes the only way to find stable

meanings and compensate for a sense of confusion, lost authenticity, and inner emptiness; but it is a self-defeating exercise, one that creates and reinforces the very circumstances it seeks to correct. This then is the bottom line: Tech.'s managed culture allows management ... to accomplish corporate goals not by enhancing the employees' experiential life but, if anything, by degrading it.

> (Kunda, 1991, pp. 30–1)

So, even when corporate culture programmes fall well short of the ideal of creating 'charged up people (who) search for appropriate adaptations' (Peters and Waterman, 1982, p. 51), they are capable of exerting an insidious, self-disciplining power. In the absence of a well-organized, supportive counter-culture, the very process of devaluing corporate ideals tends to produce confusion and emptiness, thereby making employees enduringly vulnerable to the (precarious) sense of stability and identity provided by a dramaturgical, cynical, instrumental compliance with corporate values.

Existential separation and the limits of humanism

The experience of personal meaninglessness, Giddens (1991) observes, is intensified in the context of 'late modernity' where there is an institutionalized 'existential separation' from 'the moral resources necessary to live a full and satisfying existence' (p. 91). In the pluralized life-worlds of modernity, human beings are required to make their own identity, yet lack access to the 'moral resources' that are critical for fulfilling this requirement. Or, as Giddens puts it, with direct relevance for a critical appreciation of the corporate culture phenomenon,

> The reflexive project of the self generates programmes of actualization and mastery. But as long as these possibilities are understood largely as a matter of the extension of the control systems of modernity to the self, they lack moral meaning.

> (Giddens, 1991, p. 9)

In elaborating this argument, Giddens (1991) suggests that submission to authority 'normally takes the form of slavish adherence to an authority figure, taken to be all knowing' (p. 196). Absent from his analysis is the contemporary corporate equivalent of this phenomenon in which submission, facilitated by the identity-protecting device of cool alternation, is to an organizational ideal that is simultaneously an ego-ideal (Schwartz, 1987a, 1987b) – a syndrome that is no less crippling in its impact upon human existence than doggish devotion to a deified individual.

Expressive of the efforts to achieve the 'actualization and mastery' of human labour power, corporate culturism is at once a condition and a consequence of 'existential separation'. As argued earlier, its programmes are very much an extension and refinement of 'the control systems of modernity' that, as Weber recognized, are devoid of moral meaning. Even when these programmes fail to secure unequivocal commitment, they can be effective. For, as Kunda's (1991) study shows, corporate culturism can accommodate 'cool alternation' in which employees at once are distanced from, and compliant with, core corporate values. Corporate culturism thus reproduces the conditions of demoralization and degradation for which it is presented as a remedy.

[...]

The theory and practice of corporate culturism has been criticized because it promotes practices and institutions that unnecessarily suppress and impede the nurturing of emancipatory contingencies. The position that underpins this criticism shares Deetz's (1992) view that

> Anything that influences the continued formation or deformation of the human character has ethical implications. While no one is in a position to define the social good or what the human character ultimately should be like, the full representation of differing people and their interests would seem to be fundamental to ethical choices regarding development ... I do not agree with the postmodernist claim ... that all moral democratic impulses are by necessity disguised dominations or nostalgia for the past. ... The modern enlightenment project based upon reason and technology may well be dead, and with it the liberal ideals and utopian visions it spawned. But this need not be seen as simply dumping us into a reactive amoral postmodern

> reality. Perhaps it better lays the foundation for a new age of responsibility.
>
> (Deetz, 1992, p. 3)

The objection to corporate culture philosophy has not been that 'strong' cultures alienate individuals from their 'real', essentially free, selves. Rather, the complaint – articulated most explicitly through a critical review of Weber's distinction between instrumental rationality and value-rationality – is that corporate culturism contrives to eliminate the conditions – pluralism and the associated conflict of values – for facilitating the social process of emotional and intellectual struggle for self-determination.

Conclusion

When reflecting upon the 'wonderful combination' of security and autonomy attributed to the cultural discipline of McDonald's and similar 'excellent' companies, it is difficult not to admire the audacity of the corporate culture gurus, and to marvel at the ease with which their wares have been enthusiastically consumed.

Much of the appeal of corporate culturism, it has been suggested, arises from the individualizing impact of modernizing forces that relativize meaning and demystify authority. In a situation where 'everything that is solid melts into air' (Marx and Engels, 1967, p. 83), self-identity is rendered unstable and insecure by the unrelenting, market-driven pressure to become 'somebody'. Employees' willingness to subjugate themselves to corporate culturism is procured by the sense of identity, security and self-determination that devotion to corporate values promises to deliver. Corporate culturism, it has been argued, preys upon the vulnerability of modern individuals who, as Giddens (1991) has argued, are burdened with the responsibility of choosing between 'a puzzling diversity of options and possibilities' (p. 3), but lack access to the cultural and intellectual resources that are relevant for responding to this predicament in ways that are not self-defeating.

In the name of moral renewal, corporate culture programmes celebrate, exploit, distort and drain the dwindling cultural resource of caring, democratic values. In the doublethink, monological world of corporate culture, the values of community and autonomy are simultaneously celebrated and contradicted. Like the Party member in Orwell's Oceania, the well-socialized, self-disciplined corporate employee 'is expected to have no private emotions and no respites from enthusiasm ... the speculations which might possibly induce a sceptical or rebellious attitude are killed in advance by his early-acquired inner discipline' (Orwell, 1989, p. 220). Under the guise of giving more autonomy to the individual than in organizations governed by bureaucratic rules, corporate culture threatens to promote a new, hypermodern neo-authoritarianism which, potentially, is more insidious and sinister than its bureaucratic predecessor (Ouimet, 1991; Willmott, 1992). Far from lifting or diluting management control, corporate culturism promotes its extension through the design of value systems and the management of the symbolic and emotional aspects of organizational membership.

Having said that, culture strengthening programmes can, and perhaps invariably do, fall well short of the ideal of securing unequivocal devotion to, and conformity with, corporate values. In the West, at least, an ethos of individualism sits uneasily with the collectivist aspirations of corporate culture. In the absence of institutional arrangements (e.g. lifetime employment) and ideologies (e.g. of interdependence) that cushion conflicts of interest between buyers and sellers of labour, there is a tendency for the enactment of values to be based upon instrumental compliance rather than internalization or even identification. The skilful parodying of corporate culturism is one manifestation of this phenomenon (Kunda, 1991). However, despite evidence of the distancing of employees from corporate values, there is as yet little sign of sustained questioning of, or organized resistance to, the implicit political philosophy of corporate culturism.

The challenge is to contribute to the fostering of discourses and practices in which a commitment to a dialogical process of self-formation and determination supplants corporate culture doublethink. In seeking guidance for this project, we may do worse than turn to Weber's (1948) essay on 'Science as a Vocation' where he sketches the contribution of academics to challenging the received wisdom of 'party opinions'. The primary task of a useful teacher, Weber submits,

is to teach his students to recognize 'inconvenient' facts – I mean facts that are inconvenient for their party opinions. And for every party opinion there are facts that are extremely inconvenient, for my own opinion no less than others. I believe the teacher accomplishes more than a mere intellectual task if he compels his audience to accustom itself to the existence of such facts. I would be so immodest as even to apply the expression 'moral achievement', though perhaps this may sound too grandiose for something that should go without saying.

(Weber, 1948, p. 147).

In a post-empiricist era, Weber's appeal to 'facts' must of course be problematized: the modernist idea that opinions can be corrected by the compelling reality of facts is no longer plausible. In the contemporary era, where the truths of modernism are increasingly questioned, the role of the intellectual is not to correct opinion with fact but, rather, to participate in the development of what Foucault (1984, p. 74) has termed 'a new politics of truth' in which the normativity of knowledge is more fully appreciated. A basic assumption of this article has been that grasping the normativity of 'party opinions' – such as those articulated by the gurus of corporate culture – can make a valuable contribution to a project that is post-modern *and* emancipatory.

References

ANTHONY, P. D. (1989) 'The paradox of the management of culture or "he who leads is lost" ', *Personnel Review*, Vol. 19, No. 4, pp. 3–8.

BERGER, P. L. and LUCKMANN, T. (1966) *The Social Construction of Reality*, Harmondsworth, Penguin.

DEETZ, S. (1992) *Democracy in an Age of Corporate Colonization*, Albany, NY, State University of New York Press.

FOUCAULT, M. (1984) 'Truth and power' in Rabinow, P. (ed.), *The Foucault Reader*, Harmondsworth, Penguin.

GIDDENS, A. (1984) *The Constitution of Society*, Cambridge, Polity.

GIDDENS, A. (1991) *Modernity and Self-Identity*. Cambridge, Polity.

GOFFMAN, E. (1959) *The Presentation of Self in Everyday Life*, Harmondsworth, Penguin.

HABERMAS, J. (1987) *The Theory of Communicative Action*, Vol. 2, *Lifeworld and System*, Cambridge, Polity.

HOPE, V. (1991) 'Buying into corporate culture; A study of strategic change in a leading insurance company', Working Paper, Cranfield School of Management.

KNIGHTS, D. and WILLMOTT, H. C. (1987) 'Organizational culture as management strategy', *International Studies of Managment and Organization*, Vol. XVII, No. 3, pp. 40–63.

KUNDA, G. (1991) 'Ritual and the management of corporate culture: A critical perspective', Paper presented at the 8th International Standing Conference on Organizational Symbolism, Copenhagen, June.

MARX, K. and ENGELS, F. (1967) *The Communist Manifesto*, Harmondsworth, Penguin.

ORWELL, G. (1989) *Nineteen Eighty-Four*, Harmondsworth, Penguin.

OUIMET, G. (1991) 'The impact of organizational hypermodernity on managers' psychic equilibrium', Paper given at the 10th Colloquium of the European Group for Organizational Studies, Vienna, July.

PETERS, T. J and WATERMAN, R. H. (1982) *In Search of Excellence: lessons from America's best-run companies*, New York, Harper Row.

SCHWARTZ, H. (1987a) 'Anti-social actions of committed organizational participants', *Organization Studies*, Vol. 8, No. 4, pp. 327–40.

SCHWARTZ, H. (1987b) 'On the psychodynamics of organizational totalitarianism', *Journal of Management*, Vol. 13, No. 1, pp. 45–54.

WEBER, M. (1948).'Science as a vocation' in Gerth, H. and Wright Mills, C. (eds) *From Max Weber: essays in sociology*, London, Routledge Kegan Paul.

WILKINSON, A., ALLEN, P. and SNAPPE, A. (1991) 'TQM and the management of labour', *Employee Relations*, Vol. 13, No. 1, pp. 24–31.

WILLMOTT, H. C. (1992) 'Postmodernism and excellence: the de-differentiation of economy and culture', *Journal of Organizational Change Management*, Vol. 5, No. 1, pp. 58–68.

Source: Willmott, 1993, pp. 536–52.

ORGANIZING IDENTITY: MAKING UP PEOPLE AT WORK

Paul du Gay

CHAPTER SIX

Contents

1   Introduction

Not long ago, the suggestion that culture would emerge as a central topic of conversation in the board-rooms of large organizations and become represented as a crucial mechanism in the battle to make enterprises more efficient, effective and profitable would have been laughed out of court. And yet, as we saw in the previous chapter, organizational reform programmes throughout the 1980s and 1990s have been dominated by discussions of culture. Meanwhile, those of us working in large and not so large organizations during this period are very likely to have found ourselves subjected to 'culture change' programmes as part of attempts to alter the way we relate to and perform our work.

The emergence of culture as a prime moving force in the world of business organization comes as something of a surprise given the traditionally lowly status culture has enjoyed in relationship to economics, for example. The language of economics is often held to provide us with 'hard' knowledge of the world because it deals with seemingly clear, objective, material processes. In contrast, the language of culture seems to deal with the 'soft', less tangible elements of life – signs, images, meanings and values – which are often assumed to be unable to offer clear, unequivocal and hence 'hard' knowledge. Indeed, for a very long time, the cultural dimensions of life were considered, primarily but not exclusively by Marxist theorists, to be 'superstructural' phenomena, dependent upon and merely reflecting the primary status of the material base.

The obsession with culture – with norms, values, beliefs and so forth – within the world of business and management has undermined these traditional assumptions and placed questions about *the production of meaning* at the heart of debates about contemporary organizational life. As Graeme Salaman indicated in the previous chapter, the contemporary turn to culture within organizations is premised in part upon a belief that 'rationalist' forms of organizational management – such as Taylorism – systematically destroyed meaning at work, and that a foremost necessity for organizations is to 'make meaning' for people at work, in order to compete effectively in the turbulent, increasingly global, markets of the present.

As we have seen, culture is accorded a privileged positioning in this endeavour because it is seen to structure the way people think, feel and act in organizations. The aim of 'managing culture' is to produce the sorts of meanings that will enable people to *identify* with the organization for which they work and thus enable them to make the right and necessary contribution to its success.

This focus upon culture as a means of changing the way people conceive of and relate to the work they perform suggests that its deployment as a managerial technique is intimately bound up with questions of *identity.* According to the cultural theorist Renato Rosaldo (1993, p. xi), it is a pronounced feature of the present that 'questions of culture ... quite quickly become ... questions of identity'. In this chapter, we seek to assess this claim by exploring the ways in which the turn to culture within the world of business and organizations impacts upon and reconstructs economic identities – not simply those of employees, whether workers or managers, but also those of consumers.

A crucial feature of the chapter is the way it treats these economic processes and identities as *cultural* phenomena. As earlier chapters in this book have argued, what we think of as 'economic' processes depend on 'meaning' for their effects and have particular cultural conditions of existence. In other words, before one can seek to manage something called an 'economy' or even something called an 'organization', it is first necessary to conceptualize or represent a set of processes and relations as an 'economy' or an 'organization' which is amenable to management. Economic discourse, like any other, depends upon a particular mode of representation: the elaboration of a language for depicting a particular domain in a certain way that claims both to grasp the 'reality' of that domain and literally to re-present it in a form amenable to deliberation, argumentation and intervention.

The rest of the chapter is divided into three sections. In section 2, I explore the pitfalls of attempting to allocate an objective, essential, 'once and for all' meaning to work and instead suggest that the experience and identity of work are historically and culturally constructed. What it means to be a 'worker', 'manager', or any other form of economic actor, varies across time and context and has no 'suprahistorical' essence or 'spirit'. Rather it is the product of changes in ways of representing and acting upon – what we term *governing* – economic life.

In section 3, I examine how contemporary changes in practices of governing organizational life create new ways for people to conduct themselves at work. In this section, I argue that new *discourses* of organizational reform attempt to transform the meaning and reality of work and to construct new forms of work-based identity. A particular focus of this section is the way in which contemporary discourses of organizational reform blur some established differences between the spheres of production and consumption, work and leisure, creating certain similarities in the forms of conduct and modes of self presentation required of people across a range of different domains.

In section 4, I explore some of the subjective effects of the blurring of the relations between production and consumption by way of a brief examination of contemporary changes in the government of organizational life in the service sector. I focus on services precisely because it is in service organizations that economic success is most visibly premised upon the production of meaning and where the construction of what I term *hybrid work identities* is perhaps most pronounced. By the term 'hybrid work identities' I am referring to the ways in which employees in contemporary service work are encouraged to take on the role of both worker and customer in the workplace.

2 Approaching work identity

Whether one is in or out of it, actively seeking it, preparing to meet it for the first time, and certainly whether or not one likes doing it, paid work significantly shapes the lives of most people in late modern societies. Indeed, who and what we consider ourselves and others to be as persons is frequently articulated in relationship to 'work'.

> ACTIVITY I
>
> When you meet someone for the first time how often do you reach for the question 'What do you do?' as a means of establishing contact and getting to know them? What does that suggest to you about the importance we allocate to work in our type of society and about the assumptions we routinely make concerning the relationship between work and identity?

Classifying someone's social identity on the basis of their location within – or without – the division of labour is an activity we have all probably engaged in at some point. As we have seen in other parts of the course, however, while such classificatory practice is a constitutive element of everyday social interaction it is not always entirely innocent. For what we sometimes risk assuming when we 'read off' identity from occupation is that the meaning and identities associated with a particular form of work are *objectively* present within that form of employment; that the occupation in question has certain essential qualities that remain the same throughout time and which tend 'naturally' to produce certain sorts of social and behavioural characteristics amongst its practitioners. In this sense, people become simply the 'bearers' of the occupational roles they inhabit.

Such a logic, which we can readily recognize in popular, 'common-sense' representations of occupations such as accountancy, estate agency, social work and so on, is not without its parallels in academic sociology, however. Just as many 'common-sense' representations of work and identity tend towards *essentialism* – how many times have you heard people express the sentiments 'Typical bloody accountant', for example? – so too, historically, have certain critical accounts of work experience and identity. In the rest of section 2, I seek to explore the problems and pitfalls of allocating *essentialist* meanings to work and to highlight the ways in which work meanings and identities are *culturally* and *historically* constructed phenomena.

2.1 Economic identities as contingent identities

In his 1938 lecture entitled 'A category of the human mind: the notion of person, the notion of "self" ', the anthropologist Marcel Mauss (1979) articulated what was to become one of the most scandalous axioms of the social sciences: the idea that the 'person' is a culturally and historically malleable creation. Since then, detailed anthropological and historical researches have indicated that the modern western conception of the person as a largely coherent, rational, conscious and self-directed individual by no means offers the last word on human personhood. As Mauss (1979, p. 90) himself argued, 'who knows if this "category", which all of us here today believe to be well founded, will always be recognized as such? It was formed only for us, among us.'

Mauss's argument regarding the cultural and historical contingency of identity and personhood can be productively applied to the arena of work and employment. Indeed, we do not need to look very far to begin to appreciate the contingency of work identity, for rarely a day goes by without a story appearing in the media concerning the effects of new information technologies or of increasingly competitive globalized markets on the structure and experience of work.

There can be little doubt that, in recent years, profound and ongoing changes in the industrial and occupational structures of modern western societies have posed serious questions about the 'identity' of a modern economy (conceived of in terms both of the dominance of large-scale manufacturing industry and of a national system of independent sectors), and about the identity of the 'modern industrial worker' (defined as a white, male breadwinner working full-time). For developments such as the growth of service industries, the increasingly global organization of production and exchange, and the growth of a female, predominantly part-time, labour force, have revealed the 'constructedness' of ostensibly stable, unified and 'natural' economic identities. In so doing they have served to indicate that rather than being an 'essentially' unchanging material 'base' – remaining basically the same through all the changes it undergoes – the 'economic' is itself a culturally and historically malleable category, and thus, that any established

contingent identity   economic identity is basically a **contingent identity**.

Let me explain what I mean by this in slightly more detail. At a simple level, to suggest that something is contingent amounts to saying that the conditions of existence of any entity are *exterior* to that entity and not interior to it. In other words, a contingent identity can never manage to constitute itself fully because it relies upon something *outside* of itself for its very existence. Thus, a contingent identity only constitutes itself in relation to *that which it is not*. However, because that identity would not be what it is outside of its relationship with the force opposing it, the latter is also part of the conditions of existence of that identity. Following the social theorist Ernesto Laclau, it is therefore possible to say that any social identity is basically

dislocation   **dislocated**. By this term Laclau (1990, p. 39) is referring to the ways in which any identity 'depends upon an outside which both denies that identity and provides its conditions of possibility at one and the same time'. This means that every identity is basically an *ambiguous* achievement, being dependent upon its ability to define *difference* and 'vulnerable to the entities it would so define to counter, resist, overturn or subvert definitions applied to them' (Connolly, 1991, p. 64).

However, as Laclau (1990, p. 45) goes on to suggest, if any identity is basically a contingent identity then power is always inscribed in the relation an established identity bears to the difference it constitutes. Thus, to study the conditions of existence of any established identity is to delineate the power relations making it possible.

This may seem rather complicated, so let's return to the examples cited earlier to put some substantive meat on these theoretical bones. In her discussion of the relationship between modern work and welfare regimes, the political theorist Carole Pateman (1989, pp. 186–7) draws attention to the contingent character of the 'modern industrial worker' and the power relations inscribed within that particular creation. Rather than being a universal, gender-free 'individual', she argues, the 'modern industrial worker' is a male breadwinner who has an economically dependent wife to take care of his daily needs and look after his home and children. For Pateman, the 'identity' of the modern industrial worker was established in large part through the power and status afforded to men as husbands, and the constitution of women as their economic dependants or 'housewives' relegated to the private sphere of the home. The stable, public identity of the modern industrial worker was therefore established through the positioning of women as 'other' within the domestic sphere.

However, as Pateman (1989, p. 196) goes on to indicate, the historically contingent character of this breadwinner/dependant dichotomy has been dramatically revealed as the conditions of its existence have been increasingly undermined in the 1980s and 1990s. Changes in women's social and economic positions, technological and structural transformations within the global economy, the increase in female employment and the persistence of high levels of male unemployment, have put into question the conditions through which the seemingly fixed, stable economic identity of the modern worker was established. As a result, what it means to be a worker is no longer as clear and uni-dimensional as perhaps it once appeared to be.

Similarly, the identity of the modern national economy conceived of both in terms of a system of internally related sectors with links out to the wider international economy, and in terms of the dominance of manufacturing industry as its prime 'engine of growth' and provider of 'real jobs', has been problematized by a number of important developments. For example, the organization of production and exchange on an increasingly global basis has led to the 'dislocation' of national economies. Rather than systems of interconnected but discrete sectors whose boundaries correspond to those of the nation-state, national economies are fast becoming sites across which capital, goods, and services flow internationally at varying rates (see Chapter 1 of this book).

Finally, the predominance of service industries within contemporary western societies has problematized the identity of a modern economy structured in the image of manufacturing industry (Allen and du Gay, 1994). If, for example, the identity of 'real work' is associated with employment in manufacturing and is established in relation to the 'unproductive' labour of services, what is the status of that identity when the overwhelming bulk of employment in western societies is now located in services? Once again, the contingency and 'constructedness' of an apparently 'given' economic identity is put into question as the conditions of its existence are challenged.

However, it is precisely the contingency and historicity of economic identities that have been denied by certain critical analyses of work and employment. By conceiving of economic categories and objects as essences rather than as cultural and historical constructs, these accounts have proved unhelpful guides to understanding the transformations in economic life outlined above. In the next part of this section, I outline – in admittedly simplified terms – one of the most influential approaches to work identity – what we might term a crude economistic model – and indicate some of its inherent explanatory weaknesses.

2.2 The subjects of production

One of the most enduring dualisms to be found within certain strands of economic sociology – particularly, but by no means exclusively, sociology of a Marxist persuasion – is that which posits an essential structural antagonism between the identities and interests of 'labour' or 'wage earners' on the one hand, and 'capital', or 'employers' on the other; and which then seeks to explain the course of social and cultural relations at work in terms of this 'objective' or 'fundamental' antagonism. Most of you will be familiar with this dualism at an everyday level; you may have deployed it yourself at your place of work, for example, to describe a situation or allocate blame for an event that has occurred.

A typical statement of this dualism is provided by the social theorist W. Baldamus: 'As wages are costs to the firm, and the deprivations inherent in effort mean "costs" to the employee, the interests of employer and wage earner are diametrically opposed' (1961, p. 33).

We can map the two poles of this dualism quite easily. At one extreme there stand the 'workers'. With nothing to sell but their labour power, their economic 'identity' and 'interests' can, it seems, be clearly delineated. Failing the downfall or overthrow of existing capitalist relations, the workers' 'objective' interests consist in increasing wages, reducing working hours, minimizing 'effort' and imposing various constraints upon the activities and ambitions of employers. At the opposite pole is 'capital' and its army of 'servants of power': management. Their 'objective' interests are linked to the perpetual expansion of profit through increasing productivity, de-skilling work, keeping wages low, weakening the collective power of workers and reducing their capacity to disrupt the process of accumulation, while simultaneously casting a cloak of 'ideological legitimacy' over the essentially exploitative nature of employment relations.

FIGURE 6.1 A popular representation of the 'essential antagonism' between 'workers' and 'management': *I'm All Right Jack* (1959).

All this seems quite logical. Indeed, it is very logical, but perhaps that is the problem. It is a bit too 'logical', but not perhaps *sociological* enough. Let me unpack this somewhat elliptical statement. One of the first things to note about this approach is that its analysis of capitalist relations of production consists of a relationship between economic categories, of which social actors only form part insofar as they are the bearers of them. In this analysis the wage earner does not count as a human being, of flesh and blood, but as a bearer of the category 'seller of labour power'. To show that capitalist relations of production are *intrinsically* or *essentially* antagonistic would therefore mean demonstrating that the antagonism stems *logically* from the relationship between the 'objective' categories 'buyer' and 'seller' of labour power. But is it the case, for example, that the relationship is fundamentally conflictual because it is based on unequal exchange and because the employer extracts surplus value from the wage earners? As Laclau indicated (1990, p. 9), the answer to this point is negative as it is only if actual wage earners *resist* such extraction that the relationship becomes antagonistic; and there is nothing in the abstract or 'objective' category 'seller of labour power' to suggest that such resistance is a *logical* conclusion.

In denying that capitalist relations of production are essentially antagonistic, it is important to specify what exactly I am disagreeing with. Obviously, I am not suggesting that no conflicts exist between workers and employers in the world as we know it; rather I am denying that these antagonisms arise from a *logical* analysis of the wage labour/employer relationship. What I am objecting to is the evacuation of meaning, agency and historical contingency from the analysis, due to the reduction of social actors to the 'objective' categories of buyer and seller of labour power.

Once these categories are re-integrated into the socio-cultural relations forming the agents that are their bearers, we can easily imagine a multitude of antagonisms emerging between those human agents and the relations of production in which they participate – for example, when a certain standard of living becomes impossible as wages fall below a certain level; or when fluctuations in the labour market affect housing conditions or the worker's access to consumer goods. In this case, however, as Laclau (1990, p. 9) has suggested, the antagonism is not *internal* or *intrinsic* to capitalist relations of production (in which the worker counts merely as the bearer of the category 'seller of labour power'), but results from the interaction between the relations of production and the worker's identity outside of them. S/he cannot simply be reduced to the status of wage labourer alone for that identity is only ever partially constituted – i.e. it is contingent. As we have already seen, a contingent identity can never manage to constitute itself as an essence because it relies on something outside of itself – its 'constitutive outside' – for its very existence.

Let us take a closer look at these two perspectives. In the dualistic scenario, economic actors are represented simply as the bearers of preformed interests and identities. Anything they do is interpreted in terms of pre-established criteria, with the result that concrete, lived history is reduced to a series of 'empirical variations' on a constant theme. In other words, this objectivist conception of identity always looks for essential characteristics behind the contingency of historical circumstance.

Viewed from the lofty heights afforded by this 'objective' God's-eye position, social actors always appear to be following a pre-written script; one that is basically stable and unchanging, unaffected by the contingencies of culture and history, and which appears to allocate no active role to, and require no active involvement from, its cast of characters. What we have here, then, is an objective, essentialist and subjectless account of work identity.

In contrast to this position, our second approach takes as its starting point the *dislocated* nature of any identity. As a result, the mode of understanding the concrete construction of work identity is completely modified, since contingency and historical specificity are seen to be constitutive of the very identity of social agents.

Rather than two preformed, objective entities, 'wage earner' and 'employer', the interplay of whose respective 'interests' acts as the central generating mechanism of work relations, this approach stresses that the meaning of the terms 'worker' and 'employer' are historically and culturally contingent, dependent upon their positioning within particular discursive contexts. What 'identities' these two economic categories achieve is a product of concrete, cultural and historical circumstance, not an objective, pre-determined 'given'.

The contemporary programmes of organizational reform described by Graeme Salaman in the previous chapter, seem to be implicitly infused with this second assumption, rather than the first, for they do not take the meaning of work as read or as objectively pre-established. As we have seen, the contemporary obsession with 'culture change' within organizations is precisely concerned with inculcating *employers* and *employees* with new work habits, dispositions and forms of conduct – i.e. with constructing new work meanings and identities. Rather than viewing work interests and identities as set in stone and unamenable to change, management consultants such as Tom Peters and Rosabeth Moss Kanter think and act as if these were 'up for grabs'. We may not like the meanings and identities they offer up, but I think we have to agree with the cultural critic Patrick Wright (1987, p. 8) when he suggests that, unlike crude economistic critiques, the work of these consultants entails 'no break with everyday experience' as it 'brings the life world along with it'. In other words, it engages with human agents and tries to win over or otherwise engender – by fair means or foul – their identification, rather than simply taking it for granted. For the proponents of the 'cultural turn' within organizations, then, the subjectivity and identity of workers and employers is a matter of real, practical import.

2.3   The production of subjects

The twentieth century has witnessed a huge number of attempts to shape and regulate the relations that individuals have with society's productive apparatus. Many of these programmes of organizational reform – like the contemporary Corporate Culture phenomenon, discussed in the previous chapter – have claimed to be able to restructure the employment relationship so as to be able to make work more subjectively meaningful for those performing it, whilst simultaneously increasing profitability. These different discourses of reform have represented the subjectivity of the worker not only as an object to be developed rather than repressed, but also as a crucial determinant of organizational success. Through the medium of a variety of technologies of regulation – by which I mean certain techniques that rely upon human scientific knowledge to channel human conduct into certain reproducible patterns – they have attempted to indicate that productive work can satisfy the worker, that the activities of working can provide meaningful experiences for those performing them, and that work can be an important source of personal identity.

As the sociologist Nikolas Rose has argued:

> Employers and managers equipped with these new visions of work have thus claimed that there is no conflict between the pursuits of productivity, efficiency, and competitiveness on the one hand and the humanization of

work on the other. On the contrary, the path to business success lies in engaging the employee with the goals of the company at the level of his or her subjectivity, aligning the wishes, needs and aspirations of each individual who works for the organization with the successful pursuit of its objectives. Through striving to fulfil their own needs and wishes at work, each employee will thus work for the advance of the enterprise: the more the individual fulfils him- or herself at work, the greater the benefit to the company.

(Rose, 1990, p. 56)

It is undoubtedly true that these discourses and technologies of work reform have played, and continue to play, an active role in reproducing hierarchies of power and reward at work, and that they have been consciously deployed at various times to attenuate the power of trade unions and their prerogatives for the representation of collective interests and the defence of collective 'rights'. However, it is equally important to note that they are not simply 'ideological' distortions, as the labour/capital dualism suggests. In other words, they are not merely functional responses to, or legitimations of, pre-established economic interests. Rather than simply reflecting the needs of a pre-given reality, they themselves actively construct the 'reality' of work life, and create new ways for people to conduct themselves at work. Rather than existing 'objectively preformed' outside of culture and history, as the labour/capital dualism suggests, the identity that economic actors come to have is discursively constituted as a product of changes in the ways of representing and acting upon – or **governing** – economic life.

governing

READING A

Now read 'Governing economic life' by Peter Miller and Nikolas Rose, included as Reading A at the end of this chapter.

In this piece, Miller and Rose develop some concepts derived from the work of Michel Foucault in analysing the discursive character of economic activity. This is quite a difficult piece to read as it uses a very specialized theoretical vocabulary. As you read it, jot down what you take to be the key themes and concepts that the authors raise. In particular, think about:

1 what the authors mean by the term 'government';
2 the importance of language and representation to the organization of economic life;
3 the role of 'technologies' in realizing economic aims and objectives;
4 the ways in which economic government operates through subjects.

In this article, Miller and Rose argue that economic objects are discursive in character. They suggest that it is only possible to manage or administer an object called an 'economy' or an 'organization' once you have conceptualized or represented a set of processes, activities or relations as an 'economy' or an 'organization'. To 'govern' an organization or an economy thus depends upon

representation

a particular mode of **representation** – the elaboration of a language for thinking about a particular object in a certain way that claims both to grasp the nature of the reality of that object and literally to re-present it in a form amenable to deliberation, calculation and intervention – and upon particular **technologies** – those mechanisms which seek to translate image and thought into practicable form.

technologies

In this sense, the term **government** does not simply refer to 'the Government' or to 'the State' but to a diversity of ways of managing social reality. One can talk of governing a school, a hospital, a family, a child and so on. The term helps us to realize the multiplicity of ways in which domains of activity are managed relative to the ways they are conceptualized or represented, and are hence made amenable to certain forms of intervention; it thus enables us to become aware of the variety of mechanisms through which management interventions are implemented.

government

Miller and Rose go on to suggest that programmes of government are always 'personal' matters in that they operate through subjects. They offer particular conceptions of the capacities and attributes of those to be governed and construct certain ways for people to conceive of and conduct themselves. Because 'government' is a form of power, referring, as Foucault (1980, p. 221) put it, to the ways in which 'the possible fields of action of others' are structured, it is intimately connected with shaping, guiding or otherwise affecting the conduct of persons.

Precisely because programmes of government operate through subjects, they presuppose, rather than repress or annul, the capacity of individuals as *active agents*. As Foucault famously argued:

> when one defines the exercise of power as a mode of action upon the actions of others, when one characterizes these actions by the government of men by other men – in the broadest sense of the term – one includes an important element: freedom. Power is exercised only over free subjects, and only insofar as they are free. By this we mean individual or collective subjects who are faced with a field of possibilities in which several ways of behaving, several reactions and diverse comportments may be realized. Where the determining factors saturate the whole there is no relationship of power.
>
> (Foucault, 1982, p. 221)

Because programmes of government are dependent upon the ways in which individuals conduct themselves, their success is not automatically guaranteed. The relationship between government and governed therefore depends upon what Foucault termed 'an unstable conjuncture' because it passes through the manner in which individuals are willing to exist as particular subjects. If individuals refuse to, or otherwise cannot, conduct themselves as certain sorts of subject, then the programmes of government which depend upon the emergence of that sort of subject for their effectivity will simply be unable to function.

2.4   Summary

We have covered a lot of tricky theoretical ground in section 2 and so it is worth taking a breather for a moment to review very briefly where we have come from and where we have got to.

Through an analysis of a still influential conception of work identity – one which sees a fundamental, 'objective' antagonism between 'labour' and 'capital' – I have sought to explore the problems and pitfalls of attempting to allocate an *objective, essential* meaning to work, and to highlight the ways in which work meaning and identity are *culturally* and *historically* constructed phenomena.

I have thus stressed the benefits of what is elsewhere referred to as a *social constructionist* approach (see **Hall**, ed., 1997; **Woodward**, ed., 1997) to analysing work identity and meaning, in preference to approaches that seek to explain social processes through the attribution of certain timeless *essences* to them. I have sought to do this most directly through the introduction of a particular conceptual vocabulary, derived largely, but not exclusively, from the work of Michel Foucault, which provides tools for analysing economic activities, objects and agents as *discursive* constructs.

In the following section, I seek to deploy some of the theoretical tools outlined above to analyse the discursive construction of work identities.

3   Governing organizational life in the present

The idea that organizations need to change, and to change dramatically and immediately, appears to be one of the axioms of the present age. Rarely a day goes by without a new pundit appearing in the press or on TV exhorting organizations to 'de-layer', 'downsize', 're-engineer' or 'enterprise up' in order simply to ensure their continued survival. While these pundits frequently disagree about what precisely is driving this urgent need for 'change' they nonetheless all assume that 'change' is absolutely necessary and that the imperatives of 'change' require quite similar responses from organizations.

Indeed, it is quite interesting to note how ostensibly different texts, from the popular books of management 'gurus' such as Tom Peters and Rosabeth Kanter (whose work you were introduced to in the previous chapter), through official reports published by bodies such as the Confederation of British Industry and the World Bank, to policy statements produced by both major political parties in the United Kingdom, draw upon a similar vocabulary in seeking to delineate the problems facing organizations and the solutions they should adopt. While different texts highlight different combinations of phenomena – such as the dislocatory effects consequent upon the increasing deployment of new information and communication technologies, or those associated with the competitive pressures resulting from increasingly 'global' systems of trade, finance and production – they all agree that organizations now operate in an environment characterized first and foremost by *massive uncertainty*. In such an environment, only those organizations that can rapidly and systematically *change their conduct* and *become ever more enterprising* will survive and prosper.

Invariably, organizations are offered stark alternatives: to survive in the dislocated, increasingly competitive and chaotic global economy, they 'must either move away from bureaucratic guarantees to ... flexibility... or stagnate' (Kanter, 1990, p. 356). The message is loud and clear:

> In this environment, bureaucratic organizations ... – public and private – increasingly fail us. Today's environment demands institutions that are extremely flexible and adaptable. It demands institutions that deliver high quality goods and services, squeezing ever more bang out of every buck. It demands institutions that are responsive to customers, offering choices of non-standardized services; that lead by persuasion and incentives rather than commands; that give their employees a sense of meaning and control, even ownership. It demands institutions that empower citizens rather than simply serving them.
>
> (Osborne and Gaebler, 1992, p. 15)

The language deployed in this quotation from two leading American management consultants, David Osborne and Ted Gaebler, is probably familiar to you in some shape or form. Those of you working in large, or not so large, organizations – whether public or private – have probably been exposed to some of its key terms – the exhortation to be more 'efficient' (get 'more bang out of every buck' as they so colourfully put it), to be more responsive to 'customers', to feel a greater sense of 'ownership' of the work you perform – while those of you who are not currently engaged in paid work have probably nonetheless found these key terms cropping up in your newspapers or on your radio and television sets, as the government vows to slim down bureaucracy in the public sector, for example, in order to make state organizations more efficient, effective and competitive.

The fact that the sorts of statements deployed by Osborne and Gaebler regularly crop up in other institutional settings indicates that they are part of a wider **discourse** of organizational reform. As you are aware from Reading A, a discourse can be seen as a group of statements that provide a particular language for talking about and acting on a particular object. When statements about an object or topic are made within a certain discourse, that discourse makes it possible to construct that object in a certain way. It also limits the other ways in which the object can be constructed.

discourse

As we have seen, a discourse does not consist of one statement alone, but of several statements working together to form what Michel Foucault terms a *discursive formation*: 'Whenever, between objects, types of statement, concepts, or thematic choices, one can define a regularity (an order, correlations, positions and functionings, transformations), we will say, for the sake of convenience, that we are dealing with a *discursive formation*' (Foucault, 1972, pp. 37–8). The statements fit together because any one of them implies a relation to all the others: they refer to the same object, share the same style and support what Foucault describes as 'a strategy... a common institutional ... or political drift or pattern' (quoted in Cousins and Hussain, 1984, pp. 84–5).

So how are we to characterize this discourse of which the statements articulated by Osborne and Gaebler are a constitutive element? According to Osborne and Gaebler themselves, the programme of organizational reform they advocate offers a new method of governing organizational and personal conduct which they term *entrepreneurial governance*.

Similarly, successive Conservative administrations in Britain have represented their major political programme of reforms – such as privatizing the public utilities, bringing business disciplines to bear upon public institutions such as the National Health Service and the Civil Service through the introduction of 'internal markets', 'Next Steps' agencies, performance-related pay and so forth – as part of an ongoing process of turning the UK into an 'enterprise culture'.

It is this notion of 'enterprise' which occupies the crucial position in contemporary discourses of organizational change: providing a critique of existing organizational arrangements and offering itself as a solution to the problems caused by 'massive uncertainty' in the 'external environment' through delineating the principles and practices of a new rationality of organizational governance.

3.1 Unpacking 'enterprise' as a rationality of government

So what might it mean to refer to **enterprise** as a rationality of government? Following Miller and Rose, I have referred to 'government' in general terms as those strategies and techniques for acting in various ways on the conduct of others, in a range of sites and under the aegis of a range of different authorities.

As Osborne and Gaebler's comments quoted above indicate, a key feature of 'enterprise' as a principle of government is the role it allocates to the commercial enterprise form as the privileged model for the conduct of conduct. Within this discourse, the commercial enterprise is consistently represented as the preferred model for any form of institutional organization of goods and services. Similarly, particular habits of action that display

discursive formation

enterprise

enterprising qualities – such as initiative, risk-taking, self-reliance and personal responsibility – are represented as the most appropriate forms of conduct on the part of those concerned (whether individuals or collectivities) within any organizational domain, whether public, private or voluntary.

As the social theorist Graham Burchell (1993, p. 275) has suggested, the defining feature of enterprise as a rationality of government is thus 'the generalization of an "enterprise form" to all forms of conduct – to the conduct of organizations hitherto seen as being non-economic, to the conduct of government, and to the conduct of individuals themselves'.

While the concrete ways in which this rationality of government has been put into practice have varied quite considerably, the forms of action it has made possible for different institutions and different types of person – schools, general practitioners, housing estates, prisons and so on – do seem to share a general consistency and style.

One characteristic feature of this style of government is the crucial role it allocates to **contract** in re-defining organizational relationships. The changes affecting schools, hospitals, government departments and so on, in the United Kingdom, have often involved the re-constituting of institutional roles in terms of *contracts strictly defined*, and even more frequently have involved a *contract-like way* of representing relationships between institutions, and between individuals and institutions (Freedland, 1994, p. 88).

contract

An example of the former, for instance, occurred when fund-holding medical practices contracted with hospital trusts for the provision of health care to particular patients, where previously that provision was made directly by the National Health Service. An example of the latter is the relationship between central government departments and the new executive or 'Next Steps' agencies – where no technical contract as such exists but where the relationship is governed by a contract-like 'Framework Document' which defines the functions and goals of the agency, as well as the procedures whereby the department will set and monitor performance targets for the agency.

This process, which the French social theorist Jacques Donzelot (1991) has termed 'contractual implication', typically consists in assigning the performance of a function or an activity to a distinct unit of management – individual or collective – which is regarded as being accountable for the efficient (i.e. 'economic') performance of that function or activity.

By assuming active responsibility for these activities and functions – both for carrying them out and for their outcomes – these units of management are in effect affirming a certain type of identity. This identity is basically entrepreneurial in character because 'contractualization' requires these units of management to adopt a certain entrepreneurial form of relationship to themselves 'as a condition of their effectiveness and of the effectiveness of this type of government' (Burchell, 1993, p. 276). To put it another way, contractualization makes these units of management function like little businesses or 'enterprise forms'.

According to the social theorist Colin Gordon (1991, pp. 42–5), entrepreneurial forms of government such as contractualization involve the reconceptualization of different domains of existence – whether schools, hospitals or charities – as economic entities. 'This operation works', he argues, 'by the progressive enlargement of the territory of economic theory by a series of re-definitions of its object.' He continues, 'economics thus becomes an ''approach'' capable in principle of addressing the totality of human behaviour, and, consequently, of envisaging a coherent, purely economic method of programming the totality of governmental action' (ibid., p. 43).

What Gordon is getting at here is the way in which the discourse of enterprise applies an economic rationality to all domains of existence, making formerly diverse institutions and practices amenable to representation, calculation and intervention in terms of economic criteria.

For many commentators, the growing dominance of the discourse of enterprise heralds the return of Adam Smith's famous *homo economicus* or 'economic man' to the centre stage of history. However, Gordon cautions against too hasty an identification between Smith's eighteenth-century creation and the subject of the discourse of enterprise.

For Gordon, the subject of enterprise is both 'a reactivation and a radical inversion' of Smith's original. The reactivation consists 'in positing a fundamental human faculty of choice, a principle which empowers economic calculation effectively to sweep aside the anthropological categories and frameworks of the human and social sciences' (ibid.). The great innovation occurs, in his opinion, in the conception of the economic agent as an inherently manipulable or 'flexible' creation.

Whereas the original *homo economicus* was conceived of as a subject the well-springs of whose activity were ultimately 'untouchable by government', the subject of enterprise is imagined as an agent 'who is perpetually responsive to modifications in its environment'. As Gordon points out, 'economic government here joins hands with behaviourism' (ibid.). By this Gordon means that economic theories of rational utility maximization are crossed with psychological theories of motivation to create a new, hybrid version of *homo economicus* which differs in important ways from its original manifestation. In its contemporary form, the economic subject is not simply an 'enterprise' but rather 'the entrepreneur of himself or herself'. The

entrepreneur of the self

subject of enterprise is 'an **entrepreneur of the self**' (Gordon, 1987, p. 300).

This idea of an individual human life as an 'enterprise' suggests that no matter what hand circumstance may have dealt a person, he or she remains always continuously engaged (even if 'technically unemployed') in that enterprise, and that it is 'part of the continuous business of living to make adequate provision for the preservation, reproduction and reconstruction of one's own human capital' (Gordon, 1991, p. 44).

Once a human life is conceived of primarily in entrepreneurial terms, the 'owner' of that life becomes individually responsible for his/her own self-advancement and care; within the ideals of enterprise, individuals are charged with managing the conduct of the business of their own lives. The vocabulary of enterprise re-imagines activities and agents and their relationship to one another according to its own ideals. Thus, the entrepreneurial language of responsible self-advancement and care, for example, is linked to a new perception of those who are 'outside civility' – those who are excluded or marginalized because they cannot or will not conduct themselves in an appropriately 'entrepreneurial' and hence 'responsible' manner. As we have seen in the UK context, pathologies that were until recently represented and acted upon 'socially' – homelessness, unemployment and so forth – have become re-individualized through their positioning within entrepreneurial discourse and hence subject to new, often more intense, forms of surveillance and control. Because pathological subjects are now represented as responsible individuals with a moral duty to take care of themselves, they can blame no one but themselves for the problems they face. This individualization of social problems is evidenced in the UK by the introduction of a new terminology to describe the unemployed person – 'job seeker' – and the homeless person – 'rough sleeper'.

Because a human being is considered to be continuously engaged in a project to shape his or her life as an autonomous, choosing individual driven by the desire to optimize the worth of his or her own existence, life for that person is represented as a single, basically undifferentiated, arena for the pursuit of that endeavour. As previously distinct forms of life are now classified as 'enterprise forms' the conceptions and practices of personhood – or forms of identity – they give rise to are remarkably consistent. Thus, as schools, prisons, charities, and government departments, for example, are re-presented as 'enterprises', they all accord an increased priority to the development of the 'enterprising subject' for their own success. In a very real sense then, as Rosabeth Kanter (1990, pp. 9–10) has suggested, the 'enterprising subject' is a 'new culture hero'.

As I suggested earlier, this conception of the individual as an 'entrepreneur of the self' is firmly established at the heart of contemporary programmes of organizational reform. In keeping with the entrepreneurial mix of economic and behaviourist psychological discourse that we examined above, contemporary programmes of organizational reform characterize employment not as a painful obligation imposed upon individuals, nor as an activity undertaken to meet purely instrumental needs, but rather as a means to self-development, 'self responsibility' and individual empowerment.

Organizational success is premised upon an engagement by the organization of the self-managing and 'self-optimizing' capacities of individuals as subjects, no matter what their formal organizational role or status. This ambition is to be made practicable within the workplace through the medium of those 'technologies' that Miller and Rose refer to in Reading A – techniques for reducing dependency by reducing management strata ('de-layering' or 'down-sizing'), for encouraging the breaking down of occupational boundaries through the development of 'special project teams', for stimulating individual entrepreneurship through the introduction of new forms of staff evaluation and reward ('performance-related pay') and so on.

Performance-related pay, for example, whose deployment, particularly within the public sector in the UK, has grown dramatically in recent years, often involves the development of an ongoing 'contract' between an individual employee and his/her line manager whereby that employee's pay, or part of it, is made more dependent upon whether he or she has met, exceeded, or failed to meet certain performance objectives (Milward et al., 1992, pp. 268, 361; Marsden and Richardson, 1994).

Thus, performance management and related techniques – individual appraisal and development – involve a characteristically 'contractual' and 'entrepreneurial' relationship between individual employees and the organization for which they work. This involves 'offering' individuals involvement in activities – such as managing budgets, assessing staff, delivering services – previously held to be the responsibility of other agents – such as supervisors and personnel departments. However, the price of this involvement is that individuals themselves must assume responsibility for carrying out these activities and for their outcomes. In keeping with the principles of enterprise as a rationality of government, performance management and related techniques function as 'responsibilizing' mechanisms, which are held to be both economically desirable and personally empowering.

This requirement that individuals become more personally exposed to the risks of engaging in a particular activity is represented as a means to their empowerment because within entrepreneurial discourse, individuals can only be 'free' if they are 'enabled' to build resources in themselves rather than relying on others to take risks and bear responsibilities on their behalf. According to Rosabeth Kanter, 'entrepreneurial strategies are more motivating for people' because they allow everyone the opportunity to be in business for themselves 'inside the large corporation'. They are also better for business because the corporation itself 'should reap benefits too, in increased productivity' (Kanter, 1990, pp. 357–8).

ACTIVITY 2

Turn to the article from *The Financial Times* reproduced on pages 305–6. This piece reports on a new system of organization for airport check-in staff introduced by British Airways in 1990, designed to 'increase the staff's work satisfaction and to improve the service they give customers'. As you read through this short article think about the ways in which the changes British Airways made, and the vocabulary they used to describe them, relate to the principles and practices of enterprise that I have just been describing. In particular, think about the sorts of subject-positions that these changes make available for staff to occupy.

This example tells us some interesting things about work culture and identity in the present. Notice, for example, the ways in which change is articulated according to principles that share distinct 'family resemblances' to those we have described as 'entrepreneurial'. Many of the presuppositions we noted above, that people should be active not passive, that individual responsibility is both personally empowering and economically desirable, are deployed by British Airways to explain and justify this re-organization. These changes are articulated within a particular discourse, one we can recognize as basically entrepreneurial in character.

This immediately takes us into the realm of *culture* and *identity*, for as we have seen throughout this chapter in particular, discourses create meanings for objects, activities and persons.

The changes that British Airways inaugurated did not leave the activity of 'checking-in' unaltered, for the discursive register through which that activity is represented and given meaning has been reconceived. Similarly, while the people doing the checking-in are the same people, the vocabulary through which they are encouraged to relate to their work, each other and themselves has been subtly changed. As we can see, the discourse through which change is articulated offers them new subject-positions which they are encouraged to occupy. They are being offered the opportunity or 'freedom' to take more responsibility for their own self-organization and management. This is not without cost, however, for they must now take responsibility for the outcomes of this new arrangement. It is they and not supervisors who are held to be responsible for their own organizational conduct.

As the article acknowledges, this 'responsibility has also brought its cares'. Staff are now under more 'peer pressure' to perform because they have been made more responsible to each other than they were before. Because any identity is basically relational in terms of its conditions of existence, any change in the latter is bound to affect the former. In this case, the employee's relations with her employing organization are discursively re-imagined. Rather than having the same identity – the employee – in a new situation, we have instead a new situation in which a new form of work-based identity has emerged.

We can also see that these changes are made practicable through the *medium* of a particular technique or technology known as the 'self-managing team'. This technology is inscribed with certain psychological assumptions about human motivation and behaviour, in which individuals are represented as being more likely to work creatively and enthusiastically if they are subjectively implicated in the work they perform, if it is made more intimately their own affair and they are enabled to feel personal 'ownership' of it.

WORKERS KEEP THEMSELVES IN CHECK

John Gapper finds a new system of organisation at Gatwick Airport

The smiling British Airways staff checking in bags in the North Terminal at Gatwick Airport are more worried than they look these days. Since March, they have not been able to rely on supervisors to tell them what to do.

The change to working in teams which are unsupervised for large parts of their shift is intended to increase the staff's work satisfaction and to improve the service they give customers. However, the responsibility has also brought its cares.

'The first few weeks, I went home each night a nervous wreck,' said Ms Liz Nicoletti, a BA customer service agent for 11 years. 'I was worrying about whether there were people on the desks and who was doing what.'

Ms Nicoletti was feeling a bit calmer yesterday. But she is still having difficulty coming to terms with being part of a team of 16 people who must organise themselves rather than simply being in a pool of 210 staff.

After a briefing at the beginning of each $8^3/_4$-hour shift with the leaders of the teams - known as customer services executives - the members of the team are assigned to a zone in the check-in area and left to control it.

The notion is a novel one for many of the staff, who were previously more highly controlled.

They used to be responsible to a group of 22 supervisors and underneath them to 18 'allocators.' Allocators were the equivalent of foremen - who told them where and when to work.

Since 25 March, when the scheme started, there have been considerable teething problems. Mostly, they have been caused by a lack of staff - about a dozen extra fulltimers were needed, and staff turnover has led to shortages.

About 170 of the agents working in the check-in section of BA's passenger services division at Gatwick

Responsibility: before the new system staff had felt efforts were not being recognized.

are women. Some of them believe that the idea of working in teams is a good one, but are disappointed by the way in which it is working in practice.

'I think the idea is a good one, but we were sold it as being beneficial to us and it is not like that at the moment,' said Ms Pauline Scales, sitting at a desk in one of the three check-in zones for charter and scheduled flights. Others are harsher still. Mr Alan Peckham who was working next to Ms Scales, thought the idea of splitting the check-in staff into zones was divisive and would lead to rivalries that would damage service.

But managers and supervisors are less despondent. They say that peer pressure has already led to agents supporting each other rather than seeking informal breaks. There was an agent at nearly all the desks yesterday morning.

It is still a frustrating time for BA's management at Gatwick Airport. They point at the unhappiness and low morale caused by the previous working practices according to staff attitude surveys - but the new system is still bedding down.

One of the frustrations is that, unlike the proposed change to 12-hour shifts for engineers at Heathrow which caused an unofficial strike there, the team-working idea is not intended to save money. Instead, it is about quality.

The origins of the changes lie in the move to the new North Terminal in spring last year, which coincided with the takeover of British Caledonian by the BA. Caledonian was then re-launched as the charter wing of BA.

Ms Laura Rowe, passenger services manager at Gatwick, says that the moves left unsolved problems of merging the different cultures and working practices of check-in staff who had worked separately for BA and Caledonian.

The attitude survey carried out last March disclosed a low level of morale, says Ms Rowe. The staff felt their efforts were not being recognised, they were being treated like children, and were not given responsibility.

Managers attributed much of this to the heavily supervised working system, where the staff simply waited to be instructed about their tasks. 'They had a very strong feeling of them and us,' says Mr Peter Cole, one of the 27 new customer service executives.

Ms Rowe was also convinced that service to customers would be improved if the staff felt better about the way in which their work was organised. She referred to the results of a study of staff at work in banks in the US.

BA management had set up a study group of managers, supervisors and agents which looked at team-working experiments in other companies, including US carriers. This group devised the model which was put into practice in March. This allows for 27 customer service executives handling 18 teams of agents.

On any morning, there should be one team for each zone of check-in desks, plus two teams working beyond the customs control point. The system also includes a plan for one 'day relief' team to fill in for absences in other teams, and a 'quality team' with the responsibility for looking at how the rostering is working and thinking of ways the service could be improved.

In practice, BA has not yet managed to recruit enough people to put a 'quality team' in place. It has suffered from the high employment levels in the Crawley area which means that employers must compete vigorously in order to recruit staff.

But Ms Rowe can detect some hopeful signs already. She says there is no longer a queue of agents outside her door with complaints about their allocators.

Clear lines of responsibility have been established and are operating.

She believes the check-in teams, which have to handle a throughput of about 10,000 passengers daily, will start to work more effectively when the summer rush eases and there has been time to fine-tune and get used to the system.

'It was risky to do it, but it would have been risky not to do it because morale was so low,' she says. 'If we had not made a change, I don't think we could have reached the level of customer service we have declared for ourselves.

(Source: Financial Times, 23 June 1990)

3.2   Enterprise and the blurring of boundaries

Within entrepreneurial discourse, paid work (no matter how objectively 'alienated', 'deskilled' or 'degraded' it may appear to social scientists) is represented as a crucial element in the path to individual responsibility, freedom and self-fulfilment. However, the forms of conduct which individuals are encouraged to adopt at work are not exclusive to that domain. Within entrepreneurial discourse, as we have already seen, the enterprise form is represented as the 'generalized principle of functioning' of the entire social fabric. This means that there is no domain of activity where entrepreneurial conduct is not appropriate because every individual life is, in effect, structured as an enterprise of the self which each person must take responsibility for managing to their own best advantage.

As a number of sociologists have pointed out, entrepreneurial discourse effectively blurs traditional distinctions between different social spheres by making certain (entrepreneurial) forms of conduct appropriate to the functioning of all of them. According to the US sociologist Charles Sabel (1991, pp. 42-43), for example, whereas it once seemed easy for at least a proportion of the population (mainly men, of course) to know where work stopped and leisure began, these days it is a lot harder to know when work is over or, indeed, whether it ever actually is:

> Work in the restructured economy simultaneously increases and limits autonomy in the world of life outside of it. Employees who are encouraged to think of themselves as entrepreneurs, to treat their employer as a market ... are forced to manage resources and risks in ways which make it easier for them to imagine changing the conditions of their own lives ... But this enhanced autonomy is simultaneously qualified by the same situation that produced it. Just as the firms form networks with one another and their environment in order to keep abreast of local knowledge, so do individuals secure their long-term employability through participation in neighbourhood groups, hobby clubs, or other professional and social networks outside of the firm. Only those who participate in such multiple, loosely connected networks are likely to know when their current jobs are in danger, where new opportunities lie, and what skills are required in order to seize these opportunities. The more open corporate labour markets become, the greater the burden these networks will have to bear and the greater will be the economic compulsion to participate in the social activities they organize ... Hence, ... it is becoming harder to say when one is working. Activities at work become preparation for turning the family into a family enterprise that absorbs all leisure; family and leisure activities become preconditions of employability. Anticipation of these possibilities undermines the distinctions between *work, leisure* and *family.*
>
> (Sabel, 1991, pp. 42–3)

What Sabel is getting at here is that the forms of conduct expected of employees at work are now remarkably similar to those required of them outside of work. They and their families live life as 'an enterprise' in every sphere of existence, whether at work or at play, in order to guarantee their survival and reproduction. As a result, traditional boundaries between work and non-work, public and private spheres, are increasingly thrown into question.

However, Sabel also goes on to stress that while the discourse of enterprise can be seen to blur traditional distinctions between sets of activities, this does not signify the disappearance of boundaries *per se* but rather their re-articulation according to new principles. The discourse of enterprise *does not defy classification,* it simply *categorizes in a different way.* As Sabel (1991, p. 46) argues, a world in which the boundaries within and between firms, between work and non-work, and between public and private spheres, are blurring is 'not a world without boundaries. New boundaries, indeed, new kinds of boundaries, are being drawn even as the old fade.'

The discourse of enterprise thus reconceptualizes activities, their agents and their relationship to each other according to its own classificatory ideals. For example, as we saw earlier, the entrepreneurial language of responsible self-management is linked to a new perception of those 'outside civility' – the excluded and the marginalized – who cannot or will not conduct themselves in an appropriately 'responsible' manner. If you as an individual are homeless or unemployed, for example, then it is now your own individual responsibility to deal with that situation. If your own individual efforts do not succeed then it will be assumed that it is your individual choice to live that particular lifestyle. As we saw earlier the reconceptualization of the homeless person as a 'rough sleeper' and the unemployed person as a 'job seeker' are effects of the individualization of the social domain that entrepreneurial discourse engenders.

In this scenario, no matter how constrained by external or internal factors any person may be, people are increasingly obliged to construe their lives in terms of its choices. Individuals are expected to understand their own particular life-course as the outcome of such choices, and to account for their lives in terms of the reasons for those choices.

Thus, the price of being offered more 'autonomy' at work is accepting responsibility for one's use of that autonomy and for the outcomes its exercise produces. This means that 'managerial units' such as individuals or families are more exposed to the costs of engaging in any activity and more dependent on their own resources for successfully carrying it out. Once inside the discursive world of enterprise, therefore, one cannot hand one's autonomy back. Instead, one is forced, in effect, to exercise it continuously in order to guarantee one's own survival.

4 The culture of the customer

The sociologist Nikolas Rose (1990, pp. 102–3) has suggested that the representation of the person as above all else a choosing, enterprising subject, entails a significant shift in the relations that have traditionally been held to exist between the realms of 'production' and those of 'consumption'.

According to Rose, over the past fifteen years or so the most powerful images of the economic function of the citizen have been decisively altered. The much vaunted 'protestant work ethic' had proclaimed a set of values for the citizen as producer – where hard work was a moral, personal, and social good, where dedication to labour was to be maintained and gratification deferred, and where a stable pattern of expectations over a working life was to be ensured by a reasonable certainty of continued employment in a single industry, rising wages, and a predictable (and predictably gendered) life-cycle of youthful independence, marriage and family. However, Rose continues, the discourse of enterprise reconceptualizes the economic role of the citizen in a fundamental way, privileging an **ethic of consumption** over the traditional productionist 'work ethic':

ethic of consumption

> The primary image offered to the modern citizen is not that of the producer but of the consumer. Through consumption we are urged to shape our lives by the use of our purchasing power. We are obliged to make our lives meaningful by selecting our personal lifestyle from those offered to us in advertising, soap operas, and films, to make sense of our existence by exercising our freedom to choose in a market in which one simultaneously purchases products and services, and assembles, manages, and markets oneself. The image of the citizen as a choosing self entails a new image of the productive subject. The worker is portrayed neither as an economic actor, rationally pursuing financial advantage, nor as a social creature seeking satisfaction of needs for solidarity and security. The worker is an individual in search of meaning, responsibility, a sense of personal achievement, a maximised 'quality of life', and hence of work. Thus, the individual is not to be emancipated *from* work, perceived merely as a task or a means to an end, but to be fulfilled *in* work, now construed as an activity through which we produce, discover and experience ourselves.

(ibid.)

This new privilege accorded to the consumer as the main agent of economic life has had considerable impact upon the government of organizational life. At an institutional level, meeting the demands of the 'sovereign consumer' has become an overriding imperative of organizational reform (Keat and Abercrombie, 1990; du Gay and Salaman, 1992). If you remember from section 3, the American management consultants Osborne and Gaebler suggested that a crucial feature of a successful – and hence enterprising – organization was its 'responsiveness' to the needs of customers. Similarly, the organizational changes we examined at British Airways were represented and justified in terms of providing improved customer service. Indeed, in domain after domain, 'the customer' has come to occupy a hallowed place in the vocabulary of organizational life. From the hospital to the railway station, and from the classroom to the museum, 'patients', 'passengers', 'pupils' and 'visitors' have been translated into 'customers'. In this way the 'customer' acts as a discursive device for the reconstruction of organizational relations. These references to the 'customer' form a crucial part of contemporary attempts to bring 'market discipline' to bear on the internal life of organizations.

Contemporary programmes of organizational reform such as Total Quality Management (TQM) or Business Process Re-engineering (BPR) (see the previous chapter) allocate crucial significance to the 'customer' not only in terms of the relation between the company and its external environment, but also in relation to the ways in which the internal life of the organization is conceived and structured. As the sociologist Stephen Hill (1991, pp. 399–400) has argued, the foremost principle of TQM is that 'quality is defined as conformance to the requirements of the customer'. However, the term 'customer' does not simply refer to relations between an 'inside' (the company) and an 'outside' (individual consumers). Rather, relationships between employees and departments within individual firms are also construed in terms of the customer model: employees become each other's customers.

> There are internal as well as external customers ... An organizational unit receives inputs from the previous process and transforms these to produce outputs for the next ... As a 'customer', a unit should expect conformance to its own requirements, while as a supplier it has an obligation to conform to the requirements of others.
>
> (Hill, 1990, p. 400)

In this manner, the internal life of the organization is conceived of and structured *contractually* as an assemblage of *customer/supplier market relations.*

This focus on **consumer sovereignty** is a pronounced feature of programmes of organizational reform in both private and public sectors – even senior bureaucrats in the British home civil service, for example, are to be found referring to their own Ministers as customers! – and of restructuring programmes within 'manufacturing' as well as 'service' industries. Indeed, the ubiquity of the language of the market and consumer sovereignty within and across sectors and industries suggests the ways it is serving to *blur traditional distinctions between these different domains.* A focus on the customer is conceived of as a crucial device for making organizations act in ways that most fully express the qualities of free enterprise and market competitiveness. For, within the discourse of enterprise:

consumer sovereignty

On the one hand, the conduct of commercial enterprises is presented as a (indeed the) primary field of activity in which enterprising qualities are displayed. And given that these qualities are themselves regarded as intrinsically desirable... this serves to valorize engagement in such activities and hence, more generally, the workings of a free market economy. On the other hand, however, it is also claimed that in order to maximize the benefits of this economic system, commercial enterprises must themselves be encouraged to be more enterprising, i.e. to act in ways that fully express these qualities. In other words, it seems to be acknowledged that 'enterprises are not inherently enterprising', and enterprising qualities are thus given an instrumental value in relation to the optimal performance of a market economy.

(Keat, 1990, pp. 3–4)

Within the discourse of enterprise, then, 'staying close to the customer' is presented as a crucial form of enterprising conduct that every organization must endeavour to learn in order to optimize both its own potential and that of the economy and society more generally. Representations of 'the customer' act as devices for restructuring organizations in order to make them more clearly conform to the dictates of entrepreneurial rationality. In so doing, however, they serve to blur traditional distinctions between production and consumption, public and private sectors and, increasingly, to realign the relations between workers, managers and consumers. For organizations which structure their internal workings in the image of customer–supplier relationships make it less easy to visualize where the 'inside' and the 'outside' of organizational life begin and end. With workers and managers becoming each others' customers, and customers being used to manage employee relations (see Reading B), the clear boundaries that were held to separate the categories of 'worker', 'manager' and 'customer' seem increasingly hazy.

READING B

Turn to Reading B entitled 'Consumer's reports: management by customers in a changing economy' by Linda Fuller and Vicki Smith, reproduced at the end of this chapter.

In this piece, Fuller and Smith explore the changing relationship between production and consumption through an examination of the use of customer feedback mechanisms as a means of managing staff involved in face-to-face service delivery work.

As you read through this piece, consider the following questions:

1   What main reasons do Fuller and Smith offer for the growing use of customer feedback mechanisms in service industries?

2   How is the growing use of these mechanisms related to changing conceptions about the service worker's role in securing profit?

3   In what ways does the integration of the customer into the organizational life of the firm change the relationships between workers, managers and consumers?

In this article Fuller and Smith focus on the growing use of customer feedback mechanisms in service industries in the United States. As we saw earlier, people engaged in paid work in advanced industrial societies such as the United Kingdom and the United States are more likely to be employed in services than in manufacturing work and it is in service industries, as Fuller and Smith suggest, where customer feedback is being used most intensively as a form of organizational governance.

According to Fuller and Smith, a focus on consumer sovereignty is most pronounced in those organizations where the quality of interactive – or 'face-to-face' – service delivery has become an important source of value. As 'quality of service' has become represented as 'a prime determinant of service firms' competitive success or failure' (Fuller and Smith, 1991, p. 2), so the figure of 'the customer' has invaded the internal world of the service organization providing the rationale for new forms of organizational and personal conduct.

The customer has become implicated in the management of the firm, they argue, primarily because the perceived importance of quality service to securing profit poses a problem of organizational control for service employers.

Because labour effectiveness – the quality of interactive service offered by workers to customers – is now seen as crucial to organizational success, employers in services no longer believe they can simply force or order staff to produce it. As Fuller and Smith argue, old strategies of organizational governance, such as 'simple' or 'bureaucratic' control, can engender hostility amongst the staff who are charged with continually providing 'a good-natured, helpful and friendly attitude toward customers'. Because this task is now seen as crucial to the securing of surplus value or profit, new forms of control have been sought by employers which both enhance staff's self-direction of their own work while at the same time enabling employers to channel that 'self-direction' along the paths most appropriate to the production of increased profit. This is where the customer comes in. It is the use of customer feedback which employers hope will solve this dilemma of 'control'.

As the customer will provide the benchmark against which the worker's performance is to be judged, this is held to remove managers entirely from the 'control' equation. In this way, 'customers' are held to establish 'transparent' evaluations untainted by the hands of management. This is represented by management as 'pure' feedback (though of course the criteria of evaluation are management's own!). At the same time, the fact that customers can potentially evaluate the service interaction at any time may serve as a continuous, though invisible, check on service workers' conduct.

'The knowledge that any interaction could flair into an antagonistic encounter, if the worker fails to provide service that satisfies the customer, may shape and reshape a worker's behaviour' (ibid., 1991, p. 11). In this way, the presence of the customer helps to shape workers' relationship to their own conduct – to their mode of self-presentation – turning them into the self-governing subjects desired by service employers.

Although Fuller and Smith suggest that management by customers has major implications for the reconstruction of work identities, they do not make this the prime focus of their analysis. While they indicate the ways in which the links between workers, managers and customers have become both more complex and tightly interwoven, they are less interested in analysing the ways in which the important role allotted to the customer in the internal world of service organizations provides the rationale for the *cultural* reconstruction of work identities.

In the following section I make this cultural reconstruction my main focus of analysis, indicating the ways in which, through the medium of a variety of human technologies of interpersonal management, employees engaged in service work have been encouraged to develop particular pre-dispositions and capacities which are aimed at winning over the 'hearts and minds' of customers. In particular, I focus upon the ways in which employees in services are encouraged to assemble and deploy their own experience and identity as *consumers* in their paid work of delivering 'quality service' to customers.

4.1   Making up people at work

In her book, *The Managed Heart* (1983), the American sociologist Arlie Hochschild examined the ways in which flight attendants were trained to offer quality service to their passengers (see Reading A in **Shilling**, 1997). Hochschild termed this process one of **emotional labour** because it involved staff learning to manage their emotions in order to project a particular image of themselves – and the organization for which they work – and to produce a certain set of meanings for customers in order to ensure those customers continued to fly with that particular airline. Through their involvement in particular practices – such as role playing – airline staff were encouraged to put themselves in their customers' shoes, and to learn how to offer the sort of service they themselves would ideally like to receive. As part of this process of imaginative identification, employees were taught to view the arena in which they worked as their own 'home' into which customers came as their 'guests'. Thus, 'quality service' was represented as something that had to be learnt and as something that required *workers* to instrumentally assemble, manage and market aspects of their experience as *consumers*. Workers were not born with the capacity or disposition to provide 'quality service'. Rather they were worked on and in turn worked on themselves (including their bodily comportment) to become

emotional labour

the sorts of people that would offer quality service. In other words, they were **made up** as service workers.

making up people

This may seem to you like rather an odd phrase to use. So what does it mean? Well, on the one hand, 'making something up' suggests the construction of a fiction. But in what sense can the 'worker' be represented as a fictional character? On the other hand, the idea of being 'made up' suggests a material–cultural process of formation or transformation ('fashioning') whereby the adoption of certain habits or dispositions allows an individual to become – and become recognized as – a particular sort of person.

What both these versions of 'making up' share is a concern with 'invention'. They serve as a corrective to the tendency to regard a given activity or characteristic as in some sense 'natural'. As we saw earlier, what it means to be a worker has varied historically in relationship to shifting rationalities of organizational governance. Similarly, we also noted that the dispositions, actions and attributes that constitute 'work' have no essential or natural form and, for that reason, had to be approached as a series of historically and culturally specific assemblages. To be 'made up' – in the second sense of that term – as a 'worker' is therefore to acquire that particular assemblage of attributes and dispositions which defines a particular set of work activities at any given period or in any given context.

As we saw in Reading B, service workers are increasingly represented as self-directing subjects. If the 'emotional labour' of offering customers 'quality service' could not be fully secured or effectively guaranteed through a system of close supervision and formal rules, then other systems would have to be found which attempted to minimize the potential area of error in the exercise of employee discretion. Thus the emphasis of governing organizational life shifted away from formal direction as to how work must be done to 'implicit' expectations as to how work should be done; in other words, towards a system which Miller and Rose in Reading A termed 'government at a distance'.

When government takes place through close supervision and technical rules it is hardly a problem should the worker possess a distinct cultural identity. However, once government is operating through 'the worker's "normative orientations", the necessary control in work will depend on the removal of any basic cultural differences between him and his superiors [sic]' (Wickham, 1976, pp. 9–10, quoted in Townley, 1989, p. 106). In other words, this 'normative regulation' or 'government at a distance' rests on an identification between the individual employee and the goals and objectives of his or her employing organization. As Fuller and Smith (1991, p. 13) indicated in Reading B, employees need to 'become aware of their central role in adding value ... through quality labour and to be able automatically, as if by second nature, to balance competing demands for highly individualized quality-service delivery and bottom-line financial consideration'. Here the emphasis on direct control is transformed into an emphasis on culturally produced self-control. Thus the government of the service organization is now held to operate through the subjectivity of the individual employee.

So how precisely and practically is the self-directing service worker 'made up'? Through what technologies are the self-regulating capacities of service workers as subjects aligned with the organizational goal of maximizing quality service?

READING C

Now turn to the reading by Paul du Gay, entitled 'Adding value to yourself', reproduced as Reading C at the end of this chapter.

This is a brief extract from my own research work into the reconstruction of work identities in the British retailing industry during the 1980s and 1990s. This piece focuses upon the growing use of technologies of personal and interpersonal management in retailing and the ways in which these served to 'make up' retail workers as particular sorts of person.

As you read it, try to answer the following questions:

1   In what ways do these technologies cut across traditional divisions between work and non-work life?

2   What sort of presuppositions about human motivation are at work in the operation of these technologies?

3   How do these technologies work to implicate employees in the government of the organization for which they work?

As the examples cited in this reading indicate, traditional distinctions within British retailing between work and consumption, and between what is properly 'inside' and what 'outside' the orbit of the organization, are increasingly blurred by the introduction of these technologies of personal and interpersonal management. In every case, retail employees found themselves acting partly as consumers – whether through being made to provide a 'customer report' on the conduct of their line manager or through being trained to deploy their experience and knowledge as 'shoppers' in their 'work' of providing service.

These technologies, like those we examined earlier in the case of British Airways, are also infused or inscribed with certain presuppositions about human motivation. Once again, we can see the rationality of the 'enterprising self' at work. In the case of the Quality Team programme being introduced at Company A, for example, senior management indicated that they were acting on the assumption that people who feel they have more control over their work are more likely to work harder. The central word here was 'feel'. Senior management at Company A had absolutely no intention of surrendering their overall strategic control of the company. Rather, they were seeking to enhance that strategic control through a calculated redistribution of responsibility – what we might term a process of 'controlled de-control' – that would have the effect of making individual members of staff more personally liable for the economic success of the organization.

4.2   Services : a 'hybrid' identity

As we saw in Reading C, the technologies of personal and interpersonal management being introduced within contemporary British retailing are designed to stimulate and channel – to govern rather than repress – the subjectivity of employees. Thus, these technologies play their part in 'making up' the retail worker as a particular sort of person – as an enterprising subject. Through their training in transactional analysis, for example, employees are not only being taught how to produce meaning for customers and a sale for their company, they are also being taught to conduct themselves as certain sorts of person – as self-regulating, self-actualizing, responsible individual actors who are perpetually responsive to fluctuations in their environment. In this way, service work in occupations such as retailing concerns the simultaneous production of *profit*, of *meaning* and of *identity*. This observation holds for financial and commercial service work as much as it does for the more direct servicing work found in parts of the retail, hotel and tourist-related trades. In finance, for example, particularly merchant banking, the elements of communication, display and presentation are not simply restricted to the culture of the 'deal' (Michie, 1992). Financial

FIGURE 6.2 Managing the transaction: personal service in a British supermarket.

networks, especially global networks, are essentially socio-cultural networks in which 'relationship management' holds the key to profitable success. Insofar as global financial centres are effectively characterized by streams of information, each of which is open to interpretation and each with its own contacts, one of the significant skills within international finance is the ability to make and hold contacts, to construct relationships of trust, and to be part of the interpretation of what *is* really happening.

FIGURE 6.3   Maintaining trust in a major financial centre: the dealing floor of a large merchant bank.

As Nigel Thrift (1994), amongst others, has suggested, far from there being a reduction in the need for face-to-face contact as a consequence of the globalization of finance, there is now a greater emphasis on 'the presentation of self, face, work, negotiating skills ... because of the increasing requirement to be able to read people... because of the increasingly transactional nature of the business relationships between firms and clients'. Trust in this context is something that has to be continually worked on and actively maintained rather than simply assumed from one's standing.

Even if we take an example of service work which contrasts sharply with the customer-oriented services of global finance, that of contract security work, the qualities of display, communication and presentation are still crucial components (Allen and Pryke, 1994). Security work is reactive, whether on night or day shift. During the day, guards monitor arrivals and departures with a brief to control entry and exits. 'Emotional labour', however, is not a significant aspect of security work. The work of security is primarily performative – involving a standardized body and a range of ritualized and codified gestures. Security guards produce a controlled space simply through their uniformed presence. Being male and often over six foot in height adds to the performance and communicates authority. There are few spoken lines to the performance, as it is the body itself which signifies. In this instance, the skills involved are those of presentation management and they are as constitutive of the work in question as the forms of emotional labour and relationship management referred to earlier are of those different forms of service work.

In each of these instances, service work can be seen to be a peculiarly **hybrid** creation. Because contemporary service work is both an economic and a cultural phenomenon – the production of profit in services being intimately bound up with the production of meaning, with the 'signifying' work of presentation, communication, and display – the identity of services is simply not amenable to representation in terms of a binary divide between 'economics' on the one hand, and 'culture' on the other. Rather than being 'solely' either an 'economic' or a 'cultural' phenomenon, service work is a hybrid of both.

hybrid

FIGURE 6.4 Contract security: a different form of service work.

5 Conclusion: the cultural economy

At the beginning of this book we introduced you to the idea of the 'cultural economy'. Given the antipathy that has often been assumed to exist between the terms 'culture' and 'economics', the notion of the 'cultural economy' was intended to strike you as a little strange. We hope by now that you have begun to see why we attached such importance to it.

As we indicated earlier, we think it is a useful notion for three main reasons:

1   It suggests that the economic, just like any human domain of existence, is a cultural phenomenon. As we have argued throughout this book, what we think of as 'economic' processes depend on 'meaning' for their effects and have particular 'discursive' conditions of existence.

2   It indicates the ways in which the production of 'culture' in its contemporary manifestations cannot be divorced from industrial processes and forms of economic organization (see Chapters 1, 2 and 3 of this book). At the same time as elaborating this point, however, we have continually sought to show that the production of culture cannot be reduced to a question of 'economics' alone. Processes of production and systems of organization are themselves cultural phenomena in that they are assemblages of meaningful practices that construct certain ways for people to conceive of and conduct themselves at work. As we have seen in this chapter and Chapter 5, attempts to 'govern' organizational life operate through cultural practices – they are dependent upon particular modes of representation and construct specific forms of work-based identification.

3   It indicates the growing importance of 'culture' to doing business in the contemporary world. Throughout this book, we have noted how the conduct of contemporary economic life is increasingly 'culturalized'. As we saw in Chapters 1 and 4, more and more of the goods and services available for consumption are 'cultural' goods, in that they are inscribed with particular meanings and associations as they are produced and circulated in a conscious attempt to generate desire for them amongst consumers. The aestheticization of seemingly banal phenomena – such as stamps and bank accounts – indicates the extent to which we now live in an economy of 'signs'. The growing importance of signification does not end with the goods and services that corporations produce, however, for as we saw in Chapter 5, the internal life of organizations is increasingly the subject of cultural reconstruction. The cultural intermediaries of management consultancy are involved in attempts to change the meaning of organizational life and to reconstruct people's relationship with the work they perform.

The implications of their 'meaning-making' practices for the construction of work identity have been the specific focus of the present chapter. The chapter began by exploring the pitfalls of attempting to allocate an objective, essential, once-and-for-all meaning to work. Instead, it was suggested that the experience and identity of work are historically and culturally constructed. I argued that what it means to be a 'worker' or 'manager', or any other form of economic actor, varies across time and cultural context and has no suprahistorical essence or spirit. Rather it is the product of changes in ways or representing and acting upon – or governing – economic life.

Having delineated a particular way of thinking about the cultural construction of work identity, I moved on to examine how contemporary changes in the practices of governing economic life created new ways for people to conduct themselves at work. In section 3, I argued that new discourses of organizational reform attempted to transform the meaning and reality of work and to construct new forms of work-based identity. A particular focus of this section was the way in which contemporary discourses of organizational reform served to blur established differences between the spheres of production and consumption, work and leisure, creating certain similarities in the forms of conduct and modes of self-presentation required of people across a range of different domains.

In section 4, I explored some of the ways in which workers in certain service industries were being discursively constituted – or 'made up' – as enterprising subjects. I focused on services because it is in this sector that economic success is most visibly premised upon the production of meaning and where the constructions of what I termed 'hybrid' work identities is most pronounced. In other words, through analysing developments in this sector it is possible to see all the elements of our 'cultural economy' intersecting.

References

ALLEN, J. and DU GAY, P. (1994) 'Industry and the rest: the economic identity of services', *Work, Employment and Society,* Vol. 8, No. 2, pp. 255–71.

ALLEN, J. and PRYKE, M. (1994) 'The production of service space' in *Environment and Planning D, Society and Space*, Vol. 12, No. 4, pp. 453–76.

BALDAMUS, W. (1961) *Efficiency and Effort*, London, Tavistock.

BURCHELL, G. (1993) 'Liberal government and techniques of the self', *Economy and Society*, Vol. 22, No. 3, pp. 266–82.

BURCHELL, G., GORDON, C. and MILLER, P. (eds) (1991) *The Foucault Effect: studies in governmentality*, Brighton, Harvester Wheatsheaf.

CONNOLLY, W. (1991) *Identity/Difference*, New York, Cornell University Press.

COUSINS, M. and HUSSAIN, A. (1984) *Michel Foucault*, Basingstoke, Macmillan.

DONZELOT, J. (1991) 'The mobilization of society' in G. Burchell et al. (eds) *The Foucault Effect*, Brighton, Harvester Wheatsheaf, pp. 169–79.

DU GAY, P. and SALAMAN, G. (1992) 'The cult(ure) of the customer', *Journal of Management Studies*, Vol. 29, No. 4, pp. 616–33.

DU GAY, P. (1996) *Consumption and Identity at Work*, London, Sage.

FOUCAULT, M. (1972) *The Archaeology of Knowledge*, London, Tavistock.

FOUCAULT, M. (1980) *Power/Knowledge*, Brighton, Harvester Wheatsheaf.

FOUCAULT, M. (1982) 'The subject and power' in H. L. Dreyfus and P. Rabinow (eds), *Michel Foucault: beyond structuralism and hermeneutics*, Brighton, Harvester Wheatsheaf, pp. 208–26.

FREEDLAND, M. (1994) 'Government by contract and public law', *Public Law*, Spring, pp. 86–104.

FULLER, L. and SMITH, V. (1991) 'Consumers' reports: management by customers in a new economy', *Work, Employment and Society*, Vol. 5, No. 1, pp. 1–16.

GORDON, C. (1987) 'The soul of the citizen: Max Weber and Michel Foucault on rationality and government' in S. Whimster and S. Lash (eds), *Max Weber: Rationality and Modernity*, London, Allen and Unwin, pp. 293–316.

GORDON, C. (1991) 'Governmental rationality: an introduction' in Burchell et al., pp. 1–51.

HALL, S. (ed.) (1997) *Representation: cultural representations and signifying practices*, London, Sage/The Open University (Book 2 in this series).

HILL, S. (1991) 'How do you manage a flexible firm? The Total Quality model', *Work, Employment and Society*, Vol. 5, No. 3, pp. 397–415.

HOCHSCHILD, A. (1983) *The Managed Heart*, Los Angeles, University of California Press.

KANTER, R. M. (1990) *When Giants Learn to Dance*, London, Unwin Hyman.

KEAT, R. (1990) 'Introduction' in R. Keat and N. Abercrombie (eds), pp. 3–10.

KEAT, R. and ABERCROMBIE, N. (1990) *Enterprise Culture*, London, Routledge.

LACLAU, E. (1990) *New Reflections on the Revolution of our Time*, London, Verso.

MARSDEN, D. and RICHARDSON, R. (1994) 'Performing for pay? The effects of "merit pay" on motivation in the public service', *British Journal of Industrial Relations*, Vol. 32, No. 2, pp. 243–61.

MAUSS, M. (1979) *Sociology and Psychology*, London, Routledge and Kegan Paul.

MICHIE, R. C. (1992) *The City of London: continuity and change, 1850–1990*, London, Macmillan.

MILLER, P. and ROSE, N. (1990) 'Governing economic life', *Economy and Society*, Vol. 19, No. 1.

MILWARD, N., STEVENS, M., SMART, D. and HOWES, W. R. (1992) *Workplace Industrial Relations in Transition*, Aldershot, Dartmouth.

OSBORNE, D. and GAEBLER, T. (1992) *Re-inventing Government*, Reading, MA, Addison Wesley.

PATEMAN, C. (1989) *The Disorder of Women*, Cambridge, Polity Press.

ROSALDO, R. (1993) *Culture and Truth*, London, Routledge.

ROSE, N. (1990) *Governing the Soul: the shaping of the private self*, London, Routledge.

SABEL, C. (1991) 'Moebius strip organizations and open labour markets: some consequences of the reintegration of conception and execution in a volatile economy', in P. Bourdieu and J.S. Coleman (eds) *Social Theory for a Changing Society*, Boulder, CO, Westview Press, pp. 23–54.

SHILLING, C. (1997) 'The body and difference' in Woodward, K. (ed.) Ch. 2.

THRIFT, N. (1994) 'On the social and cultural determinants of international financial centres: the case of the City of London' in S. Corbridge, R. Martin and N. Thrift (eds) *Money, Space and Power*, Cambridge, Blackwell.

TOWNLEY, G. (1989) 'Selection and appraisal: reconstituting social relations?' in J. Storey (ed.), *New Perspectives in Human Resource Management*, London, Routledge, pp. 92–108.

WOODWARD, K. (ed.) (1997) *Identity and Difference*, London, Sage/The Open University (Book 3 in this series).

WRIGHT, P. (1987) 'Excellence', *London Review of Books*, May, pp. 8–11.

READING A:
Peter Miller and Nikolas Rose,
'Governing economic life'

[...]

First, let us consider the notion of government. Michel Foucault argued that a certain *mentality*, that he termed 'governmentality', had become the common ground of all modern forms of political thought and action. Governmentality, he argued, was an 'ensemble formed by the institutions, procedures, analyses and reflections, the calculations and tactics, that allow the exercise of this very specific, albeit complex form of power' (Foucault, 1979, p. 20). And, he claimed, since the eighteenth century *population* had appeared as the terrain *par excellence* of government. Authorities have addressed themselves to the regulation of the processes proper to the population, the laws that modulate its wealth, health, longevity, its capacity to wage war and to engage in labour and so forth. Thus, he implies, societies like our own are characterized by a particular way of *thinking* about the kinds of problems that can and should be addressed by various authorities. They operate within a kind of political *a priori* that allows the tasks of such authorities to be seen in terms of the calculated supervision, administration and maximization of the forces of each and all.

This way of investigating the exercise of political rule has a number of advantages. Firstly, it refuses the reduction of political power to the actions of a State, the latter construed as a relatively coherent and calculating political subject. Instead of viewing rule in terms of a State that extends its sway throughout society by means of a ramifying apparatus of control, the notion of government draws attention to the diversity of forces and groups that have, in heterogeneous ways, sought to regulate the lives of individuals and the conditions within particular national territories in pursuit of various goals. Rather than 'the State' giving rise to government, the State becomes a particular form that government has taken, and one that does not exhaust the field of calculations and interventions that constitute it.

It is to the analysis of these aspirations and attempts that the notion of government directs us. This path may appear to lead, in a rather idiosyncratic way, to a familiar and well-trodden field – that of the historical and contemporary analysis of economic and social policy. However, the apparent familiarity of these concerns is likely to mislead. It is true that the earliest forms of governmentality in Europe went under the name of the science of 'police', and that 'police' and 'policy' share a common root. But the analysis of policy suggested by the concept of government implies that the very existence of a field of concerns termed 'policy' should itself be treated as something to be explained. It draws attention to the fundamental role that knowledges play in rendering aspects of existence thinkable and calculable, and amenable to deliberated and planful initiatives: a complex *intellectual* labour involving not only the invention of new forms of thought, but also the invention of novel procedures of documentation, computation and evaluation. It suggests that we need to consider under what ethical conditions it became possible for different authorities to consider it legitimate, feasible and even necessary to conduct such interventions. It suggests that the concerns that have occasioned and animated policy are not self-evident. The emergence of unemployment, crime, disease and poverty as 'problems' that can be identified and construed as in need of amelioration is itself something to be explained. It points to the diversity of the groupings that have problematized such aspects of existence in relation to social and political concerns, and that have developed and sought to implement policies. These are not just 'political' authorities, in the traditional sense, but also those whose basis is intellectual, spiritual, and so forth. It implies that there is no smooth path of development of evolution of policies, but that the lasting inventions have often arisen in surprising and aleatory fashion and in relation to apparently marginal or obscure difficulties in social or economic existence, which for particular reasons have come to assume political salience for a brief period.

Hence the notion of government highlights the diversity of powers and knowledges entailed in rendering fields practicable and amenable to intervention. It suggests that the analysis of 'policy' cannot be confined to the study of different administrative agencies, their interests, funding, administrative organization and the like. A complex and heterogeneous assemblage of conditions thus makes it possible for objects of policy to be problematized, and rendered amenable to administration.

Of course, these dimensions can be studied, and have been studied, without drawing upon the notion of government. But the approach suggested by these writings of Michel Foucault has two further features that we consider important. Policy studies tend to be concerned with evaluating policies, uncovering the factors that led to their success in achieving their objectives or, more usually, deciphering the simplifications, misunderstandings, miscalculations and strategic errors that led to their failure (e.g. Williams et al., 1986). We, on the other hand, are not concerned with evaluations of this type, with making judgements as to whether and why this or that policy succeeded or failed, or with devising remedies for alleged deficiencies (cf. Thompson, 1987). Rather, we are struck by the fact that this very form of thinking is a characteristic of 'governmentality': policies always appear to be surrounded by more or less systematized attempts to adjudicate on their vices or virtues, and are confronted with other policies promising to achieve the same ends by improved means, or advocating something completely different. Evaluation, that is to say, is something internal to the phenomena we wish to investigate. For us, this imperative to evaluate needs to be viewed as itself a key component of the forms of political thought under discussion: how authorities and administrators make judgements, the conclusions that they draw from them, the rectifications they propose and the impetus that 'failure' provides for the propagation of new programmes of government.

'Evaluation' of policy, in a whole variety of forms, is thus integral to what we term the *programmatic* character of governmentality. Governmentality is programmatic not simply in that one can see the proliferation of more or less explicit programmes for reforming reality – government reports, white papers, green papers, papers from business, trade unions, financiers, political parties, charities and academics proposing this or that scheme for dealing with this or that problem. It is also programmatic in that it is characterized by an eternal optimism that a domain or a society could be administered better or more effectively, that reality is, in some way or other, programmable (cf.

Gordon, 1987; MacIntyre, 1981; Miller and O'Leary, 1989b; Rose and Miller, 1988). Hence the 'failure' of one policy or set of policies is always linked to attempts to devise or propose programmes that would work better, that would deliver economic growth, productivity, low inflation, full employment or the like. Whilst the identification of failure is thus a central element in governmentality, an analysis of governmentality is not itself a tool for social programmers. To analyse what one might term 'the will to govern' is not to enthusiastically participate in it.

The discursive character of governmentality

Governmentality has a discursive character: to analyse the conceptualizations, explanations and calculations that inhabit the governmental field requires an attention to language. There is nothing novel in the suggestion that language and politics are interrelated, nor even in the suggestion that the relation between the two is neither one of simple homology or reflection, nor one of ideological mystification, but is mutually constitutive (e.g. Shapiro, 1984; Connelly, 1987; Taylor, 1987). In relation to economic policy, a number of studies have directly addressed the discursive constitution of the domain and the component parts of the economy. They have demonstrated the conceptual conditions under which it came to be possible to conceive of a specifically economic domain composed of various economic entities with their own laws and processes that were amenable to rational knowledge and calculation, and hence to various forms of regulatory intervention (Burchell et al., 1985; Hopwood, 1987; Loft, 1986; Tribe, 1978; Thompson, 1982; Tomlinson, 1981a, 1981b, 1983). [...]

Our approach has much in common with this. But we would like to place these concerns within a rather different framework. On the one hand, we suggest that policy should be located within a wider discursive field in which conceptions of the proper ends and means of government are articulated: an analysis of what Michel Foucault terms 'political rationalities'. On the other hand, we argue for a view of 'discourse' as a technology of thought, requiring attention to the particular technical devices of writing, listing, numbering and computing that render a realm into discourse as a knowable, calculable and administrable object.

'Knowing' an object in such a way that it can be governed is more than a purely speculative activity: it requires the invention of procedures of notation, ways of collecting and presenting statistics, the transportation of these to centres where calculations and judgements can be made and so forth. It is through such procedures of inscription that the diverse domains of 'governmentality' are made up, that 'objects' such as the economy, the enterprise, the social field and the family are rendered in a particular conceptual form and made amenable to intervention and regulation.

[...]

All government depends on a particular mode of 'representation': the elaboration of a language for depicting the domain in question that claims both to grasp the nature of that reality represented, and literally to represent it in a form amenable to political deliberation, argument and scheming. This gives us a clue to a further way in which language is significant for government. For it is in language that *programmes of government* are elaborated, and through which a consonance is established between the broadly specified ethical, epistemological and ontological appeals of political discourse – to the nation, to virtue, to what is or is not possible or desirable – and the plans, schemes and objectives that seek to address specific problematizations within social, economic or personal existence. For example, in the early years of this century in Britain, the language of national efficiency served both to establish the proper role of government and the kinds of problems that it could and should address, to organize disputes between different political forces, and to articulate a range of different programmes that addressed themselves to managing specific aspects of the economic life and health of the population (Miller and O'Leary, 1987; Rose, 1985). Language here serves as a *translation mechanism* between the general and the particular, establishing a kind of identity or mutuality between political rationalities and regulatory aspirations.

The forms of political discourse characteristic of 'governmentality' open a particular space for theoretical arguments and the truth claims that they entail. The government of a population, a national economy, an enterprise, a family, a child, or even oneself becomes possible only through discursive mechanisms that represent the domain to be governed as an intelligible field with its limits, characteristics whose component parts are linked together in some more or less systematic manner (Burchell et al. 1985; Hopwood, 1984, 1985, 1986; Miller, 1989; Miller and O'Leary, 1989a; Rose, 1990). Before one can seek to manage a domain such as an economy it is first necessary to conceptualize a set of processes and relations as an economy which is amenable to management. The birth of a language of national economy as a domain with its own characteristics, laws and processes that could be spoken about and about which knowledge could be gained enabled it to become an element in programmes which could seek to evaluate and increase the power of nations by governing and managing 'the economy'. 'Government' that is to say, is always dependent on knowledge, and proponents of diverse programmes seek to ground themselves in a positive knowledge of that which is to be governed, ways of reasoning about it, analysing it and evaluating it, identifying its problems and devising solutions. Theories here do not merely legitimate existing power relations but actually constitute new sectors of reality and make new fields of existence practicable. Hence, as well as establishing the place of certain objects and problems within the legitimate obligations and powers of rulers, and enabling them to be formulated programmatically, it is through language that governmental fields are composed, rendered thinkable and manageable.

In drawing attention to the role of language in government in this way, we do not wish to suggest that the analysis of political power should become a sub-department of the history of ideas, nor that our concern should be with the problem of meaning. The features of language that we have described have a more active role than this, one perhaps best captured in the term *intellectual technology*. Language, that is to say, provides a mechanism for rendering reality amenable to certain kinds of action. And language, in this sense, is more than merely 'contemplative': describing a world such that it is amenable to having certain things done to it involves inscribing reality in the calculations of government through a range of material and rather mundane techniques (Rose, 1988; cf. Latour, 1987a). The events and phenomena to which government is to be applied must be rendered into information – written reports, drawings, pictures, numbers, charts, graphs, statistics. This information must be of a particular form – stable, mobile, combinable and comparable. This form enables the pertinent features of the domain – types of goods, investments, ages of persons, health, criminality, etc. – to literally be re-presented in the place where decisions are to be made about them (the manager's office, the war room, the case conference and so forth). From the eighteenth-century invention of statistics as the science of state, to the present attempts to evaluate the economic life of the nation by measuring the money supply or the efficiency of health services by turning their endeavours into cash equivalents, programmes of government have depended upon the construction of devices for the inscription of reality in a form where it can be debated and diagnosed. Information in this sense is not the outcome of a neutral recording function. It is itself a way of acting upon the real, a way of devising techniques for inscribing it (birth rates, accounts, tax returns, case notes) in such a way as to make the domain in question susceptible to evaluation, calculation and intervention.

The technologies of government

'Government', of course, is not only a matter of representation. It is also a matter of intervention. The specificity of governmentality, as it has taken shape in 'the West' over the last two centuries, lies in this complex interweaving of procedures for representing and intervening (cf. Hacking, 1983). We suggest that these attempts to instrumentalize government and make it operable also have a kind of 'technological' form (cf. Foucault, 1986; pp. 225–6). If political rationalities render reality into the domain of thought, these '*technologies of government*' seek to translate thought into the domain of reality, and to establish 'in the world of persons and things' spaces and devices for acting upon those entities of which they dream and scheme.

We use the term 'technologies' to suggest a particular approach to the analysis of the activity of ruling, one which pays great attention to the actual mechanisms through which authorities of various sorts have sought to shape, normalize and instrumentalize the conduct, thought, decisions and aspirations of others in order to achieve the objectives they consider desirable. To understand

modern forms of rule, we suggest, requires an investigation not merely of grand political schema, or economic ambitions, nor even of general slogans such as 'state control', nationalization, the free market and the like, but apparently humble and mundane mechanisms which appear to make it possible to govern: techniques of notation, computation and calculation, procedures of examination and assessment; the invention of devices such as surveys and presentational forms such as tables; the standardization of systems for training and the inculcation of habits; the inauguration of professional specialisms and vocabularies; building design and architectural forms – the list is heterogeneous and is, in principle, unlimited.

[...]

It is through technologies that political rationalities and the programmes of government they articulate become capable of deployment. But this should not be understood simply as a matter of the 'implementation' of ideal schemes in the real, still less as the extension of control from the seat of power into the minutiae of existence. By drawing attention to the technological dimension of government, we do not mean to summon up an image of a 'totally administered society'. It is true that, in certain European countries, the early versions of 'police' were inspired by the utopian dream that all regions of the social body could be penetrated, known and directed by political authorities. But, as Michel Foucault has pointed out, nineteenth-century liberalism marks the point from which this dream was abandoned in those nations that called themselves liberal democracies. The problem became, instead, one of governing a territory and a population that were independent realities with inherent processes and forces. With the emergence of such an idea of 'society', the question became 'How is government possible? That is, what is the principle of limitation that applies to governmental actions such that things will occur for the best, in conformity with the rationality of government, and without intervention' (Foucault, 1986, p. 242).

It is for these reasons that we have suggested the need for the analysis of the 'indirect' mechanisms of rule that are of such importance in liberal democratic societies: those that have enabled, or have sought to enable *government at a distance*. In conceptualizing such indirect mechanisms by which rule is brought about, we adapt for our own ends Bruno Latour's notion of 'action at a distance' (Latour, 1987b, pp. 219 ff). He develops this notion in answering the question 'how is it possible to act on events, places and people that are unfamiliar and a long way away?' Eighteenth-century French navigators could only travel to unfamiliar regions of the East Pacific, colonize, domesticate and dominate the inhabitants from their European metropolitan bases because, in various technical ways, these distant places were 'mobilized', brought home to 'centres of calculation' in the form of maps, drawings, readings of the movements of the tides and the stars. Mobile traces that were stable enough to be moved back and forward without distortion, corruption or decay, and combinable so that they could be accumulated and calculated upon, enabled the ships to be sent out and to return, enabled a 'centre' to be formed that could 'dominate' a realm of persons and processes distant from it. This process, he suggests, is similar whether it is a question of dominating the sky, the earth or the economy; domination involves the exercise of a form of intellectual mastery made possible by those at a centre having information about persons and events distant from them.

[...]

'Governmentality' is embodied in innumerable deliberate attempts to invent, promote, install and operate mechanisms of rule that will shape the investment decisions of managers or the child care decisions of parents in accordance with programmatic aspirations. But such attempts are rarely implanted unscathed, and are seldom adjudged to have achieved what they set out to do. Whilst 'governmentality' is eternally optimistic, 'government' is a congenitally failing operation. The world of programmes is heterogeneous and rivalrous, and the solutions for one programme tend to be the problems for another. 'Reality' always escapes the theories that inform programmes and the ambitions that underpin them; it is too unruly to be captured by any perfect knowledge. Technologies produce unexpected problems, are utilized for their own ends by those who are supposed to merely operate them, are hampered by underfunding, professional rivalries,

and the impossibility of producing the technical conditions that would make them work – reliable statistics, efficient communication systems, clear lines of command, properly designed buildings, well framed regulations or whatever. Unplanned outcomes emerge from the intersection of one technology with another, or from the unexpected consequences of putting a technique to work. Contrariwise, techniques invented for one purpose may find their governmental role for another, and the unplanned conjunction of techniques and conditions arising from very different aspirations may allow something to work without or despite its explicit rationale. The 'will to govern' needs to be understood less in terms of its success than in terms of the difficulties of operationalizing it.

[...]

In the remainder of this paper, we wish to illustrate some of the mechanisms to which we have drawn attention by means of a number of examples. None of these is intended as an exhaustive historical account of policy development and implementation, let alone an evaluation of policies or the politics behind them. Our concern is with 'governmentality' in the sense in which we have discussed it above, with the mentalities that have constituted the changing attempts to modulate economic activity, the varying vocabularies through which economic activity has been rendered thinkable, the different problems that have concerned them, the role of intellectual technologies of theorization and inscription within them, the diversity of regulatory technologies that have been invented together with the difficulties of implanting them and the key role that has been taken by expertise.

[...]

Governing the psychological world of the enterprise

Governing involves not just the ordering of activities and processes. Governing operates through subjects. The individual manager who comes to think of investments in terms of the discounting of future cash flows is a resource for a strategy of government oriented toward economic growth. Government to that extent is a 'personal' matter, and many programmes have sought the key to their effectiveness in enrolling individuals as allies in the pursuit of political, economic and social objectives. To the extent that authoritative norms, calculative technologies and forms of evaluation can be translated into the values, decisions and judgements of citizens in their professional and personal capacities, they can function as part of the 'self-steering' mechanisms of individuals. Hence 'free' individuals and 'private' spaces can be 'ruled' without breaching their formal autonomy. To this end, many and varied programmes have placed a high value upon the capacities of subjects, and a range of technologies have sought to act on the personal capacities of subjects – as producers, consumers, parents and citizens, organizing and orienting them in the decisions and actions that seem most 'personal', and that confront them in the multitude of everyday tasks entailed in managing their own existence.

Experts have played a key role here. They have elaborated the arguments that the personal capacities of individuals can be managed in order to achieve socially desirable goals – health, adjustment, profitability and the like. They have latched on to existing political concerns, suggesting that they have the capacity to ameliorate problems and achieve benefits. They have allied themselves with other powerful social authorities, in particular businessmen, translating their 'lay' problems into expert languages and suggesting that rational knowledges and planned techniques hold the key to success. They have problematized new aspects of existence and, in the very same moment, suggested that they can help overcome the problems that they have discovered. And they have acted as powerful translation devices between 'authorities' and 'individuals', shaping conduct not through compulsion but through the power of truth, the potency of rationality and the alluring promises of effectivity.

Again, we will take our examples from economic life, focusing here upon the internal world of the enterprise and the management of the productive subject. The government of economic life across the twentieth century has entailed a range of attempts to shape and modulate the relations that individuals have with society's productive apparatus (Miller, 1986b; Rose, 1990). In the process, the activities of individuals as producers

have become the object of knowledge and the target of expertise, and a complex web of relays has been formed through which the economic endeavours of politicians and businessmen have been translated into the personal capacities and aspirations of subjects.

[...]

Governing the autonomous self

The forms of political rationality that took shape in the first half of this century constituted the citizen as a social being whose powers and obligations were articulated in the language of social responsibilities and collective solidarities. The individual was to be integrated into society in the form of a citizen with social needs, in a contract in which individual and society had mutual claims and obligations. A diversity of programmes for social security, child welfare, physical and mental hygiene, universal education and even for the form and content of popular entertainment operated within this rationale and numerous technologies were invented – from social insurance to the child guidance clinic – that sought to give effect to it.

Whilst the decade or so after the Second World War may be seen as the culmination of this period, marked by attempts to weld these diverse programmes and technologies into a coherent and centrally directed system, the past decade has seen an apparently decisive displacement of these political rationalities. Not only within the revived vocabulary of neo-liberalism, but also in many of the political programmes articulated from the centre and the left of the political field as well as from radical critics of the present, the language of freedom and autonomy has come to regulate arguments over the legitimate means and ends of political power.

No longer is citizenship construed in terms of solidarity, contentment, welfare and a sense of security established through the bonds of organizational and social life. Citizenship is to be active and individualistic rather than passive and dependent. The political subject is henceforth to be an individual whose citizenship is manifested through the free exercise of personal choice amongst a variety of options (cf. Meyer, 1986). Programmes of government are to be evaluated in terms of the extent to which they enhance that choice. And the language of individual freedom, personal choice and self-fulfilment has come to underpin programmes of government articulated from across the political spectrum, from politicians and professionals, pressure groups and civil libertarians alike.

This new political language may be seen as an ephemeral phenomenon, as ideology, or as merely a reprise on the atomistic individualism characteristic of capitalism. However the perspective we have sketched out in this paper would suggest a different approach, one that emphasized the manner in which this new language served not only to articulate and legitimate a diversity of programmes for rectifying problematic areas of economic and social life, but also enabled these programmes to be translated into a range of technologies to administer individuals, groups and sectors in a way that was consonant with prevailing ethical systems and political mentalities (Rose, 1989b). We can illustrate this by focusing upon one particular notion that has been so central to the doctrines of the new right in Britain, Europe and America – that of 'enterprise'.

The language of enterprise has become so significant, we suggest, because it enables a translatability between the most general *a priori* of political thought and a range of specific programmes for administering the national economy, the internal world of the firm and a whole host of other organizations from the school to the hospital. But further, it enables such programmes to accord a new priority to the self-regulating capacities of individuals (cf. Gordon, 1987). At the level of the macro-economy, the argument that an economy structured in the form of relations of exchange between discrete economic units pursuing their undertakings with confidence and energy will produce the most social goods and distribute them in the manner most advantageous to each and to all has not spelt an end to programmes for the 'government' of economic life. Rather it has given rise to all manner of programmes for reforming economic activity in order to construct such a virtuous system, and to a plethora of new regulatory technologies that have sought to give effect to them (see Thompson, 1990; Rose and Miller, 1989).

Within these rationalities, new relations can be formed between the economic health of the nation and the 'private' choices of individuals. The citizen is now assigned a vital economic role in his or her activity as a consumer. To maintain the economic health of the societies of the west, construed both in terms of budgetary discipline and high levels of employment, a constant expansion in consumption is required. Economies are successful to the extent that they can promote this, at one and the same time proliferating and differentiating needs, producing products aligned to them and ensuring the purchasing capacity to enable acts of consumption to occur. However, whilst the language of the consumer and consumer responsiveness structures political argument, providing the rationale for programmes of reform in domains as diverse as the organization of the car industry, delivery of health care and the organization of water and sewage systems, consumption is itself shaped by a differentiated range of practices and techniques whose mentalities are not those of government but of profit. This reveals the extent to which certain conditions of existence are necessary for particular political rationalities to be made operable. In this case, the rationalities of autonomy have become operable, in part, because of the emergence of a plethora of discourses and practices for shaping and regulating the conduct, choices and desires of individuals: popular television and entertainment, and particularly the transformation of the world of goods through expert techniques of product differentiation, targeting and marketing.

Thus whilst the aim of maximizing consumption may be a matter of state, the executive power operates in an indirect manner upon it, by policies on advertising, interest rates, credit and the like. The language of enterprise again forms a kind of matrix for thought here, consumers being considered as, in a sense, entrepreneurs of themselves, seeking to maximize their 'quality of life' through the artful assembly of a 'life-style' put together through the world of goods. Within this politico-ethical environment, the expertise of market research, of promotion and communication, provides the relays through which the aspirations of ministers, the ambitions of business and the dreams of consumers achieve mutual translatability. Design, marketing and image construction play a vital role in the transfiguring of goods into desires and vice versa, imbuing each commodity with a 'personal' meaning, a glow cast back upon those who purchase it, illuminating the kind of person they are, or want to become. Product innovation and consumer demand are connected through the webs of meaning through which they are related, the phantasies of efficacy and the dreams of pleasure which guide both. Through this loose assemblage of agents, calculations, techniques, images and commodities, consumer choice can be made an ally of economic growth: economic life can be governed through the choices consumers make in their search for personally fulfilling forms of existence.

The rationalities of personal autonomy and self-fulfilment are also linked to a transformation in programmes and technologies for regulating the internal world of the enterprise (e.g. Peters and Waterman, 1982; see Rose, 1990). Once again, expertise plays a vital translating role, promising to align general politico-ethical principles, the goals of industry and the self-regulatory activities of individuals. The vocabulary of enterprise provides versatile tools for thought: the worker is no longer construed as a social creature seeking satisfaction of his or her need for security, solidarity and welfare, but as an individual actively seeking to shape and manage his or her own life in order to maximize its returns in terms of success and achievement. Thus the vocabulary of entrepreneurship does not merely seek to shape the way bosses calculate and activate business strategies in the external world of the market, but also can be formulated by the experts of management into a new set of techniques for ensuring business success. In these programmes, the world of the enterprise is reconceptualized as one in which productivity is to be enhanced, quality assured and innovation fostered through the active engagement of the self-fulfilling impulses of the employee from lowliest worker to highest manager, aligning personal desires with the objectives of the firm. Organizations are to get the most out of their employees, not by managing group relations to maximize contentment, or by rationalizing management to ensure efficiency, but by releasing the psychological strivings of individuals for autonomy and creativity and channelling them into the search of the firm for

excellence and success. Psychological consultants to the organization provide the techniques for charting the cultural world of the enterprise in terms of its success in capitalizing upon the motivations and aspirations of its inhabitants. And these experts have invented a whole range of new technologies in order to give effect to these programmes, techniques for promoting motivation through constructing a regime of values within the firm, for reducing dependency by reorganizing management structures, for encouraging internal competitiveness by small group working, for stimulating individual entrepreneurship by new forms of staff evaluation and reward.

The 'autonomous' subjectivity of the productive individual has become a central economic resource; such programmes promise to turn autonomy into an ally of economic success and not an obstacle to be controlled and disciplined. The self-regulating capacities of individuals are to be aligned with economic objectives through the kinds of loose and indirect mechanisms that we have described earlier: the capacities of language to translate between manager, programmes, technologies and self-regulatory techniques, and the particular persuasive role of expertise. Significantly, these programmes do not merely seek to instrumentalize the aspirations of workers, but also seek to act upon the selves of managers. There is no opposition between the modes of self-presentation required of the manager and the ethics of the personal self, indeed becoming a better manager is to become a better self, and innumerable training courses and seminars operate in these terms. The values of self-realization, the skills of self-presentation, self-direction and self-management are both personally seductive and economically desirable. Again, expertise plays the role of relay, teaching managers the arts of self-realization that will fulfil them as individuals as well as employees. Economic success, career progress and personal development intersect in this new expertise of autonomous subjectivity.

No doubt there is a considerable discrepancy between the images portrayed in the proliferating texts written along these lines, and the reality of the practices of management. And, no doubt, the promises of this new generation of programmers of the enterprise will soon be deemed to have failed: increased productivity, improved flexibility and enhanced competitiveness will still prove elusive goals. But it is more than ideology that can be observed here. As with the previous illustrations, what is at issue here is the establishing of connections and symmetries, at both the conceptual and practical level, between political concerns about the government of the productive life of the nation, the concerns of owners of capital to maximize the economic advantages of their companies, and techniques for the governing of the subject. Expertises of the enterprise play a crucial role in linking up these distinct concerns into a functioning network. Their languages and techniques provide both the necessary distance between political authorities and organizational life, and the translatability to establish an alliance between national economic health, increased organizational effectiveness, and progressive and humanistic values.

The rapprochement of the self-actualization of the worker with the competitive advancement of the company enables an alignment between the technologies of work and technologies of subjectivity. For the entrepreneurial self, work is no longer necessarily a constraint upon the freedom of the individual to fulfil his or her potential through strivings for autonomy, creativity and responsibility. Work is an essential element in the path to self-realization. There is no longer any barrier between the economic, the psychological and the social. The government of work now passes through the psychological strivings of each and every individual for fulfilment.

References

BURCHELL, S., CLUBB, C. and HOPWOOD, A. G. (1985) 'Accounting in its social context: towards a history of value added in the United Kingdom', *Accounting, Organizations and Society*, pp. 381–413.

CONNELLY, W. (1987) 'Appearance and reality in politics' in M.T. Gibbons (ed.), *Interpreting Politics*, Oxford, Basil Blackwell.

FOUCAULT, M. (1979) 'On governmentality', *I & C*, Vol. 6, pp. 5–22

FOUCAULT, M. (1986) 'Space, knowledge and power' in P. Rabinow (ed.), *The Foucault Reader*, Harmondsworth, Penguin.

GORDON, C. (1987) 'The soul of the citizen: Max Weber and Michel Foucault on rationality and government' in S. Lash and S. Whimster, *Max Weber, Rationality and Modernity*, London, Allen & Unwin.

HACKING, I. (1983) *Representing and Intervening*, London, Cambridge University Press.

HOPWOOD, A. G. (1984) 'Accounting and the pursuit of efficiency' in A.G. Hopwood and C. Tomkins, *Issues in Public Sector Accounting*, Oxford, Philip Allan.

HOPWOOD, A. G. (1985) 'Accounting and the domain of the public: some observations on current developments', The Price Waterhouse Public Lecture on Accounting, University of Leeds. Reprinted in A.G. Hopwood (1988) *Accounting from the Outside: the collected papers of Anthony G. Hopwood*, New York and London, Garland.

HOPWOOD, A. G. (1986) 'Management accounting and organizational action: an introduction' in M. Bromwich and A.G. Hopwood (eds) *Research and Current Issues in Management Accounting*, London, Pitman.

HOPWOOD, A. G. (1987) 'The archaeology of accounting systems', *Accounting, Organizations and Society*, pp. 207–34.

LATOUR, B. (1987a) 'Visualization and cognition: thinking with eyes and hands', *Knowledge and Society: studies in the sociology of culture, past and present*, Vol. 6, pp. 1–40.

LATOUR, B. (1987b) *Science in Action*, Milton Keynes, Open University Press.

LOFT, A. (1986) 'Towards a critical understanding of accounting: the case of cost accounting in the U.K.', *Accounting, Organizations and Society*, pp. 137–69.

MACINTYRE, A. (1981) *After virtue: a study in moral theory*, London, Duckworth.

MEYER, J. (1986) 'The self and the life course: institutionalization and its effects' in A. Sorensen, F. Weinert and L. Sherrod (eds) *Human Development and the Life Course*, Hillsdale, NJ, L. Erlbaum.

MILLER, P. (1986) 'Psychotherapy of work and unemployment' in P. Miller and N. Rose (eds), *The Power of Psychiatry*, Cambridge, Polity Press.

MILLER, P. (1989) 'Managing economic growth through knowledge: the promotion of discounted cash flow techniques', working paper.

MILLER, P. and O'LEARY, T. (1987) 'Accounting and the construction of the governable person', *Accounting, Organizations and Society*, pp. 235–65.

MILLER, P. and O'LEARY, T. (1989a) 'Hierarchies and American ideals, 1900–1940', *Academy of Management Review*, pp. 250–65.

MILLER, P. and O'LEARY, T. (1989b) 'Accounting expertise and the entrepreneurial society: new rationalities of calculation', paper presented at Conference on Accounting and the Humanities, University of Iowa, September 1989.

PETERS, T. J. and WATERMAN, R. H. (1982) *In Search of Excellence*, New York, Harper & Row.

ROSE, N. (1985) *The Psychological Complex: psychology, politics and society in England 1869–1939*, London, Routledge & Kegan Paul.

ROSE, N. (1988) 'Calculable minds and manageable individuals' *History of the Human Sciences*, vol. 1, pp. 179–200.

ROSE, N. (1989) 'Governing the enterprising self', paper presented at Conference on the Values of the Enterprise Culture, University of Lancaster, September 1989.

ROSE, N. (1990) *Governing the Soul: the shaping of the private self*, London, Routledge.

ROSE, N. and MILLER, P. (1989) 'Rethinking the state: governing economic, social and personal life', working paper (available from the authors on request).

SHAPIRO, M. (ed.) (1984) *Language and Politics*, Oxford, Blackwell.

TAYLOR, C. (1987) 'Language and human nature' in M.T. Gibbons (ed.), *Interpreting Politics*, Oxford, Basil Blackwell.

THOMPSON, G. (1990) *The Political Economy of the New Right*.

TOMLINSON, J. (1981a) 'Why was there never a "Keynesian Revolution" in economic policy', *Economy and Society*, Vol. 10, pp. 73–87.

TOMLINSON, J. (1981b) *Problems of British Economic Policy 1700–1945*, London, Methuen.

TOMLINSON, J. (1983) 'Where do economic policy objectives come from? The case of full employment', *Economy and Society*, Vol. 12, pp. 48–65.

TRIBE, K. (1978) *Land, Labour and Economic Discourse*, London, Routledge and Kegan Paul.

WILLIAMS, K. et al. (1986) 'Accounting for failure in the nationalised enterprises: coal, steel and cars since 1970', *Economy and Society*, Vol. 15, pp. 167–219.

Source: Miller and Rose, 1990, pp. 1–31.

READING B:
Linda Fuller and Vicki Smith, 'Consumers' reports: management by customers in a changing economy'

Introduction

There is growing consensus among sociologists and industrial relations experts that macro-economic changes of the 1980s have led employers to change the organization of the American workplace in fundamental ways. Researchers use various conceptualizations to describe these broad economic changes, ranging from 'the permanently new economy' (Ritzer, 1989) to 'postindustrial capitalism' (Heydebrand, 1989) and 'the new rules of competition' (Hage, 1988). Referring to a core set of phenomena, such as increased competition from foreign industry, a more quality-conscious consumer population, rapidly changing product markets, deregulation and new technologies, these changes have prompted US industrial and service sector firms to seek new ways to increase their productivity and competitiveness (Hage, 1988; Heydebrand, 1989; Schoenberger, 1989; Wood, 1989).

In this paper we explore how competitive pressures resulting from such factors have affected strategies of control in the workplaces of 'interactive service employees' (Leidner, 1988) whose primary job task is directly serving customers. The category of interactive service work encompasses a large group of workers, in many different industries, whose jobs display wide variation in terms of routinization and amount of customer interaction. At one extreme are fast food workers and telephone operators, at the other are workers in the child care, automobile sales and service, and financial industries.

We argue that the strategies managers use to control interactive service workers are linked to their objective of eliciting *quality service work*. To encourage quality service work, service employers must look for management methods that de-emphasize obtrusive managerial or bureaucratic control and give greater leeway to employees when working with customers. One such method is the utilization of consumer feedback to manage employees. Consumer feedback has been used by

companies in the past but, we argue, may become more important as managers increasingly perceive the customer/worker interaction to be a source of profitability.

Quality of service and theories of control

As pressures for profitability in the service sector have increased, service firms have been forced to search for new ways to compete for customers. One of these has been to stress not only the content of services but also their quality (Hochschild, 1983; Noyelle, 1987; Albrecht, 1988; Hirschhorn, 1988). A corporate ideology of quality has emerged, reflected in managerial assertions that customers' loyalty depends on the treatment they receive from service workers, as well as corporate reorganization policies, trade journals and advertising. In employers' eyes quality of service has become an important source of value (Hirschhorn, 1988) and a prime determinant of service firms' competitive success or failure (Koepp, 1987).

At one level management's definition of quality service is simple: quality service is being delivered when customers keep coming back and when they recommend a particular company to their friends. On the other hand exactly what prompts a customer to return and to recommend a company's service varies tremendously from individual to individual. As a consequence interactive service workers are required to make on-the-spot, subtle judgements about what would please individual customers hundreds of thousands of times daily in the American workplace. In other words, workers must continually utilize their 'tacit knowledge' (Manwaring and Wood, 1984) to determine what constitutes quality service. For one customer this might be friendliness, for another (or the same one at a different time) it might be speed, for yet another it might mean taking the time to share information and knowledge or just to chat, for still others quality service might mean service delivered by an employee who is flirtatious, solicitous, or deferent. In other words, to perform quality-service labor an employee must tailor delivery to the idiosyncratic and changeable needs of individual customers.

Since what is considered quality service varies so greatly by individual customer, how can managers and employers ever make sure that their employees are delivering it? How can they be certain that such an intangible product as service meets consumers' subjective needs and preferences? Here, previously identified methods of control have proven insufficient, if not counter-productive. For example, continuous simple or direct control by managers (Edwards, 1984), a potentially abrasive type of management that can engender hostility among employees, may be untenable for ensuring the delivery of quality service. One of the main things quality-service workers must 'produce' over and over again every workday is a good-natured, helpful and friendly attitude toward customers, a productive task they are likely to perform poorly when relations with their superiors are intrusive or overtly antagonistic.

Similarly, bureaucratic control, which prespecifies the 'rules, procedures, and expectations governing particular jobs' (Edwards, 1984, p. 130), may be insufficient for ensuring that workers interact satisfactorily with customers. Quality service requires that workers rely on inner arsenals of affective and interpersonal skills, capabilities which cannot be successfully codified, standardized, or dissected into discrete components and set forth in a company handbook. Indeed, to the extent that managers succeed in perfecting bureaucratic control over quality-service labor, they may extinguish exactly those sparks of worker self-direction and spontaneity that they are becoming ever more dependent upon.

Claiming that simple or bureaucratic control methods are insufficient and possibly counter-productive is not to say that they are not utilized in interactive service workplaces. Many fast food restaurants make regular use of a quintessential combination of technical and simple control – automatic cameras mounted in the ceiling which continuously photograph employees. Furthermore, as we discuss later, customer management can be used to bolster systems of bureaucratic control. Different forms of control are often used together, but we maintain that reliance on simple, bureaucratic and even technical forms of control to manage interactive service workers is particularly problematic given the dynamics of the work itself in the new competitive environment.

In an effort to deal with the control dilemma before them, many firms have turned to what we call consumer control or management by customers. We wished to discern whether customer control allowed management to execute the three principal functions of control systems underscored by Edwards (1984) – direction, evaluation, and discipline – yet simultaneously allow interactive service workers, even those in comparatively routinized jobs, to make skilled judgements necessary to provide quality service under fluctuating circumstances.

[...]

In sum, we understand customer control as a management response to an old, but somewhat altered, imperative: to simultaneously exclude workers from exerting genuine control yet secure their participation in the process of production (Cardan, n.d., p. 123). Profitable production under capitalism has always required that managers convince or coerce workers to do what they want them to, when they want them to and how they want them to. In other words, the expenditure of labor power must occur under the employer's command. Profits invariably suffer when workers are prohibited from exercising some degree of autonomy on the job.

Employers of interactive service labor continue to face the traditional dilemma of achieving a balance between managerial control and worker self-direction. What is distinctive about interactive service labor, however, is that the most profitable resolution of this dilemma obligates that employers expand, to a greater or lesser degree, workers' control over their own labor. This, of course, does not mean managers of interactive service workers now turn a blind eye to the direction, evaluation and discipline of employees. Rather, it means they must continue their search for new management techniques which simultaneously maintain their own control prerogatives but interfere as little as possible with employees' ability to exercise the amount of self-direction necessary to deliver quality service.

Customer control mechanisms: how they work and why they are used

[...]

Managing workers with customer feedback

We expected that a principal reason employers and managers would use customer management would be to monitor workers to evaluate whether they were delivering quality services to consumers. Furthermore, we expected that they would use these data to reward workers who succeeded in this task and discipline those who did not. What evidence is there that companies utilize customer input to carry out these objectives?

First, in every business in which we conducted interviews it was possible to identify individual workers through company-instigated or company-encouraged feedback mechanisms. Thus, approximately one-third of the comment cards available at the point of the service transaction included a line on which customers were invited to write employees' names. On the remaining two-thirds of the cards employees' names were not solicited specifically but easily could be discerned from other information already known or requested from the customer, such as the time and date of customer interaction, or the department, floor and/or store to which the customer's comments pertained. Importantly, employees in the companies we studied frequently wore name tags. Five of our respondents showed us examples of customer-supplied information, demonstrating how easily and regularly they were able to identify individual employees by name even when names were not overtly solicited. Comments such as: 'Pam was great' and 'Susan stunk' appeared on one hospital's monthly summary of its discharged survey. The comment: 'The blonde lady in the produce department doesn't like management' (store and date identified), was offered by one supermarket patron whose phone complaint was received by the chain's president. As one middle manager stated, the customer survey is important for monitoring workers because: 'It's like a report card on individual employees.'

Second, surveys and shoppers relayed detailed information about individual employee's behavior and attitudes. The following questions from printed surveys indicate the specificity, and often the subjectivity, of the information customers were asked to provide about employee behavior:

- Were your nurses *concerned?*
- How was the *temperature* of your food?
- Was our employee *knowledgeable?*
- Was our employee *quick* and *efficient* at the cash register?
- Were you greeted *graciously?*
- How was your salesperson's *appearance?*
- Was our employee *cheerful?*
- Approximately how many minutes did you wait to receive service?

  (no wait; 1-2; 3-4; 5-9; 10+)

Third, such detailed feedback about specific employees derived from customers was funneled into employees' personnel files and often used in bureaucratic systems of evaluation and discipline. A brief sketch of one firm illustrates the dynamics that can lead a company to implement customer management and subsequently to link this with its overall and thoroughly bureaucratized system of monitoring and evaluating employees. With the objective of maintaining current and attracting new customers 'Amer-Insure', a large insurance company, turned an aggressive eye to improving customer service in the early 1980s. The company manager we interviewed claimed that:

> Customer service is one of the top important factors in our competitive position. The survivors in the insurance industry are determined more by their service than by their product. The products are the same, with a few exceptions. Once there's a product innovation by one company, it's not long before everyone has it. People will pay more for good service; it's the cutting edge. It will determine who makes the cut and who does not.

This company implemented an extensive and rigorously-monitored system for securing customer feedback, including written surveys that were mailed to customers and unannounced visits by anonymous shoppers in selected regions. 'Amer-Insure's' shoppers were retired claims adjusters who would 'buy' insurance, a dummy file would be opened on them and eventually (after a dummy accident or theft) they might 'make claims'.

Once 'Amer-Insure' began to gather this feedback, it revised its employee performance evaluation form to include a customer service section, putting customer service on an 'equal level with other job responsibilities here at Amer-Insure.' Customer feedback was routed into workers' personnel files, on the basis of which periodic quantitative performance reviews used to determine raises, promotions and the like were prepared. Acceptable customer service ratings are now a condition of employment at this firm.

[...]

A union official representing grocery workers provided further evidence of management use of consumers' reports to control employees, as well as insight into the increasingly complex relations between workers and customers that this establishes. According to him, not only was customer feedback used to initiate the first stages of disciplinary action against supermarket employees (warnings and written conduct reports), but such information also provided the grounds for temporary suspensions and on-the-spot terminations. Moreover, should an employee file a grievance in response, customers nearly always became involved in the arbitration proceedings that followed. The union, usually in management's presence, interviewed the complaining customer and sometimes customers were subpoenaed to arbitration hearings where they were, as in an ordinary trial proceeding, sworn to testify under oath and examined and cross-examined by union and company counsel.

Using customer feedback to manage managers

Consumers' reports provided data for managing individual service workers, but they were also a source of data about the *overall* quality of each separate service delivery site. Such data thus gave upper levels of company management evidence about how well middle-level managers were doing their jobs. Middle managers were expected to use detailed data about customer/worker interactions as a basis for promoting quality service; how well they succeeded was reflected in the feedback that was channelled to the higher reaches of corporate management. Indeed in 80% of the diverse businesses in which we conducted interviews top-level managers and employers suggested that managing middle-level managers was as important

a reason for gathering customer feedback as managing workers.

To begin with, like workers, middle-level managers could often be individually identified in consumers' reports, either by name or indirectly through customers' identification of particular work shifts, store locations, or dates. Additionally, in every company we studied, ultimate control over some of this customer information was held, not by middle managers, but at the highest management levels. For example, in all firms at least one of the mechanisms employed to gather customer feedback was initiated by corporate management, which then gathered and analyzed the ensuing data itself; furthermore, a great deal of the consumer information collected was regularly reviewed by top officers in the organization. The president of a supermarket chain claimed personally to read forty to fifty customer comment cards daily; in two hospitals summaries of all patient feedback were reviewed monthly by their presidents, vice-presidents and boards of directors.

Third, customer data were often aggregated and analyzed by service delivery unit, allowing top management to control middle managers through comparison. The owners of a restaurant chain broke down the information they collected from patrons by restaurant and by management shift and posted it in their eating establishments, thereby setting up an explicit comparison amongst middle managers. Similarly, an auto manufacturer summarized its customer data by dealership, the main purpose of which was to facilitate inter-dealer comparisons. Corporate-level management, furthermore, used this information to discipline and control middle managers. Middle managers were clearly expected to demonstrate to top managers an awareness of the weak spots highlighted by customer feedback, to provide explanations for these and eventually to rectify their performance.

[...] A customer relations manager in a hotel chain reported that when top management received the results of customer surveys they wrote to middle managers, informing them of problems and complaints; middle managers had to respond within 30 days, notifying upper-level management of the ways in which they had rectified any faulty conditions. If no response was made by 30 days corporate management instigated formal proceedings against the manager via his or her superior. [...]

In sum, our data indicate that middle- and upper-level managers were using devices such as customer surveys, shoppers and comment cards to provide data on how well services were being sold. In all the firms we studied, diverse mechanisms were used to obtain information about service workers' and middle managers' attitudes and overall presentation of self, as well as the latter's success in eliciting high-quality service from workers. At a time when all these firms saw quality service as integral to their profitability, consumer feedback was an increasingly important foundation for monitoring, evaluating and disciplining workers precisely at the point where they understood profits to be created: the customer/worker interaction. As one bank manager noted: 'Without the responses from our customers, we will be unable to improve the quality of our workers in order to compete with other financial institutions.' Moreover, approximately three-quarters of our respondents indicated that they were in the process of refining and strengthening the mechanisms through which they collected and used customer feedback or that they would soon do so.

Discussion

We have discussed the ways in which service companies collected customer feedback and used it to manage both individual employees and the work of middle managers, the latter often measured by the totalistic picture of the workplace that customer feedback provides. We begin this section by highlighting four implications that may follow from systems of customer management. Although only suggestive, they nevertheless point to important foci of study for workplace sociologists concerned with power, hierarchy and control in a changing economy.

First, customer management may increase the complexity of authority and power arrangements at the workplace. Because the customer/worker interaction is used as the primary measure of workplace performance, the power to control workers and mid-level managers may appear to be removed from upper management's hands and redistributed to a company's clients, customers, passengers, patients, etc. In fact, however, feedback from consumers strengthens employers' hold over

the workplace by providing them with an additional source of data they can use for control, evaluation and discipline.

As management continually impresses the importance of the customer/worker interaction on its employees, consumer feedback may appear to be a more legitimate basis on which to reward and discipline service workers than information provided by managers. Experientially it is the customer who knows how a worker delivers service, not the manager. Positioned as agents in the management circuit, customers, rather than managers, are set up as the ones who must be pleased, whose orders must be followed, whose ideas, whims and desires appear to dictate how work is performed. Workers are judged on their interactions with customers *by* customers themselves. It would then appear that managers, in using customer data to control employees, were acting more as customers' agents or intermediaries, and less out of the managerial privilege accorded by their superordinate positions in the social relations of production.

Yet, while customer management techniques appear to dilute management responsibility for how employees are directed, disciplined and evaluated, in essence workers gain an additional boss. Managers now have formally designated accomplices in controlling workers, insofar as they exploit customers for their observations about how service is delivered. In sum, consumers' reports broaden *managerial* power, augmenting it with *customer* power; conflicts between employers and employees may thus be reconstituted as conflicts between employees and customers.

A second implication of our research is that customer management may make organizational power a constant yet elusive presence. The fact that customers potentially can evaluate the service interaction at any time may serve as a continuous, though invisible, check on service workers' interactions with the public. The knowledge that any interaction could flair into an antagonistic encounter, if the worker fails to provide service that satisfies the customer, may shape and reshape a worker's behavior. Organizational power is a constant in the sense that workers may always feel someone is looking over their shoulder.

[...]

[Third,] even by 'soft' social science criteria, the data which underpin such customer control practices hardly warrant the scientific label. Samples tend not to be representative (Lewis, 1983), survey responses tend to be biased toward negative evaluations because of the self-selection problem (Trice and Layman, 1984) and response rates are generally poor: 20–65% in the companies we studied. Furthermore, though survey and industry specialists have collaborated to devise reliable and valid instruments for gathering information on customer satisfaction, their measures [...] are often crude, yielding results that: 'defy meaningful interpretation' (Lewis and Pizam, 1981, p. 38).

As a consequence, data that claim to capture the reality of workers' and middle managers' performance may, in fact, severely distort it. The murkiness of much customer feedback data was revealed in the comments of a union official representing supermarket workers. To begin with, he argued, such information was very subjective. 'You're often dealing,' he explained, 'with how a customer interprets something – a mannerism, a tone of voice of something like that. "She just threw the change back at me." "He didn't smile at me!" These are very gray areas.' In addition, this official was familiar with cases in which customers had registered phony complaints against workers, occasionally in response to material incentives businesses offered customers who provided feedback. As a result he was adamant that any disciplinary action inspired by customer feedback had to be scrutinized especially closely by the union.

Finally, customer control may prompt various contradictions and resistances, ruptures in the organization of work that sociologists may want to investigate. First, insofar as it positions customers to assume antagonistic, adversarial roles in relation to employees it may spawn resentment, perhaps overt resistance, amongst workers and middle managers. We uncovered limited evidence of worker resentment of and resistance to customer control practices. One quarter of our interviewees stated that employees had become sensitive about customers providing negative reports on their work. Because of its deceptive character, shopping in particular may engender misgivings on the part of workers. Indeed, a manager in a large hotel

reported that her desk clerks had been so angry about the prospect of being anonymously observed by shoppers that one shift staged a 'smile strike', treating each and every customer that day in a rapid, affect-less fasion. In certain circumstances, customer control practices may thus produce precisely the opposite kind of service delivery from what management is trying to encourage and this in turn might force the curtailment or tempering of such methods. Our understanding of this possibility would be greatly enhanced by research on workers' responses to customer control, specifically how they negotiate or comply with, or resist, consumers as managers (Rafaeli, 1989).

Alternatively, workers and mid-level employees may attempt to appropriate, interpret or collect customer feedback data to protect themselves from the customer data collected by their superiors. The interpretation of data can also be the object of intense contestation, tacking significant organizational costs onto top management's attempt to use them to control employees. Thus, in a bank we studied, it was virtually impossible to rely exclusively on consumer feedback as a basis for serious disciplinary action because, at most, the use of these data would prompt a series of prolonged discussions and mediations between the criticized worker and various personnel and grievance groups in the corporation. Finally, we learned that auto dealers' efforts to protect themselves from reprisals based on the consumer feedback gathered by manufacturers has not only prompted many to collect their own data but has also spawned independent businesses that collect customer feedback solely for dealers.

We note one final issue of interest to sociologists studying changes in the contemporary workplace. Our research found evidence of increased managerial enthusiasm for employee *self control* used in conjunction with, and, perhaps, in response to the failures of, customer management. According to certain managers and employers we interviewed, employees must come to internalize the appropriate 'values'. They must become aware of their central role in adding value to products and services through quality labor and to be able automatically, as if by second nature, to balance competing demands for highly individualized quality-service delivery and bottom-line financial considerations, variously described as efficiency, profitability, productivity, growth and so forth.

We uncovered a number of attempts to operationalize employee self control in the companies we studied, including an employee self-evaluation procedure in one supermarket chain. But the seriousness with which some firms have come to regard employee self control was clearest in a discussion of structural changes in the company that had proceeded the furthest with its implementation. For many years every regional office in this corporation had had its own customer affairs department. Rather than expanding these departments as part of their efforts to improve customer service, however, top corporate managers abolished them all. In their place they created very small customer relations units on a temporary basis. This action only makes sense if understood as part of a corporation-wide effort to institute employee self control. Explained a man who headed one of these newly created units:

> My customer relations unit should never become permanent, or it will become a corporate dumping ground, as the customer affairs departments had turned into. Employees dumped all the responsibility for customer service with the customer affairs department. That would defeat our whole purpose. We want every employee to internalize responsibility for customer service. My unit's job is to disseminate this philosophy to every individual. Once we've done that we (the unit) disappear.

Such corporate attempts to convince workers to manage themselves, used in conjunction with customer management, can form the twin pillars of continuous, unobtrusive control systems, whereby managers attempt to insure the delivery of quality service by enlarging the arena of employee self-direction.

References

ALBRECHT, K. (1988) *At America's Service*, IL, Dow Jones-Irwin.

CARDAN, P. (n.d.) *Redefining Revolution*, London, Solidarity.

DALLOS, R. (1987) 'Airlines spy on selves in service war', *Los Angeles Times*, July 21, pp. 1 and 16.

EDWARDS, R. (1984) 'Forms of control in the labour process: an historical analysis' in F. Fischer and C. Sirianni (eds) *Critical Studies in Organization and Bureaucracy*, Philadelphia, Temple University Press.

HAGE, J. (1988) *Innovating to Adapt Strategy and Human Resources to Rapid Technological Change*, MA, Lexington Books.

HEYDEBRAND, W. (1989) 'New organizational forms', *Work and Occupations*, Vol. 16, pp. 323–57.

HIRSCHHORN, A. (1988) 'The post-industrial economy: labour, skills and the new mode of production', *Service Industries*, January.

HOCHSCHILD, A. (1983) *The Managed Heart*, Berkeley, CA, University of California Press.

KOEPP, S. (1987) 'Whatever happened to good service', *Time*, February 2, pp. 48–57.

LEIDNER, R. (1988) *Working on People: the routinization of interactive service work*, PhD, Department of Sociology, Northwestern University.

LEWIS, R. (1983) 'When guests complain', *The Cornell H.R.A. Quarterly*, August, pp. 23–32.

LEWIS, R. and PIZAM, A. (1981) 'Guest surveys: a missed opportunity', *The Cornell H.R.A. Quarterly*, November, pp. 37–44.

MANWARING, T. and WOOD, S. (1984) 'The ghost in the machine: tacit skills in the labour process', *Socialist Review*, vol. 74, pp. 57–86.

NOYELLE, T. (1987) *Beyond Industrial Dualism*, Boulder and London, Westview Press.

RAFAELI, A. (1989) 'When cashiers meet customers: an analysis of the role of supermarket cashiers', *Academy of Management Journal*, Vol. 32, pp. 245–273.

RITZER, G. (1989) 'The permanently new economy: the case for reviving economic sociology', *Work and Occupations*, Vol. 16, pp. 243–72.

SCHOENBERGER, E. (1989) 'Multinational Corporations and the New International Division of Labor: a critical appraisal' in S. Wood (ed.) pp. 91–101.

TRICE, A. and LAYMAN, W. (1984) 'Improving guest surveys', *The Cornell H.R.A. Quarterly*, November, pp. 10–13.

WALL STREET JOURNAL (1990) 'Chain finds incentives a hard sell', July 5, B1 and B4.

WOOD, S. (ed.) (1989) *The Transformation of Work? Skill, Flexibility and the Labour Process*, London, Unwin Hyman.

Source: Fuller and Smith, 1991, pp. 1–16.

READING C:
Paul du Gay, 'Adding value to yourself'

[...]

As several commentators have argued (Hollway, 1984, 1991; Rose, 1990), during the past decade there has been a substantial growth in the practical involvement of psychological expertise in the everyday life of the modern business enterprise with psychologically trained experts carrying out such tasks as selection, appraisal, promotion and job evaluation either as permanent employees or as private consultants.

Although, at first sight, the image of the entrepreneur seems far removed from the world of psychotherapeutics this opposition does not appear to hold. As Rose (1990, p. 14) has argued,

> therapeutics can forge alliances between the liberation of the self and the pathways to personal success, promising to break through the blockages that trap us into powerlessness and passivity and underachievement. Hence therapeutics can appeal to both sides of the employment contract: it will make us better workers, at the same time, it will make us better selves. Therapy can thus offer to free each of us from our psychic chains. We can become more enterprising, take control of our careers, transform ourselves into high fliers, achieve excellence and fulfil ourselves, not *in spite of* work, but *by means of* work.

In other words, psychotherapeutic technologies of the self are designed to cut across divisions between 'work' and 'non-work' life, between both the 'top' and 'bottom' and the 'inside' and 'outside' of the corporation. Within the discourse of enterprise there is no longer room for any contradiction or conflict between the motives and desires of the employee as an individual and the goals and objectives of the organization for which he or she works. The individual human being at work, as much as outside of it, is considered to be engaged in a project to shape his or her life as an autonomous individual driven by motives of self-fulfilment. In short, no matter what role they may perform, all people produce themselves at work.

There is a considerable amount of evidence from within the retailing industry that suggests that

enterprising technologies of regulation are being deployed quite extensively by retailers, that these technologies are covering a much wider range of employees, and that in certain important respects they are blurring the distinction between what it means to be a consumer and what it means to be a retail employee.

At the British multiple mixed retailer W.H. Smith, for example, up to 300 middle managers were assigned for 'retraining' following a large-scale survey of management style in which staff were asked to comment upon their manager's performance across a wide range of competencies. During 1990 and 1991 the company surveyed 3,500 of its 16,000 staff in 'one of the first schemes in Britain allowing staff to assess managers'. Each employee was asked to complete, anonymously, a questionnaire rating his or her manager's qualities. On a scale of 1–5, the 400 managers whose performance was assessed rated an average 4.52 for being 'prepared to make decisions', but only 3.12 for being 'someone I could go to if I have personal problems'. Other low ratings included 'someone who keeps me motivated', 'someone who is prepared to change his or her view if I have something useful to add', and 'someone who creates a happy working environment'.

The company's retail and personnel training manager said that senior management had expected managers to perform better in traditional roles because the company had trained them to do so in the past: 'these are things we have concentrated on, and they are the traditional measures of a good manager, but we are now saying that a manager's job is broader than it was in the past and we are asking more of them.' As a result of the exercise, all managers deemed to require 'retraining' attended an assessment centre where they were interviewed by an occupational psychologist, informed of their individual result, and offered guidance on how to work on themselves in order to better themselves and become more motivational and inspirational managers of people.

While at first sight, this exercise seems to have had little to do with 'saturating the company with the voice of the customer' (Whiteley, quoted in Miller and O'Leary, 1993, p. 198), nothing could be further from the truth. Attempts by retail organizations to re-imagine the role and conduct of store managers –

turning them from direct controllers to empowering facilitators of staff – are constitutive elements of governing in an enterprising manner; in other words, they are essential components of creating a 'customer-driven company'. As this example highlights, market-orientated organizational reforms often serve to turn employees into each other's customers as well as encouraging them to focus upon the needs of (external) traditional customers (Hill, 1991). Retail employees, like staff in other service industries, are increasingly encouraged to take on the role of both customer and servicer in the workplace, through, for example, providing 'consumer reports' on their own managers (just as customers are encouraged to provide reports on the quality of service they receive from staff at the point of purchase), as well as providing quality service to external customers. In these ways, work and consumption relations become increasingly enmeshed (see, for example, Fuller and Smith, 1991).

Similarly, at British department store chain Dickens & Jones, senior management's 'pursuit of service excellence' led to an exercise analogous to that at W.H. Smith, this time aimed primarily at shopfloor staff. The company employed the services of a private consultancy to act as anonymous 'professional' shoppers who systematically surveyed the performance of sales employees against a predetermined and weighted set of means. Although these professional shoppers remained anonymous, staff were informed of their presence and the purpose of the exercise. Over a one-month period, 184 full- and part-time staff in London were individually assessed on four separate occasions, each time by different consultant shoppers. Emphasis was placed on manner of approach, attitude/rapport, efficiency and farewell. The score was recorded then tabulated to arrive at an overall assessment. These were communicated to staff, individually, in the form of an appraisal and then used 'to reward levels of excellence and/or identify training needs'. In order to celebrate individual 'heroes', senior management at the company presented each employee attaining 80 per cent or over with a gift voucher and certificate, and then invited them to attend a champagne party in their honour.

Two crucial points emerge from examining these cases. First, in both, a distinct interrelation can be delineated between enterprising 'technologies of power' – an objectivizing of the work-based subject through the use of devices of calculation: an examining, quantifying and grading of individuals – and enterprising 'technologies of the self' – practical psychotherapeutic counselling through which people can work upon themselves to better themselves, as workers and human beings. Through the deployment of such technologies senior management at these companies have shifted the form of control exercised over staff away from close, formal direction towards a more entrepreneurial, indirect form of government – or controlled decontrol – which relies for its effectiveness upon the self-regulating capacities of its employees as subjects.

Secondly, in both cases the technologies deployed have had the effect of blurring distinctions between work and consumption identities. Both examples gave practical effect to the objective of 'saturating the company with the voice of the consumer'. In the first case, shopfloor employees were re-imagined as internal 'customers' providing consumer reports on their managers. In the second example, shopfloor staff were assessed and rewarded in terms of the degree to which their conduct conformed to the requirements of external customers. As these examples indicate, the delivery of quality service – to both internal and external customer – is deemed to necessitate employees becoming aware of their crucial role in 'adding value' through quality 'emotional labour', both to themselves and to the company for which they work.

According to both the managing and retail operations director at company *B*, the 'excellent customer service demanded by our customers' entailed a new approach to the recruitment, selection and training of both managers and staff. No longer content to 'recruit in haste and repent at leisure', senior management were looking for a particular 'type of personality' to service their stores. The personnel and training department at company *B* was charged with developing a number of programmes to give effect to these aspirations. In conjunction with a range of other departments, as well as a private management consultancy, they worked to create a formal 'person specification' for the job of sales assistant which would act as a guide for store managers in selecting 'staff with the right image and attitude'. At the same time personnel and training staff were also considering the introduction of psychometric testing for sales assistant positions. With regard to training, the emphasis shifted away from a primary concern with technical skills – till operation and dressing-room procedures – towards a more concerted focus on the development of interpersonal skills and self-learning. The behavioural and attitudinal characteristics of shopfloor employees as individuals were now seen to be of vital importance: 'we are saying that personality and the way people behave are as important to us as any other factor.'

At some of the company's newer stores, staff were being trained to view customer care as a series of skills which could be learnt. Through interpersonal training in transactional analysis, for example, staff in these stores were taught how to 'effectively manage a transaction with a customer'. In transactional analysis each individual is represented as exhibiting three types of 'ego states' in social relations: those of Parent, Adult and Child. Thus any interaction between two individuals can be analysed in terms of whether it is Parent-Child, Adult–Adult, Adult–Child etc., and therefore effectively managed to obtain a favourable outcome.

> So when a customer comes in you identify whether they're Parent, Adult or Child, and you respond accordingly to get an 'uncrossed' transaction. If they come in and you want to move them out of one mode and into another, then you respond to their stimulus and then you move into Adult, or Parent, or Child and it works ... We want 'uncrossed' transactions and not 'crossed' ones because they work in a positive direction. It's all about being aware of what mode the customer is in and responding accordingly.

Training in transactional analysis at company *B* was an attempt to provide staff with a new way of seeing, and intervening in, social relations. Moreover, not only was transactional analysis deployed to assist staff in managing customer interactions 'in a positive manner', it was also deemed to provide a technique for helping staff to help themselves; that is, to turn themselves into empowered human beings. According to *B*'s

training manager, it was this 'self-producing' aspect of transactional analysis that was highlighted to staff:

> the first thing they realize is that transactional analysis and customer care, or 'how to handle other people', is a *skill*. It's 'my skill is being challenged here. Because I'm not stretching myself I'm not dealing with this customer the right way.' And once they realize it's a skill, and they can do something about it, they take it on board. It's very much an empowering thing that way. If they have a customer who goes away still arguing then they've failed. The challenge is to turn the customer around and that's how the whole thing is sold.

The deployment of transactional analysis in customer-care training was a crucial aspect of what senior management regarded as a move towards 'enterprising up' the company and its staff, making them more 'customer driven'. Via the medium of 'soft', 'cultural' technologies such as transactional analysis, employees at company *B* were being encouraged to become aware of their central role in adding value both to themselves and to the company for which they worked by providing quality service to customers. It was through such mechanisms that the quest for 'emotional proximity' between customer and organization was operationalized and that specific ways for the shopfloor employees of company *B* to conduct themselves were delineated. In other words, these micro-technologies were deployed to align the self-actualizing capacities of retail employees as subjects with the organizational goal of staying 'close to the customer'.

Although several similar mechanisms were deployed at company *A* to ensure the delivery of their Secure Shopping Strategy, the centrepiece of the company's attempts to become more customer driven was the introduction of their Quality Team (QT) programme. In a speech to staff launching the company's strategy in-store, the managing director highlighted the introduction of QTs as the key to the future success of the business.

> There are many exciting aspects to our Secure Shopping Strategy but I highlight in particular the introduction of Quality Teams into every area and department of the company which will

allow all of you to become involved in a very real and meaningful way in changing some of the things we do for the better. I strongly believe that throughout this huge company amongst our staff there is an enormous wealth of talent, experience and skills that is not being allowed to be used fully. At last we will have a means of taking full advantage of that and I hope allow everyone to feel that they are contributing to our progress in a very positive way.

[...] QTs were articulated as an integral component of *A*'s 'overall business strategy'; in other words, they were represented as a mechanism intended to promote continuous business improvement. According to senior management within the company, QTs constituted the central technique through which the 'hearts and minds' of the company's workforce would be harnessed to the pursuit of 'staying close to the customer'. Quality teams were seen to be the key

> to changing round the way we think of our front-line troops. And throughout the company there is this recognition now that they have got a very major contribution to make. They know all the wrinkles. They actually know half the answers. And we're beginning to grow more and more aware that 75 per cent of our problems are management driven, it may be 90 per cent for all I know. And actually staff have 90 per cent of the answers: 'Why are they doing it this way? If only they'd listen to us.' So this Quality Team approach, I believe, is the beginning of the answer because it's starting to say, 'We need you. You've got talent. You know the wrinkles. Tell us and we, the managers, will listen to you' ... so we're in a way turning our managers – and management is about controlling and suppressing isn't it? – into leaders. And leadership is about giving people countless opportunities to grow, to develop and contribute. But you don't do that overnight. That's ten years' work.

Quality teams were established at each level and in each function of the business and involved all members of the company (indeed membership of a QT was mandatory, not voluntary). The 'senior' QT comprised the Board of Directors of company *A*, and the 11–12 people sitting on that forum

established the overall strategic goals – the 'Whats': What We Want to Achieve. These 'Whats' were then 'cascaded' down to the next level QT chaired by the line manager from the immediate 'superior' QT. This QT then discussed the 'Hows': How they would deliver the 'Whats' that had been established by the 'superior' QT. The commitments made at this level were then cascaded down to the next 'subordinate' QT and continued in the same fashion right down to the front-line QTs in-store, which were chaired by the branch manager.

As this brief outline suggests, the QT system was very hierarchical. QTs were not an alternative to line management; rather, as a senior manager indicated, they 'simply involve everyone in analysing and achieving strategic objectives in a multi-level, multi-functional organization', and 'form a platform for the implementation of any major change in the future'.

In-store the Chair of the QT set the agenda indicating the 'Whats' cascading down from the immediately superior QT. The Chair's role was to guide the meeting imperceptibly and certainly not to hijack it or dominate it, ensuring that everyone got involved, that the group agreed to a series of 'Hows', and that everyone was personally committed to their implementation. In other words, the Chair had to encourage the group to gel without appearing to be in control. Guidelines on managing QTs stressed that 'self-regulation is a key motivation' and that 'self-monitoring is a key to commitment'.

QTs were sold to staff very much as a freedom package; as an opportunity for them to become more personally involved in the running of the business, and, simultaneously, to develop themselves as individuals. Emphasis was placed on getting staff to see the 'hows' formulated by the group as the result of their own autonomous deliberation; that they 'owned' the QT process. 'Recognition and celebration of success' were also represented as vital ingredients of the QT system. '[M]ore and more now QTs are involving those front-line people in making their contribution to the delivery of Secure Shopping. And you know as well as I do that if it's your idea, you're obviously much more committed to it than if I impose my ideas upon you. The obvious stuff, psychologically.'

Through the technology of QTs, staff at *A* were encouraged to imagine that they 'owned' the business for which they worked. The psychotherapeutic presuppositions that permeated the QT – self-monitoring as the key to commitment and so forth – structured it as a rational technology of the personal and interpersonal. Thus QTs could be seen to provide their members with an 'ethical' exercise, in Foucault's use of that term, aimed at producing a particular kind of relation to self, and, through this, the ethical demeanour and standing of a particular kind of person: the enterprising self. Here, once again, the onus on direct control was transformed into an emphasis on regulation through self-production. Via the technology of QTs, as with the other techniques outlined earlier in the chapter, the government of company *A* has come to operate through the 'soul' of its individual employees.

Technologies such as transactional analysis and quality teams are designed to incite and channel – to govern rather than simply to repress – the subjectivity of service workers. These technologies are fashioned first and foremost to assist staff in managing the service interaction; that is, to produce a pleasurable meaning for the customer and a sale for the company. At the same time, however, they are also deemed to provide service staff with the practical means of empowering themselves at work. In this way, service in occupations such as retailing can be seen to concern the simultaneous 'production of meaning' and 'production of profit'. The two goals are symbiotic. Moreover, the effective management of the service relation is deemed to provide meaning and fulfilment for the producer of the service, the retail employee, as well as the consumer of that service, the customer (Allen and du Gay, 1994, p. 267).

[...]

References

ALLEN, J. and DU GAY, P. (1994) 'Industry and the rest: the economic identity of services', *Work, Employment and Society*, Vol. 8, No. 2, pp. 255–71.

FULLER, L. and SMITH, V. (1991) 'Consumers' reports: management by customers in a new economy', *Work, Employment and Society*, Vol. 5, No. 1, pp. 1–16.

HILL, S. (1991) 'How do you manage a flexible firm? The Total Quality model', *Work, Employment and Society*, Vol. 5, No. 3, pp. 397–415.

MILLER, P. and O'LEARY, T. (1993) 'Accounting expertise and the politics of the product: economic citizenship and modes of corporate governance', *Accounting, Organizations and Society*, Vol. 18, Nos 2/3, pp. 187–206.

ROSE, N. (1990) *Governing the Soul: the shaping of the private self*, London, Routledge.

Source: du Gay, 1996, pp. 138–45.

Acknowledgements

Grateful acknowledgement is made to the following sources for permission to reproduce material in this book:

Cover

Advertisement storyboard: Whitbread Beer Company/Bartle Bogle Hegarty.

Chapter 1

Text

Reading A: Hannerz, U. (1993) 'The withering away of the nation?', *Ethnos*, Vol. 58, Nos 3-4, National Museum of Ethnography, Sweden; *Reading B:* Angell, I. (1995) 'Winners and losers in the information age', *LSE Magazine*, Vol. 7, No. 1, London School of Economics; *Readings C and D:* From *Newsweek*, 24 April 1995, © 1995 Newsweek, Inc. All rights reserved. Reprinted by permission; *Reading E:* Wilk, R. (1995) 'The local and the global in the political economy of beauty: from Miss Belize to Miss World', *Review of Political Economy*, Vol. 2, No. 1, Routledge.

Figures

Figure 1.1: Newsweek cover, 24 April 1995, © 1995 Newsweek Inc. All rights reserved, reprinted by permission. Photograph by Donal Holoway; *Figures 1.2, 1.3, 1.4, 1.5:* Martin Parr/Magnum; *Figure 1.6: Newsweek* cover, 26 June 1995, © 1995 Newsweek Inc. All rights reserved, reprinted by permission. Photograph Cleaver/Wide World/Associated Press; *Figure 1.7: Newsweek* cover, 14 August 1995, © 1995 Newsweek Inc. All rights reserved, reprinted by permission. Illustration by Charles Burns.

Chapter 2

Text

Jackson, T. (1995) 'Masters of the moving image', *Financial Times*, 2 August 1995; Roberts, J. L. (1993) 'Missing links: entertainment giants, like Sony, see little of synergy's benefits', *The Wall Street Journal Europe*, 30 March 1993. Reprinted by permission of the Wall Street Journal, © 1993 Dow Jones and Company, Inc. All rights reserved worldwide; Skapinker, M. (1994) 'Designer stubble that got burnt', *Financial Times*, 22 June 1994; *Reading A:* Adorno, T. and Horkheimer, M. (1979) *Dialectic of Enlightenment*, Verso, by permission of the Tanja Howarth Literary Agency; *Reading B:* Gendron, B. (1986) 'Theodor Adorno meets the Cadillacs' in Modleski, T. (ed.) *Studies in Entertainment*, Indiana University Press.

346 PRODUCTION OF CULTURE/CULTURES OF PRODUCTION

Figure

Figure 2.2: Press Association.

Chapter 3

Text

Reading A: Roche, D. (1994) *The Culture of Clothing: dress and fashion in the 'ancien régime',* Librairie Arthème Fayard/Cambridge University Press; *Reading B:* Coleridge, N. (1988) *The Fashion Conspiracy*, William Heinemann Ltd. Copyright © Nicholas Coleridge 1988; *Reading C:* Belussi, F. (1987) *Benetton: information technology in production and distribution. A case study of the innovative potential of traditional sectors*, Science Policy Research Unit, University of Sussex.

Figures

Figures 3.1, 3.5, 3.6, 3.7: M. Chandoha Valentino; *Figure 3.2:* Photographed from L. Roger-Miles, *Comment Discerner les Styles du VIIIe au XIXe Siècle, Vol. 3, Le costume et la mode*, Edouard Rouveyre, 1898; *Figure 3.3:* Drawing by R. Chast, © 1988 The New Yorker Magazine, Inc.; *Figure 3.4:* Mansell Collection; *Figure 3.8:* Courtesy of Ralph Lauren; *Figure 3.9:* Courtesy of Benetton.

Chapter 4

Text

Reading A: Wernick, A. (1991) *Promotional Culture*, Sage Publications Ltd. © Andrew Wernick 1991; *Reading B:* Westall, C. (1985) 'A breakthrough in the study of women', *Campaign*, 22 November 1985, Haymarket Marketing Publications Limited/McCann-Erickson Advertising Ltd, © Christine Restall 1985; *Reading C:* Bourdieu, P. (1984) *Distinction: a critique of the judgement of taste*, Routledge.

Figures

Figure 4.1: Royal Mail/Bartle Bogle Hegarty; *Figure 4.3:* The Whitbread Beer Company/Bartle Bogle Hegarty; *Figure 4.4:* Heineken/Collett, Dickenson & Pearce & Partners; *Figure 4.5:* Levi Strauss & Company/Bartle Bogle Hegarty; *Figure 4.6:* Courtesy of the International Wool Secretariat/Bartle Bogle Hegarty; *Figure 4.7:* Copyright Biff.

Chapter 5

Text

Reading A: Deal, T. E. and Kennedy, A. A. (1991) *Corporate Cultures: the rites and rituals of corporate life*, Penguin Books Ltd; *Reading B:* Willmott, H. (1993) 'Managing culture in modern organizations', *Journal of Management Studies*, Vol. 30, Blackwell Publishers Ltd;

Figure

Figure 5.3: Courtesy of Professor Rosabeth Moss Kanter.

Chapter 6

Text

Gapper, J. (1990) 'Workers keep themselves in check', *Financial Times*, 23 June 1990; *Reading A:* Miller, P. and Rose, N. (1990) 'Governing economic life', *Economy and Society*, Vol. 19, No. 1, Routledge; *Reading B:* Fuller, L. and Smith, V. (1991) 'Consumers' reports: Management by customers in a changing economy', *Work, Employment and Society*, Vol. 5, No. 1, The British Sociological Association; *Reading C:* du Gay, P. (1996) *Consumption and Identity at Work*, Sage Publications Ltd.

Figures

Figure 6.1: CHARTER/Kobal Collection; *Figure 6.2:* John Lewis Partnership; *Figure 6.4:* Courtesy of the British Security Industries Association.

Photograph

p. 21: Courtesy of British Airways.

Every effort has been made to trace all copyright owners, but if any have been inadvertently overlooked, the publishers will be pleased to make the necessary arrangements at the first opportunity.

The publishers would like to thank the following organizations for help in the preparation of this book: Bartle Bogle Hegarty; The Disney Store, Milton Keynes; Dixons Group/Currys, Milton Keynes; Hilton International.

Index